10/02

D1126434

Meramec Library
St. Louis Community College
11333 Big Bend Blvd.
Kirkwood, MO 63122-5799
314-984-7797

WITHDRAWN

FRONTIER BLOOD

NUMBER NINETY
The Centennial Series of the
Association of Former Students,
Texas A&M University

St. Louis Community College
at Meramec
Library

Frontier

The Saga of the Parker Family

TEXAS A&M UNIVERSITY PRESS

Blood

Jo Ella Powell Exley

COLLEGE STATION

Copyright © 2001
by Jo Ella Powell Exley
Manufactured in the
United States of America
All rights reserved
First edition

The paper used in this book
meets the minimum requirements
of the American National Standard for Permanence
of Paper for Printed Library Materials, z39.48-1984.
Binding materials have been
chosen for durability.

LIBRARY OF CONGRESS CATALOGING-IN-PUBLICATION DATA

Exley, Jo Ella Powell, 1940–

 Frontier blood : the saga of the Parker family / Jo Ella Powell
Exley.—1st ed.

 p. cm.—(The centennial series of the Association of Former
Students, Texas A&M University ; no. 90)

 Includes bibliographical references and index.

 ISBN 1-58544-136-8 (alk. paper)

 1. Pioneers—Texas—Biography.   2. Parker family.   3. Frontier
and pioneer life—Texas.   4. Parker, Cynthia Ann, 1827?-1864.
5. Parker, Quanah, 1845?-1911.   6. Comanche Indians—Texas—
History—19th century.   7. Indian captivities—Texas.   8. Texas—
History—19th century—Biography.   9. Pioneers—Southern
States—Biography.   10. Frontier and pioneer life—Southern States.
I. Title.   II. Series.

F385.E95   2001

976.4'004974'00922   2001002241

To Jim & Emily,

my ever-faithful helpers

CONTENTS

PART V. QUANAH

ILLUSTRATIONS

PREFACE

Quanah Parker, the last chief of the Comanches, was half white. He led his people in both war and peace. Although several books have been written about Quanah and his mother Cynthia Ann Parker, no biography has previously been published on the Parker clan, a sometimes strange and often brilliant people. Their obsession with religion and their desire for land brought them into contact with American Indians on the frontier in Virginia, Georgia, Tennessee, Illinois, and finally Texas and affected not only their lives but also the course of American history.

The cast of characters is fantastic. Elder John, the patriarch, was a footwashing Predestinarian Baptist preacher also known as "Squealing Johnny" because of his preaching style. Elder John's first son was Daniel, religious fanatic, disseminator of the strange Two-Seed doctrine, and hated perpetrator of the anti-missionary movement that tore the Baptist Church apart during the eighteenth century. Elder John's granddaughter, Rachel, was a young wife and mother held captive by Comanche Indians for thirteen months. Rachel's father, James, was a sometime Baptist preacher accused of counterfeiting, theft, and worse. He spent years searching for Rachel and three other relatives captured in the Fort Parker massacre. James's nephew John was rescued after four years but ran away and returned to the Indians. And finally, the most famous Parkers of all were Cynthia Ann and Quanah. Cynthia Ann, captured at the age of nine, was adopted by a band of Comanches, married a chief, and bore three children. One of them was Quanah. When most of the Comanche bands had gone to the reservation, he led his band until there was no more hope for freedom. Then on the reservation in Oklahoma he became the greatest peace leader of the Comanches.

The Parkers were quintessential pioneers—tough, wily, brave, even foolhardy, willing to risk everything for their religion, for personal freedom, and for rich, virgin land. Their coexistence with the Indians lasted for at least one hundred years, and their spilled blood mingled with that of their Indian foes. But at last the pioneer and Indian blood was mixed in one man, and the tragedy, misery, and hatred were expiated as he led his people to successful lives near the Wichita Mountains in Oklahoma.

Parts of this story have been told but never before with such scope and depth. Included in *Frontier Blood* are excerpts from the short autobiography of Daniel Parker, from Rachel's two narratives of her Indian captivity, from James Parker's account of his search for Rachel and the other captives, and from several autobiographical accounts that Quanah dictated to his friends. I have included lengthy quotations from these people and others who lived during this period because their actual words give a true feeling of what it was like to live on the frontier in the eighteenth and nineteenth centuries. They give interesting details of their daily lives, which would be lost in paraphrasing. We also have the rare opportunity to hear the voices of backwoodsmen, the flowery presentation of the educated, the incomparable rhetoric of frontier preachers and politicians, and the poetic words of the Indians. More important, the speakers characterize themselves and others as they speak.

In addition, I have included many letters and documents in the text because in the past their contents have sometimes been misrepresented. Readers can judge firsthand what is the truth.

In the sixteen years that I researched and wrote this fascinating story, I was greatly aided by my husband Jim and my daughter Emily; both encouraged me and patiently bore with my endless reading, typing, and visits to the library as well as accompanying me on research trips to places such as Tennessee, Oklahoma, New Mexico, East Texas, and the Panhandle and Big Bend of Texas. I would also like to thank the people who helped me on these research trips.

My husband and I spent a wonderful day with Ruth Parker Carter, driving through the countryside in Tennessee looking for creeks and old churches. Clark Hitt and Judge Charlie Bell took me to Mule Creek and the Pease River battle site. Mac Conaway and Gary B. Sanders escorted Emily, Jim, and me to the Adobe Walls battle site in the Texas Panhandle and entertained us for the day. Marilyn and Jerry Palmer took me to Cynthia Ann Parker's original burial plot and to the location of Fort Houston in Palestine, Texas. In West Texas my family and I spent a wonderful day with Dr. David Murrah exploring the breaks and Staked Plains as we toured the site of the battle at Blanco Canyon and then viewed Mesquite Creek, thought to have been the camping place of Quanah and his band when they finally agreed to surrender. A special thank-you goes to Jerry McClung, who gave me immense help with research. My family and I spent a wonderful day with Jerry and her husband Paul in the Wichita Mountains, haunts of the Comanches. Then they introduced us to Dr. Jacquetta Parker McClung,

Quanah's great-great granddaughter, who shared with us her family photograph album.

Many librarians and archivists have given their time and assistance, and I can never properly thank them, but I would like to mention some by name. My friends the late Bill Richter and Ralph Elder have provided invaluable help through the years. In Katy, Texas, Myrtle Ross, Kathy Green, and Terry Dingley have ordered hundreds of books for me through interlibrary loan as well as giving me continual encouragement. At the Fort Sill Museum Judy Crowder and Towana Spivey located primary material.

My friends also provided encouragement and help. Bobbie and Bill Peace researched archives in Santa Fe. My dear cousin David Lewis Barkin, now deceased, provided a sketch of the location of Isaac Parker's cabin in Birdville, Texas, and did research for me in the Haltom City Library. Others who have helped me are Elvis Allen, Jim Barnhart, Ellen Brown, Scott Burgan, Gilbert Cuthbertson, Ted Davidson, Pauline Dollar, T. R. Fehrenbach, the late J. Evetts Haley, Max Harper, Paula Marks, Marian Meyer, Jerry Melcher, Robin Montgomery, Burney Parker, the late Joe Bailey Parker, R. E. (Jack) Plummer, Myldred Stebbins, Tera Stubblefield, Donald Stubblefield, Vyrtes Thomas, Robert Weddle, and Vera Wimberly.

Many friends and acquaintances have read all or part of the manuscript and offered helpful advice: my husband Jim Exley, Charles Bennett, Mike Goins, the late Marj Gurasich, Nelda Hammett, the late Margaret Henson, and Steve Hudson.

To all the others who have helped me through the years, I express my sincere gratitude.

PART I

DANIEL

CHAPTER 1

A Poor Sinner

IN THE VALLEY of Elk Creek in the Wichita Mountains, a young woman gave birth. Her husband, who was a Comanche war chief, was far to the west leading his men in battle against the Navajos. The woman had cropped hair and skin tanned by the sun, but out of the dark face smiled the clear blue eyes of a white woman, Cynthia Ann Parker. The son in her arms was Quanah, who would become the last principal chief of the Comanches. The last chapter in the story of the Parker family and their quest for freedom was about to begin.[1]

The events that culminated in this unusual birth began on the East Coast when the Parker clan became inextricably linked with the Baptists in the colonial United States. The story of the Parkers is centered around a quest for freedom, civil as well as religious. The patriarch of the Parker clan was John Parker, who was a Predestinarian Baptist minister. John was born in Baltimore County, Maryland, on September 6, 1758, and according to family tradition was the descendant of Puritans who had fled from England because of religious persecution.[2] Sometime before 1777 John and his family moved to Culpeper County, Virginia, in the foothills of the Blue Ridge Mountains.[3] Baptist congregations had existed in Virginia as early as 1714, but they had been scattered and insignificant. In 1754 missionaries from New England began their work in the South.[4] They were Free Will Baptists, unlike most of the old settlers, who were Predestinarian Baptists. From 1760 until 1770, phenomenal growth occurred in the Free Will churches. Mammoth camp meetings brought hundreds into the fold. Excesses of emotion sometimes produced strange effects, as one eyewitness describes: "Some screaming on the ground, some wringing their hands, some in extacies of joy, some praying, others cursing and swearing, and exceedingly outrageous. We have seen strange things today."[5]

The era from 1768 to 1770 is known as the Period of the Great Persecution. Because of their rejection of the established religion and their insistence upon separation of church and state, many Baptist ministers were arrested for disturbing the peace, and more than thirty were thrown into dungeons. Culpeper County was in the center of this religious controversy.[6] Whether participant in or observer of the turmoil, John Parker was imbued with the tenets of the Baptist religion, and his beliefs were to cause profound effects on his family for generations.

In 1777, nineteen-year-old John Parker, like many other Baptists, went to fight in the American Revolution. He volunteered in October and served twelve months under Captain Fields in Colonel Slaughter's Virginia Regiment in General Nathanael Greene's Brigade.[7] Two years later he returned to find his sweetheart, Sarah (Sallie) White, waiting. She was the daughter of Benjamin White who, according to family legend, was the first county judge of Culpeper County.[8] Sallie and John were married in November of 1779 in his parents' home.[9] Shortly after the wedding, John was drafted for another twelve months of service, this time under Captain Collier in Colonel William Alexander's Virginia Regiment.[10] John later stated that during his second year of service he "marched through Winchester Virginia, thence through Benton town, Pennsylvania & was stationed on a peak called 'Ten Mile'," and that he was in no "engagement with the enemy." After the war John returned home, and on April 6, 1781, the Parkers' first child was born.[11] John and Sallie gave him the name of Daniel, and like his namesake, he was cast into a lion's den, but it was one of his own making.

Other children were born in quick succession. On their farm, the Parker family struggled to survive. Then a new land beckoned: the fertile fields of Georgia, suitable for growing cotton to trade with the English for cash, a chance to improve their lot rather than subsisting on a small farm with corn for their animals and a vegetable garden for themselves, never getting ahead.

When the Parkers moved to Georgia in about 1785, the population of Georgia was 82,000. Slavery was an important institution, and rum was one of the major exports. The Creeks and Cherokees had not yet been removed from the state, and the settlers fought bitterly with them. The Parkers lived on the Savannah River in Franklin County, land that had been occupied by the Cherokee Indians shortly before the Parkers' arrival.[12]

Daniel was five or six years old when the family moved to Georgia. In his autobiography he describes his education: "When but a small child, my parents moved to the State of Georgia, where I was raised without an education, except to read in the New Testament, but very imperfect, when quite small, and to shape letters with a pen, and indeed to this day I have never examined the English Grammar five minutes, neither do I understand even one rule in the Arithmetic. I do not name these things to boast of my ignorance, but for truth's sake, and that God may have the glory of what little he has done by and through me, and not the wisdom of this world."

The Parkers were probably subsistence farmers. As a young man, Daniel spent many happy hours in the wilderness near his home, where he said that for five years he "ranged the woods as a hunter, nearly as much in company with Indians as with the whites."

Daniel grew up in a highly charged religious atmosphere since, as noted, his father was a Predestinarian minister. The only mention Daniel makes of his father in the thirty-page autobiography is to give his name as John Parker and to state that he was still living when the work was written in 1831.

Daniel does mention his mother several times, describing her as a "God-fearing woman" who often talked to her children about religion. Once when Daniel was about eight years old, she gathered her brood of four children about her and very plainly explained to them "the great danger of sin, our need for a Saviour, and that we should fear and worship God." Daniel describes his reaction: "This left a lasting impression on my mind, to dread sin, for fear of the wrath of God, and torment of hell." However, since he had been brought up in a Predestinarian Baptist home, he decided that if he were one of the elect, he would be saved, and if he were not one of the elect, he would not be saved, so he didn't need to worry about it.

When Daniel was about seventeen, he heard a sermon by Elder Moses Sanders in which Sanders expounded upon the wickedness and presumptuousness of the stance Daniel had adopted. Daniel was shaken, but he was "so much in love with sin that I still gave latitude to my youthful vanity." Then there began a four-year torment for Daniel. He states: "It never once entered my mind that I might be under conviction, and that perhaps the Lord was preparing me to partake of his love." Daniel viewed himself as such "a lump of sin and corruption" that it was "presumptuous wickedness" to ask God for His mercy.[13]

What were the heinous sins of which Daniel was guilty? He does not explain exactly, but the temptations were many to a young man of twenty on the Georgia frontier. Some frontier settlements were models of order and law-abiding people, but others were morasses of sin and depravity.[14] No matter which type was found in Daniel's neighborhood, there was a place where the young men met on Sunday, the day for socializing. Typical frontier amusements were card playing and horse racing. Usually the pioneer, no matter how poor, owned the best horse he could afford. In the gambling that accompanied the card playing and horse racing, sometimes the stakes were high; a young man could lose several months' worth of hides he had laboriously collected. Another temptation was alcohol, which often led to vicious fights in which the opponents tried to gouge out each other's eyes or slice each other to ribbons.[15] Worst of all were the cruel games such as "whip races." Two men tossed a coin to decide who would be the first to wield a five-foot-long rawhide whip. The men were placed fifteen feet apart at the beginning of a quarter-mile course. At the drop of a handkerchief, the two men would make a mad dash to the finish line with the whip holder getting in as many slashes as he could. At the finish line the men would trade places, and the second man would get in as many blows as he could. Often the second man was in no shape to run, much less administer a whip while doing so.[16]

William Ross, a contemporary of Daniel Parker, lists what the Baptists called "outbreaking sins." He explains: "Sinners were advised to shun outbreaking sins if possible, such as horse-racing, card-playing, cock-fighting, profanity, drunkenness, and fiddling and dancing especially." In discussing his sinful condition, Daniel states: "I had never used profane language, or particular out-breaking acts of wickedness." Daniel fervently prayed: "*Lord save* . . . I have sinned against thee, the best of all beings, and upon whose mercies I have lived, whilst rebelling against thy government."

After four years of mental torture, Daniel was keyed up to a high emotional pitch. At this time he happened to attend an evening religious service in the home of the Smith family nearby in Franklin County. As he traveled alone the four or five miles to the neighbor's home, he fervently meditated and came to the conclusion that if he were not one of the elect, God was entirely just in condemning him to the everlasting torment in hell that the Predestinarian preachers so vividly described.

It so happened that Elder William Denmon, who preached that night, described a man in the same sort of torment Daniel had been suffering. Then to Daniel's surprise, instead of declaring that such a man was not one of the elect and was condemned to hellfire, Denmon declared: "This is the way that the Lord brings sinners to the knowledge of truth." Daniel's reaction was immediate: "I felt to my soul the truth of the declaration, and reflected that had the words been declared by an angel from heaven, there could not have been more truth in them."

On the way home, Daniel started to reflect on his past sins as he had on the way to the meeting. To his surprise, he found that things had changed: "It appeared clear to my view that the Saviour had put my sins all away. . . . I felt as if I was an entire new creature, filled with astonishment at the change of things while viewing God's works and ways, in saving me a poor sinner."

The day following this religious experience, Daniel was sent to find some escaped horses in the wilderness adjacent to the family farm, and he felt that the two days he spent alone were "the two happiest days I ever spent on earth . . . my soul united in the glorious theme. The bar was taken away which had stood between me and a throne of grace, and I thought an access to a throne of grace was one of the greatest blessings ever bestowed on man."[17]

In spite of Daniel's glorious experience, he began to doubt he was one of God's elect. This dread thought often cast the Predestinarian Baptists into deep depression. They believed that Satan, who often appeared as an angel of light, might have tricked them into believing they were among God's elect when in reality they were doomed to eternal hellfire. There was no hope for the nonelect. Nothing they could do would save them. The doubters could often be heard singing the sorrowful old hymn:

> Tis a point I long to know,
> Oft it causes anxious thought;
> Do I love the Lord or no?
> Am I his or am I not?[18]

Daniel went through this harrowing experience. "My mind became dark, my heavenly views and happy feelings gone, and I concluded that I was a poor deceived wretch, that my case was now worse than ever." After two months of worse torment than before, Daniel finally had another intense religious experience. He had been visiting some of his neighbors, who had been discussing the Universalist doctrine they had recently heard preached. Parker remarked that "such a doctrine might do them, but it would not do me." As he traveled home, the sun was setting. He was thinking he was lost, and the Universalist doctrine could not help him either. He describes his second "awakening": "(O! shall I ever forget that spot and moment of time?) The first thing I was capable of recollecting, I was about forty yards from that spot, walking fast, rubbing my hands together, and praising God, I believe, with a vocal voice, for salvation by grace. About one hundred and fifty yards further on my way, was the place I had previously concluded to pray, as it would be about the time I generally retired for that purpose. When I came to the spot, it struck my mind, and I knelt down, but soon found that I could not pray, because I had every thing that I wanted. I felt more like praising God than praying; at the same time these words were running through my mind: 'We know that we have passed from death unto life, because we love the brethren.' At length they were applied with such power to my soul, that I arose to my feet, and cried out, I do know that I do love the brethren. I then thought that I never should doubt again, and that I wanted to tell every body about the goodness of the Lord, but before I met with any person, I had so got out of that notion, that I held my peace."[19]

Thus ends part one of Daniel Parker's autobiography. The last sentence underlines Parker's extreme honesty and hints at a feeling of guilt that he may have had about his initial inability to proclaim what he felt was the great gift that God had given him—the gift of grace, of eternal life in heaven.

Immediately after Daniel's second religious experience, he felt a call to the ministry. He resisted this call because he felt inadequate. "I had been raised without an education, in an uncultivated part of the world, and (I think) had then, never seen a newspaper in my life, and was unable to have written a letter to a friend." He explains that at the time he did not realize what he believed to be true later—that the ability to preach was God-given, having nothing to do with education. Daniel states that he "shrank back from so great a work, and plead with the Lord to send some other one, (believing that I was more unfit for that work than any other converted man,) or let me alone until I was by age and improvement better qualified for the work." Daniel at length felt that all of his objections were answered by God, who was calling him to preach, and "that the help was in him, that he was my strength, and that he would be with me and do his work by or through me." Thus Daniel became, as he said, "willing with trembling" to enter the ministry. He emphasizes that he never once felt that God wanted him to attend a theological institution in order to be qualified to preach.

While Daniel was agonizing over whether or not he should be a minister, he did not attend church. He had never previously made "a profession of religion" because he felt that he could live just as clean a life outside the church as in it. He also felt that since he had such a "desperate wicked heart to grapple with" and that the cause of religion was "so dear and precious," he would "rather die than to disgrace it." Eventually, what Daniel felt was his call to preach finally caused him to make a public profession of faith.[20]

A person was not immediately accepted into the Predestinarian Baptist

Church upon a public profession of faith. A solemn ceremony preceded acceptance into a church. First the members of the church gathered in the meeting house or a member's home if there were no official church building. A hymn was sung with the minister "lining it out." Since many people of that day could not read even if they had hymnals, the minister would read a line of a hymn and the congregation would then sing it. Then a prayer was offered, with each member praying in turn. Next the pastor started the old practice of "renewing covenant," in which members would tell about their feelings, trials, hopes, and joys during the past month. In the next part of the ceremony, the "door was opened" for members to relate their "experiences of grace." The Predestinarian Baptists enjoyed relating their conversion experiences in which they first became gloriously aware of the fact that they were among God's elect. Even as they visited in one another's homes on nonreligious occasions, they would relate these experiences, which seemed to create a strong bond among them.[21]

The next step in becoming a member of the church was an examination in which the minister questioned the candidate on "points of doctrine and experience." Members of the congregation also questioned the candidate, and sometimes a person was gently told to wait a little while longer. However, most of the time the candidate was accepted, and the church proceeded with plans for the baptism.

Baptism was a high point for those whom these old Baptists called "born again" Christians. Most of the churches were built on the banks of creeks, and in the mountains and foothills the spring water ran over rock bottoms where fish could be seen swimming in the depths. In spring, summer, and early fall, yellow daisies, white Queen Anne's lace, and purple violets lined the banks. The members of the congregation walked to the stream. The minister and the candidate waded into waist-deep water, and then the minister held the candidate in his arms and gently lowered him backward into the water of the stream, where he "put on the Lord Jesus Christ, and made the oath of allegiance to the king of Zion," in the words of one old-timer. The members then retired to the meeting house, where the minister gave a brief address, and then all partook of the Lord's Supper.[22]

In that day of few amusements, in order to break the monotony of life, sometimes large groups of people came to baptisms, especially when a number of people had been converted in a camp meeting. One such baptism turned into a farce as hundreds of nonmembers looked on, climbing trees, falling out of them, and cursing and swearing, but usually the baptisms were solemn occasions enhanced by the grandeur of nature.[23]

Daniel Parker was received into Nail's Creek Church in Franklin County, Georgia, and was baptized on January 3, 1802. A short time later, he was "licensed to preach."[24] Licensing, the first step to becoming a minister, was a simple affair. A man would voice a desire to preach, and the local congregation merely voted on the candidate. Sometimes a modest man with obvious ability would be encouraged to apply for a license. After he was licensed, he would travel about preaching in various churches. When a church "called" a man to be their pastor, he would then be ordained by a board of elders and become a full-fledged minister.[25]

Three months after Daniel Parker's baptism, he married Martha (Patsey) Dickerson on March 11, 1802.[26] In his autobiography, Parker never mentions her name and does not give the date of their marriage, merely stating: "About this time [the time of his baptism] I married, and became concerned with the cares of a family." Shortly after Daniel's marriage, he became dangerously ill. As his wife and his mother hovered over him, he told them, "I am not going to die now." They gently replied, "It looks as if you cannot live." With supreme confidence Daniel replied, "I am confident that the Lord has work for me to do, and I will not die until I have done it." Daniel soon recovered.[27]

⇜ CHAPTER 2 ⇝

The Wrong Road

O N JUNE 23, 1803, the Parker clan started on a trek to Tennessee.[1] Since Daniel was only twenty-one years of age, he followed the leadership of his father. The other members of the immediate family were Daniel's mother and seven brothers and sisters, his wife Patsey, and their five-month-old daughter.[2] Often whole congregations of Baptists would emigrate across the mountains, holding church services as they went.[3]

The economic slump that followed the American Revolution lasted until 1820, especially affecting the southern states along the eastern seaboard. Farmers could not sell their abundant crops, and many were ready to push on to a better land. Earlier, the Baptists had won religious freedom in Virginia when they had succeeded in abolishing the taxation used to pay the Anglican clergy. When the Episcopal churches were deprived of the sixteen thousand pounds of tobacco they had annually received from the government, the established church was broken up, and many shells of empty churches with their attendant graveyards could be seen in Virginia and the Carolinas. The Baptists followed this triumph with a wholehearted participation in the Revolutionary War, which impressed both Thomas Jefferson and Benjamin Franklin and was instrumental in effecting the separation of church and state. The lower middle-class farmers of Virginia, North Carolina, and Georgia were also tired of the snobbery of the Virginia planters and longed for the equality that the frontier offered in Kentucky and Tennessee.[4]

As the small farmers were struggling to make a living in the early 1800s, they started hearing reports of a beautiful, fertile land beyond the Appalachian Mountains, which everyone called Cumberland. The travelers reported that it was a vast area of lush forests, clear streams, rolling hills, and valleys and meadows covered with wildflowers. Besides, it was a hunter's paradise. It was reported that some "long hunters" had killed hundreds of bear, buffalo, and deer in a few days.[5] At Bledsoe's Lick in Sumner County, where the animals came to get salt at the sulfur springs, sometimes the buffalo were so thick that a man could not ride his horse through them.[6] One old settler called the Cumberland "the most magnificent park the world had ever seen." At first the southerners did not believe the reports of the incredible beauty and fertility of the area, but as more and more reports began to come in, a mass exodus started from Virginia, the Carolinas, and Georgia.[7] Whenever the pioneers emigrated to new lands, there were tearful farewells because they knew that they would probably never again on this earth see the friends and relatives left behind. The Parkers turned toward "the land of the setting sun" as they crossed the Appalachian Mountains in the northwest corner of Georgia. As Daniel and the numerous members of his family were traveling over the mountains and rivers of Georgia and Tennessee to reach their destination, Daniel, always the mystic, felt that in his mind's eye he had seen almost the whole route, and he felt right about every path they took until they turned onto what was called the Caney Fork Road on the west side of the Cumberland Mountains. Daniel felt that instead, he should go up "the road that lead by Waltan's ferry at or near the mouth of the Caney Fork [River]." He became so preoccupied with his strange feeling that he said to his mother, "I am going wrong." His mother asked, "Why do you think so?" Not wanting to explain, he brushed off the question by vaguely replying, "Perhaps I have taken the wrong road, and left my course."[8]

After two months of travel across bumpy roads often through dangerous Indian country, the Parkers finally arrived at their new home a few miles southwest of Nashboro, now known as Nashville. In 1803 Nashboro was a raw frontier village of some one hundred houses of log and frame, a water mill, a ferry, three taverns, a courthouse, and two springs. Lawbreakers were sometimes punished by branding or having their ears clipped.[9]

Daniel and Patsey settled on Turnbull Creek in Dickson County. Elder John, Sallie, and their other children settled a few miles away on what was called Parker's Fork of Turnbull Creek.[10] The area was beautiful, with steep, timber-covered hills and a multitude of spring-fed creeks and rivers. On the hills and in the narrow valleys along the streams, wildflowers bloomed in a profusion of white, yellow, purple, and blue. When the Parkers arrived, it was, as Daniel said, a "wilderness" of giant oaks, sweet gums, sycamores, and canebrakes where huge fields of cane higher than a man's head grew so thickly in the creek and river bottoms that one could not walk through

GENEALOGY 1

John Parker family

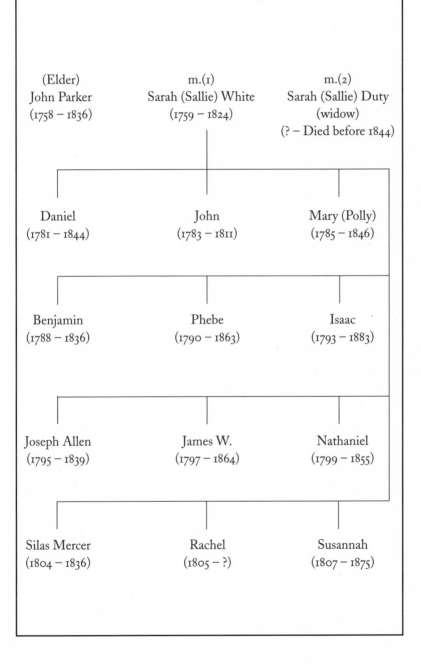

| (Elder) John Parker (1758 – 1836) | m.(1) Sarah (Sallie) White (1759 – 1824) | m.(2) Sarah (Sallie) Duty (widow) (? – Died before 1844) |

| Daniel (1781 – 1844) | John (1783 – 1811) | Mary (Polly) (1785 – 1846) |

| Benjamin (1788 – 1836) | Phebe (1790 – 1863) | Isaac (1793 – 1883) |

| Joseph Allen (1795 – 1839) | James W. (1797 – 1864) | Nathaniel (1799 – 1855) |

| Silas Mercer (1804 – 1836) | Rachel (1805 – ?) | Susannah (1807 – 1875) |

them. Early settlers shunned them but later learned that they grew on some of the richest land.[11]

There were few settlers in Dickson County in the years that Daniel and his family lived there. It was on the edge of Indian lands, and two forts or blockhouses had been built with walls made of logs capable of withstanding either bullets or arrows. An uneasy peace existed between the Indians and the whites, and while Elder John and his family were living in the area, the Indians went on an extensive raid, killing a number of people. In 1806 the first general store was established, and the proprietor sold "dry goods, notions, groceries, and whiskey." The first saloon, then called an "ordinary," was licensed the same year. Corn mills, so vitally important to the early settlers, who frequently ate corn pone, corn meal mush, and hoe cakes, were located on Jones Creek, Yellow Creek, and Piney River. From the earliest settlement, numerous "still-houses" were scattered about the country, and the average output of beer was one barrel per day.[12]

Spiritual affairs were progressing also. Daniel and others in his family were busily collecting members for what eventually became Turnbull Church, established in 1805.[13] It was customary for Baptist congregations to purchase a blank book when they first began to meet and to record the minutes of the monthly business meetings. Although the ink has faded, and some of the pages are stained with water, the Turnbull Church book has survived.

Near the front of the book, a list of some twenty members is given. The Parker families attending Turnbull Church were Elder John and his clan and John's nephew Moses Parker and his family. At the beginning, the meetings were held in the cabin of Elder John Parker. On May 28, 1806, Daniel Parker's ordination is recorded as follows: "Having set apart the Date above written for a time of Grace and final perseverence of the Saints in Grace to Glory having sat apart the day and Date above written for a time of fasting and prayer for the purpose of ordaining our beloved Daniel Parker Jun who has Labored amongst [us] word and [deed] and being . . . Regularly Examined by our Beloved Brothers in the [faith] John McConnico, John Turner, John Reson."[14] After the examination, ministers were ordained by the laying on of hands and through prayer.[15]

On another page Daniel's wife is mentioned: "Saturday before the second Lord's day in July [1806] met at Brother John Parkers on Turnbulls Creek . . . opened a door for the Reception of members Rec-d by Experience Betsey Jones & Patsey Parker by Experience." The phrase "received by experience" indicates that Patsey Parker had not been a member of the

Predestinarian Baptist Church before this time but had recently undergone an "experience of grace," which convinced her that she was one of "God's elect."

The entry for October of 1806 refers to Elder John:

> Therein Received a letter from Brother John Parker and received the same—Then the church sent a Letter to Buffellow church the Contents is as follows—We Rec-d a Letter from Nails Creek church in Georgia in answer to our Petition to them for the Liberating John Parker to his preaching Gift Honery [honorary?] Brethern as his Membership is or near Received by you and not wishing to do anything that Might Cause a wound or Grief to you we wish you to Consider the Matter and Send us a Letter to that a Mount—The Church in Georgia gives us Liberty to Receive him as dealing with him in Gospel order if we think he ought to be Restored.

The cryptic entries continue in December of the same year: "Agree to send for brother White and brother Whitset and brother Turner to met in the Saterday before the 5 Lords Day in mrch in order to restore brother Parker." The situation seemed to get more serious in March of 1807. "The Church met and set in Conferance and took up the Reference concerning Bro. parker and appointed the Saterday before the fourth Lords day Bros Whetset and Bro Turner to meet on that day to help us all. . . . notified Buffelo and Big harper." The story continues: "April the twenty th day 1807 this is to certify that the helps came forward from Mill Creek yallow Creek and Buffalow Creek Churches in order to look into the stand of brother John parker he being absent nothing done. . . . May the 9th day of 1807 The Church met to gather after prayers bussiness began the Church she is without a pastor."[16] Evidently, for some unknown reason, in Georgia, Elder John had been banned from preaching. The Nail's Creek Church in Georgia agreed to restore Elder John, but there was some doubt among the members of neighboring churches in Tennessee. A meeting was called, Elder John did not show up, and in effect resigned as pastor of Turnbull Church.

Daniel Parker had had a bad feeling about going to Dickson County. He was ready to leave after staying three years: "Through the course of this time, the exercise and distress of my mind under a conviction that I was not in my proper lot, or station, was more than tongue or pen could describe, and the want of room forbids me to notice the particular impressions of mind, and remarkable turns of providence, all uniting to confirm the fact, that I was not in the place to which God had appointed me to." Still he was undecided: "Being well pleased with the country where I was, my worldly interest, (to my view,) the natural ties of affection to my relations, and friends, with my love to my brethren, and their apparent respect for me, all united to keep me in disobedience." After another period of intense mental anguish, Daniel decided to go to Bledsoe's Creek in Sumner County, Tennessee.[17]

The countryside around Turnbull Creek had a wild beauty with its deep forests and steep slopes, but the gently rolling hills around Bledsoe's Creek with their borders of trees and meadows of bluish grass were like an enchanted park. Indian tribes, long since dead when Daniel arrived, had chosen this area for their home. Seven Indian mounds, four hundred feet high and conical in shape, dotted the approach to Bledsoe's Creek. The area was heavily wooded with poplar, ash, walnut, sugar maple, redbud, and blackhaw. In early spring when the trees were tinted with the gold and green of new leaves, the flowering trees burst into bloom in the woods—the white of the dogwood, the blazing pink of the redbud, the poplar with its tuliplike blooms, and the blackhaw with snow white clusters of flowers.

Gently sloping banks held streams that rushed over rapids in the spring and slowed to a ripple in August. Daniel Parker settled into a church called Hopewell on the banks of Bledsoe's Creek. A path led down to Bledsoe's Creek. On the banks the wildflowers grew waist high. A rocky ledge on the sandstone bottom formed a pool of clear, cold spring water, perfect for baptizing. Daniel had chosen a beautiful place for his new church home.[18]

Daniel Parker was a strange combination, a pragmatic mystic. He was an old pioneer preacher who wrestled with Satan and with nature, and in his description of his new home, he gives no hint of its beauty. "Here I found a little church called Hopewell, on Bledsoe's Creek, to which I became a member, and extensive bounds without a Baptist preacher in it, and through which they rarely passed. Here I felt myself at home, tho in very low circumstances as to this world's goods. I had a wife and two small children, and my wife in a very low state of health, near lying-in with a third; had a horse, and little or no money. I soon paid for a cow by my labor, and provided bread and meat for my family, and though I then had no prospect of ever owning a home for my family, yet I felt a calm serenity of mind, believing that I was doing my duty, and that the Lord would provide for me."[19]

Daniel then began what was in actuality missionary work. The frontier Baptist preacher was a rare breed. These "farmer preachers," unlike the Methodist circuit riders, received no salary for their work. They worked hard, just as the members of their flocks did, clearing land, splitting rails for fences, planting crops, and raising hogs, cattle, and horses.[20]

In sparsely settled country, a few people would band together to form a church. Most Baptist preachers served several churches. Some congregations had as few as eight people and met in the homes of members. Others numbered one hundred or more and constructed a crude log building for a church, with a platform for the minister and a fireplace at one end. Baptist ministers were often invited to preach at sister churches, and the more popular preachers, like Daniel Parker, spent a great deal of time traveling.

Each weekend the Baptist preacher would leave his farm on either Friday evening or Saturday morning, depending on how far he had to travel. Often he would conduct services on both Saturday and Sunday. One of the important sacraments of the Predestinarian Baptists was the ritual washing of each other's feet, in which members demonstrated their humility and love for each other. People came from miles around to participate and to join in Christian fellowship.

Daniel Parker was happy with his new church home even though he and his family were nearly destitute. After five years Daniel and Patsey had collected enough money to buy some land. In 1811 Daniel paid 425 dollars for "a little spot [215 acres] of poor land on what is called the Ridge near the head of Cany Fork of Drakes's Creek, having no improvement on it."[21] He worked hard when he was at home, often at night, so that he would have time to preach during the weekend. Daniel's sincerity and effectiveness as a preacher was spreading his fame, and he had many calls to preach and to administer to the suffering. He refused pay because he felt "so unworthy." Farming was his only means of support, and he states: "Sometimes it really appeared as if my family must suffer. I had but one horse to do all my work and riding, and I well recollect using him for two years in that gravelly country, without a shoe on his foot, because I was not able to get him shod without going in debt. I was afraid to do that, and was too proud to beg, often going on foot fifteen or twenty miles to my appointments, my wife having to shift for her little children as she could, attend to her business in the house, and mine out of doors, in my absence, being deprived of the common necessaries of life, (perhaps not one pound of coffee in a year,) except that of substantial food, and that at times appearing so coarse, that she at length (for the only time in her life,) observed to me, that she thought I would have to take in my appointments, or we should certainly come to want. I replied "I hoped not; if we have meat and bread, there is no danger of suffering, and I will try to keep that."

In spite of his words to his wife, Daniel doubted that he could both continue to accept all of his calls to preach and at the same time provide even "coarse" food for his family. After much soul-searching, Daniel as usual arrived at an answer that put his religion above all else in his life. He decided to continue preaching whenever and wherever he was called because "the Lord had as yet provided for me. . . . But when they [his wife and children] did come to actual suffering, then I might know that I had gone too far, and that it was my duty to stop, and stay more at home, for the benefit of my family."[22] He continued to preach, and not only did he and his family survive, but eventually they acquired great wealth.

Daniel's single-mindedness and preoccupation with religion sometimes caused him to do strange things. John Bond, who knew Daniel, relates the following anecdote:

He was a poor man, and had settled in Sumner County with an increasing family—worked hard and preached much. He once had an appointment at night, some four or five miles from home. The day being very warm, while hoeing corn, he had rolled up his pants nearly to his knees. The sweat and dust had made mortar on his feet and legs, while he worked on watching the sun so as to start just early enough to meet his appointment. Laying aside his hoe, he hastened off without shifting clothes or even washing. He reached the place in due time—commenced preaching, and continued some time before he looked down and discovered his ridiculous figure. He afterwards said that it made him feel a little bad at first, but his subject was so absorbing, he had no time to look at his legs and feet.[23]

In spite of his eccentricities, Daniel was growing in power and influence. He was invited to preach in Nashville by a Brother Foster, one of the most prominent Baptists of that day. On the appointed day, the people filed into the meeting house, which was soon crowded. Brother Foster was sitting next to Parson Blackburn, a Presbyterian minister who was considered to be the best orator in the state. One of Daniel's fellow ministers tells the story:

The house was soon crowded, and Parker commenced preaching. In a little time his neck-tie became too burdensome, as it was an article he was not much addicted to wearing, drawing it off he laid it aside, continuing his discourse in the meantime. He soon finds it necessary to relieve himself of his coat; and next his vest is laid aside. At this stage of the stripping process, Blackburn whispers to Foster, in an ironical way, "Will he pull his shirt off?" After preaching was over, Foster, who was highly insulted at Blackburn's question, asked him, "What do you think of Bro. Parker now?" He replied, "It is a pity that man has not a good education, and some refinement. He might have made a right good preacher." Foster replied with a snarl, "He is the best preacher in the State as he is."[24]

Evidently, removing his coat and hat was somewhat of a ritual with Parker. James Ross, who heard Daniel preach once at an association meeting held at Spring Creek Church in about 1820, describes "the man and his methods": "He was a small, dry-looking man, of the gypsy type, with black eyes and hair and dark complexion. On rising to the pulpit to speak, he soon gave us to understand that he meant business,—pulled off his coat and vest, laid them deliberately on the pulpit near him, and unbuttoned his shirt collar. After this preparation it is almost incredible with what ease and fluency he spoke. He seemed full of his subject, and went through it in a way that was truly wonderful."[25] Parker was an outstanding speaker, and a good and kind man, but he was implacable, a man of the past who could not accommodate change. He spent his life fighting battles, and most of them were with his fellow Christians.

When Daniel Parker first arrived in Sumner County in 1806, he found that there were many Methodist preachers in the area, and since the Baptists had no ministers, the Methodists preached to the Baptists as well as to their own flocks. Daniel describes the situation as he saw it: "I had until this time, been altogether raised and traditionized to the backwoods, or frontier country, having no learning, and being rough and course in my language and manners, I made but a poor appearance as a preacher, and those Methodists at first appeared as if they thought me hardly worth notice, but at length they, by their conduct, seemed to think it might be better to put me out of their way, before I did them much harm, and so they engaged in war against me." This challenge put Daniel into a quandary because he did not know what it was his duty to do. He felt that he did not truly understand what the Baptist faith was, and even though he had heard many men preach and talk about different points of doctrine, he felt that he did not have a true understanding of the "merit" and "consistency" of the different tenets of the church.[26]

He meditated for about three months and came to the conclusion that "the Lord gave me to see and feel that it was my duty to draw the sword of

truth, go forth in his name, and fight for the truths of the gospel."[27] During
this period, Daniel formulated the method for ascertaining what he felt to
be the truth in matters of faith, a method he used throughout the rest of his
life, attracting thousands to his fold at some points in his career but finally
burying himself and his followers in the strange and obscure doctrine of
Two Seedism.

Daniel, in his supreme self-confidence, states how he arrived at the "truth":

> All I know, was what little I was taught in the Bible by my experience,
> in the teaching, as I trust by the spirit of God in my own mind. This
> taught me that salvation was wholly of grace. The way I came to be what
> I now am in doctrine, my mind would first become weighted with some
> particular point of doctrine, feeling a weight and deep interest in know-
> ing the truth on that subject my mind would be drawn out to the lord
> and his word for instruction. . . . Thus I was brought from point to point,
> or thing to thing, in my mind, distinguishing between truth and error,
> until I am what I am; and I am confident, that had there been no other
> man on earth, holding the principles I do, that I should have been just
> what I am, for I never received those principles from man, that makes
> me an old predestinarian Baptist.[28]

His choice of words, "old predestinarian Baptist," points up one of the
guiding forces in Parker's life: ultraconservatism. Throughout his life he
believed in the old Calvinistic faith.[29] Daniel Parker was a pioneer Baptist
preacher of the old school, jealous of any encroachment upon his freedom
but at the same time imposing the restrictive doctrine of Calvinism upon
his followers. The idea of "unconditional election," meaning that certain
people are predestined to eternal bliss, and other people to eternal damna-
tion, is comforting to those who are convinced that they are numbered
with the elect.

Armed with his "sword of truth," Daniel entered into the fray with the
Methodists. He states: "I did not sheath my sword to let any error pass that
came in the way, but with what I called my old Jerusalem Blade, which had
two edges, and cut every way, I laboured to cut off every thing that was
seeming to touch the crown on the Redeemer's head, or remove the rights
and foundation of the of church of God."[30] An anonymous writer, who was
an "eye and ear witness" to many battles in the war, recorded his impressions in the biographical sketch he wrote about Daniel. The writer first
imagines how the Methodists felt:

The course that has marked the workers of Iniquitty in all ages of the world, began to show its deformed head, while the enemies of truth ware useing every exertion in thear power to amalgamate the world and Religion together. He [Daniel Parker] feerlessly, declared to the flock. Come out of her my people, and as the Lord had made him the instrument in his hand—of bringing home to the church many of the captured children of Zion the craft was in danger. The silver shrines for the Goddess Diana began to fall in value. now something must be done to get red of this verry troublesom fellow. They cryed out, our Craft is in danger— help wisdom of the world or we shall soon be left in possession of our art alone—with out a market for one of our silver shrines (or man made preachers).[31]

In 1808 Daniel Parker was challenged by a Reverend Cook to a public debate on the subject of baptism. The two men met near Gallatin, Tennessee, and according to the biography writer, the debate was so clearly won by Daniel that a number of the Methodists were converted to the Baptist faith. Another memorable encounter took place in late summer about 1811 when Daniel was preaching near his home in eastern Sumner County. After the sermon, the Reverend Samuel King, who was "considered to be the champion of the Methodist order," berated Daniel, saying: "You are our Enemy to truth, and your Doctrine come from Hell and will go back thear again—and you are preaching the Devils Doctrine. Your doctrine is fals, and I consider you a dangerous man, as you are in no wise bound to the truth. I dare you to meet me on the subject of your Doctrine (useing his own words) I hoist my batry piece of my Artilery, and Ile crumble your Hellish doctrine to its original nothing."[32]

Daniel replied: "Mr. King I am not fond of controversy. I preach the Doctine [*sic*] as revealed to me by the King of Zion. I am reddy Sir to acknowlege you my superior in point of Education and worldly acquirements. But my masters kingdom is not of this world, neither has this world any knowledge of that kingdom by nature, consequently, I feel no danger, for christ has said he will be with me, and I believe his promise. he had been with me thus fare & will certainly be with me to the end, no uncerconised Philistine shall Bid defiance to the Armies of Isreal. In the strenth of Isreal's God Ile meet you, in fare investigation of the doctrine that I preach, and I will show the falscity of the Doctrine you preach."[33]

Daniel reluctantly agreed to meet King "in public controversy." In his autobiography Daniel states: "Mr. King was considered a man of talents,

and of considerable information, and feeling myself to be so ignorant, knowing that I was without information, except what little I knew, in or of the
Bible." Parker decided to study "some few pamphlets" on the subject of
Baptism in order to prepare for the "debates." Suddenly he realized that
the information he read was secondhand and that "if they [the pamphlets]
were true, the authors had got the truth from the Bible; that it was still in
the Bible, and as free for me as for them, and that to the Bible I should go,
to know the truth." After carefully studying the Bible, Daniel felt enlight-
ened on "every point I needed," and he went into the fray with "undaunted
feelings." Daniel says: "I felt secured in having the Lord and his word on
my side."[34]

At this time, listening to speakers, religious as well as political, was popular
entertainment, and oratory had been raised to the position of a fine art.
The setting for the debates was probably out of doors since there were no
churches in the area large enough to hold the crowds the spectacle would
draw. The debates might have been held at one of the Methodist camp
meeting grounds. Often these meeting places were in the midst of a forest.
At one end of a clearing filled with crude benches provided for the congregation would be several wooden platforms upon which the speakers stood.
A circus atmosphere attended the first debate. The biography writer describes some of the incidents that took place. He praises Daniel for his
"forbearance" when "censorious epithets ware thrown out against him."[35]
While Daniel was speaking, "Mr. King in presance of the audience, would
grin, and disfigure his face. Getting behind P. in the stand [he] would draw
back his fist as though he intended to strike him." Daniel retained his com-
posure in spite of King's antics. Both Daniel Parker in his memoirs and the
biography writer state that Daniel was clearly the winner in the debates.
Daniel says that he lost no Baptist members "in all my bounds" but that
many Methodists were converted to the Baptist faith.[36] The writer cites as
evidence of Daniel Parker's victory "that not one of his (King's) friends
attempted to deny it aftewards, as we ever hird of."[37]

After Daniel Parker's battle with the Methodists was over, old cam-
paigner that he was, he entered into the bitterest and most protracted controversy of his strife-filled life. What made the conflict even more tragic
was that it was with his own kind, the Baptists.

This internecine conflict began in 1815. At that time Daniel was moderator or chairman of the Concord Association, a loose-knit group of
churches in a large area north of Nashville and east of the Cumberland
Mountains.[38] Ever jealous of their independence, the Baptists had no overall

structure like those of Methodists, Presbyterians, and other denominations but were loosely organized by geographical areas into what were called associations. Representatives from each congregation attended annual meetings to worship and discuss church business. These associations also helped new congregations get started and advised the older ones, especially in cases of disagreements.

On September 9, 1815, the Concord Association received a letter from Elder Luther Rice, agent of the Baptist Board of Foreign Missions for the United States.[39] Daniel says of his initial reaction to the idea of missions: "At the first view I was wonderfully pleased with the prospect of the gospel being extended with such rapidity, but having learnt in the time of my Methodist war, that nothing but Bible truth would stand the test, my mind was directly turned to my Bible, to see if the plan proposed by the mission principle was the Lord's way of sending the gospel and christianizing the world; so as I came to a knowledge of the mission plan, I compared it with the Lord's way of doing business, and I was sorry to find that they did not fit or work together."[40] Daniel also objected to the organizational superstructure of missions, which necessitated paid missionaries and central boards curtailing the freedom of members of the Baptist Church.

According to Daniel, in spite of his conviction that "there was evil in the mission principle," he kept quiet in order to see how the churches would vote in the Concord Association meeting of 1815. At that time he was the pastor of three churches and one "arm" or branch. All of the members of his flock who attended the association meeting voted against the mission principle, and a large majority of the churches as a whole voted against it, thus defeating it for that year.[41]

Meanwhile, a group of Baptists in Sumner County had formed a missionary society independent of the Concord Association. At the 1816 meeting another letter from the Baptist Board of Missions was read. According to Daniel, "Here, for the first time, I took a public and pointed stand against the mission principle and its objects." The extremely powerful and popular Daniel Parker "told the Association in plain terms, that if they did not drop the correspondence and cease their missionary operations, he would burst the Association." Since the members of the association knew how powerful and shrewd Daniel was, they disbanded the missionary society and severed connection with the Baptist Board of Missions. Daniel had meditated and struggled with his conscience for a year. He was pitting himself against his beloved Baptists, his brethren. Daniel states in his autobiography, "This was a hard time." As a finale to the 1817 meeting, Luther Rice preached and afterward passed the collection plate for foreign missions. When Parker was asked if he had contributed, he reportedly said that "no, he had no counterfeit half dollars; if he had he would have thrown in, but as he had none he would not throw away good money for such an object."[42]

Daniel Parker had reached the climax of his life. He had allied himself forever with the harsh doctrine of what came to be known as anti-missionism, which he would watch become more unpopular with each passing year of his life. In his autobiography Daniel reveals his feelings: "Until this time, I had lived in perfect peace with the Baptists, all in love, fellowship and union; but from that time until now, the greatest enemy I ever had in human shape is the mission spirit or principle, by men who call themselves Baptists, because I remain where they left me, and will not sacrifice the faith of God's elect."[43]

The next step in the evolution of Daniel's faith was his adoption of the strange doctrine of Two Seedism.

CHAPTER 3

Plain and Unpolished—
The Diamond in the Rough State

AFTER DANIEL PARKER had ceased fighting with the Methodists and had "smashed" the missionary movement in the Baptist Concord Association in 1816, he felt restless. He describes his feelings in his autobiography: "My mind was roving in the defiance of the truth against error, and where error was prevailing most against truth, there was the place that I felt like I ought to be, and though I often felt too mean and worthless to say I was one of the Lord's preachers, yet sometimes I felt as if something like the care of all the churches lay on my mind, and that God required of me to defend the cause of truth . . . and to maintain the rights of his church, not having the mission errors particularly in view."[1]

In this state of mind, Parker visited the Wabash area of southern Illinois. He felt that "the errors of the christian society (so called) were taking deep root there, and the truth of God in the Baptist cause was not fully maintained in some parts of that country, I thought perhaps I might be of as much use there as any place I could go." As an afterthought he added, "I could do better for my family by going to a new country."[2] As was usual with the Parkers, most of the family decided to move as a group.

Elder John and Sallie had at that time eleven living children. Their son John, born about 1783, had been killed near the beginning of the War of 1812 while fighting Indians near Cape Girardeau, Missouri.[3] His wife had gone back to Georgia.[4] Some of Daniel's brothers and sisters had married by this time and had children. A long wagon train pulled out in the fall of 1817. One of the popular roads from Tennessee to Illinois ran beside the rivers, following the Cumberland west to where it met the Ohio River on the border of Kentucky and Illinois. There the road crossed over the Ohio River and followed it for about seventy miles until it reached the Wabash, which forms the boundary between Illinois and Indiana. About 120 miles upriver lay Fort Lamotte, Illinois.[5]

When the Parker family arrived at the fort on a cold December day in 1817, the Sauk and the Fox Indians were hostile because of the tide of settlers flowing into their lands. During the War of 1812, these tribes had joined with the British and had annihilated a group of settlers and soldiers near Fort Dearborn, located on land in present-day Chicago. After the War of 1812 had ended in 1814 with the defeat of the British and the Indians, an uneasy peace ensued, with intermittent uprisings causing the settlers to flee to safety in blockhouses or forts. One of these disturbances occurred about the time the Parker clan arrived, and they were forced to take refuge in Fort Lamotte for a short while.[6] The huge family must have caused some consternation when they arrived at the cramped quarters of the fort.

Illinois was admitted to the Union one year after the Parkers' arrival. The population of the state was forty thousand in fifteen counties with two hundred Baptists scattered about in ten churches.[7] Because of the Indian problem, settlement of the state was slow until Black Hawk and his people were finally subdued in 1831 at the massacre at Bad Axe River.

There was a sharp dichotomy between the settlers who came from the East and those who came from the South. The easterners usually had the advantage of more education and often came to Illinois with more capital and material possessions. One southern woman complained, "I am getting skeery about them 'ere Yankees; there is such a power of them coming in that they and the Injuns will squatch out all the white folks."[8]

Fort Lamotte was surrounded by a number of Indian burial mounds. The countryside was beautiful with rolling prairies and primeval forests of oak, hickory, walnut, hackberry, sycamore, pecan, and cottonwood along the rivers and creeks.[9] The timber along the waterways made fingerlike projections into the prairies. Crawford County had a greater percentage of timber-covered land than open land, and some of the prairies were completely surrounded by trees.[10] An early traveler described the beauty of the land: "In summer the prairie is covered with a tall grass, which is coarse in appearance, and soon assumes a yellow color, waving in the wind like a crop of corn. In the early stages of its growth the grass is interspersed with little flowers, the violet, the strawberry blossom, and others of the most delicate structure. When the grass grows higher these disappear, and taller flowers displaying more lively colors take their place; and still later a series of still higher but less delicately formed flowers appear on the surface. While the grass is green these beautiful plains are adorned with every imaginable variety of color. It is impossible to conceive of a greater diversity. . . . In the summer the plants grow taller, and the colors more lively; in the autumn another generation of flowers arises which possess less clearness and variety of color and less fragrance."[11]

The principal river was the Wabash, and the area was drained on the north and west by Lamotte Creek. Although the prairies and river bottoms were swampy, the land was rich, black loam in some places and sandy soil in others, providing good farm land in most areas. Daniel Parker had finally found the rich land he had sought so long.[12]

Hard work and danger lay ahead for the Parkers. The Indians still roamed the forests, and the howls of wolves and the screams of panthers chilled the hearts of the settlers on long, lonely nights in their cabins. Deadly, mysterious milk sickness was a threat, and mosquitoes spread bone-racking malaria, which was called "ague," "agy," or "ager."[13] One old settler told a newcomer that she feared he was "in for a smart grip of agy." Later after he had recovered, she commented, "beat all the shakes I ever saw, he shuck the hull cabin."[14] The tough pioneers paid little attention to such a minor complaint as malaria, dismissing it by saying, "He ain't sick; he's only got the ager."[15] In spite of everything, the pioneers saw a "vision of loveliness," and when their town was laid out, they called it Palestine.[16]

Daniel was no longer a poor man. Before moving to Illinois, he had bought land in Robertson, Dickson, and Sumner counties in Tennessee and in Logan County, Kentucky.[17] He had also received a land grant of thirty-six acres in Sumner County. Evidently, he had given up his idealistic attitude toward acquiring material wealth. In his autobiography he states that when he first arrived in Tennessee, "I avoided every thing like trade or traffic for speculation, lest I should bring a reproach on the tender cause of God."[18] During the time Daniel spent in Illinois, he continued to buy and sell land, accumulating a considerable amount in Crawford, Clark, and Coles counties.[19]

The other members of the prolific Parker clan also prospered. They built their log cabins and settled in and around Crawford County. In about 1824, Elder John, Sallie, and other members of the family moved to present-day Coles County, where they were the first white settlers. According to family legend, Elder John preached the first sermon in Coles County in a small log cabin. The entire adult white population of the county was there—all eleven of them, all Parkers. Elder John called himself a "Two-Seed Baptist traveling preacher" and always closed his sermon with these words, "Brethren, we have wandered far into the wilderness, but even here death will find us." Elder John preached all over Illinois, first in homes and later in schoolhouses, but he did not have a reputation for piety. Family legend has pictured Elder John as a character—hard drinking, fun loving, and not adverse to bending the rules when it suited his fancy. When he fought in the American Revolution, he was known as "High Johnny" because of his high spirits. A story told about him was that he once closed a sermon with the announcement that he would be back "to preach at that place, that day in four weeks if it was not a good day for bee-hunting." In Tennessee the cryptic minutes of the Turnbull Church had told their story.[20]

Although the members of the Parker family always ended up living in the same general area, an ever-widening rift seemed to be occurring between Elder John and Daniel. Daniel's life centered around his God, and he always began his life in a new place with religious activities. On his arrival in Illinois he organized the Lamotte Baptist Church, the first church in Lamotte Township. Also, he immediately began to participate in civic affairs. Between the years of 1817 and 1824 he was a road supervisor, a caretaker of the poor, and a land custodian for the school district.[21]

Daniel entered state politics for the first time when he ran for a seat in the senate in 1822. Four men were running for the post, and of the 364 votes cast, he received 134. When he went to take his seat in the legislature, the state capital was located in the middle of a wilderness. The state house was a two-story frame building with low ceilings and a plain interior.[22] While serving in the legislature, Daniel was on the committee for internal improvements and worked diligently, submitting many resolutions and petitions for building roads and for constructing a canal to link the Illinois River with Lake Michigan.[23]

Another contribution Daniel made had to do with the slavery question. The Illinois constitution, written in 1818, prohibited slavery, but as more and more slave owners moved into the state, they began to agitate to legalize slavery. A bitter fight began in the legislature in 1823. One of the arguments of the pro-slavery faction was that since the French, who had been the first white inhabitants of Illinois, were allowed to own slaves, others should have the right also. In the midst of a heated argument on this point, one venerable gentleman, the state senator from Union County, arose and stated that "fittener men [than I am] mout hev been found to defend the masters agin the sneakin' ways of the infernal abolitioners; but havin' rights on my side, I don't fear, Sir. I will show that are proposition is unconstitutional, inlegal, and forenest the compact. Don't every one know, or leastwise had ought to know, that the Congress that sot at Post Vinsan [Vincennes], garnisheed to the old French inhabitants the right to their niggers, and haint I got as much rights as any Frenchman in this State?"[24]

After a bitter fight, the pro-slavery faction finally managed to pass a resolution calling for an election in which the people would be asked to decide whether or not to call a convention to amend the state constitution to permit slavery. The pro-slavery faction, knowing that they had a two-thousand-vote majority in the state, were ecstatic. They celebrated with an "impromtu jollification." First they formed a torchlight procession. Shouting, blowing tin horns, and beating on drums and pans, they marched down the streets of Vandalia until they reached the residence of Governor Edward Coles. There they emitted a cacaphonous "medley of groans, wailings and lamentations." After repeating their performance in front of the boardinghouses where their other opponents were staying, they held a banquet. One of the toasts was made to "the state of Illinois: the ground is good; give us plenty of negroes and a little industry and she will distribute her treasure."[25]

Daniel was a member of the determined little band in the legislature that fought against the faction favoring slavery, and he actively campaigned against the proposed pro-slavery constitutional convention. A letter he and fourteen other legislators wrote to the *Illinois Intelligencer*, a Vandalia newspaper, was published in the March 8, 1823, issue. In it they addressed the citizens of Illinois: "Selected by our fellow citizens to stand for a while upon the political watchtower, as sentinels for the public safety, we feel it our incumbent duty to sound the note of alarm, and to apprize you, that a portion of your rulers have formed the systematic design, to expunge from your constitution its fairest feature, and entail upon yourselves and your posterity the evils of slavery. . . . The song of the siren may be sung, but listen not to the notes of her melody." The fourteen legislators also proclaimed that slavery was "an usurpation, whose prohibition is written by the finger of God upon his works." They continued by stating that slavery "is appropriating the fruits of *their* [the slaves'] labor to feed *our* mouths. *Unjust*, because it is sinking them in mental degradation, to support us in indolence and ease." They concluded: "In the name of unborn millions who will rise up after us, and call us blessed or accursed, according to our deeds—in the name of the injured sons of Africa, whose claims to equal rights with their fellow men will plead their own cause against their usurpers before the tribunal of Eternal Justice, we conjure you, fellow citizens, to PONDER UPON THESE THINGS."[26]

Excitement built to a fever pitch. One of the anti-slavery legislators was burned in effigy, and the residence of Governor Coles was mobbed. The contest is described by an eyewitness: "Old friendships were sundered, families divided and neighborhoods arrayed in opposition to each other. Threats of personal violence were frequent, and personal collisions a common occurrence. As in times of warfare, every man expected an attack, and was prepared to meet it. Pistols and dirks were in great demand, and formed a part of the personal habiliments of all those conspicuous for their opposition to the Convention measure."[27] The populace became totally absorbed in the election. The "old preachers" railed against slavery and the proposed convention. Thousands of handbills and pamphlets were printed. An eyewitness describes the situation: "These missive weapons of a fiery contest were eagerly read by the people. The state was almost covered with them; they flew everywhere, and everywhere they scorched and scathed as they flew. . . . Almost every stump in every county had its bellowing, indignant orator on one side or the other, and the whole people for the space of eighteen months did scarcely anything but read newspapers, hand-bills, and pamphlets, quarrel, argue and wrangle with each other whenever they met together to hear the violent harangues of their orators."[28]

After more than eighteen months of contention, election day finally arrived. The "aged, the sick, and the crippled" were transported to the polls, sometimes from long distances. "Settlers from Peoria traveled one hundred miles by horseback and wagon to vote in Springfield. The Covenanters of Randolph County put aside their religious scruples against voting and voted, probably for the only in their lives. The turnout in the 1824 poll was overwhelming: 11,612 votes were cast. (Only 4,707 votes were cast in the next presidential election.) The anti-slavery group won with a majority of 1,668, and slavery was forever barred from Illinois."[29]

William Henry Perrin, who knew Daniel during his Illinois political career, sums up his character: "He was plain and unpolished—the diamond in the rough state—honest to a fault, kindly, and of justest impulses, a noble type of race fast fading away."[30]

Even though Daniel devoted a great deal of energy to politics, he seemed to have plenty left over for his consuming passion, religion. In the summer of 1818 when Daniel was still just settling in as pastor of Lamotte Prairie Baptist Church in Crawford County and Little Village Baptist Church in Lawrence County, the man who would soon become his bitterest enemy was crossing the Mississippi River and making his way into the fertile fields of Illinois. John Mason Peck was a Baptist missionary from New York. He and his wife had traveled twelve hundred miles, arriving at his headquarters in St. Louis on December 1, 1817, at almost exactly the time that Daniel Parker had arrived in Crawford County, Illinois, one hundred miles away. By October of 1818, Peck had formulated the constitution of his first missionary society and was soliciting money for his and Isaac McCoy's missionary work among the Indians. He also intended to establish seminaries for training teachers and ministers.[31]

In the years that followed, as John Mason Peck was organizing the missionary effort in western Illinois, Daniel Parker was organizing the anti-missionary fight in the eastern part of the state. Peck, who had hated Daniel from the start, attributed Daniel's anti-missionary zeal to jealousy, especially of the saintly Isaac McCoy, who had been a missionary to the Indians since 1817. Peck publicly denounced Parker in an address at a General Union Meeting of Baptists in 1832: "Parker was not the kind of man who would suffer another to hold a more elevated place in the estimation of Baptists than himself. Hence under the show of great zeal for the cause of Christ it became necessary for him to undermine McCoy's influence and that of his friends. His indefatigable zeal, which would have done honor to a good cause, and the prejudices of the people, enabled him at last to accomplish his object in part."[32]

Although Peck was hardly an objective observer, he was right in surmising that some of the antipathy of the anti-missionary people toward missions was due to the pioneer preachers' jealousy of the well-educated eastern "upstart" missionaries. The pioneer preachers felt that a college education was not necessary because if a man were truly called by God to preach, he could by diligent and prayerful study of the Bible learn God's word and communicate it to his congregation. In addition, the pioneer preachers resented being asked to send money to the East to educate what they called "man-made preachers." In a letter to the *Illinois Intelligencer* Daniel attacked the editor of a religious magazine called *Family Visitor:*

> Sir, I have been at a loss to know what tribe you are of, until I got your paper of August 24; then, sir, I began to suspect you for an Ishmalite, or at best part, Ashdod, that speaks half of each tongue, and cannot speak the Jewish language. Sir, if you be either of these, come out from behind the curtain like a man, and own your name; and then perhaps you will be at no loss to know what these hints, phillippick, & squibs mean, that you talked about; for the artillery of heaven is levelled against the workers of iniquity; and the phials of the wrath of God is preparing to be poured out upon all them that have the mark of the beast; and the sword of the Lord and of Gideon is ready to slay the enemies of God. . . . Sir, when

you talk about men teaching and sending out well taught preachers, in the way you do, and boasting of theological institutions, and seminaries of learning, &c. you show a plain mark of the beast, and manifest the wickedness of your heart—and that you are under the influence of a spirit, that would dethrone God; sap the foundation of the christian religion; raise anti-Christ to his full power; exalt those Popes that are training up men to preach; establish priestcraft; and lead the public to believe that no man is qualified to preach but classical men and thereby make them believe that those men whom God has called are fools or imposters; and by these means bring on an awful persecution (as soon as the beast has power) against the true Church of Christ.[33]

In his memoirs Peck compares the old western preachers with the young easterners. In so doing, he shows his mixed feelings toward both. He also shows the disparity between his ideas about religion and those of Daniel Parker:

Many of our frontier preachers, who never knew any rules for the interpretation of Scripture, but their own fancy, or as some of them mistakingly thought, the Spirit of God taught them the meaning—had some queer speculations. . . . A good English dictionary and a careful examination of the meanings of words, with a smattering of the elements of rhetoric, about "tropes and figures," and a slight touch of logic and mental philosophy would have been of great service to this class of preachers. But some of them were as much afraid of a dictionary as they were of a missionary.

It would be a capital thing if we could preserve the golden mean in the education of ministers, and especially young ones. . . . They are taught—or rather in our modern institutions, they are carried over superficially, a wide field in science and literature, and learn very little of THAT BOOK, doctrinally, practically and spiritually, which God has given, and out of which he has commanded them to teach the people. Some of these illiterate old men have studied the Bible carefully, and with prayer, and guided by plain common-sense, and deep reverence for the things of God, overflow with true Biblical knowledge, and spiritual emotions; though they sometimes make blunders in speech and miss the meaning of figurative language. And yet young preachers who have dabbled a little in Latin and Greek, are apt to turn up their noses at these old fathers. Such is poor human nature in young and old.[34]

Did Peck ever realize that he too was a victim of "poor human nature" as he railed against the pious and sincere Daniel Parker?

Another objection to the missionaries had to do with their efforts to Christianize the Indians. One anti-missionary minister claimed: "Missionaries use the poor heathen as mules or oxen; whipping them if they travel too slowly, and hitching them outdoors like beasts of burden. They send home false reports of success to their employers, for the purpose of retaining their incomes. See the great increase of vice, crime, dishonesty, theft, drunkenness, licentiousness, among the heathen after this spurious christianity.... When one scheme becomes a little stale they start another, so as to keep the minds of the people sufficiently excited to part with their money to these greedy beggars, who keep much of the money they get to pay themselves for begging, and the object for which they beg is little cared for."[35]

The other side of the story was pictured in a letter written in 1824 by William Polk, a friend of Isaac McCoy. Although Polk had fought against the Indians in the War of 1812, he became a supporter of them after witnessing their degradation as they were camped around Vincennes, Illinois. Their craving for alcohol and the greed of some of the traders and store owners had caused the Indians to be stripped of their possessions and the necessities of life. Polk wrote: "[If] Christians who now oppose missions as useless Could see the wretched situation of these Children of the forest and witness their gratitude in Receiving Cloaths to Keep them warm and could hear some of them . . . singing 'Jesus sought me when a stranger', [they] would be ashamed of their opposition."[36]

Daniel stated his primary objection in letters, pamphlets, and sermons preached in Illinois, Indiana, Kentucky, Tennessee, and North Carolina, feeling that "there was too much difference between the word of God and the mission principle."[37] He elucidated this point in a pamphlet entitled *A Public Address to the Baptist Society and Friends of Religion in General on the Principle and Practice of the Baptist Board of Foreign Missions for the United States of America,* published at his own expense in 1820. Parker states: "The colonization of the heathens ought to be conducted under the direction of our civil government, or a society formed for that express purpose, not under the character of any society of religion whatever. But we rejoice in all good that is done in translating the Bible, or educating the heathens and are willing to give our aid in counsel or money, provided it can be done and not dishonor the cause of religion."[38]

Meanwhile, the "two questions" were wreaking havoc all over Indiana and Illinois as Parker's supporters presented them year after year in every association meeting until every association had taken sides. A heated contest took place at the 1822 meeting of the Wabash Association—Daniel Parker pitted against John Mason Peck—a contest of "giants."[39] Peck describes his bitter enemy:

Mr. Parker is one of those singular and rather extraordinary beings whom Divine Providence permits to arise as a scourge to his church, and a stumbling-block in the way of religious effort. Raised on the frontiers of Georgia without education, uncouth in manners, slovenly in dress, diminutive in person, unprepossessing in appearance, with shriveled features, and a small, piercing eye, few men, for a series of years, have exerted a wider influence on the lower and less educated class of frontier people. With a zeal and enthusiasm bordering on insanity, firmness that amounted to obstinacy, and perseverance that would have done honor to a good cause, Daniel Parker exerted himself to the utmost.... He possessed a mind of singular and original cast. In doctrine he was an Antinomian from the first, but he could describe the process of conviction, and the joys of conversion, and of dependence on God, with peculiar feeling and effect.... He fully believed, and produced the impression on others, that he spoke by immediate inspiration. Repeatedly have we heard him when his mind seemed to rise above its own powers, and he would discourse for a few moments on the divine attributes or some doctrinal subject with such brilliancy of thought, and force and correctness of language, as would astonish men of education and talents. Then, again, it would seem as though he was perfectly bewildered in a mist of abstruse subtleties.[40]

In spite of his many good qualities, Peck was undoubtedly a snob. The "slovenly dress" by which he characterized Daniel was the typical garb of the pioneer preacher: well-worn, plain clothes made of broadcloth or even homespun. Peck at one point in his autobiography describes a poverty-stricken pioneer family as "ignorant, filthy, wretched squatters." He also states: "We had met with so little encouragement in visiting, conversing, and praying with this class that we concluded to pass them by."[41] Peck's autobiography is filled with mundane matters—descriptions of people, places, and events—whereas Parker's autobiography almost completely omits temporal affairs, being a soulful outpouring of his feelings about his relationship with his God.

For two years Peck and Parker debated in association meetings and even in the state capitol, but Daniel Parker's Calvinistic brand of religion was doomed in an America increasingly intent upon the right of individuals to decide their own destiny in this world as well as in the next. He compounded the slowly mounting antipathy to his religious views with the introduction into his religious philosophy of the strange concept now called Two Seedism. In 1826 Daniel published *Views on the Two Seeds*. Underneath the title is a quotation from Genesis 3:15: "And I will put enmity between thee and the woman, and between thy seed and her seed." The doctrine is based on a belief that God created Adam with the seed of Christ in his spirit. After Eve ate the forbidden fruit in the Garden of Eden, the seed of Satan was also implanted in the human spirit. From that time on, according to Daniel, "womankind is capable of producing children from the seed of Christ—the elect of God—and of the seed of Satan—the non-elect or fallen." Therefore, the fate of a person was determined by which seed grew in his soul.[42]

The publication of this pamphlet caused another rift in the already sorely beleaguered Baptist Church. Even Parker's home church at Lamotte Prairie was split asunder. A second Baptist church was established in the neighborhood and "made it a cause for exclusion when one of their number joined the 'Parkerites.'"[43] The furor cast Daniel into a deep depression. As he describes his feelings in his autobiography, he seems almost suicidal: "One evening, while solemnly reflecting on the state of things, knowing from every appearance that death somewhere must be the result, and striving to become reconciled in mind to die, rather than cause a distress in the church."[44]

However, Daniel received what he felt was another divine revelation: "The whole course of my ministry seemed opened to my view. The truth for I which I had so long been contending, particularly the doctrine of the union, appeared so glorious, that I felt as if I would as soon surrender the Bible as that truth. . . . I felt that if God would support me by his grace, that I would choose to die even at the stake, rather than surrender his cause."[45]

Parker printed another pamphlet, *Second Dose of Doctrine on the Two Seeds*.[46] In addition, he began publication of the *Church Advocate*, a religious journal written and edited in his log cabin home and published in Vincennes, Indiana, every month for two years. In it he referred to himself as "an old backwoods hunter."[47] Daniel, who had always denounced religious periodicals, justified his change in attitude with the following statement: "Although I am not much in favor of religious periodicals, yet finding so many errors

ingeniously circulating through that medium [Peck had just begun publishing a monthly journal called the *Pioneer*], against which I felt it my duty
to set up truth, and viewing that I could not do so in a durable and extensive way by traveling and preaching, I engaged in publishing the *Church
Advocate*."[48]

Although the anti-mission battle continued to rage in Illinois and the
rest of the nation for many years, Daniel must have known that his power
was waning. He ran for a seat in the Illinois House of Representatives, a
lower position than the one he had held previously, and was defeated.[49] His
publications were not selling well, and he had gone into debt to pay the
printer. He felt that he did not have time to "attend to my temporal business."[50] There were only a few churches in Illinois that espoused the Two
Seed doctrine and none in Parker's home county. His own anti-mission
stronghold, the Wabash Association, had stated in its 1931 "Circular Letter":
"Zion is almost forgotten. But little prayer for her, for sinners, ourselves or
our brethren is now felt or done. Watching over each other for evil becomes
more common than for good. Church discipline becomes more resorted to
for the purpose of excluding than for the object of reclaiming."[51]

The last few paragraphs of Daniel's autobiography, published in the final issue of the *Church Advocate*, convey a deep sadness: "My readers, I
must now bid you adieu until eternity decides all disputes, and though a
narrow bound may be my circle, yet through grace I shall mourn with the
afflicted children of Zion, regardless of all the abuse I may receive from the
enemy, rather than exchange the glories of the cross of Christ for the honours
of the world. . . . My day of trial will soon be over. I freely forgive all my
enemies for their trespasses against me, but their wickedness against the
Lord, his church and truth, is between them and the God with whom they
have to do."[52]

Daniel Parker was fifty-one years old. He was tired, but not defeated.
He wanted a new start in a land where he could be free to lead his flock
without constant strife. He turned his eyes toward virgin land—the wilderness of Texas.

Daniel was not the only member of the Parker clan who was feeling the
confinement of a settled area. Palestine had grown into a town of five or six
hundred inhabitants, and Crawford County was one of the most thickly
settled counties in Illinois.[53] According to family legend, in 1832 Daniel
and his brothers Benjamin, James, and Joseph made a scouting trip to Texas.[54]
Another unsubstantiated story is that Daniel went to call on the Mexican
authorities and requested that he be allowed to establish a church in Texas.

The Mexican authorities denied his request, but he decided that God had directed him to Texas to minister to these people who were "blinded by Catholicism." Again Daniel felt that God would provide some means for him to fulfill His will and thought of a plan in which he would organize a church in Illinois and move it to Texas in order to stay within the letter of the law. As the story goes, Daniel went to Stephen F. Austin and asked permission to bring an established church to Texas, and Austin assented. A verifiable fact is that Daniel Parker on March 16, 1833, took an oath of allegiance to the Mexican government and also vowed that he would return with his family by January 1, 1834.[55]

Daniel lost no time in returning to Illinois to carry out his plan. On July 26, 1833, in the Lamotte Regular Baptist Church meeting house, the Pilgrim Regular Predestinarian Baptist Church of Jesus Christ was organized with charter members Daniel and Patsey Parker, John Parker, Phoebe Parker, Julious and Rachel Christy, and Sally Brown. All were Daniel and Patsey's children and in-laws except for the Christys. The first meeting of the new church was on August 11, 1833, at Daniel and Patsey's home, where four new members were received. Two were the Parkers' daughter and son-in-law, Stephen and Anney Crist. Julious and Rachel Christy had decided to leave the congregation and were granted letters of dismission.[56]

As was customary, friends and relatives joined the emigrating group. Most of the children of Elder John and Sallie eventually moved to Texas. Nathaniel stayed in Coles County and served in the state legislature numerous times, and Mary Parker Kendrick had remained in Tennessee. Joseph Allen Parker and his family did not go with the first group but did arrive in Texas in June of 1834. Susannah Parker Starr and her family stayed in Illinois but emigrated in 1848 when her husband's doctor advised him to move to a warmer climate.[57]

With Daniel were his brother Silas and wife Lucy and their children Cynthia Ann, John, and Silas Jr. Daniel's brother Isaac and his wife and children were also in the wagon train. Elder John, who was seventy-five years old, went along also. His wife Sallie had died on July 28, 1824, or, in Daniel's words, had "gone home."[58] On March 21, 1825, in Knox County, Indiana, Elder John had married Sarah (Sallie) Duty, the widow of Richard Duty. Several of her daughters had married into the Parker family.[59] Daniel and his wife Patsey were accompanied by most if not all of their eleven children and their families. Daniel's brother James and his family had struck out on their own and did not go with this group. In all, some thirty ox-drawn wagons pulled out of Crawford County, Illinois, in the fall of 1833, and others were picked up along the way. Making their way to Texas were Parkers, Browns, Kennedys, Jordans, Greenwoods, Lagos, Bennetts, Crists, Faulkenberrys, Eatons, Frosts, Davidsons, Sadlers, and some others.[60]

It was a pleasant time of year to travel. Unlike the harrowing trips across the desert to California in later years, earlier trips across the South and the Midwest were usually pleasant times of fellowship and excitement. The men hunted and fished to provide fresh meat, and a high point was the discovery of a bee tree. Added to the pleasure of this group was religious zeal, and the joy of bringing a new religion to the wilderness. The pilgrims stopped each Sunday and held worship services. The anonymous writer of Daniel's biographical sketch describes the scene: "The members [of the Pilgrim Baptist Church] and company generly had provided themselves with tents. On a Sabath eve they would pitch thear tents with a vew of reatiring tell monday. . . . Ther was the wilderness home of the savage made vocal with hymns of praise to the most high God. . . . Such was [the] adroitness in perserving order in the church, that not one singel difficulty occured, during the travel."[61]

The pilgrims traveled across Illinois and crossed the Mississippi River at Chester, Illinois. During most of the trip they had to make their own roads. After crossing the Mississippi, they went down through Missouri, Arkansas Territory, and Louisiana. On October 20, 1833, they held a business meeting in Claiborne Parish and received seven new members into the church. They crossed the Sabine River at Gaines' Ferry, and they were finally in Texas, their new home, in November of 1833. While they were camped near San Augustine, Texas, a spectacular meteor shower occurred, later known as "the night the stars fell." John Harvey Greenwood, who was in the wagon train, tells the reaction of the people: "The old women seemed to think that the day of judgement had come like a thief in the night. We had two Baptist preachers in the crowd, my father Garrison Greenwood and Daniel Parker but the Lord had not revealed anything of this kind to them therefore they could not lend us much comfort in this trying hour. So the remainder of the night was spent in prayer."[62]

The immigrants made their way to Nacogdoches, then a small Mexican-type town. They stayed there several days and then went to Bedias Bayou and camped for a few days near the Indian village. The Bedias were a small tribe and were friendly to the settlers at this time. While the pilgrims were camped in this place, they were visited by Sam Houston: "He rode up to our camp on a thorobred Mexican or Indian horse, and old-style

Mexican saddle, a long hair rope on his horse's neck. . . . Houston wore a broad brim sombrero, a buckskin coat with long fringe hanging down the sides, leggins of the same kind of buckskin and moccasins on his feet. He stayed at our camp and talked with us for several hours and gave us much valuable information about this country."[63]

In December some of the members split off and traveled to present Limestone County. Daniel and his remaining followers traveled only a few miles south and settled, and on January 20, 1834, the first recorded meeting in Texas of the Pilgrim Regular Predestinarian Baptist Church, and possibly the first Baptist church service in Texas, was held in Daniel Parker's cabin on Holland's Creek on the outskirts of the present town of Anderson.[64] Daniel is credited with performing the first wedding ceremony in Grimes County when in the summer of 1834 he married Henry Fanthorp and Rachel Kennard in their future home, a log cabin with a stone chimney at each end.[65]

After a short stay on Holland's Creek, Daniel and some of his followers built Fort Brown on San Pedro Creek near present-day Grapeland but later moved a few miles northwest to Daniel's headright of about 4,600 acres of land near present-day Elkhart. There he established the home base for his religious activities and the headquarters for his vast empire of land.[66]

PART II

RACHEL

CHAPTER 4

Father, Forgive Them

RED-HAIRED RACHEL PARKER was named after the lovely girl in the Bible, she whose beauty had caused Jacob to labor fourteen years for her hand in marriage. Even though Rachel was only a young girl, she was a pioneer, and she must have known that her marriage to Luther Thomas Martin Plummer would mean land for her and her husband, forty-six hundred acres. But Rachel and L. T. M. paid for their land—they paid the highest price of all.[1]

The father of Rachel Parker was James W. Parker, who was born in Georgia on July 4, 1797, the ninth child of Elder John and Sallie Parker. He immigrated with his parents and brothers and sisters first to Tennessee and then to Illinois, where at the age of nineteen he married Martha (Patsey) Duty. Surprisingly, the ceremony was performed by Daniel's enemy, missionary Isaac McCoy. On March 22, 1819, Rachel was born, an obscure pioneer child but destined to become one of the most famous women on the frontier. James was fairly prosperous and was obviously respected since he was twice elected justice of the peace, but the land around Crawford County was swampy and unhealthy, and three of James and Patsey's children died. The death rate among children was high during that time, but in the tough Parker clan, few children died. Amazingly, all of James's eleven brothers and sisters lived to adulthood. James said that the death of his children was the reason he decided to move to Texas.[2]

Although it appears that James accompanied his brothers Daniel, Benjamin, and Joseph on their exploratory trip to Texas in 1832, he was not living in Illinois at that time.[3] Since 1830, he and his brother Joseph had been living with their families in Conway County, Arkansas Territory. In a letter to Stephen F. Austin written at San Felipe and dated June 29, 1832, James W. Parker informs Austin that he has spent three months "exploring your colony" and requests permission to settle twenty-five or thirty families in Texas. "Some of them professors of religion (Baptist) they want the liberty of concience and of worshiping accordingly. . . . I am determind on becomeing a resident if I can do So on any principals that I can live by." James gives his permanent address as "Peconery post office, Conway County, Arkansas Territory."[4] At that time many prospective colonists lived in Arkansas Territory for a while, waiting until it seemed safe to move to Texas. A number of Indian tribes inhabited Texas, including the ferocious Comanches. The Parkers had lived near and sometimes fought against various tribes of Indians since the first Parker had set foot on American soil, but they had never come up against Plains Indians. Another problem was that war with Mexico was imminent.

As Daniel was organizing his church in Illinois, James and his family had made their way to Texas sometime before August of 1833. Daniel and his caravan arrived in November of that year.[5] James moved around a great deal, staying at different locations on the Angelina, Colorado, and Brazos rivers. He left the Colorado River valley because of trouble with Indians, saying: "Many of my neighbors were killed and scalped by the savage foe, during my stay here; among whom were Messrs. Christian and Strother; Mr. Wilbarger was literally shot to pieces, scalped, and left as dead. We found him soon after, and with great care and attention his life was preserved."[6]

The land that James eventually chose was not in Austin's Colony but in Sterling C. Robertson's Colony, farther north, and on April 1, 1835, James, his brother Silas, and his son-in-law L. T. M. Plummer each received a league and a labor of land, about forty-six hundred acres. There must have been rejoicing and praising of God when the Parkers heard that their land grants had been approved—forty-six hundred acres each for James, L. T. M., and Silas. The next task was to build a fort on the land near "the head-waters of the River Navisott," near present-day Groesbeck. James states that he and Silas built Fort Parker in 1835, but surely the other men in the area helped. Contemporary documents indicate that the fort was in existence in July of 1835. Its twelve-foot-high log walls, with tops hewn to sharp points, enclosed four acres. Blockhouses were built on two corners to be used as lookout posts and bastions for firing at attacking Indians. Attached to the inside walls of the fort were six tiny cabins. Facing south was a huge double gate, the only other entrance being a small gate adjacent to the southwest blockhouse, through which the inhabitants could go to fetch the clear, cold water of a spring.[7]

The Parkers must have been proud of their little empire—thousands of

Replica of Fort Parker near Groesbeck, Texas. Courtesy Joseph E. Taulman Collection, the Center for American History, the University of Texas at Austin.

acres of rolling, fertile land. The vast acreage had everything the pioneers looked for. Lying at the junction of the blackland prairie and the post oak belt, it had small meadows here and there surrounded by virgin forests of oak, ash, walnut, and sweet gum, a spring for unlimited fresh water, several creeks, and a river. After wandering from Virginia to Georgia to Tennessee to Illinois to Texas, the Parkers were at last on the brink of making their fortune.

The pioneers moved into their fort, and the stage was set. Far out on the plains, the antagonists were getting ready to make their entrance. The Comanches, whose name is sometimes translated as "anyone who wants to fight me all the time," were known as the Lords of the South Plains. They held their supremacy because they could shoot clouds of arrows with amazing accuracy, ride while hanging from a horse by one foot, and were the most intrepid warriors on the plains. Two hundred years earlier they had been a starving, straggling bunch of food gatherers who wandered on foot in the Rocky Mountains and the plains. Their acquisition of the horse had changed all that, and after their appropriation of the huge herds of buffalo on the plains, they were set. Their bravery, skill as horsemen, and reputation for ferocity enabled them to occupy one of the prime hunting areas of the world.

At first the Comanches tolerated the few traders and adventurers who wandered into their midst. For seventy-five years the Comanches had raided San Antonio and the other Spanish settlements with few reprisals, but the tribe soon learned that the Texans were a new breed. As the line of settlement moved slowly northward and westward, their most beautiful haunts, those with the best grass and the clearest water, were gradually being swallowed up by land-hungry Texans. The Comanches undoubtedly knew about the fort being built on their hunting grounds. Perhaps they watched silently from the woods as it went up.

Meanwhile, the Parkers settled in. The cabins were small and cramped, but each had a fireplace, a bed attached to the wall in typical pioneer fashion, a homemade table fastened together with wooden pegs, and a bench or several stools. The dirt floor was packed hard and swept often, but still it was impossible for the women to keep their families clean. The living conditions were especially trying for families with young children. Rachel was pregnant when they moved in, and James Pratt Plummer, born on January 6, 1835, was the first child born in Fort Parker. Rachel and L. T. M. must have sat in front of the fire at night talking quietly about their vast land holdings and about where they were going to build their house. They needed a spring close by, and if they built on a hill, they could sit in the gallery and gaze at their land rolling away into the distance.[8]

They may also have discussed the political situation in Texas. The settlers were restive under the oppressive Mexican rule. Skirmishes between the colonists and Mexicans had occurred in 1832, leading to the arrest of William B. Travis and others. In 1833 Stephen F. Austin had traveled to Mexico City to confer with the authorities. While returning to Texas, he had been arrested and incarcerated in the Prison of the Inquisition in Mexico City. After almost a year, Austin was released, and seven months later in July of 1835, he was allowed to return to Texas. After such treatment, Austin gave up all hope that the colonists could settle their differences with Mexico, and he accepted the chairmanship of the provisional government at San Felipe. On September 19, 1835, the provisional government called for a consultation. Two of the Parker men rode down to San Felipe to represent their districts. James Parker was one of the representatives for the Municipality of Viesca, and Daniel Parker was a delegate from the Municipality of Nacogdoches.[9]

In 1835 San Felipe was a scraggly collection of log cabins stretching along the east bank of the Brazos River. The official opening date of the Consultation was October 15, 1835, but a quorum was not attained until November 4. The first order of business was to elect a presiding officer. Branch T. Archer was chosen, and in his inaugural address, he outlined Austin's plan of action, which included the proposition that the delegates make a declaration for the reinstatement of the Constitution of 1824 of the Republic of Mexico. Austin's strategy was to stall for time, increase Anglo immigration to Texas, and eventually break away from Mexico.[10]

According to Gail Borden Jr., publisher of the San Felipe newspaper, the Consultation continued in an orderly manner. He described the three days of debates as "lengthy and animated yet coolness and moderation pervaded throughout."[11] The delegate from Victoria, John J. Linn, disagreed. According to Linn, the atmosphere of the Consultation was that of a rough-and-tumble frontier gathering. Linn tells the story of the conflict between a Mr. Urbane and Martin Parmer, who was also known as the "Ringtailed Panther." Urbane had graciously lent the use of the building in San Felipe where the Consultation was held. Parmer complained because the stove smoked, and a corn mill used by Urbane caused a loud, irritating noise, making it difficult for the delegates to hear. When approached with the problems, Urbane suggested that they could solve the problem of the smoking stove if they removed it, and he would be glad to discontinue the use of his grist mill as long as his boarders, some of whom were delegates to the Consultation, did not mind doing without bread. He also reminded the delegates that they had the use of his hall free. The Ringtailed Panther made a motion that Urbane be fined fifty dollars for "contempt of the Consultation." The motion was defeated.[12]

On the other hand, Anson Jones did not find the situation at the Consultation amusing. "There appeared to me a plenty of recklessness and selfishness, but little dignity or patriotism. Still there were some good men there. But I felt sick at heart at the prospect. I was introduced to Bowie—he was dead drunk. . . . The first night after my arrival, I was kept awake nearly all night by a drunken carouse in the room over that in which I 'camped. . . . What made the whole thing more unpleasant to me was, that the whole burden of conversation, so far as it was, at times, intelligible, appeared to be abuse and denunciation of a man for whom I had the highest respect, Gen. Stephen F. Austin, then in command before San Antonio de Bexar, for not breaking up the siege of that place, and retreating to the east of the Colorado. . . . History will not be able to say much in favor of that 'Consultation'; nor of the Provisional Government they established. It however had the effect intended, of precipitating the final, and probably inevitable result, of an early separation from Mexico." Jones's attitude may have been caused in part by the fact that he was a member of the opposing party. In fact, his life was threatened, and he had to flee from San Felipe.[13]

Daniel Parker was one of the most visible personages at the Consultation, serving on many committees and proposing a number of resolutions. The Parkers were opposed to war with Mexico. Linn reports: "Mr. Daniel Parker, in a speech delivered on the floor of the Consultation, declared that the liberality of Mexico in her dealings with the colonists was unparalleled in the annals of time. To the head of each family a league of land was given; exemption from all taxes, custom duties, etc. for ten years. To what land could they have turned for a more liberal tender?" One of the most important resolutions Daniel proposed established the Texas Rangers. He proposed that three companies of rangers be formed, one for the area between the Brazos and Trinity rivers, one for the east side of the Trinity River, and the third for the area between the Brazos and Colorado rivers. Silas M. Parker was designated as "superintendant" in charge of "twenty five rangers whose business shall be to range and guard the frontiers between the Brazos and Trinity rivers. . . . Each ranger that [is] employed [will receive] one dollar & twenty five cents per day." Other men were assigned to the two other areas. A Committee of Five was formed in order to report on the resolution, and Daniel Parker was a member of this committee. The proposal passed and supposedly, Fort Parker was safe—a strong fortification protected by a company of Texas Rangers.[14]

The Committee of Five submitted a report containing a number of items. The last item was: "the committee . . . beg leave to report that in their opinion . . . that said officers be particular not to interfere with friendly tribes of Indians on our borders that said superintendants shall watch over the conduct of the officers and report accordingly and see that full justice is done to the bounds assigned them."

On October 18, 1835, Daniel Parker also made the following amendment to a resolution made by A. Houston, which resulted in the following:

Whereas, several of the Indian chiefs [of the Cherokee, Shawnee, and other tribes] were invited to the Consultation of Texas, to convene with them for the purpose of having their claims to their land properly adjusted by that body . . . the committee are of the opinion that it is the duty of this council to appoint three commissioners, whose duty it shall be to repair immediately to the villages of the said Indians, with full powers to hold a consultation with them, for the purpose of ascertaining their grievances, and for giving them full assurances that their case will be properly attended to, as soon as the Consultation meets.

This Committee are of the opinion that there have been unwarrantable encroachments made upon the lands occupied by the said Indians; therefore, be it resolved, by the permanent council of Texas now in session, that Peter J. Menard, Jacob Garrett, and J. L. Hood be appointed commissioners for the purpose of holding consultations with the different tribes of Indians, and giving them such assurances as may be necessary for the advancement of their rights and privileges as citizens of Texas, and for the purpose of transacting such other business as may be necesary to promote the cause of the people of Texas.

The document was signed by A. Houston, A. G. Perry, Peter J. Menard, J. L. Hood, and Daniel Parker.[15] It is impossible to determine the primary motive of Daniel and the other committee members. Did they care about the plight of the Indians, or did they merely want to placate the Indians to avoid having them join the Mexicans in the coming revolution?

On November 4, Daniel Parker tried to offer a plan for a declaration to the people of Texas. Sam Houston moved that the plan be tabled for the present and referred to the committee on the subject. The motion passed. When the committee of twelve men began the work of framing a declaration, they had at least four plans from which to work: those of Daniel Parker, Stephen F. Austin, Don Carlos Barrett, and Robert M. Williamson. All drafts have been preserved except the one written by Daniel. The final document was primarily based on the plan submitted by Austin.[16]

At one time during the Consultation, six of its members traveled to Salado Creek, twelve miles east of San Antonio, in order to address the members of the Texas army who were camped there. As the story goes, after Stephen F. Austin, Daniel Parker, Sam Houston, Branch Archer, and other distinguished orators had harangued the group for several hours, the opinion of the troops was that the dignitaries should go back to San Felipe to attend to their business while the army did the fighting.[17]

The Consultation was disbanded after a month of deliberations. The members had voted thirty-three to fourteen to remain a part of Mexico and to try to work out the differences between the settlers and the central government.[18] Daniel and James Parker were members of the peace party, but their efforts to avert war were in vain. In January of 1836, the dreaded Antonio López de Santa Anna led an army across the border into Texas. The Texans tended to hold most of the Mexican soldiers in contempt, but here was a seasoned, veteran soldier—wily, brilliant, ruthless. At forty-two years of age, General Santa Anna was slim and athletic. Middle-class by birth, he had moved up through the ranks, finally becoming dictator of

Mexico. He was hated by many in Mexico because of the ruthless methods he used in quelling rebellions, allowing his soldiers to rape and kill non-combatants and seldom taking prisoners. Also, he used opium on occasion and was a profligate and a womanizer. In a fake ceremony he "married" a young girl in San Antonio although he had a wife in Mexico.[19]

When Santa Anna entered Texas, he struck terror into the hearts of the inhabitants. As pioneer George B. Erath stated, "It became known that Santa Anna had crossed the Rio Grande with seven thousand men, and was advancing rapidly, vowing death and extermination to the American race on Mexican soil." Santa Anna divided his force into two parts, and with a contingent of four thousand men swept across Texas headed for San Antonio. The Texans, casting aside the vague, conciliatory resolutions of the Consultation, got ready for war. The Convention of 1836 was called, and the first meeting was held on March 1, 1836, at Washington-on-the-Brazos. As the convention opened, the colonists shivered in an unfinished building while a freezing norther roared outside. Daniel Parker was in attendance although he was not a delegate. He received the honor of opening the convention with a prayer. The delegates quickly got down to business. They wrote a Declaration of Independence, organized a government, and appointed Sam Houston commander in chief of the motley Texas army. Early on the morning of March 17, 1836, the delegates were informed that the Mexican army was approaching. They quickly adjourned and fled in all directions.[20]

William Barrett Travis and James Bowie with 185 men had decided to make a stand at San Antonio in an abandoned mission called the Alamo. While the convention was in progress, Santa Anna had ridden into San Antonio with five thousand troops. Flying above his head was a red flag, which meant no surrender—no quarter. The men in the Alamo fought valiantly, but they were massacred, selling their lives dearly while they bought much-needed time for General Houston to train and rally his ephemeral army.

After the Alamo fell, Santa Anna began what he considered to be a mop-up operation. The red flag still flew and Texans feared for their lives. A mass exodus of women and children and a few men began toward the Sabine River and the safety that lay in the United States. The precipitous flight, which came to be known as the Runaway Scrape, had begun as early as January 1836 in San Patricio, San Antonio, and Refugio, but the real panic began in mid-March when Houston sent dispatches to the settlers telling them to leave at once.

It was a cold March, and as luck would have it, rain set in and fell for six weeks. The settlers packed hurriedly and scoured the countryside for carts, wagons, anything with wheels so that the women and children would not have to walk. Some slaughtered chickens and other farm animals and packed food for the journey, but others left dishes and food on the table as they dashed away. As provisions ran out, nearly all suffered from hunger.

The roads were clogged with people as thousands went east toward Louisiana. Most of the vehicles were uncovered, and the travelers sat huddled together in them as the rain pelted their faces and soaked their clothes. Others walked day after day in mud and water. At night the refugees tried to start fires to prepare food and dry their clothes, ever fearful not only of the Mexican soldiers with their red flag but of Indians as well. As the refugees slept, sometimes their horses were stolen. Some slept little at night, fearing that they would have to make their way on foot.

Worst of all, disease broke out—whooping cough, sore eyes, and a measles epidemic along with colds and dysentery. Weakened by hunger, fatigue, and exposure, many sickened and died, especially the old and the very young. Their bodies and were buried beside the road. Mothers held sick children in their arms for mile after mile in the rain until they reached the Trinity River. Five hundred people were fighting for a place on the ferry when the Trinity broke out of its banks, trapping hundreds in a huge lake of water. After wandering for several days in the flooded river bottom, the refugees finally reached Liberty, where many stopped, too tired and ill to go on.[21]

Most of the Parker men did not join the Texas army but served in ranger companies at one time or other in 1836.[22] During an election held at Fort Parker on February 1, 1836, all but one of the men had voted for peace. As the entire population of Texas was streaming in an ever increasing tide to the Louisiana border, the inhabitants of Fort Parker joined the throng.[23]

Rachel and L. T. M. had a sixteen-month-old son, James Pratt, and the little family must have huddled together in the rain as they made their way down to the Old San Antonio Road and from there to the Trinity River crossing at Robbins' Ferry. When the refugees reached the Trinity, they could not cross the rain-swollen river, so they camped on its banks. They had traveled some seventy miles sloshing through mud and water.[24]

As the refugees were plodding eastward through the rain, momentous events were taking place on the coast. Sam Houston retreated before Santa Anna's seven-hundred-man detachment, considerably smaller than the attack force at the Alamo. Sensing that a showdown was coming, men who had left the Texas army at the beginning of the Runaway Scrape began to rejoin the ranks. Houston retreated closer and closer to the coast until he finally decided to make a stand in a field bounded by the San Jacinto River and Buffalo Bayou. Nerves strained from weeks of retreat, blood boiling from the slaughters at the Alamo and Goliad, the men were ready for a fight.

The Mexicans had marched into a trap. Realizing their precarious position, they spent most of the night of April 20 frantically erecting a barricade. On the morning of April 21, the Texans learned that General Martín Perfecto de Cos had crossed over Vince's bridge with 540 troops, bringing the total Mexican force to about 1,200. Houston ordered Vince's bridge destroyed, and the Texans knew it would be a fight to the finish. Houston's force consisted of 910 men.

On April 21, the weary Mexican troops waited all day for an attack, and when none came, they lay down for their afternoon siesta. Houston chose this moment to charge the Mexican camp. The slaughter that followed surpassed that of the Alamo and Goliad. The Mexicans, roused from sleep, weaponless, on foot, begged for mercy as they were shot down, hacked to pieces, or clubbed to death with rifle butts. The Texans picked them off in the water as they tried to swim the San Jacinto River. An estimated 639 were killed that day—630 Mexican soldiers and nine Texans. Sam Houston was wounded, but not seriously, and Santa Anna was captured. The independence of Texas, declared forty-seven days earlier, was secured in a short, bloody battle on the swampy plain of San Jacinto.

The Parkers, camped on the banks of the Trinity, heard the news in a few days. Surely they lifted their voices in praise that peace was restored in the land. They started back to the fort on April 23.

After their return, the settlers at Fort Parker fell back into the slow rhythm of farm life. Rachel and L. T. M. were expecting a second child in six months. Rachel was seventeen. She had been through a great deal of hardship in her short life, and there was much more to come.

The unsettling events of the war had encouraged the Indians to increase their raids in many parts of the republic. Most Texans, especially those in the outlying areas, slept fitfully if at all on the nights when a full moon lighted the way for Indian raiders.

The settlers in the vicinity of Fort Parker had been having serious problems with Indians. In February of 1835 Sterling C. Robertson, G. W. Pierson, and James W. Parker had made a peace treaty with "12 of the principal chiefs of the hostile Indians."[25] Then a few settlers on the Colorado attempted to steal horses from the Tawakonis, and the Indians retaliated by killing several settlers and stealing cattle and other stock. On July 11, 1835, Robert Morris Coleman with about eighteen men invaded the Tawakoni Indian village at Tehuacana Spring a few miles from Fort Parker. Finding themselves greatly outnumbered, Coleman and his men fled to Fort Parker and sent out a call for reinforcements, which was answered by Edward Burleson and John H. Moore, who organized four companies of volunteers and joined Coleman at Fort Parker. The whites trailed the Indians for over one hundred miles to the northwest and finally found a small encampment, which they attacked and routed, killing three and taking five or six captives.[26] Coleman's invasion of the Tawakoni village stirred up that group of Indians as well as other related tribes, and in August of 1835 they began a war upon the settlers.[27] The Cherokees in East Texas were hostile as well, and rumors of Indian attacks were rife. In November of 1835, Silas Parker was authorized to add ten men to his company of rangers, but after three months of service, the men were discharged.[28]

On January 8, 1836, Casimiro, a Comanche of the Yamparika band, presented himself to the Mexican political chief of the Bexar Department, saying, "Within three or four days, Comanches will attack the ranches and the settlers in the neighborhood of this municipality." On the same day an unnamed Comanche presented himself to the headquarters of the Commandancy of Bexar, demanding within twenty days a treaty of "Amity, Commerce & Limits." On January 17, 1836, the General Council "proceeded to the election of five commissioners to hold said treaty.... Edward Burleson, J. C. Neill, John W. Smith, Francisco Ruíz, and Byrd Lockhart were duly elected," but no treaty was made until much later.[29]

At about this time, James Riley, Thomas Riley, and Robert Coleman were attacked by forty Caddos and Comanches when the white men attempted to make a settlement on the San Gabriel River. Also in early January, the Hibbons family was attacked by Comanches while traveling to their home on the Guadalupe River, and in April most of the members of the Beales' colony were massacred by Comanches, and Sarah Ann Horn, a Mrs. Harris, and their young children were taken captive. The situation was becoming worse in the spring as Mexican agents attempted to incite the Indians. On April 11, 1836, U.S. Indian agents reported the Hainais, Nadacos, Kichais (Caddos), and Wichitas had met with members of the Comanche tribe on the forks of the Trinity River where Dallas lies today to discuss how they could use the unsettled state of the country to their advantage.[30]

Because of this unrest, the ranger companies in most parts of the state were on duty and alert. In his memoirs James W. Parker, who was the captain of the Fort Parker rangers, makes an incomprehensible statement: "I had disbanded the troops under my command, as there appeared to be but little danger of an attack, and as the Government was not in a condition to bear the expense of supporting troops, unless the circumstances were of such nature as to imperiously demand it."[31]

According to a story passed down in the LaGrone family, because of the threat of attack by Indians, Sam Houston had even ordered the inhabitants of Fort Parker to evacuate, but they had stayed. The descendants of Adam LaGrone contend that he was a scout for the ranger band at Fort Parker, and in mid-May, after learning that the fort would be attacked at dawn on May 19, he warned the Parkers, but they took no heed. Then LaGrone drew his pistol, held it on Silas Parker, and told the Parkers and their neighbors that anyone who wanted to flee to safety should do so at once. Several families fled to Nacogdoches.[32]

Still another source states that the inhabitants of the fort were warned of the impending attack by Griffin Bayne, who had been informed by a friendly Indian. Consequently Elisha Anglin, David Faulkenberry, and Silas H. Bates, who lived in cabins near the fort, removed their families to Fort Houston sixty miles northeast. A slightly different version of this story that has been passed down in the Parker family gives additional details: Elisha Anglin lived on his farm near Fort Parker. His brother Abram, who lived near Fort Houston, traded with an Indian named Jack Still. One day Still told Abram, "You had better get him [Elisha] away before so many (naming how many) moons, as the wild Indians of the Northwest are going to destroy that fort." As soon as Elisha was informed of the impending Indian attack, he and Faulkenberry moved their families and belongings to Fort Houston. Elisha tried to get the others to go, but they were determined to stay.

According to an Anglin version of the story, Adrian Anglin, not Elisha, warned the Fort Parker pioneers. In 1835 Adrian and his wife had settled in what is now Houston County, leaving their daughter Margaret Anglin Duty and her husband Richard Duty in Illinois. This younger Duty family immigrated to Texas in 1836, settling near Fort Parker. In early May an "old Indian" went to Adrian Anglin and told him that Fort Parker was going to be attacked by Indians. Anglin ignored the warning, but the next week the Indian returned, saying that "one week from today the Fort will be taken and your daughter will be taken or killed." Becoming alarmed, Anglin enlisted the help of a neighbor, Mr. Box, and they set out for Fort Parker in "an ox wagon." Before their departure, Anglin's "Indian friends" gave him a small piece of leather with marks on it to show to any Indians who might attempt to "molest" them. When the men arrived at Fort Parker, Richard Duty refused to leave "on account of business," so Anglin and Box loaded Margaret and her baby into the wagon and started out toward present-day Houston County. At sundown while they were preparing to camp on the bank of a river, they saw forty or fifty Indians in full war paint dashing toward them. Anglin "met them with a smile and shook hands with them." He then showed them the "cowhide pass" and proposed smoking a peace pipe, offering them tobacco that he kept on hand for such emergencies. The Indians conferred among themselves for a while and then mounted their horses and, with a departing "war hoop," galloped away. The refugees reached their destination without further incident.[33]

If the Parkers knew of the unrest and were warned of the Indian attack, why did James disband the ranger company? Why did ten of the men leave the fort to work in the fields? Why were the huge front gates of the fort open and Silas's gun unloaded? These questions will never be answered, but what happened on Tuesday, May 19, 1836 is horribly clear.

On May 19, ten men and a boy left Fort Parker and went into the fields to work. Among them were Rachel's father James W., her husband L. T. M., her brother-in-law Lorenzo Nixon, and her brother Wilson. Seven additional men sometimes slept in cabins on their farms, but on the night before the nineteenth they had spent the night in the fort. They were David Faulkenberry and his son Evan; Seth Bates and his son Silas; Elisha Anglin and his son Abram; and "old man" Lunn.

Left in the fort were six men: Elder John Parker, Benjamin Parker, Silas Parker, Samuel Frost and his son Robert, and G. E. Dwight. The women and children in the fort were Silas's wife, Lucy, and their children, Cynthia Ann, John, Silas Jr., and Orlena; Rachel Parker Plummer and her son James Pratt; Rachel's sister, Sarah Parker Nixon; their mother, Patsey Duty Parker, and her young son; Rachel's step-grandmother, Sallie Duty Parker (Elder John's wife); Rachel's aunt, Elizabeth Duty Kellogg, a young widow; Mrs. Frost and her children; and Mrs. Dwight and her children.[34]

At about ten o'clock in the morning a large band of Indians rode up. Rachel, who wrote two versions of her story, first listed the following tribes: "There was many of the different tribes; Tywaconies, Cadoes, Keacheys, Wakos, Towash, some Beadies, and I have but little knowledge how many others. There was of the Commanchees somewhere from six to seven hundred, they composed the strongest party." In the second version she gave no list, mentioning only Comanches and "Kitchawas" [Kichai]. Later evidence in which one of the Indians in the raid was identified as a "Caddo" from a neighboring tribe indicates that at least two tribes were involved: Comanches and Kichai, who were also called Caddos by the settlers.[35]

The first that Rachel knew about the Indians was when she heard someone yell the words that struck terror into the pioneer's soul, "Indians! Indians!" The Indians were a little more than a quarter of a mile from the fort. The inhabitants of the fort ran about in confusion. Sarah Nixon dashed out of the fort and ran to find her husband and father in the fields. The other women quickly left, carrying their babies and dragging their toddlers by the hand. Mr. Dwight gathered up his family along with Mrs. Frost and her children. Elder John and Granny Parker ran as fast as they could. Only Rachel, who was pregnant, hesitated. Her explanation was, "I was in the act of starting to my father, but I knew I was not able to take my little son."

As Dwight was herding his wife and children out of the fort, Silas yelled at him, "Good Lord, Dwight, you are not going to run? Stand and fight like a man, and if we have to die we will sell our lives as dearly as we can." Dwight promised to return after he had hidden his family in the woods. Did Silas buy time for the women and children to escape, or did his bravado seal the fate of the victims of the tragedy—himself, Benjamin, Elder John, Elizabeth Kellogg, Granny Parker, Samuel and Robert Frost, Rachel, and his own children, John and Cynthia Ann?

The Indians had stopped about two hundred yards from the fort and sent two braves to the front gate. Rachel could see that they were carrying a white flag. The braves told the settlers they had come to make a treaty with the Americans. Benjamin Parker went up to the main body of the Indians. After a few minutes he returned, saying, "I believe the Indians intend to fight. Put everything in order for defense! I'll go back to the Indians to see if a fight can be avoided." Silas told him, "Don't go. We'll try to defend the place as well as we can." Not heeding his younger brother, Benjamin walked out of the front gate to certain death. He sacrificed his life to buy a few minutes, which allowed some of the settlers to escape. Silas said, "I know they will kill Benjamin." He turned to Rachel, but instead of telling her to run away as fast as she could, he said to her, "Do you stand here and watch the Indians' motions until I run into the house for my shot pouch." As she stood watching, Benjamin was surrounded by the Indians. Deciding that the Indians were going to kill Benjamin, at long last Rachel picked up James Pratt and started running through the fort to the back gate, where she met Silas, who asked if the Indians had killed Benjamin. "No," Rachel replied, "but they have surrounded him." Silas said, "I know they will kill him, but I will be good for one of them at least."

These were the last words Rachel heard him say. Then she ran as fast as she could out the back gate and saw the Indians stabbing Benjamin with spears. The stillness of the pastoral setting was shattered by the triumphant war whoops filling the air.

Rachel describes her tardy, pitiful attempt to escape. "I tried to make my escape, but alas, alas, it was too late as a party of Indians had got ahead of me. Oh! how vain were my feeble efforts to try to run to save myself and little James Pratt." As Rachel ran with her child in her arms, a large Indian picked up a hoe he found lying on the ground and knocked her down. The Indians wrenched James Pratt out of Rachel's arms as she fainted and fell to the ground. When she came to, she was being dragged by her hair. Three or four times she tried to struggle to her feet. When she had finally regained her footing, she heard "desperate screaming," several shots, and then she heard her uncle Silas shout a "triumphant huzza as tho' he had thousands to back him." Rachel had a brief moment of hope, thinking the men from the neighboring farms had gathered and staged a counterattack. She desperately hoped that the men had come to rescue her.

But the shout was from Silas alone; he had no thousands behind him. He, Samuel Frost, and young Robert Frost were being savagely slaughtered.

Meanwhile, three other groups were struggling to escape. Elder John and Granny Parker ran as fast as they could. Granny paused to hide one hundred dollars in silver coins under a hickory bush. Elizabeth Duty Kellogg tried to help the old ones. Elizabeth, like Rachel, had waited too long to run away, tarrying to help her aged mother. The Comanches soon overtook the straggling three, stripped them of their clothes, shot Elder John with an arrow, and scalped him. They "abused" Granny Parker, ran a large knife through her breast, and left her on the ground. Elizabeth Kellogg was seized and taken away.

Another drama was unfolding in the Parker cornfield about a mile from the fort. Sarah Nixon had reached her husband, her father, L. T. M., and the other men as they worked in the field. She ran to them screaming, and then breathlessly told them about the attack on the fort. Rachel's mother with her little brood followed closely behind Sarah.

The men quickly decided that James Parker would take his family to a safe place, L. T. M. would run to enlist the help of the neighbors, and Nixon would go to the fort to try to help the others.

When Nixon arrived at the fort, he saw that the Indians had also captured Silas's wife Lucy and her two younger children. Nixon vainly attempted to aid them but was captured also. As he, Lucy Parker, and the two younger children, Orlena and Silas Jr., were being dragged back to the fort, Abram Anglin, David Faulkenberry and his son, and L. T. M. dashed up, pointed their guns at the Indians, and succeeded in rescuing the four, but Cynthia Ann and John were lost, surrounded by the Indians where they and the other captives were being beaten and "maltreated in every conceivable way."[36]

While Anglin and the other men were skirmishing with the Indians, Rachel's situation was worsening. Covered with blood, she was dragged by her hair into the midst of the main group of Indians, where she saw the mutilated body of Benjamin, his corpse filled with arrows. As the Indians rode by, they jabbed their lances into the body. Wounded, bleeding, witness to horrors beyond her imagination, Rachel was in deep despair. "I now expected that my father and husband, and all the rest of the men, were killed. I soon saw a party of the Indians coming, bringing my aunt Elizabeth Kellogg a prisoner, and some bloody scalps—among them I could distinguish that of my old grandfather, Elder John Parker, I knew it by the grey hairs. I had not yet seen my little James Pratt, and had almost entirely given him up, when at a great distance I discovered him. An Indian had him on his horse—he was crying and calling for mother, oh mother! He was just able to lisp the name of mother, being only about eighteen months old." Then an Indian woman began beating Rachel with a whip.[37]

The battle won, all the enemy having been killed or captured or having escaped—the Indians began looting and ransacking the fort. They cut open the mattresses and tore out the stuffing, filling the air with feathers. They carried off Silas's books and medicines, broke many of the bottles, and tore apart the books. The Indians often stuffed paper into their shields to make these more resistant to arrows and bullets.[38]

The Indians with their captives rode away the same way they had come, shooting arrows into the settlers' cattle as they went. In her narrative Rachel gives only a few details about the captives' first day's journey: "They soon convinced me that I had no time to reflect on what was past, for they commenced whipping me in such a manner that the wounds and bruises were not well for some weeks, in fact my flesh was never clear of wounds from the lash, and bruises from clubs."[39]

Other Comanche captives told of being stripped naked, thrown on a horse, their hands tied in front of them and their feet tied together underneath the horse. Their bare, white skins soon became sunburned. Female captives often had their long hair cropped or shorn. The captives were frequently beaten with bows, whips, and clubs, and jabbed with lances. Then there was the mental torture, remembering the screams of loved ones as they were murdered, and thinking about the coming night. The women who lived on the frontier knew what happened to female captives the first night of their capture—torture, gang rape, and perhaps slow, horrible death as the warriors danced around the campfire. But worst of all was the plight of the women whose children were also captives. Some Comanches delighted in torturing the children in the presence of their mothers. Helpless to aid the frantic little ones, at times mothers prayed for the swift death of their children.[40]

Rachel describes her particular hell in her narrative:

> About midnight they halted, but there was not near so many Indians as there was at the Fort, for they had been dropping off all the evening. . . . They now tied a plaited thong around my arms, and drew my hands behind me. They tied them so tight that the scars can easily be seen to this day. They then tied a similar thong around my ankles, and drew my feet and hands together. They now turned me on my face and I was unable to turn over, when they commenced beating me over the head with their bows, and it was with great difficulty I could keep from smothering in my blood; for the wound they give me with the hoe, and many others were bleeding freely.
>
> I suppose it was to add to my misery that they brought my little James Pratt so near me that I could hear him cry. He would call for mother; and often was his voice weakened by the blows they would give him. I could hear the blows. I could hear his cries; but oh, alas, could offer him no relief. The rest of the prisoners were brought near me, but we were not allowed to speak one word together. My aunt called me once, and I answered her; but, indeed, I thought she would never call or I answer again, for they jumped with their feet upon us, which nearly took our lives. Often did the children cry, but were soon hushed by such blows that I had no idea they could survive. They commenced screaming and dancing around the scalps; kicking and stamping the prisoners. . . . Such dreadful, savage yelling! enough to terrify the bravest hearts. Bleeding and weltering in my blood: and far worse, to think of my little darling Pratt! Will this scene ever be effaced from my memory? Not until my spirit is called to leave this tenement of clay; and may God grant me a heart to pray for them, for "they know not what they do."[41]

Rachel does not describe the sexual abuse that she and Elizabeth endured that night or in the months following, saying only: "To undertake to narrate their barbarous treatment would only add to my present distress, for it is with feelings of the deepest mortification that I think of it, much less to speak or write of it; for while I record this painful part of my narrative; I can almost feel the same heart-rending pains of body and mind that I then endured, my very soul becomes sick at the dreadful thought." Few female captives lived more than a few years after their rescue, their health broken by physical and psychological abuse.[42]

The other Parkers had fared better. After Abram Anglin, the two Faulkenberrys, and Plummer had rescued Nixon, Lucy Parker, and her two youngest children, they retreated, holding off the Indians with their rifles. After charging the whites several times, the Indians, some of whom were on foot, returned to their companions who were plundering the fort. Knowing it was useless to confront the huge band of warriors, the settlers fled toward the river, where they hoped to hide. L. T. M. asked about Rachel and James Pratt. Finding that they were not with the others, he went off into the wilderness by himself to look for them. The rest of the settlers proceeded to the river where they hid in the underbrush.[43]

Meanwhile, Abram Anglin, the Faulkenberrys, and Silas Bates stealthily made their way back to the fort. On the way, they entered the Anglins' cabin, where they were astonished by what they thought was an apparition. Anglin was frightened: "It was dressed in white with long, white hair streaming down its back. He was scared worse at this moment than when the Indians were yelling and charging. Seeing him hesitate, his ghost beckoned him to come on. Approaching the house, it proved to be old Granny Parker."[44]

Anglin and Faulkenberry cared for Granny Parker and then proceeded to the fort. They found pandemonium as the animals clamored for food. "The dogs were barking, the cattle bellowing, the horses neighing, and the hogs squealing." But there were no human sounds; the dead lay quietly in the moonlight. Anglin quickly searched for that silver Granny Parker had told him she had hidden. He found the money under the hickory bush, one hundred dollars in silver coin. The two men returned to where they had hidden Granny Parker, picked her up, and carried her to the group huddled in the river bottom. By this time Nixon had also joined them.[45]

David Faulkenberry waited until dawn and then sent Silas Bates, Abram Anglin, and Evans Faulkenberry to the fort to obtain horses and supplies.

Without burying the dead, the three men returned to the others hiding in the river bottom, bringing with them five or six horses as well as a few saddles, and bacon, and honey. The settlers then set out toward Fort Houston. For many days they did not know the fate of James Parker and those who were with him.[46]

James's contingent was composed of his wife and family (including his married daughter Sarah Nixon), Mrs. Frost and her young children, and Mr. and Mrs. Dwight and their children. To make matters worse, James's wife Patsey was eight months pregnant. The refugees had no food, no guns; everyone was barefoot except Patsey Parker and Mrs. Frost, and most of the children were dressed only in shirts. Mrs. Frost, fearing that her husband and son had been slain, was almost hysterical. Always there was the fear that the Indians were pursuing them and they would be the next to be slaughtered or captured.

That night, James decided to return to the fort to obtain food and find out what had happened to the others. When he told his charges of his plans, they objected violently, pointing out that he was the only one who knew the way to the settlement and how to avoid capture by the Indians. When they insisted that they would rather starve than risk capture, James reluctantly agreed to stay with them. After hiding them in the briars, he climbed a tree in order to survey the fort and the surrounding area. "All was silent as death. I in vain strained my eyes to see some living object, and listened to hear some human voice about the fort."[47]

Returning to the refugees, James gathered them together in preparation for the long journey ahead, some forty miles to Tinnin's settlement on the Old San Antonio Road crossing of the Navasota River. Each of the six adults picked up one child, took another by the hand, and started on their slow, agonizing journey. To avoid capture they decided to follow the river by night and to hide in the underbrush by day. Traveling through a pathless forest is not easy, but struggling through the dense undergrowth of an East Texas river bottom at night is almost impossible. Nearly every step was impeded by trees, bushes, tall grass, and, worst of all, briars and blackberry vines. The thorns tore at the children's bare arms, legs, and feet until "the blood trickled down so that they could have been tracked by it." Fearful of being discovered by the Indians, Parker made everyone walk backwards when they came to a sandy place in the river bottom. At three o'clock in the morning, the travelers were exhausted. They lay down on the grass and slept until dawn, when they resumed their weary journey. In desperation,

Parker led his charges out of the river bottom to the prairie, but there he saw so many footprints of moccasin-clad feet that he was certain the Indians were hunting for them, so he led the refugees back into the protection of the briars.

As night fell, the weary travelers were far from their destination. Not having eaten for thirty-six hours, they were famished, the children and nursing mothers suffering the most severely. Suddenly, as the refugees wearily sat on the riverbank, they saw a skunk. James immediately chased it, and as he delicately puts it, "After much trouble, I succeeded in catching it." The unfortunates then had to add the putrid odor of the skunk to their sufferings. Having nothing with which to kill the skunk, James drowned it in the river. Fortunately someone had brought "the means for striking fire," so James was able to cook the skunk. The refugees quickly devoured it, each getting only a tiny morsel. They had no other food until the evening of the fourth day, when they managed to catch another skunk and two terrapins.[48]

The refugees slowly struggled through the tangled underbrush, until finally, at the end of the fifth day, the women and children, exhausted, starving, their feet bleeding and sore, could travel no farther. They all agreed that James should go ahead to the settlement and come back to get them as soon as he could.[49]

Spurred on by the suffering of his companions, James walked all night. The first house he reached was that of a Captain Carter in Tinnin's settlement. Carter saddled five horses, and he, a neighbor, and James returned to the refugees. They found them at twilight, placed them on the horses, and all arrived at the settlement at about midnight. The next day L. T. M., having given up his solitary pursuit of Rachel and James Pratt, also arrived at the settlement.[50]

They were all alive, but where were Rachel and James Pratt and the other captives? Granny Parker, who had survived the ordeal at Fort Parker and the journey to Fort Houston, recovered but died sometime before 1844.[51]

⊰⊱ CHAPTER 5 ⊰⊱

Vengeance Is Mine

F AR TO THE NORTH, Rachel, James Pratt, and the other prisoners survived the ordeal of the first night after their capture. The
next day the Indians and their captives passed through the Cross
Timbers. Battered, bruised, degraded in mind and body, Rachel still
was able to feel wonder and excitement at the beauty of the country: "It is
a beautiful faced country—prairie and timber.—I saw a great many fine
springs. I think it was about sixty miles from the Fort to the cross timbers.
. . . This range of timber is of an irregular width, say from five to thirty-five
miles wide, and is also diversified country, abounding with small prairies
skirted with woodlands of various kinds of timber, Oaks of all kinds, Ash,
Hickory, Elm, Mulberry, Walnut, etc.: tho' there is more Post Oak on the
high lands than any other kind of timber."[1]

After the travelers left the Cross Timbers, they headed out into what
Rachel called the Grand Prairie. The captives were bound hand and foot
every night, were given no food, and were allowed barely enough water to
keep them alive. The Indians then veered to the east. After about five days
of hard riding, the victors paused long enough to divide the spoils. Elizabeth Kellogg fell to the Kichais, and Rachel was given to one band of
Comanches and Cynthia Ann and John to another. Finally the Indians
brought James Pratt to Rachel:

> My child kept crying, and almost continually calling for "Mother,"
> though I was not allowed even to speak to it. At the time they took off
> my fetters, they brought my child to me, supposing that I gave suck. As
> soon as it saw me, it, trembling with weakness, hastened to my embraces.
> Oh, with what feelings of love and sorrow did I embrace the mutilated
> body of my darling little James Pratt. I now felt that my case was much
> bettered, as I thought they would let me have my child; but oh, mistaken,

indeed, was I; for as soon as they found that I had weaned him, they, in spite of all my efforts, tore him from my embrace. He reached out his hands towards me, which were covered with blood, and cried, "Mother, Mother, oh, Mother!" I looked after him as he was borne from me, and I sobbed aloud. This was the last I ever heard of my little Pratt. Where he is, I know not.

After the division of the captives, the Indians turned to the northwest and headed deep into the Great Plains.[2]

At Tinnin's settlement on the Navasota River the Parker family was gathering. L. T. M., as noted, arrived the day after James W. and his charges had reached Tinnin's. Lorenzo Nixon, after hearing that his wife and her family were at Mr. Carter's cabin, journeyed from Fort Houston to join them. He told everyone who had been killed and who had been captured. Mrs. Frost finally learned of the death of her husband and son.

James W. Parker, fearing another attack, moved his family to Grimes' Settlement near Holland's Creek. He was "entirely without money," but through the kindness of friends, Jesse Grimes and Andrew Montgomery, James found a place for his family to stay. The house was small, with a dirt floor, and the Parkers had to share it with another family. James constructed a bed by driving four forked stakes into the ground, making a frame, attaching it to the wall, covering it with boards, and laying hay on top. He hastily provided for his family because he was determined to go back to Fort Parker to bury the dead. Just as he was about to leave, however, another misfortune occurred. As James explains, "All of my family were taken sick with the measles; but leaving them to the charity of the neighbors and to the mercy of Providence, I set off."[3]

Accompanied by thirteen other men, Parker returned to the fort. There they found desolation: crops destroyed, horses stolen, most of the cattle killed, and the household articles taken or smashed. Worst of all, the wild beasts had devoured the flesh of the dead, leaving their skeletons scattered about. The men gathered up the bones, put them in a single "rough box" and buried them in one grave except for those of Silas. James and Silas had made a pact that "whichever survived should see that his brother's body was not buried."[4]

As James assisted in the burial of the dead, he cried out, "Rest my father and rest my brothers—rest—would to God I were with you."[5] James, Benjamin, and Silas had led these people into the wilderness, where their age-old enemies had finally defeated them. Was there a special reason that the Indians had staged their devastating attack on Fort Parker? The rumors had already begun to fly, rumors that would plague James for the rest of his life.

Leaving his pregnant wife and young children, James began the search that would become an obsession, driving him even to murder. The deserted and looted Fort Parker revealed no clues as to the path the Indians had taken, so James and the other men rounded up the few cattle left and returned to Grimes' Settlement. Before James arrived at the house where his family was staying, he was met by a Dr. Adams, who told him Patsey was dying. James immediately decided that his wife's disease was "as much of the mind as of the body" and that she would not die at this time. After telling the doctor his opinion, he asked for the use of the medicines. The doctor gave them to him, and James, armed with the drugs to cure his wife, approached the cabin. A grim scene awaited him: "On my coming in the presence of my wife, I was horror-stricken. There she lay on a pallet of straw literally reduced to skin and bones; she was entirely bereft of reason, and appeared to have lost all sense of pain. Oh God! how my soul was pierced when she gazed upon me with her ghastly eyes! By her side lay my youngest child, having more the appearance of a corpse than a living being." After praying for the recovery of his wife and child, James began to care for them. There followed seven days of "unceasing watching and painful suspense" before Patsey was "restored to reason," but she and the child survived.[6]

Once James's wife and child had recovered, he moved his family even farther from the Indian country, to the cabin of Jesse Parker near Huntsville. From Benson Resinghoover James bought a large tract of land five miles east of town on the east fork of Harmon's Creek in the dense East Texas piney woods. There he built a "temporary camp" for his family. James, in a hurry to get on with his search, said, "Having fixed my family as comfortably as I could, on the 11th of July I started to see Gen. Houston."[7] Most of the people in Texas at that time felt that "Old Sam Jacinto" could do just about anything that needed to be done.

When James Parker called on Sam Houston in San Augustine, Texas, in mid-July of 1836, Houston was convalescing from a wound received at the Battle of San Jacinto.[8] James says that "all I desired, was, that he should grant me a company of men." James seemed to think that this was a simple request. But money would be required to pay the men, and the fledgling republic was virtually bankrupt. Also James did not even know what band had stolen Rachel and the others or where in the vast expanses of Comanchería they might be. Houston's answer to James was that "a treaty with the Indians would be the most effective and expeditious means of releasing the prisoners." In desperation James argued with Houston: "Such a thing as a treaty being formed with hostile Indians until they were whipped and well whipped, had never been known; and the more thorough the chastisement, the more lasting the treaty."[9]

Houston would not relent. Sorrowfully, James made his way back to Montgomery County, arriving on August 12. He does not make it clear where he had spent one entire month. Remaining with his family one day, he then went to visit Nathaniel Robbins, who had great influence with the local Indians. Robbins joined Parker, and they went to Nacogdoches, where Sam Houston had resumed his law practice.[10] The two men called on Houston and once more pleaded with him for a company of men, but he refused, still insisting that a treaty with the Indians was the best course to take. Rebuffed again, Parker, with the tenacity characteristic of his clan, decided to take another tack. He went to visit Richard Sparks, who lived a few miles from Nacogdoches, to enlist his aid in persuading Houston; but as James said, "It did no good." On August 20, James returned to Nacogdoches and discovered that his wife's sister, Elizabeth Kellogg, had been brought to Nacogdoches by some friendly Delaware Indians. The Delawares had purchased Elizabeth and asked for 150 dollars for their services. James claimed he was "pennyless" and unable to pay, so Houston paid the ransom.[11]

Elizabeth and James, accompanied by a Mr. Milligan and several other men, whom James does not identify, started on the eighty-mile journey to James's new home. On August 22, they "fell in" with a man whom James identifies only as "a Mr. Smith," who told the travelers that he had just prevented a horse raid and had shot one of the Indians involved. The travelers rode a few hundred yards from the road to look at the "dead" Indian. To their surprise they discovered that he was not dead because "the ball had merely grazed his forehead." Then Elizabeth Kellogg identified him as the warrior who had killed and scalped James's father and said that "if he was the same, he had a scar on each arm as if cut with a knife." James lost no time. "I immediately examined him, and found, with mingled feelings of joy, sorrow, and revenge, the scars as described:—joy at the opportunity of avenging the butchery of my father, and sorrow at the recollection of it. . . . What followed, it is unnecessary to relate—suffice it to say, that it was the unanimous opinion of the company, that he would never kill and scalp another white man."[12]

On the first page of his memoirs James ruminates on his feelings after his brother John had been killed by the Indians at about the beginning of the War of 1812:

> This awakened in me, feelings of the most bitter hostility towards the Indians, and I firmly resolved upon, and impatiently awaited for an opportunity to avenge his death. This, however, was never afforded me; for soon after my arrival in that country [Illinois], peace was declared, and I was thereby deprived of satiating that revenge my soul panted for, whenever I met an Indian. I say, this engendered in my heart a deadly hostility towards this race of God's creatures, which, my subsequent sufferings and heart-rending privations, produced by these blood-thirsty savages, had assisted, in no wise, to diminish. This feeling, I hope, however, is not nurtured by me to such an extent as to do violence to that holy precept of my Divine Master, who says, "vengeance is mine, and I will repay it." Though I may despise their treachery, pity their ignorance, and mourn the wrongs I have received at their hands; yet, I pray God to enable me to forgive them, and to sincerely pray for the speedy civilazation and christianization of their whole race.[13]

James and Elizabeth arrived at Montgomery County on September 6, 1836. Patsey was overjoyed to see her sister. They were both scarred by their ordeal, but they were safe and they were free. Since Elizabeth could furnish little information about the other captives, James asked several of his friends what would be the best course to follow. They advised him to go to Coffee's Trading Post on the Red River to learn the whereabouts of the captives or, if possible, to make arrangements to have them brought in.[14]

James Parker started toward Indian Territory by way of Jonesborough, Texas, on the Red River, and arrived at the settlement on September 27. He had traveled two hundred miles in twelve days and had worn out his horse, so he purchased another for the last leg of his journey, one hundred miles along a road that followed the bank of the Red River. The searcher finally arrived at Coffee's Trading Post, which was surrounded by a stockade made of tall log pickets.[15]

Holland Coffee was a notable trader of the early 1800s. He spoke seven Indian languages and was both hated and admired by his white neighbors. First they complained that he was trading guns and whiskey to the Indians in exchange for stolen livestock, and then a short while later they elected him to the Texas House of Representatives. Be that as it may, Coffee was noted for his attempts to ransom Indian captives. Sarah Ann Horn, who was captured at about the same time as Rachel, told of his futile efforts to buy her from the Comanches. Coffee shed tears when he was unable to rescue Mrs. Horn, and he left her some food and clothing. But he was successful in rescuing a Mrs. Crawford and her two children.[16]

Most traders kept a large stock of goods attractive to the Indians, such as brightly colored calico, vermilion dye, earrings, beads, tobacco, pipes, rope, axes, and knives. But the most important items of trade were guns, bullets, and whiskey.[17] Drinking by Indians added to the dangers of a frontier trading post. Sometimes they played games such as throwing coins over the trader's cabin and then scrambling and fighting for them in the dust. Most traders built forts around their trading houses with blockhouses on two corners. The inside of a trading house was like any other store of the period, with a counter across the back and boxes and barrels arranged along the walls.[18]

After arriving at Coffee's establishment, James heard that a woman who fit Rachel's description had been brought in to the trading post of a Captain Pace in Indian Territory about eighty miles east on the Blue River. James could not get his horse across the Red River, and he had lent his hunting gun to a man in Jonesborough, so he decided to set out on foot, armed only with two small pistols. His desperation is shown by his instructions to the man with whom he left his horse: "that should I not return to his house within ten days, he should let my family know that I was dead, as I had determined to return within that time, if alive." Unable to obtain good directions as there was no road, nor even a trace, he set out on foot with nothing more than a compass and some meat and bread. With the help of a Mr. Stewart he built a raft and crossed the Red River. After James had landed on the opposite shore, he lost his provisions as he struggled through the dense underbrush and swamps in the river bottom.

When night fell, James wanted to continue, but he was compelled to stop since he could not see his compass. By this time he was on a prairie. He lay down in the tall grass but could not sleep. "The thought that I was so near my child, drove sleep from my eyes. I would sometimes doze for a few moments, but would soon arouse with an effort to embrace the object of my care and pursuit."

Even though his feet were blistered and he was suffering from exhaustion and hunger, James started walking as soon as it was light. As night fell, he was still on the prairie. He built a fire and prepared for sleep when a thunderstorm erupted. When the lightning flashed, he could see that the prairie was a sheet of water. At two o'clock in the morning a norther struck. James survived the night by walking in circles in water two feet deep.

His ordeal was not over. With dawn came light but little warmth. The grass was matted with ice, making walking slow and painful. Finally James saw a grove of timber in the distance and slowly made his way there. When he finally reached the shelter of the trees, he sat on a log to rest and was almost overpowered by the desire to sleep. But he realized that if he went to sleep, he would soon freeze to death. Struggling to get up, he discovered to his horror that as he had sat, his legs had stiffened and his feet had frozen. Knowing that he would die if he were unable to start a fire and warm himself, he crawled toward a dry log he saw about fifty yards away. After inching along for an hour, he finally reached the log.

Then James cut off a piece of his shirt for wadding, loaded his pistol, fired at the log, and was able to start a fire. He had been suffering with cold before, but now the pain became excruciating as his hands and feet began to warm up. He explains what kept him going: "The hope of soon seeing my lost child, added a new vigor to my body, and summoning all my remaining strength I pursued my journey." Not having eaten for three days, James knew that he was still in danger of dying as he lay down, finally succumbing to his overpowering need for sleep. When night came, James made another fire and fell down on the ground to rest. Although the fire went out, he survived the night to wake refreshed in the morning. His clothes were frozen to the ground, his hair was matted with ice, and he was numb with cold, but he was still alive.

James arose, rekindled the fire, and after he had thawed out, continued on his journey. He began to fear that he had passed Pace's trading post, but knowing that in his weakened condition he could never make it back to Coffee's, he continued on his weary way. "The sun was now setting, and I almost hoped I would not live to see it rise. Darkness came on apace; and Oh, how horrible was the thought of having to spend another night in the wild wilderness, eight hundred miles from home, with the frozen ground for a bed, and the blue dome of heaven my only shelter. As these thoughts were revolving in my mind, I heard a calf bleat—and the songs of angels could not have been sweeter to my ears, or more charming to my soul, than was the bleat of that calf."

Hurrying on, James was soon in Pace's house, sitting in front the fireplace drinking a cup of coffee. His joy at reaching his destination was short-lived when he learned that the woman who had been ramsomed was not Rachel but a Mrs. Yorkins. James did receive some information from one of

Coffee's traders, who was at the post at the time. He told James that the Indians holding Rachel were camped only sixty miles away. The trader also informed James that the Comanches had killed Rachel's child. James's fury and desperation grew: "This intelligence kindled anew the flame that was raging in my breast; and I immediately determined to go to the camp of the Indians, and at the risk of my life, recover my daughter."

After resting for two days, James departed from Pace's. Upon reaching the vicinity of the Indian camp, he discovered the Indians had already left, but since the ground was wet, he could track them. For six days he followed them, until he reached the place where they had crossed the Red River. Since James was too weak to swim the river, and there was no timber to make a raft, he was forced to abandon his search. Defeated and dejected, he started on his long journey back by heading east along the bank of the Red River. He describes his feelings at the time: "I felt as certain as that I was then alive, that I should never again see home. Faint with hunger and fatigue, and all hopes of ever again seeing my unfortunate daughter, being, as I thought, cut off, I resigned myself to my fate. I looked down the river and saw some timber, and feeling that I would rather die among the trees than in an open prairie, thither I directed my steps; and just as the sun was setting, I reached the spot which I never expected to leave. I pray God that when the final hour does come, and He shall call me hence, that I may feel as willing to obey as I did then."

Once again James was saved by a skunk. He was so happy to see the creature that his entire outlook on life changed: "The hand of the all-wise and merciful God is stretched forth, and we are plucked from the cold embrace of the 'King of Terrors,' as a 'brand from the burning!'" James killed the skunk, roasted it, and ate enough to restore his strength. In the morning he burned some logs into several pieces and lashed them together with grapevines to construct a raft. He then floated down the river to the house of Mr. Fitzgerald, where he had left his horse. James had been gone twenty days, but fortunately Fitzgerald had not written to James's family as directed. James then felt it his duty to return home. He retraced his steps, arriving in Montgomery County on November 17.[19]

As James was frantically searching for his daughter and the other captives, Rachel was experiencing the life of an Indian captive. She omitted many details from her narrative. She did not say when the Comanche warriors with whom she was traveling finally reunited with the rest of their band. She did not relate whether she wore her own clothing or the buckskin attire of an Indian woman. The Plains Indians at times wore the clothes of their victims, and sometimes the warriors would wear the women's dresses.[20] The simply cut dresses of the pioneer women, made out of homespun or calico, would not have lasted long in the wilderness, and eventually Rachel must have donned Comanche attire. Her hair may have been cut off and braided into that of her captor to make a long scalplock.[21]

Rachel was not a true member of the tribe; she was a slave and would ever remain so. The treatment of captives depended upon age and sex. Adult males were almost always killed, sometimes tortured to death in the presence of the other captives. Some Mexican men were allowed to live and then used to tend the horse herds, which sometimes reached vast proportions. Many captive boys froze to death while guarding these herds. The young captives who were allowed to live were slaves, but if they survived, they were eventually adopted into the tribe. The boys sometimes grew up to become more relentless tormentors of their own people than the Comanche warriors themselves. A young girl was sometimes spared sexual abuse if her captor planned to adopt her, but at puberty she was usually forced to marry the warrior who had captured her.[22]

The fate of the adult female was a different matter altogether. Occasionally, a woman was taken in marriage by an Indian man, but she was always accorded a lower status, and the slightest mistake could cause her to fall back into her former state of slavery. Almost always the adult Anglo female captive became the slave of the brave who had captured her, and in some cases an unwilling prostitute, available to anyone who could pay for her or win her in a gambling game.[23]

For some reason, Rachel was given to a Comanche whom she describes only as "an old man." She says nothing else of him or of their relationship, reserving her ire for her constant tormentors, the old man's wife and daughter. Rachel's new "home" was a scattering of lodges. The size of a Comanche band varied, with groups coming and going at will. When the band was large, the lodges stretched for a mile or so along the banks of a river or creek. When the camp was made in the open prairie, the tents would be placed in somewhat random fashion with relatives camped near each other. Women carried on their work of roasting meat, tanning hides, sewing clothing, carrying wood or water, or caring for children. Braves and old men sat in groups playing games of chance, smoking, talking, or making bows and arrows. The noise level was high, women screeching, dogs barking, and children yelling as they played. A game similar to soccer was enjoyed by the women and girls, and the men and boys delighted in horse racing, foot races, and wrestling. The smells would be a combination of the delicious fragrance of woodsmoke and roasting meat and sometimes the unpleasant smell of carrion.[24]

The band to which Rachel belonged moved every two or three days unless the weather was bad, and then they stayed in one place until it improved. The road for Rachel and her new companions lay north across the headwaters of the Arkansas River in present-day Colorado. They were on the High Plains, the land of the big sky, a treeless, gently rolling sea of grass where the average speed of the relentless wind was fourteen miles an hour, harder than anywhere else in the continental United States except for the seashore. Rachel, born in Illinois, had traveled far in her short life and had crossed many prairies, but never had she seen land like that of the High Plains. The blue sky seemed boundless, because the horizon was broken by nothing at all. Rachel states: "We would travel for weeks and not see a riding switch."[25] These plains, mountains, and canyons comprised a land of few trees and scant rainfall, but it was a paradise for a nomadic people who depended mostly on wild game for food. In a few weeks it could turn from a brown, sun-baked plain of shimmering mirages into a lush grassland covered with a myriad of wildflowers of yellow, white, lavender, pink, and blue.

In some areas the rivers and springs were fouled with gypsum, but there was always good, clear water somewhere, and the Comanches knew where to find it. Along the creek beds grew wild plums and grapes. Other delicacies the land yielded were pecans, walnuts, and persimmons. In the streams and shallow lakes were thousands of ducks, geese, and other wildfowl. And there was big game—deer, antelope, bear, elk, and what has been called the commissary of the Plains Indian, vast herds of buffalo. On the High Plains, the rivers, which were small streams in most seasons, cut deep canyons such as the spectacular Palo Duro Canyon with its huge red boulders and strange rock formations sometimes resembling lighthouses. Often called the badlands, these river valleys with their sinister beauty offered protection from enemies and from the icy north winds in the winter.[26]

As the band progressed across the plains, gradually the foothills of the Rocky Mountains came into view. At first they were only a thin line on the horizon for days as the Indian band slowly made its way: men, women, and children riding, horses pulling travois, and dogs trotting patiently beside their masters. Through the foothills the caravan wound slowly higher and higher into the heart of the mountains. In July and August Rachel and the Indian band were in what she called the Snow Mountains, where "it is perpetual snow." Rachel, alone, despised, abused, eight months pregnant, was forced to shiver in the cold darkness as she watched the horses and worked on her allotment of buffalo skins. Often she had no shoes and little clothing to protect her from the cold. Sometimes in the morning her feet would feel as if they were frozen. In the mountains in about October of 1836 Rachel gave birth to her second child, a son she named Luther T. M.[27]

How did Rachel, the hated white slave, bear her child? Unlike some of the other captives, who sometimes mentioned a sympathetic or kind Indian man or woman, she described no one who befriended her or spoke a kind word. Whatever happened, Rachel, resourceful, undaunted, brought her child into the world. She says of her baby, "My little infant, tho' very small, was very pretty and bid fair to do well."[28]

Knowing that the Comanches seldom spared the lives of white babies, Rachel lived in fear. One day her fears were realized. She tells the story simply:

He was about six weeks old, when, I suppose they thought it too much trouble, five or six sturdy Indian men came where I was suckling my little infant; one of them caught it by the throat and choked it till it was black in the face, and while he was so doing the rest of the Indians were holding me, to prevent me from trying to relieve the child. At length they pulled it out of my arms by force—threw it up in the air and let if fall on the frozen ground until life was, to all appearances, entirely gone!!! They then gave it back to me. I tried to recover it, and as soon as they saw that it had recovered a little, they treated it as before several times, and then they tied a thong round its neck and threw it into the large ledges of prickly pears, which are ten or twelve feet high; they would then pull it down through the pears, which they done several times; they then tied the end of the rope to their saddles, and would drag it round me. When entirely dead, yea literally torn to pieces! one of them took it up by one leg and brought it to me, and threw it into my lap. But, in praise to the savages, I must say they gave me time to dig a small hole in the earth and deposit it away. I was truly glad when I found it was entirely over its sufferings. I rejoice now to reflect, that its soul is now in the sweet mansions of eternal day—may I be prepared to meet my little infants there. I would have rejoiced to have had the pleasure of laying my little James Pratt with it. Parents, you little think what you may come to. When we was about leaving the place, I looked with pleasure on the sweet resting place of my happy infant, and shall ever recollect the spot.[29]

Soon after Rachel buried her child, the Indians moved on to a place she described as "the country where the water gas is." She next mentions salt lakes, "where there are millions of bushels of salt . . . enough there to supply all the world."[30]

In March of 1837 the Indian band moved to the headwaters of the Arkansas River, where thousands of Indians of various tribes had gathered for a war council.[31] Rachel describes the impressive scene: "It was the greatest assemblage of people I ever saw. The council was held on a high eminence, descending every way;—the encampments were just as close as they could stand one to another, but how far they extended I know not, for I could not discern the outer edge of the encampment with my naked eye."[32] Since Rachel still had a "faint" hope of being rescued, she decided to try to learn the plans of the Indians. The proceedings were conducted in the Comanche language, which she had learned during her ten-month captivity. When she was discovered listening, she was whipped, but she returned again and again to the council in spite of the beatings. Rachel learned that the Indians were planning a massive attack on the Texans to kill or drive out all the whites. Then the Indians who grew corn would take over the farms of the Texans, and the Plains Indians who lived by hunting would jointly occupy the prairies and defend each other against attack. After the farmer Indians had raised a good supply of corn, the Indians would then band together again to attack Mexico. They expected to be joined by a number of Mexicans who were dissatisfied with the Mexican government. After conquering Mexico, the Indians planned to attack the United States and drive all the whites from the country. All agreed with the plan, but they were unable to agree upon the time of the attack. Some wanted to attack in the spring of 1838 and others in the spring of 1839. Eventually they decided to let the "Northern Indians" decide, and then send a message to the chiefs of the Comanches. While in the encampment, Rachel was approached by a Beadie Indian who told her that the Indians were going to make slaves of the white people. He then cursed her in English. These were the first words of English Rachel had heard in ten months.[33]

As late spring approached, the Indians again turned toward the coolness and beauty of the mountains. After the Comanche band left the war council, they slowly made their way into the Rocky Mountains, frequently stopping for a few days. Rachel was awed by the mountains and sometimes would climb a high pinnacle and look off into the distance as one peak after another was finally lost in the mist. In the mountains were many caves, and one day she decided to explore one of them. After repeatedly requesting permission, Rachel finally obtained the consent of her old mistress to enter the cave and to take her "young mistress" with her. Rachel made several candles out of buffalo tallow, and also took a flint and some fuel to make fire. Rachel and the young woman had barely entered the cave when the young Indian woman became frightened and wanted to turn back, insisting that Rachel accompany her. When Rachel refused, she swung at Rachel with a piece of wood. Rachel dodged and knocked her down with another piece. Rachel states, "I cared not for her cries, but firmly told her that if she attempted again to force me to return until I was ready, I would kill her." Nevertheless, Rachel accompanied the girl back to the mouth of the cave and then returned to her adventure. She was astonished by the crystalline formations which sparkled in the candlelight. Proceeding farther, Rachel found an underground stream of crystal clear water. She walked through the cave until she came to a huge waterfall, then retraced her steps and discovered that the Indians had been searching the cave for her.[34]

As time passed Rachel fell into despair. Her beautiful, innocent baby had been murdered, and she had heard no word of whether James Pratt still lived. She doubted that any member of her family was alive. Not knowing that her father was desperately searching for her, she lost all hope of ever being rescued. Frequently beaten, she was daily becoming weaker, almost broken in body and spirit, although she was only eighteen years old. At last Rachel decided she wanted to die. Although she kept a small knife for the purpose of killing herself, she was unable to bring herself to plunge it into her body. Rachel decided to provoke the Indians into killing her. One day when she and her young mistress were a short distance from the Indian village, the woman ordered Rachel to go back to get a tool the Indians used to dig roots. When she refused, the woman angrily ordered her to obey, but Rachel again refused. Screaming with rage, the woman ran at her. Although Rachel was weakened by her long ordeal, months of hatred gave her the strength to push the woman down and pin her to the ground. As the two struggled in the dust, the Indians poured out of their lodges, encircled the struggling women, and added their piercing yells to the melee.

Fearing every minute to feel a spear thrust through her body, Rachel decided that if she were going to die, her tormentor would live a cripple forever after. Rachel grabbed a large buffalo bone and began beating the young woman on the head until in some places the skull was exposed. Still no spear from the screaming Indians ended Rachel's life. Finally, the Indian woman begged for mercy, and Rachel let her go. As the woman lay in the dirt bleeding, Rachel was amazed that none of the Indians tried to kill or seize her. They did not even attempt to aid the injured woman. Finally, Rachel picked her up, carried her back to the camp, bathed her face, and gave her some water. The woman seemed "remarkably friendly," and to Rachel's amazement, the other Indians went about their affairs as if nothing had happened.

One of the chiefs came up and silently watched Rachel ministering to the injured woman. Finally, he said to her, "You are brave to fight—good to fallen enemy—you are directed by the Great Spirit. Indians do not have pity on a fallen enemy. By our law you are clear. It is contrary to our law to show foul play. She began with you, and you had a right to kill her. Your noble spirit forbid you. When Indians fight, the conqueror gives or takes the life of his antagonist—and they seldom spare them."[35]

Rachel states that these words were "like balm to my soul." But the trouble was not over. Rachel's old mistress was incensed and ordered her to collect a large bundle of straw. Rachel soon learned that the old woman planned to burn her to death, and she planned to kill herself with her knife rather than being slowly burned alive. The old woman then ordered Rachel to cross her hands in front of her so that she could tie them. Rachel refused, and the old woman lighted a small bundle of straw and threw it on her, burning her severely. Rachel warned that she would fight if the old woman burned her any more. Screaming with rage, the Indian lighted another bundle and threw it on Rachel. Determined to fight for her life, Rachel pushed her into the fire. When she stood up, Rachel pushed her down again, holding her in the fire until she was as badly burned as Rachel was.

By this time the entire band of Indians had encircled the two women. Screams of the combatants and spectators filled the air. The old woman got hold of a club and began hitting Rachel with it. Rachel wrested it from her, swung it with all her strength, and knocked the old woman to the ground. As the women fought, they fell into their lodge, breaking one side of it. Rachel overcame the old woman and again found that the other Indians made no attempt to punish her or to aid the injured woman. As Rachel treated the wounds of her fallen enemy, all were silent except the old woman, who moaned from time to time. The young woman refused to help Rachel as she dragged the injured woman into the lodge. After making the old woman comfortable, Rachel repaired the side of the lodge that had been broken.

The chiefs of the village decided that something had to be done to restore peace. The next morning twelve of the chiefs assembled in the tent used for councils and summoned the three women. As Rachel says, "With all the solemnity of a church service, [we] went to the trial." The old woman was the first to testify. She told the whole story, as Rachel says, "without embellishment." One of the chiefs asked Rachel "if these things were so." She answered, "Yes." The chief than addressed the young Indian woman: "Are these things true?" She admitted that they were. The chief then asked the three women if they had anything to say. The two Indian women answered, "No." But Rachel had a great deal to say: "I told the court that they had mistreated me—they had not taken me honorably; that they had used the white flag to deceive us, and by which they had killed my friends—that I had been faithful, and served them from fear of death, and that I would now rather die than be treated as I had been. I said that the Great Spirit would reward them for their treachery and their abuse to me."

The sentence was that Rachel was required to replace the tent pole that had been broken in the fight. She agreed on the condition that the young woman be required to help her. The young woman was ordered to do so. Rachel had learned that the Comanches had great respect for bravery and says that from this point on, "I took my own part, and fared much the better by it."[36]

The Indian band crossed the Rocky Mountains and went to a far off land. Rachel asked the Indians and the Mexican captives what the name of it was, and they said that it was the "province of Senoro," where "nearly every shrub and tree bears a thorn or briar. The timber, what little there is, is very low and scrubby. . . . I saw here some springs that were truly a curiosity. The water, or kind of liquid, was about the consistency of tar, which would burn like oil, and was yellow as gold. The earth, in many places, is also yellow. There are very few places in all this country, but what looks to be very poor. From the time that we left the country of the Rocky Mountains, and during the whole time we were in this region, I do not think I saw one tree more than fifteen feet high; and those, as before stated, covered with thorns."[37]

At this place the Comanche band camped near a small village inhabited by both Indians and Mexicans. Rachel did not know to what tribe the Indians belonged. Hope surged in Rachel's breast. Perhaps she could persuade someone to buy her. If she could only convince one of the Mexicans that she was the owner of thousands of acres of the richest land in Texas, perhaps she could escape from her hideous bondage. The Comanches did not allow Rachel to mingle with the inhabitants of the village often, but one day she managed to talk to one of the Mexican men. She begged him to buy her, telling him she had enough land in Texas to repay him fully. The

Mexican agreed but did not keep his word. When the Comanches left, they stole all the horses and killed some of the villagers.[38]

Not knowing that his daughter was a thousand miles away, James continued his frantic attempts to rescue her. As noted, he left Oklahoma Territory and returned to Montgomery County, arriving on November 17, 1836.[39] The First Congress of Texas was in session at Columbia on the steep, red banks of the Brazos River. James decided to go there and appeal to the representatives for assistance. Francis R. Lubbock, who later became governor of Texas, describes the scene in his memoirs: "I found the town of Columbia about two miles westward on the edge of a prairie dotted with live oaks. The Congress was occupying two frame houses—the larger one, with partition removed, for the Representative chamber, and the smaller one for the Senate (then having only fourteen members), the shed rooms being used for committes. . . . I took my meals with Fitchett & Gill, the tavern-keepers, sleeping under a liveoak tree at night. This was the lodging place of many."[40]

Near bankruptcy, the fledgling republic was in chaos. Sam Houston had been elected president. Depressed, overworked, and trying to conquer his alcoholism, he struggled to lead the republic. At about this time, Daniel had joined James in putting pressure on Houston to supply James with money and arms to rescue the captives. Evidently Daniel wrote, published, and sent Houston a copy of a document entitled *Pamphlet*, which has been lost. On February 13, 1837, Houston wrote Daniel the following reply:

> Your favor had reached me, and no man can regret more sincerely than I do the misfortune, which has taken place. I am not mistaken in my calculation. I did not suppose that my orders would be *viewed as too strict*. They now see how matters are to be [m]anaged. Where is the Fort on Trinity? Where is the Blockhouse? ordered to be erected by me and the ferry. This was all [supposed to be] done previous to the inhabitants returning to their homes. *Men* who do *not* obey the orders given should not expect recompense. My heart is every day thrilled with the fruits of *incaution*. All men think themselves wise. They have proven themselves so, and their evidence is written in blood. You well know my orders, and the policy which seems to be best!
>
> I have appointed Commissioners, and they have forgotten every duty! I have written to Genl Rusk in relation to matters and if my orders, are not obeyed, I am not responsible to those who do not obey me! I solace

Sam Houston,
painted by Martin
Johnson Heade.
Courtesy Texas
State Library and
Archives Commis-
sion, Austin.

myself with the asurance, that, *not one, drop of blood,* has been shed in
Texas by my order unless, it was in the Battle of "San Jacinto."

If men will not obey orders, they will find that another power, is at
least equal to *disobedience.* This power, I *will exercise!* Capt Jewell will, as
soon as it can be done place a ferry and Block-house, on Trinity; at the
crossing. This will be more, than had been done by hundreds! I hope
they will deserve the appellation of *Soldiers!* I am proud of it: They are
from my own land!

You may say to your brother that his accounts, can only be settled,
when he is here! I will do all that I can for the people in that quarter! Tell
them to obey my orders and they will not err!

As to the matters, which you write about in the *"Pamphlet,"* we will
not differ, and on this subject, *I wish your slumbers to be sound!* and your
wakings, cheerful! . . .

You know the *sacred* injunction. "*Watch,* and pray; least you enter into
temptation." Regard this!!![41]

Houston did not give in to the pressure, but James, having decided to
never cease in his efforts to release the prisoners, left Columbia and next
visited Thomas Jefferson Rusk and Isaac Watts Burton. They stated their

willingness to help James, but they could not act without the consent of Congress. Again James journeyed to Nacogdoches, this time to appeal to R. Sparks, but his efforts were in vain.

After months of traveling around the state trying to obtain government assistance, James decided to return to Indian Territory once again. He left Montgomery County on February 25, 1837, arriving on March 7 in Natchitoches, Louisiana, where he placed an advertisement in the local newspaper offering a reward of three hundred dollars for "every prisoner then among the Indians that might be brought in."

On March 10, James left Natchitoches for Monroe, Louisiana, to collect a debt so that he would have some money to pay the reward. The spring rains had filled the rivers and creeks, and James slowly made his way to Monroe, arriving on March 20. There he collected "a small sum of money," and on March 29, he left for Indian Territory. Arriving on "the last prairie on Red River" on April 2, he then made his way to Marshall's trading house on the Blue River, where he purchased one thousand dollars' worth of goods to be used as ransom and persuaded Marshall and two other men to go among the Indians to try to locate the captives.

James left Marshall's establishment and went to Smith's trading house, where he made arrangements to procure Smith's stock of goods in case he needed them to ransom the captives. There he met a Shawnee Indian who told him that a white woman had been purchased by one of Marshall's traders. James returned immediately to Marshall's but found that Marshall had gone to the traders' camp. Fearing that James would follow him and be killed by the Comanches, Marshall left the following note: "Having received good news, I start after the prisoner to-morrow morning. Mr. Sprawling has purchased a woman; I hope it is your daughter. Keep yourself here. The Cumanches are now at Coffee's. You must stay here until I come back, and if God spares my life I will have the prisoners. I have got three Indians engaged at two dollars per day. For God Almighty's sake stay here until I come back, and see what can be done."

James paid no heed to Marshall's directives: "Can it be supposed that I obeyed his directions? I did not; for I immediately started for the traders' camp, where I supposed my daughter was." Upon arriving, James was again bitterly disappointed to learn that the woman was not his daughter. He remained at the traders' camp for a month trying to obtain Rachel's release but accomplished nothing.

Undaunted, James decided on a desperate and foolhardy plan. He would sneak up to the streams near the Comanche camps and leave written messages. Knowing the captives were required get water, he hoped that Rachel would find one of his messages and meet him at a prearranged place.

James procured a good rifle, four pistols, and a bowie knife. He was joined in this adventure by a man whom he identifies only as "one of the men belonging to a trading house." The two men rode for three days and were soon deep in the haunts of the Comanches. At sundown on April 24, they decided to make camp. They hobbled their horses and lay down on the ground to sleep but soon heard Indians trying to steal their horses. James grabbed his rifle and shot an Indian who was about ten feet from him. Taking up his pistol, he shot at another Indian and missed. James and his companion then jumped on their horses and rode all night.

The next morning the two were still riding when they were startled by the crack of rifle fire. A bullet grazed James's left ear and cheek. He wheeled around, put his rifle to his shoulder, and, seeing an Indian holding an empty rifle, fired and killed him. James noticed another Indian reloading and succeeded in killing him also. Meanwhile, James's companion had slain a third. About that time the two men heard "a yell as if all the demons of hell were around us." They galloped away, eventually outdistancing their pursuers.

On April 26, James's companion left him and returned to the trading house. James then swam his horse across the Washita River and left it with some friends, thinking that if he were on foot, he was more likely to escape detection. He then swam back across the Red River and found a Comanche camp.

James spent a month lurking about the camp, hoping to communicate with one of the captives. When he needed meat, he would go about ten miles from the Indian camp, kill a buffalo, and then roast it and eat it. If no buffalo were available, he would haul water with his hat, and pour it into a prairie dog hole until the animal ran out. Often James went for days without food. Finally, he decided to return home. Returning to the "Cash Forks of the Red River," he retrieved his horse and rode back to Montgomery County after an absence of five months.[42]

James then decided to appeal once more to Sam Houston, and on June 19, 1837, he went to Houston City. The latest capital of Texas was a brand new city of tents, saloons, several cabins, and a two-story wooden capitol building painted "peach blossom," complete with a portrait gallery in one wing.[43] A recent arrival describes the populace:

> Persons came pouring in until, in a short time, a floating population had collected of some four or five hundred people. Houses could not be built near as fast as required, so that quite a large number of linen tents

were pitched in every direction over the prairie, which gave the city the appearance of a Methodist camp-ground. Some of these tents, such as were used such for groceries [saloons], were calculated to surprise one from their great size. A number of them measured more than a hundred feet each in circumference, with conical tops, thirty or forty feet in height supported by means of a pole in the center. . . . Among a population of six or seven hundred persons, where but the one half were engaged in any regular business . . . unless drinking and gambling may be considered such, riots of all kind were to be expected.[44]

James again visited Sam Houston, who was receiving visitors in the executive mansion, a two-room log cabin with a dog run between the two rooms. The reception area was sparsely furnished with a small table serving as a desk for President Houston. Pallets, trunks, and other things were strewn about the room, and the dirt floor was frequently muddy. Houston often received dignitaries in one of his favorite outfits—a velvet coat, trousers decorated with broad, gold lace, and an old-fashioned cravat.[45]

Finally, Houston relented and granted James's request for troops. Parker stated in his memoirs that Houston gave him "the commission of the Commander-in-Chief of a military company, to be denominated the 'Independent Volunteers of Texas'; without limit as to numbers." A letter dated June 10, 1837, indicates that James exaggerated somewhat. Houston states in part: "Your letter of the 6th Inst has this moment come to hand, and in reply I have to say that as war has now been declared by Congress against those Indians of the Prairies I will authorize you, to proceed to the east, and to Red River, and give the commissions sent to you to take one, authorizing the raising of 120 men and as many more volunteers as they may think fit to turn out, so as to flog those Indians. Great care must be taken, and the *commander* will be Lieut Col Horton of San Augustine selected for the expedition and one that I trust will suffer no surprise from the enemy." James quickly began looking for volunteers.[46]

The men he assembled were a distinguished lot. James's brother Nathaniel, a state senator in Illinois, came down to Texas. Another brother, Joseph, who was a prosperous land speculator, also joined the group. Others associated with the project were Joseph Williams, Daniel Montague, William Lloyd, and W. T. Henderson.[47] However, in the midst of the preparations, President Houston ordered James to "abandon the expedition and to disband the company." According to James, "It appears that he was induced to do this by the misrepresentations of some evil disposed persons. He had been made to believe that I premeditated an attack upon some friendly and well-disposed Indian tribes near the frontier of Texas; which was entirely destitute of truth."

Upon hearing the news, Nathaniel returned to Illinois. James and his brother Joseph then set out alone to Indian Territory, where they wearily rode five hundred miles in the hot sun of July and August. Worn out by malnourishment and exposure, James and Joseph became ill and were forced to return to Montgomery County, arriving on August 31, 1837.

A week later James started out on his fourth trip to Indian Territory, but his weakened condition soon compelled him to return home. A month or so later, James again made his way to the Red River. He first visited the traders he had engaged to help him. Finding that they had not heard anything, he decided to go again among the nonhostile tribes on the frontier of the United States. Several men accompanied him; he identified them only as "my companions."

James claimed that on this fifth and final trip among the Indians, a singular incident occurred. Parker and his companions had entered an Indian village somewhere near the Sabine River. All at once, James saw an Indian wearing a vest just like one he used to have, with buttons made from the rind of a gourd. After questioning the Indian, James decided that he was one of those who had participated in the raid at Fort Parker. James mounted his horse, and "Taking a 'last, fond look' at my vest—*with one eye through the sight of my trusty rifle*—I 'turned and left the spot,' with the assurance that my vest *had got a new button hole!*"

Although the enraged Indians attacked, James and the others managed to escape and make their way to the Sabine River, where they entered another Indian village. Seeing that the Indians were intoxicated, James and the other men did not get down from their horses. Suddenly, one of the Indians grabbed the bridle of James's horse and pulled out a knife. James jerked his rifle out of his saddle and knocked the Indian down, breaking the firearm in the process. The other Indians rushed the men, but they again managed to escape and continue their journey, this time homeward.

James arrived at his home on October 28, 1837. Ill and exhausted, he could not return to the frontier. Rachel had been in captivity for seventeen months. James had made five trips to the Red River area, traveled thousands of miles, and spent hundreds of dollars but still had made no progress. He had not recovered his daughter, and he did not even have a clue as to where she was. But James kept trying. He sent his son-in-law Lorenzo Nixon to find out if the traders had learned anything.[48]

CHAPTER 6

How Checkered Are
the Ways of Providence

THE PLAINS in eastern Colorado were drier and hotter than usual in the summer of 1837. The sun had set, but Rachel continued with her work. A little more than a year before, her grandfather and uncles had been killed, and she and James Pratt and the others had been abducted. Only a year, but she knew that she could not live much longer. Her hope was almost gone, but she was a Parker, and although her body and spirit were bruised, she had survived.[1]

Suddenly, Rachel noticed some men coming toward her in the semi-darkness. As they drew closer, she could see that they were Mexican traders. Comancheros visited Comanche villages to barter for horses and mules and, at times, human beings. After the transaction, the Comanches would sometimes steal the stock or slaves back from the traders.[2]

When Rachel saw the Comancheros, she felt a surge of hope that she might be rescued. The traders asked Rachel where her master was, and she took them to him. "They asked if he would sell me. No music, no sounds that ever reached my anxious ear, was half as sweet as *'ce senure.'*"

One of the traders next offered some goods in exchange for Rachel, but the old man refused the offer. Rachel trembled in fear that the trader would not offer enough. "Oh! had I the treasures of the universe, how freely I would have given it; yea, and then consented to have been a servant to my countrymen. Would that my father could speak to him; but my father is no more. Or one of my uncles; yes, they would say 'stop not for price.' Oh! my good Lord, intercede for me." She thought of her uncle Nathaniel Parker in Illinois, who was a member of the state legislature and would be glad to help her if he could, and yet her freedom—her life even—might be forfeited for a few bolts of calico or several twists of tobacco. The trader made another offer, which was also refused. He told the old man that he "could give no more." As Rachel agonized, the offer went higher, and to Rachel's wild joy, the old Indian accepted it. Rachel did not know that the traders had been instructed to pay any price for her release.

At last Rachel was free, but the pitiful creature who had once been a proud young woman had been so brutalized that she still did not think of herself as free. She spoke of her rescuer as her "new master." Rachel had only one more night to spend in her hell on earth, and as she lay sleepless in the tent of the trader, she gave thanks to God for her deliverance. The night was uneventful, and early in the morning Rachel and the traders were on the road.[3]

Although Rachel estimated that when she was ransomed, she was "five hundred miles north of Santa Fe" or somewhere "north of the Rocky Mountains," she was probably on the plains in eastern Colorado. She does not tell what route the traders took in getting to Santa Fe, stating only that "we traveled very hard for seventeen days." They may have taken either the Mountain Branch of the Santa Fe Trail or the old Comanchero trail, which skirted the mountains, swung around the southeast side of Mount Tucumcari, and then led westward to the valley of the Pecos River.[4]

Finally on the evening of the seventeenth day, the travelers saw lights in the distance. Below them in a valley lay La Villa de Santa Fe. On a typical evening in August, the acrid smell of burning piñon would fill the air as the women in the town cooked the evening meal. The trails into the valley led through corn and wheat fields burned by the sun and then past small adobe houses surrounded by fenced gardens containing the dried remains of red pepper, onion, and bean plants. The stillness was sometimes broken by dogs barking at new arrivals. Next, travelers would find themselves on narrow, winding streets with a solid line of one-story adobe houses crowding the pathway.[5]

At last Rachel and her rescuers reached the heart of the capital of New Mexico, the plaza. In 1837 New Mexico was still a province of Mexico. Rachel's destination was "the inn at the end of the trail," the best hotel in New Mexico and the home of her rescuers. Traditionally called La Fonda, which means simply "the inn," the hotel was originally the residence of the rich and powerful Ortiz family. The old Spanish-style houses of the wealthy people, or ricos, consisted of a large rectangle or square of rooms with a courtyard in the center. The rooms with their thick adobe walls were cool in the summer and easily heated in the winter with small corner fireplaces. Although the floors in the houses in Santa Fe were of hard-packed dirt, they were often covered with woven mats or brightly colored Mexican blankets. Furniture was sparse, consisting of homemade tables, benches, and chairs and possibly a carved wooden chest. In their homes, the Mexicans slept on mattresses on the floor; rolled up and covered with blankets, they served as couches during the daytime. But the hotels contained "clean, inviting" beds. In the courtyards were gardens, orchards, shade trees, and even corrals and stables in the larger establishments. At the inn Rachel met William and Mary Watt Dodson Donoho, the couple who had sent the Comancheros with orders to pay any price for her release. The Donohos had also arranged for the ransom of Mrs. Harris and were in the process of ransoming Sarah Ann Horn, the two English ladies who, sixteen months previously, had been abducted from Beales' colony near the Rio Grande.[6]

William and Mary Donoho were from Columbia, Missouri, and had lived in Santa Fe for only a few years. In 1833 they had loaded up a number of wagons with trade goods, collected 150 men to accompany them, packed up their infant daughter, and started down the Santa Fe Trail. Mary Donoho was the first female U.S. citizen to live in Santa Fe, and the Donohos' second daughter and first son were the first Anglo children born there. The Donohos welcomed Rachel and gave her a home:

> I hope that every American that reads this narrative may duly appreciate this amiable man, to whom, under the providence of God, I owe my release. I have no language to express my gratitude to Mrs. Donoho. I found in her a mother, to direct me in that strange land, a sister to condole with me in my misfortune, and offer new scenes of amusement to me to revive my mind. A friend? yes, the best of friends; one who had been blessed with plenty, and was anxious to make me comfortable; and one who was continually pouring the sweet oil of consolation into my wounded and trembling soul, and was always comforting and admonishing me not to despond, and assured me that every thing should be done to facilitate my return to my relatives; and though I am now separated far from her, I still owe to her a debt of gratitude I shall never be able to repay but with my earnest prayers for the blessing of God to attend her through life.[7]

Rachel went to sleep that night in a bed enclosed by four walls. No longer would she lie in a tent or outside on the hard ground with only a buffalo robe to cover her. In the morning she would be awakened by the bells of La Parroquia, the ancient parish church near the plaza. To the east were the peaks of the Sangre de Cristo (Blood of Christ) Mountains, some-times visited by the Comanches, and on the west were the Jémez Moun-tains, a favorite hunting ground of the Apaches.[8]

Situated in the midst of the haunts of the Comanches, Apaches, and many other Indian groups, the citizens of Santa Fe and the inhabitants of the nearby ranches had been harried for centuries. Although the popula-tion of the town was about three thousand, with another three thousand in the vicinity, the capital of New Mexico was not a bustling, thriving me-tropolis but a decaying, shabby town. The Republic of Mexico was in fi-nancial trouble. To make matters worse, in the summer of 1837 New Mexico was gripped by a drought, and the days were hot and still. The town with its crumbling adobe walls and narrow streets was a strange sight for the eighteen-year-old girl who had traveled so far to many places never seen by her countrymen. As Rachel regained her strength somewhat, she must have walked out onto the plaza. There she saw no fountains or walks or carefully tended plants, but a large rectangular space with hard-packed dirt that turned to mud when it rained. If Rachel walked around the plaza, she would have come upon a stone sundial with its somber message, "Vita fugit—sicut umbra," meaning "Life flees like a shadow."[9]

On the north side of the plaza was the Governor's Palace, a rectangular one-story adobe building. More than two hundred years old, the palace had a flat roof, a long porch that ran along the front, spacious rooms with dirt floors and exposed roof beams, and a large courtyard in the center. Two of its most notable features were glass windows and several strings of the dried ears of Indians, draped across the walls of one of the rooms. At one time bounty hunters were paid for each Indian they killed, and the ears were supplied as proof of their deeds. Behind the Governor's Palace and attached to it was a presidio or fort that enclosed about one acre. Inside its walls were other government buildings and living quarters for the soldiers.[10]

On the south side of the plaza was the military chapel, La Capilla de Nuestra Señora de la Luz (Chapel of Our Lady of Light), commonly known as La Castrense. Because of lack of funds to pay the chaplains, it had been closed before Rachel arrived in Santa Fe. Its adobe walls were crumbling and its copper bells were silent, but it still stood with its facade of "a large rectangular slab of freestone, elaborately carved. It represented Our Lady of Light in the act of rescuing a human being from the jaws of Satan whilst the angels are crowning her." Inside the crumbling building was an enor-mous, exquisite altar screen carved from white stone and painted with blue, red, yellow, green, and black.[11] The east and west sides of the plaza were lined with shops and a few dwellings belonging to the ricos. As Rachel walked around the town, every once in a while she could get a glimpse through a covered walkway and see the courtyard of a spacious home with trees, bushes, flowers, and perhaps a mockingbird in a cage.[12]

Rachel must have been shocked by what most visiting Americans felt to be the licentiousness of Santa Fe. The fandangos, bailes, and gambling were foreign to the young girl who had been brought up in one of the strictest religious sects of the day. Most of the Mexican women wore short skirts, low-cut blouses, shawls, and numerous rings, bracelets, and necklaces. They gambled and smoked cigarritos made of cornhusks filled with finely chopped tobacco. Even the sounds of the town were strange—the drums and fife of the soldiers, and the church bells that always seemed to be ringing. The smells were pungent—the familiar farm smell of manure from the horses and mules, but most of all the unique smell of Mexico—a spicy mixture of fried onions, red pepper, and sizzling meat.[13]

Did the people of Santa Fe welcome Rachel or did they consider her degraded and shun her? Rachel states in her memoirs that in an outpouring of generosity, a number of people donated 150 dollars to finance her return to Texas, but the money was embezzled by an unscrupulous clergyman. Bitterly disappointed, Rachel had to wait. The Donohos could have financed her return, but perhaps they feared sending her off again into the territory of the Comanches. It was eight hundred miles to Fort Parker, and Rachel and her escort would have to travel through mountains, deserts, and the heart of Comanchería. It would take much more than 150 dollars to ensure her safe conduct to Texas.[14]

Besides, the Donohos had more important matters to worry about in the hot, still days of early August. The people of Santa Fe always lived in danger of Indian attack.[15] In addition to the "horse Indians" as the Comanches and Apaches were called, the Pueblo Indians had become a threat. The oppressive measures in the revised Mexican constitution, such as centralization of powers and new taxes, were causing unrest in New Mexico in the summer of 1837.[16]

The Pueblo Indians hated their Hispanic masters. It was prophesied among the Indians that a new race would soon appear from the east to release them from their bondage. Repressed and kept in perpetual poverty by the Hispanic ricos, the Pueblos in every part of New Mexico were "ripe for insurrection."[17]

The Pueblo Indians' dissatisfaction came to a head when a new governor, Colonel Albino Pérez, was sent from Mexico City to rule New Mexico;

the previous governors had been local men. Even more galling was the fact that new taxes were levied to support the new regime. Although there was unrest, no violence erupted until a local alcalde was imprisoned by the new governor. When the alcalde was liberated by a mob, a general insurrection began.[18]

The Donohos, who had traveled eight hundred miles to make a home in New Mexico, were without doubt exceedingly alarmed. They had lived in Santa Fe for four years and invested thousands of dollars in their hotel and trading house, but they had their three children to think about as well as themselves, Rachel, and Mrs. Harris. Famine threatened as the drought continued, and as the August heat increased, the news became more and more alarming. At La Cañada, a small town about twenty-five miles north of Santa Fe, the principal warriors of all the northern pueblos had gathered.[19]

Governor Pérez issued orders for the militia in each town to be called to active duty, but he managed to muster only about two hundred men. Most were the warriors of the pueblos of Santo Domingo, Chochití, and Sandía. Foolishly, the governor marched with his small force out of Santa Fe toward La Cañada. At Black Mesa, a few miles from La Cañada, the governor and his men were ambushed by two thousand Pueblo Indians, and all but twenty-three of the governor's soldiers deserted him. The beleaguered remnant fought their way back to Santa Fe, arriving on August 8, but that night they were captured as they tried to flee to the south. The governor was shot and killed, his body stripped and mutilated, his severed head stuck on a pole and carried to the rebel camp near the Church of Nuestra Señora de Rosario northwest of the city. The rebels yelled at Pérez's head, "Ah, you robber! You will no longer extort taxes; you will no longer drink chocolate or coffee!" Then they kicked the head about the streets, hacked it with their sabers, poked it with arrows, and declared that anyone who buried the naked, headless corpse would be put to death.[20]

District Judge Santiago Abreu was tortured before he was killed. First he was placed in stocks. Then his hands were hacked off and waved in his face as the revolutionaries asked him such questions as: "Why did you use these hands to make life miserable for the people of New Mexico?" After further mutilations Abreu was finally put to death. About ten more men were slaughtered, their bodies left rotting in the August sun as the animals stripped the flesh from their bones. Rachel seemed strangely unaffected by these events and barely mentions them in her memoirs, saying only: "Soon after I arrived in Santa Fe, a disturbance took place among the Mexicans. They killed several of their leading men."[21]

The American traders, who numbered about two hundred, filled five or six hundred guns with powder and shot and sat in front of the shops surrounding the plaza. The Pueblo Indians, who had for centuries tilled their land and tended their cattle and sheep, looted the town, but did not harm the Americans. They elected their own governor, José Gonzales, a creole from Taos and one of the leaders of the insurrection. Gonzales was a buffalo hunter, described by Padre Don Francisco Madariaga as "without civil virtues and so ignorant that he was unable to sign his own name." On August 10, Gonzales was installed as governor of New Mexico in a ceremony that took place at the Church of Nuestra Señora de Rosario. Then the revolutionaries carried Gonzales through the streets in a sedan chair, shouting: "Long live Christ and death to the robbers!"[22]

William and Mary Donoho had had enough. Hurriedly packing their belongings into wagons, they gathered up their children, Rachel, and Mrs. Harris and, banding together with other disillusioned Americans, prepared to leave the beautiful Santa Fe valley forever.[23]

Days of preparation were usually necessary for the eight-hundred-mile journey along the Santa Fe Trail. First the wagons and teams had to be gathered together. In the 1830s the traders usually used a wagon called the Pittsburgh wagon, a modified version of the Conestoga wagon. Each Pittsburgh wagon was drawn by at least six mules or oxen and carried about three thousand pounds of goods. The Donohos probably transported as much as they could of their merchandise and household goods. Provisions for each person would also have to be included: fifty pounds of flour, fifty pounds of salted meat, twenty pounds of sugar, a little salt, and ten pounds of coffee if it were available. Sometimes such luxuries as beans and crackers were added.[24]

Rachel gives no details about the caravan in which she traveled. Most consisted of about forty wagons. Traders and other travelers banded together when traveling the Santa Fe Trail. The larger the caravan, the less the danger of attack by the Indians who frequented almost every mile of the trail.

The teamsters gathered their wagons together in the plaza. The hour for departure set, the leader of the wagon train would yell, "Catch up! Catch up!" Immediately noise and confusion would fill the air as the wagon drivers began hitching up their teams. The men would yell and curse as the mules and oxen balked and struggled to get away. Then the rattle of harness, the jingle of chains, and the incessant braying of the mules and bawling of the oxen would be heard. Finally, one by one, the drivers would call out, "All's set!" and at last the captain would shout, "Stretch out!" Then the air would be filled with the "heps" of the drivers, the cracking of whips, the creaking of wooden wheels, and the rumbling of wagons. The last call was "Fall in!" and finally the wagons stretched out along the four sides of the plaza.[25]

As the wagons rumbled out of the plaza, they made a sharp turn and passed San Miguel Church. Then the trail turned to the right to pass the house of a rico. Surely the Donohos were sad to be leaving the Santa Fe valley with its mild winters and bright, crisp summers, but they were going home—back to friends and relatives. Rachel must have had mixed feelings as she left the town to go back to the haunts of the Comanches. She must have known that after the caravan reached the plains, she would not see a house for over a month, but at times she would see Indians in the distance. Rachel was making another trip across the treeless plains, this time riding on a hard wagon seat instead of on horseback or walking beside a travois loaded with the household goods of her Comanche master. The grueling eight-hundred-mile trip would take her even farther from Fort Parker than she had been when she was in Santa Fe. Rachel had not recovered her strength in the few weeks that she had spent in Santa Fe, and now she had to face another trek across the seemingly endless plains.[26]

The Santa Fe Trail had two main routes and several minor deviations, but the first leg of the journey from Santa Fe was always the same—one hundred miles to Las Moras Creek. Since the wagon trains traveled between twelve and fifteen miles a day on average, and a good deal less in the mountains, many days would pass before the Donoho caravan reached the village of Las Vegas. First the travelers had to cross the Santa Fe valley. As they turned their wagons almost due east, they came to a hill. One last look at the rectangular fields and flat-roofed houses, and the travelers were on their way to the United States.[27]

The caravan traveled to a place called Arroyo Hondo, six miles from Santa Fe. The refugees next struggled through a dense piñon forest on a rough and winding road. A steep, jagged spur of a mountain had to be crossed, and then the wagons entered an immense canyon where they rumbled through deep ravines, across scattered rocks, and around huge boulders. Again the road became steep and made a dangerous "S" curve. The teams had to be doubled to drag the heavy wagons to the tops of the hills. With a mountain on one side and a deep ravine on the other, the road was barely wide enough for a wagon to pass. The teams were then reduced to four or six oxen so that they could negotiate the sharp curves without tumbling over the precipice. The travelers were lucky if they made three to six miles a day on this stretch. At last the pass was reached, and they found themselves surrounded by the twelve-thousand-foot peaks of the Sangre de Cristo Mountains.[28]

As the wagons rolled on, they passed through the village of San Miguel del Vado, where they forded the Pecos River. Twenty-five miles up the road, the travelers descended into the Gallinas River valley and soon found themselves rumbling through the streets of Las Vegas, originally known as Nuestra Señora de los Dolores de Las Vegas (Our Lady of Sorrows of the Meadows), which was a village of about one hundred adobe houses. A plaza was used both for protection against the Indians and as a market-place.[29]

Twenty miles beyond Las Vegas at the Moras Creek crossing, the Santa Fe Trail divided into two main branches, northern and southern. The southern route was known as the Cimarron Cut-off, the Desert Route, or the Dry Route. The older of the two, it was also the shorter route and for the most part passed through wide open country with few obstructions for the bulky wagons. On the other hand, it was filled with dangers. It led through the hunting grounds of a number of Indian tribes: the Arapahoes, Pawnees, Cheyennes, Kiowas, Apaches, and, the most deadly of all, the Comanches. Even more frightening was the Jornada or Water Scrape, a forty-mile stretch between the Cimarron and Arkansas rivers where in most seasons there was no water.

Rachel did not specify in her memoirs which route the Donoho caravan took, but her description of the route as "a vast region of prairie, which is nearly one thousand miles across" indicates that the Donohos chose the Cimarron Cut-off, which was by the far the more popular route in 1837.[30]

Finally, after two months of grueling travel across mountains, deserts, plains, and rivers with quicksand, in a land inhabited by hostile Indians, the travelers could see a group of buildings on the horizon and knew that they had reached Independence, Missouri, and were home at last. In Rachel's case the name Independence was ironic. She had been free of Comanche bondage for several months but would never be free of the feelings of degradation.[31]

Independence, founded in 1827, was the principal jumping-off point for western trappers, traders, and travelers. The returning teamsters often signaled their arrival with gunshots so they could be sure of receiving a proper welcome. The town had an international flavor with four languages commonly spoken: English, French, Spanish, and German. In the numerous saloons, prosperous traders in broadcloth and stovepipe hats rubbed shoulders with Indians, French Canadian trappers, Mexican drovers, and American gamblers.[32]

In spite of its character as a wild boomtown, Independence was a haven for Rachel. She says, "I received many signal favors from many of the inhabitants, for which I shall ever feel grateful." With its churches and its neat square and brick two-story courthouse, it must have reminded her of Palestine, Illinois. The river, and the little patches of woods interspersed with lush prairie grasslands, was much like the terrain around her birthplace, which she had left only four years before.[33]

After a short stay in Independence, the Donohos, Rachel, and Mrs. Harris moved in with Mary Donoho's mother, Lucy Dodson, who lived in Pulaski County, Missouri. Later, Sarah Ann Horn was also welcomed into Lucy Dodson's home. While Rachel was in Missouri, she constantly inquired about her relatives in Texas, and one day she received a letter from G. S. Parks, who informed her that he had heard that her father and husband were alive. Month after month passed, and as Rachel says, "It was now in the dead of winter and no prospect of getting to my relatives. My anxiety grew so high that I could not sleep. Every evening I made it my invariable rule to pray, mingled with my tears, to the Almighty God to intercede for me, and in his providence to devise some way for me to get to my people. I was often tempted to start on foot." Mary Donoho tried unsuccessfully to console her unhappy visitor. "Despite all the kind entreaties of that benevolent woman, Mrs. Donoho, I refused to be comforted; and who, I ask, under these circumstances, could have been reconciled?"[34]

On January 20, 1838, a notice appeared in the Houston newspaper *Telegraph and Texas Register:* "December 1837, Mrs. Plimmer from Robertson's Colony, Texas was lately purchased from the Camanche Indians—she is at Independence, Missouri. She states she has three children and one sister yet with the same tribe. The above named lady has red hair. For further information apply to Wm. T. Smith, Columbia, Boon county, Missouri. Mrs. Harris has been likewise purchased from the Indians, and can be found at the same place. She was also taken from Texas."[35]

Although filled with errors, the advertisement was effective. One evening as Rachel was in her room trying to pray but finding it impossible, she walked to the door and there she saw her brother-in-law, Lorenzo Nixon. She tried to run to him but was too weak. Rachel describes her feelings at the time: "I was so much overjoyed I scarcely knew what to say or how to act." The first questions Rachel asked Lorenzo were: "Is my husband and father alive? Is mother and the children alive?" In spite of her weakness and poor health, Rachel was determined to return to Texas. "Every moment was an hour, and it was now very cold weather, but I thought I could stand any thing if I could only get started towards my own country."[36]

In the winter of 1837–38, Rachel started on the long trip home. The Donohos furnished her with a horse and William Donoho accompanied Rachel and Lorenzo. Rachel does not describe the journey from Missouri to Texas, saying only: "We had a long and cold journey of more than one thousand miles, the way we were compelled to travel, and that principally through a frontier country."[37]

As Rachel approached the home of her parents, she became more and more eager to see her loved ones:

> Finally on the evening of the 19th day of February, 1838, I arrived at my father's house in Montgomery county, Texas. Here united tears of joy flowed from the eyes of father, mother, brothers and sisters; while many strangers, unknown to me, (neighbors to my father) cordially united in this joyful interview. . . . I am now once more in the company of dear father and mother and other friends, and moreover have the great pleasure of embracing my beloved husband. But oh! dreadful reflection, where is my little children? One of them is no more—I buried its bloody body in those vast regions of prairies—but I hope its soul is now in Heaven. My body is covered with scars which I am bound to carry to my grave; my constitution broke—but above all and every trouble which haunts my distracted mind is WHERE IS MY POOR LITTLE JAMES PRATT!"[38]

Rachel's return was recorded in the Houston *Telegraph and Texas Register* for March 3, 1838: "Mrs. Plummer, who was captured by the Comanches in the spring of 1836, has returned to her relatives. She has prepared a brief sketch of the country through which she has passed with these Indians, and a narrative of her adventures, which will be presented to the public in pamphlet form in the course of a few weeks."[39]

Rachel's father explains the events that led to Lorenzo Nixon's appearance in Missouri.

> I arrived at home, from this tour [to Indian Territory], on the 28th of October. Finding that my health was much impaired from travelling, I started my son-in-law, (Mr. Nixon,) to see what my traders had done. On the 30th, at a late hour of the night, a Mr. G. S. Parks arrived at my

house, and informed me that he had met Mr. Nixon, and that he had directed him to go on to Independence, Missouri, where Mrs. Plummer was, she having been brought into that place by some Santa Fe traders.

Reader, I leave you to your own conceptions of what were my feelings on hearing this joyful news. My wife rushed eagerly to my side to hear the glad tidings, and so overjoyed was she to hear that her child was yet alive, that she fell, senseless, in my arms, whilst my little children gathered around me, all anxiously inquiring: "Father, does sister Rachel still live?"

How chequered are the ways of Providence. Though my sorrows and sufferings, for the past two years, had been greater than it would be thought human nature could bear, the joy I felt that night overbalanced them all, whilst I poured forth to Almighty God, the humble thanks of a grateful heart for the merciful deliverance of my child from a cruel bondage. How truly does the inspired writer say, that "He that chasteneth when it seemeth fit, and maketh the sorrowful heart to rejoice in due season."

On the 19th of February, Mr. Nixon and Mrs. Plummer arrived at my house, and great indeed was the joy on her return to the bosom of her friends. She presented a most pitiable appearance; her emaciated body was covered with scars, the evidences of the savage barbarity to which she had been subject during her captivity. She was in very bad health.

Rachel was home at last, but a long and happy life did not await her; one tragedy would follow another.[40]

PART III

JAMES W.

⊰⊱ CHAPTER 7 ⊰⊱

The Tongue of Slander

J AMES W. PARKER was forty-one years old and at the lowest point of his life. Three years earlier he had been at the pinnacle, a respected leader instrumental in obtaining for his family a vast empire of some of the richest land in Texas. Although he still owned thousands of acres, now he was weighed down with the deaths of five people at Fort Parker. Other members of his family were still in captivity: his nephew John, his niece Cynthia Ann, and his grandson James Pratt. He had with him only a "pityful remnant" of his once numerous and strong family. How had he come to this? Some of the mysterious activities of James W. Parker will never be understood, but clues can be found in obscure documents and letters.

In the fall of 1838 and the winter of 1838–39, a series of events occurred that have not been completely explained. A letter James W. Parker wrote to Mirabeau B. Lamar, president of the Republic of Texas, offers some insight into what was happening at the time. In this letter James petitioned for protection from "certain armed forces—citizens of the county of Nacogdoches, San Augusteen Shelby and Montgumery and prehaps others." According to James, these vigilantes conducted mock trials and sentenced individuals in order to induce them to implicate others. James does not state of what crime the victims had been accused. One settler said the vigilante group calling themselves the Regulators had set out in the summer of 1838 to "ferret out horse thieves and counterfeiters."[1]

The Republic of Texas to which Rachel returned in February of 1838 was in deep trouble. The majority of Texans had expected to be annexed by the United States immediately after they had obtained their independence, but the slavery question had prevented annexation, and in 1839 there seemed to be no chance of statehood in the near future. In addition, an extreme money shortage caused many problems. Cattle and hogs became means of exchange, with a cow worth ten dollars and a hog one dollar. Promissory notes were often used, but since they exchanged hands as many as five times, they often caused serious problems when the bearer finally tried to collect from the original signer. One counterfeiter in San Felipe was considered by some to be a public benefactor because he was facilitating monetary exchange.[2]

Even more serious were the threats from the Indians and from Mexico. The Mexicans were attempting to incite the Indians against the Texans, and even the formerly friendly tribes were becoming restive as the settlers pushed relentlessly northward and westward. Settler George Bernard Erath gives his view of the situation:

> There were two very different kinds of Indians in Texas: Caddos, half civilized from Louisiana, mixed with remnants of other tribes from farther east, and the wild Indians, also immigrants, but of a much earlier date than the Caddos. Among the wild Indians the Comanches were the most powerful: they claimed the sovereignty of Texas, and treated all other tribes as vassals. They regarded the whites on the Colorado and west of it as a different race from those on the Brazos and in the east generally. In fact, they regarded the whites, like themselves, as divided up into tribes, and so made war on the western whites while they considered the eastern ones their friends. The Caddos were much better informed, and knowing the difficulties that might arise from the wild Indian depredations, they did not themselves go to the Colorado River. But the people of the Colorado believed that the Caddos harbored their enemies and traded with them for stolen horses; in their vexation they even accused the Brazos whites of such conduct.[3]

Thus, the Colorado settlers suspected the Brazos settlers, including the inhabitants of Fort Parker, of unscrupulous dealings with the Indians. After the massacre, rumors drifted from settlement to settlement. Some of them were about James W. Parker.

When Rachel reached her father's home in Montgomery County in February of 1838, the rumors had been growing and festering like an ugly sore for more than two years. In spite of his many problems, James was a prosperous man. He lived two miles east of Huntsville, which consisted of two log houses and a sawmill. James owned a farm and must have owned a mill since he called his home "Parker's Mill." His land was in the pine belt of Texas, a thickly wooded area with tangled underbrush and sandy soil. The settlers grew corn and cotton as cash crops and such vegetables as beans, potatoes, and pumpkins for the table. Some owned a few cattle and hogs, and the men hunted small game as well as deer and bear. The favorite spot for bear hunting was a sharp bend in Atkins Creek. The dogs would drive the bears into this area, where the men would kill them.[4]

Other entertainment was provided by the district court, which met in the town of Montgomery once a month. A festive atmosphere prevailed as settlers from miles around poured into the county seat to see who was suing whom and to watch the show. The town was filled with the usual mixture of men and women found on the frontier. Some of the men wore broadcloth suits and stovepipe hats while others wore homespun or buckskin trousers and shirts. Most of the women donned their Sunday best dresses of calico, but some wore silk dresses brought from their home states or made of fabric imported from New Orleans. The old settlers, sometimes called "buckskin people," often resented the newcomers, who were usually more affluent and flaunted their wealth with fancy clothes, the finest horses, and perhaps even a carriage. One of the local characters was the Wild Man of the Woods, who wore a snakeskin vest. Sam Houston may even have been there. He probably would have left his black velvet suit with the gold lace in Houston City, in favor of his Mexican blanket coat with buckskin britches or, more probably, a broadcloth suit.

The citizens of the Republic of Texas were a litigious group, suing one another at the least excuse. Many of the cases involved hogs, which wandered about freely and were sometimes appropriated by a neighbor for a quick feast. Another frequent cause for a lawsuit was nonpayment of debt. On a winter's day late in the year of 1838, James rode into Montgomery, and as he was sitting on his horse, for some unknown reason he was accosted by William W. Shepperd, a prosperous local citizen.[5]

Why Shepperd chose this particular day to revile James will probably never be known, but his approximate words have been recorded for posterity in a slander case James filed requesting ten thousand dollars in damages. The accusations Shepperd made were serious. His words are quoted in the complaint James filed: "You (meaning the said James W. Parker) were notoriously known in Illanois to be a counterfeiter and [also as a] counterfeiter and horse thief in Texas." Shepperd even said the horse that James was riding was stolen and that he was associated with the Indians in a plan for stealing horses. These accusations were made in the presence of a number of people. The reason given for the attack was that "William W. Shepperd well knowing the premises and envying the said James W. Parker [his] good name fame and Reputation and maliciously intending to deprive him of same did speak rehearse pronounce and publish the false scandalous and malicious words stated."[6] Obviously there was more to it than that. This verbal attack on James occurred "on or about the third day of December in 1838." Sometime in the winter of 1838–39, vigilantes attacked James's home.[7] It is probable that the vigilante attack and the public accusations were related.

Another probable cause for the vigilante attack on James were rumors implicating him in an atrocity that had occurred two years earlier twenty miles from Montgomery at Roan's Prairie. On March 8, 1837, a man named Levi Taylor had been killed by Indians while he was in a creek bottom searching for a lost cow. His wife had taken their three children, ranging in age from two to six years, and sought refuge at the residence of Joshua Hadley, who lived in a two-story house with a log fort nearby. One night about a month later, a band of Indians attacked. The Indians were repulsed, but Mrs. Taylor insisted on fleeing to the house of another neighbor who lived half a mile away. The Hadleys tried to restrain her, but dragging her children with her, the hysterical woman fled into the night.[8]

James W. Winters, a member of the party who pursued the Indians, later reported:

> The attack was made in the night, and Mrs. Taylor tried to leave the house with her children, three in number—two boys and a girl. The Indians found them out in their flight, and killed the mother and little girl and shot one of the boys in the hand with an arrow. This occurred near where the town of Anderson now is. Mrs. Taylor was delivered of another child in her dying struggle after being shot. . . . After an organization took place Jerry Washam was chosen captain, and the pursuit of the Indians commenced. They had taken a westerly course out of the country. The command crossed the Navasota River and went up between that stream and the Brazos, passing within three miles of Fort Parker. Twenty-five miles beyond the fort, at a horseshoe-shaped prairie belted by timber, the Indians scattered and the trail was hard to keep. . . . The Indians were all on foot and not more than ten in number. They were trailed across the prairie on the other side of the timber, and here they again scattered and it was impossible to follow them, so the pursuers commenced their return.[9]

For some reason, James was suspected of being involved in the murder of Mrs. Taylor and her daughter. During the winter of 1838–39, while he was away, vigilantes went to his home in Montgomery County. James described the incident in the letter he wrote to Lamar: "thay have come to the residence of your Memoralist in his absence and told his family that thay meant to kill him and threated his soninlaw, (Goion) [going on ?] that if he did not leve the house of your Memorialist, (his home) thay would whip him and destroy the property." When James returned and learned what had happened, he went into hiding and directed his family to go to Houston City, which was seventy miles away through a heavily forested area. Although there was a dirt road from Huntsville to Houston, the refugees were compelled to hack their way through the tangled underbrush in order to hide from the vigilantes. According to James, "my family . . . wase so exposed to the cold rain and inclemenency of the weather as not only to endanger all thare lives but has actually taken Four of my belovd. of my family to thare long home."[10]

Rachel was pregnant as she and the other members of her family slogged through the rain and mud to Houston. Her third child had been conceived shortly after she was reunited with her husband. While in Houston, Rachel and the other refugees may have lived for a time with James's younger brother Joseph Allen Parker, who had amassed vast land holdings.[11]

Houston City had changed in the two years from the time when James had visited Sam Houston in his presidential shack. It was still a wild boomtown, hogs roamed about, and the streets were rivers of mud when it rained, but the population of the little city had grown to two thousand, and a two-story courthouse built of planks instead of logs had been erected. Houston had two theaters and three newspapers but no church. A writer for the *Morning Star* complained: "It is a source of much astonishment, and of considerable severe comment upon the religious character of our city, that while we have a theater, a court house, a jail and even a capitol in Houston we have not a single Church."[12]

During this time Rachel published the first version of the story of her captivity. In the preface she states, "I had written this narrative partly in Santa Fe and part in Missouri, and completed it at my father's in Texas. . . . I have had again to draw off my travels, trusting a great deal to my recollection, though the facts here stated are facts, and such as will never be erased from my memory. I know the scattered situation of my mind is such that I could not connect subjects or sentences—but I hope that the public will view my errors with an eye of charity." The preface ends with the information: "Dated at Parker's Mill in Texas, Montgomery county, September 23d, 1838."[13]

By January, James evidently felt safe enough to venture to Houston to join the members of his family. Tired of the pervasive rumors, he wrote and published a five-page pamphlet entitled *Defence of James W. Parker, against Slanderous Accusations Preferred against Him.* After a lengthy passage asserting his innocence, James lists the charges against him:

> The first is, that at the time I resided in what was called Parker's Fort, on the head waters of the Navisota, I was associated with the Indians in a plan for stealing horses from the whites—that it was my practice to purchase the shares of the Indians in the stolen property, and to pay them in counterfeit money—that the Indians in attempting to pass this counterfeit money were detected and punished, and in revenge for the fraud practised on them by myself, attacked the fort, killing part of the residents, and taking captive others. The second charge made against me is that of circulating counterfeit money: that in the state of Illinois, where I formerly resided, I was in the constant practice of passing counterfeit money, and that in Texas I was both a counterfeiter and a horse-thief. A third charge is, that I was the murderer of Mrs. Taylor and her daughter, in the spring of 1837, and that the main object was to rob the house of Major Hadly. And besides these specific charges, the public mind had been poisoned with charges, rumors, and reports of crimes committed by me of every character and degree, from the lowest in the catalogue of petty villainy, up to the most atrocious of which human depravity is capable; and yet so artful have I been, or so sluggish and blind has been public justice, that up to the present moment none have attempted to place me at the bar of a court and before a jury of my country, to answer a part or all of these charges. . . . I am placed before the people of Texas in the attitude of a criminal, the grossest delinquencies are imputed to me by the tongue of slander . . . I here make the denial and challenge the proof.

> To the first accusation, relative to the causes which produced the attack on Parker's Fort, I can only reply by a solemn denial of ever having at any time or for any purpose formed a league with the Indians, or having passed to them counterfeit money. This is all which is left to me, or to any man who is placed in the condition of maintaining the negative. Let the accuser show the proof, or any thing resembling proof, positive or presumptive, direct or circumstantial, and I should be willing to abide the event. . . .

> To the second charge, of my conduct in Illinois—if there was any foundation for that charge, it is susceptible of clear and ready proof. I

resided for many years in that state, was generally known in the section of the country of my residence, and filled an office [justice of the peace] the duties of which, I say in defiance of my persecutors, were discharged to the satisfaction of the neighborhood, and without the slightest imputation ever having been cast on me. I repeat the same denial and defiance as it regards my conduct in Texas. . . .

The third charge, of my being the murderer of Mrs. Taylor and her daughter, was attempted to be fixed on me, as I have heard; but so completely were these assassins of character baffled in the attempt, and so satisfactorily was it shown that I was travelling and in a different part of the country at the period when the murder was perpetrated, that the bloodhounds of malice were compelled to abandon that chase, and resort to their usual mode of attack, by bold and impudent assertion, or sly and dark insinuation. . . .

I have served my country, faithfully served it, here and elsewhere, and always given satisfaction to the candid and unprejudiced in every station in which I have been called to act. I have served in the field as a soldier, and in peace as a magistrate, and in the Consultation of Texas as a member, and my success engendered malice in the hearts of some who, if they could not elevate themselves to my level, were determined to drag me down to theirs. . . .

Hear me patiently, judge me candidly and impartially; dismiss from your minds any prejudices you may have imbibed, and come to the decision on my case with a determination to decide according to the facts exhibited. A trial will soon take place, which must enable my enemies to support the charges against me, it they are susceptible of being supported by proof; or which will result in declaring the innocence of,

Your fellow citizen,
JAMES W. PARKER.

The pamphlet is "Dated at Houston, January the 22d, 1839"[14]

All the events that occurred immediately before and after the publication of this pamphlet are not known. Rachel and L. T. M.'s son Wilson P. was born on January 4, 1839, and by mid-March, Rachel was dying. James says of her illness, "During her protracted illness, she was seldom heard to murmur at her own sufferings, past or present, which she knew would soon end; but her whole soul appeared continually engaged in prayer to God for the preservation and deliverance of her dear and only child, James Pratt, from the inhuman bondage he was suffering." Rachel often told her father that "this life had no charms for her, and that her only wish was that she might live to see her son restored to his friends." She did not receive her wish. Rachel died on March 19, 1839. James says only: "In about one year from the time she returned to her paternal home, she calmly breathed out her spirit to Him who gave it, and her friends committed her body to the silent grave." Rachel was twenty years old at the time of her death. Her infant son lived two days longer, dying on March 21, 1839.[15]

To add to his troubles, James was involved in several lawsuits besides his action against William W. Shepperd. He was twice sued in Harris County for nonpayment of debt. In one suit the firm of Hedenberg and Vedder, merchants who sold bulk goods on consignment and by auction, claimed that James owed them five hundred dollars. On June 27, 1839, in their deposition, they stated that they wanted payment because James was leaving the city.[16]

It was time for James to take the "pitiful remnant" of his family and flee back to his home, for an enemy more deadly than vigilantes had hit—the dread yellow fever had turned Houston into a city of death. On October 14, 1839, Houston resident Millie Gray recorded in her diary that one-third of the people were ill with the fever. She added: "Sickness—Sickness—Sickness—Sickness all around and many deaths. . . . 6 or 7 deaths every day from yellow fever." On November 8, 1839, James's brother Joseph Allen Parker died of yellow fever. Joseph's wife Lucinda Richardson Parker died from the same cause at about the same time.[17]

In September of 1839 James was back in Montgomery County. Not only that, he was back in court. The courthouse must have been very familiar to James. It was a log cabin to which had been added a "bar, judges seat, jury boxes, et cetera." This time James was suing Caswell B. Bledsoe (usually spelled "Bloodsaw" by the county clerk) and Appleton Gay. Bledsoe owned 640 acres near Montgomery, and Gay was a thirty-three-year-old planter who also owned 640 acres as well as thirteen slaves, seven horses, and a silver watch. In spite of their flamboyant names, evidently neither of the men could write since they both signed their names with "their mark," which was a jagged "X." James was trying to collect seven hundred dollars from the men. It seems that he had obtained a promissory note from a man named E. M. Fuller, who had received the note from Bledsoe and Gay.[18]

The case dragged on until finally on April 21, 1841, the lawyer of Bledsoe and Gay presented the following argument to the court: "Defts say that the promissory note in plffs Petition set fourth and sued upon [was] executed to receive the payment of a wager made and bet upon a horse race, and that said horse race was prooved to be run by the contrivance of the payre of said note and others combined for the purpose of cheating and defrauding your Defts and that said note was fraudulently and unjustly obtained and ought not to be paid by your Deft[s]—and said Defts pray for all such relief as may be allotted by equity and good conscience."[19]

Horse racing was popular in the Republic of Texas. Tracks were built in Houston and Galveston, and soon almost every plantation had a private track. Races were usually between only two horses. Jockeys removed shoes and shirts and sometimes even trousers so that they would be lighter. Wagers were made, and at times planters callously bet slaves, who were torn from their families if the master's horse did not run fast enough. The case of Bledsoe and Gay vs. Parker was finally settled when the defendants agreed to pay court costs, but James did not receive the seven hundred dollars.[20]

A third case also involved a horse and a promissory note. James sued for 150 dollars. The case was dismissed and James had to pay court costs this time.[21]

◁≫ CHAPTER 8 ≪▷

The House of God

IN 1840 THERE were indications that James Parker was trying to mend his tattered life. Financially, he was better off than most of his neighbors. Among his assets were twelve hundred acres of land in Montgomery County, to which he did not have a clear title, as well as three slaves, thirty cattle, one gold watch, and one silver watch.[1] Once a year he still went to the "Indian country" to see if he could find his niece Cynthia Ann, his nephew John, and his grandson James Pratt.

During the year of 1840, James returned to the political scene. Journeying to the new capital at Austin, he proposed a plan to the legislature, requesting permission to raise an army of four thousand men who would capture Santa Fe, thereby validating Texas' claim to New Mexico. In addition, the men would make a treaty with the Indians entitling the whites to preempt the land along the Santa Fe Trail. Each soldier would receive 360 acres as a reward for his participation in the project. The legislators did not act on the proposal.[2]

Religion was also vitally important to James at this time. Two years earlier, on July 25, 1838, a little church had been formed near James's home. It was called the Mount Pleasant Church of the Regular United Baptist Faith and Order and the members first met at the schoolhouse in the dense woods near James Dean's residence on Harmon's Creek. At times the members met at the "brick academy" on land now located within the Huntsville penitentiary walls. Elder Allen G. Samuels was chosen as pastor, and his descendants say he started the church.[3]

The church drifted peacefully along for two years. A minor problem occurred when Elder Samuels could not get to the services because he lived too far away and he had "lost his horse." A more severe problem arose when Samuels was accused by several members of the church of "the high crime of living in adultry with his presant wife," but he was subsequently cleared of this charge. On May 7, 1840, the Mount Pleasant Regular Baptist Church received James's daughter Sarah Parker Nixon by "experience," and on June 13, 1840, the church minutes contain the following entry: "Receved . . . Bro. James W. Parker, by relation and Recantation Believing it to be the Duty of the Church to Receve all who brings forth prety meats for Repentence, that is of the faith of this Church and Comes into gospel order." James had publicly repented of some sin or infraction of church rules and had been reinstated.[4]

On July 11, 1840, Elder Daniel Parker and Deacon Isaac Parker from the "Pilgrim church of the regular Baptist faith and order in Shelby County" visited Mount Pleasant Church and "pronounced her a church legally autherised to do and perform the business pertaining to the House of God in union with the Church of the regular Baptist order."[5]

Much had happened to Daniel Parker in the last four years. To the best of his ability, Daniel had led his flock in peace and in war. In 1836 during the Texas Revolution, the members of Pilgrim Church had fled from their homes, many of them settling in Shelby County along the Louisiana border. Two years later the congregation was still divided, with meetings being held both at Daniel Parker's house on San Pedro Creek and at the schoolhouse at Lathom's and Peirpont's Settlement in Shelby County.[6]

As we have seen, the year of 1838 was a time of great turbulence in Texas. Mexican agents such as Vincente Cordova had long sought to incite the Indians in East Texas to attack the Texans. Since the members of the Texas Senate had refused to ratify the treaty Sam Houston had made with the Cherokees and their associated bands, "Shawnee, Delaware, Kickapoo, Quapaw, Choctaw, Biloxi, Ioni, Alabama, Coushatta, Caddo of the Neches, Tahocullake, and Mataquo," which would have given them the vast land holdings that they had occupied for many years, they were ripe for rebellion.[7]

On October 5, 1838, members of the Killough, Woods, and Williams families who had settled on lands promised to the Cherokees were attacked by Indians and Mexicans. Eighteen of the settlers were killed or captured. According to a legendary story, after Isaac Killough and his two sons were murdered, his wife Urcey ran out of the house screaming at the attackers, telling them to kill her also. The Mexicans cursed her and yelled, "Go back in the house." She finally obeyed, and she and two other women who were in the house were spared. The survivors of the massacre started out on foot to Nacogdoches. A group of Cherokees found them, took them to their village, where they fed them, and then escorted them to Lacy's Fort near present-day Alto. Although the Cherokees denied that they or any of their associated tribes were involved in the massacre, many settlers were convinced that they were.[8]

In response, Major General Thomas Jefferson Rusk called up the East Texas militia, and Daniel's sons, Daniel Parker Jr., Dickerson, and Benjamin, volunteered to serve under Captain William Turner Sadler, as did most of the able-bodied men of the neighborhood. The militiamen marched toward the Kickapoo village where the Indians and Mexicans were staying. On October 15, 1838, the men camped in a wooded area near Kickapoo Town. A heavy mist descended during the night, and the Indians and Mexicans took this opportunity to attack Rusk's forces early on the morning of October 16. Colonel Hugh McLeod identified the aggressors as "a motley gang—Mexicans, negroes, Coshattees, Caddoes & some thought Keechies." The militia rallied and charged, and the Mexicans fled in confusion, but the Kickapoos fought the militiamen for three days and were easily defeated. A Cherokee warrior named Tail was found among the dead.[9]

Captain Sadler and the other volunteers from the San Pedro Creek area rode wearily home. The families of Captain Sadler, John Edens, Martin Murchison, James Madden, and Robert Madden had "forted up" in the sturdy log cabin of John Edens on San Pedro Creek a few miles from Daniel Parker's place. When the militiamen reached home, a terrible sight awaited them. The cabin had been attacked by Indians believed to be Kickapoos.

When the men had left to fight, six women and about nine children had gathered in the cabin of John Edens. The women were Mrs. John Edens, Mrs. Martin Murchison, Mrs. William Sadler, Mrs. James Madden, Mrs. Robert Madden, and a sixty-year-old slave named Patsy. They had been left in the protection of four armed men. The cabin consisted of two rooms with a dog run between them. The women and children went to bed in one of the rooms, and the four men occupied the other. Suddenly, a dozen or so Indians broke down the door of the room occupied by the women and children and, using knives and tomahawks, began clubbing and stabbing the terrified victims. Mrs. Sadler and Mrs. Murchison were immediately killed. The Indians then set fire to the house. Mrs. Edens, who was wounded, ran from the house into a nearby field, where she collapsed and died.

Early in the attack, Patsy grabbed one-year-old Melissa Edens and ran a mile to a neighbor's cabin. Meanwhile, Mrs. Robert Madden, who had been clubbed three times with a tomahawk, had managed to run from the burning room and collapse on the bed in the room where the men were staying. The four men had all escaped to the woods. When Patsy returned from leaving the child at the neighbor's house, she rushed into the burning cabin and, finding Mrs. Robert Madden unconscious on the bed, dragged her out just as the roof fell in. Patsy also pulled Mrs. James Madden out from under an eve of the cabin minutes before a burning wall collapsed. She then placed the two women in her cabin in the yard and took care of them until morning, when help arrived. Six of the children were killed and their bodies were destroyed in the fire. The charred remains could not be identified. One child may have been taken captive.

The militiamen returned from their victory in time to bury the remains of the victims. It is thought that Daniel Parker performed the last rites as the autumn leaves swirled to the ground. According to Daniel's great grandson Ben J. Parker, at that point Daniel's sympathetic attitude toward the Indians changed, and he wanted them all killed or driven out of East Texas.[10]

In 1839 Daniel again attempted to serve his country when he was elected to serve in the House of Representatives of the Fourth Congress of Texas, but the drafters of the constitution had included the following provision in the First Section, 5th Article: "Ministers of the gospel being, by their profession dedicated to God and the care of souls, ought not to be diverted from the great duties of their functions: therefore, no minister of the gospel, or priest of any denomination whatever, shall be eligible to the office of the executive of the republic, nor to a seat in either branch of the congress of the same." When Daniel was told that he could not serve in the legislature because he was a minister, he replied that he "certainly would like to preach to them, for apparently they needed to hear a good sermon."[11]

The rest of Daniel's life centered around his church work. After eleven years of laboring in Texas, Daniel and his co-workers thought there were enough members to form an association, but the move was initiated by James Parker's Mount Pleasant Church rather than by Daniel Parker's Pilgrim Church. James was sent as a delegate to the organizational meeting held in October of 1840 at Douglass, Texas. After much discussion, led chiefly by Daniel, the members agreed on "articles of association," and the Union Association of Regular Predestinarian Baptists was founded. The number of members in 1840 was fewer than one hundred.[12]

A few months later, an acrimonious controversy began in the Mount Pleasant Church. The church minutes for February 13, 1841, contain the following statement: "Brother James W Parker informed the Church, that Sundry charges had been perferd against him, but after collecting all the information we can on the Subject. Say that we have no Gospel charge against him." Other statements in the minutes of February 13, 1841, indicate that the Mount Pleasant Church was experiencing grave problems in regard to the constitution of the church. Although it is difficult to determine exactly what happened, this much is clear. In early February of 1841 James W. Parker was charged by a member or members of the church with some sins or crimes. At the meeting on February 13, 1841, a rule was added to the constitution making it illegal to excommunicate a member without a unanimous vote. At a March or April meeting, not recorded in the Church Book, James was excommunicated by the Mount Pleasant Church, and Elder Samuels and his wife Nancy left the church. The anti-Parker faction called Elder Sutton to be their pastor. At the May 8, 1841, meeting, a confrontation occurred. James and three of his allies, "Brother Edmond, Sisters Susanah Tinsley [and] Sarah [Parker] Thomas, alias Sarah Nixon," left the meeting house, taking the Church Book with them. The Parker faction held services somewhere else, and since James had the Church Book, he wrote his version of the proceedings, as he had been doing since the dispute had begun.[13]

After the long, hot summer during which the feud between the "constitutional party" and the "unconstitutional party" continued to rage among the ten or fifteen Baptists of Mount Pleasant Church, James turned his thoughts to other matters. In September of 1841, he heard about two children who had been taken to a place he called the "Chickasaw Depot," which was probably Boggy Depot in present-day Atoka County, Oklahoma.[14]

James was ill with fever when he heard about the children, but he mounted his mule and started anyway. Again he headed up the route he had traversed at least once a year for the last five years. When James reached Indian Territory, he made his way to what was called the Texas Road, which ran from Colbert's Ferry near Preston, Texas, northwest to Fort Gibson. For thirty-five miles the road, which was very rough, ran through a heavily timbered, mountainous area. Boggy Depot was one of the towns that lay along the road. James arrived in Boggy Depot on September 22 and immediately found himself in great danger. The Chickasaws and Choctaws were extremely hostile to anyone who was a Texan. James solved the problem by pretending to be a citizen of Arkansas.[15]

James soon perceived that he was in even greater danger from another enemy. He states: "There were many Indians at the Depot when I arrived, and to my horror I found that many of them were of the same tribe to which the Indian belonged that had on my vest." In spite of the circumstances, James was determined to fulfill his mission. He went to the trading house of Robert M. Jones, a mixed-blood Choctaw who was a wealthy plantation owner and the principal trader in Boggy Depot. James states that Jones informed him that "the children that had been brought in were not those I was looking for, but said that his traders knew of some children among the Cumanches that no doubt were those I was in search of."

Since Jones's traders were about to leave on a commercial expedition among the Comanches, Jones told the headmen to "purchase these children at any price" and promised to reimburse the traders himself. It happened that James knew one of the traders, an elderly Delaware Indian named Frank. Frank took James aside and told him that he was in danger. Pointing out an Indian in the crowd around the trading post, Frank told James that the man said James had killed his brother. James continues the story: "Maj. Jones gave me the same caution that old Frank, the Delaware, had given me, and added, that he would invite me to stay at the Depot that night, but he knew if I staid the Indians would steal my mule." After Jones had walked away, the Indian that Frank had pointed out walked up to James and asked him when he was leaving and what road he planned to take.

Knowing that Jones would not protect him, James decided to leave immediately. He noticed that his interrogator and forty or fifty other Indians mounted their mules and started off down the road to Fort Towson. James "studied a few moments" and formulated a plan. He surmised that the Indians had secreted themselves in some heavy brush lying two miles from town. After waiting an hour, James proceeded down the Fort Towson road, intending to turn off about a mile from town at the Blue River road. His plan was thwarted when he encountered two Indians at the fork. Thinking that the Indians would shoot him on the spot if he turned off the Fort Towson road, he nonchalantly continued on his way. He soon realized that the two Indians were following him. When a sharp bend in the road hid James from the Indians' view, he veered off the road and, whipping and spurring, his mule, he took off in an easterly direction. He soon found himself in a muddy prairie. After the mule had struggled through the muck for about eight miles, James spied a "high piece of land," made his way to the highest point, and stopped there in order to let his mule rest and to look back over the prairie.

From there he could see the Indians about two miles behind him heading straight in his direction. Mounting his mule, James again whipped and spurred the animal for two hours until he arrived at a mountain. The mountain seemed insurmountable, but James urged his tired animal ahead, and after "much labor and danger to myself and mule" they reached the top as the sun was setting. James climbed a tree to look for the Indians. Seeing nothing of them, he got back on his mule and descended from the mountain. At midnight he found the Blue River road and traveled down it until he crossed the Blue River. Finding a good hiding place, he lay down and slept until daybreak. In the morning he continued down the road and was soon out of danger from Indians.

James arrived home on October 8, 1841. He states, "My family and friends were as much grieved as myself, at my disappointment in not finding the children." James had risked his life once again in his relentless quest to rescue all of his relatives from the Comanches.[16]

The Mount Pleasant Church minutes for October 8, 1841, state that Daniel Parker preached that day. Evidently James had stopped by Shelby County and Daniel had accompanied him to Montgomery County for a visit. The minutes do not state what text Daniel chose for his sermon. A good choice would have been Exodus 5:1, "Let my people go."[17]

⋙ CHAPTER 9 ⋘

Sundry Charges

T HE NEXT FOURTEEN months of James's life were relatively uneventful. Mount Pleasant Church grew rapidly, adding ten members. Five were slaves, and one was owned by James Parker. One member, Sister Elizabeth Barnett, was excommunicated for unspecified "immoral conduct." During the nineteenth century, the charge of immoral conduct against white women in Baptist churches was most often based on social dancing. James was active in the church, recording the minutes of business meetings, visiting "delinquent" members, attending the association meeting, and serving on the "presbytry" to create a new church in Mustang Prairie, a settlement in present-day Houston County, and on November 17, 1842, the minutes of Mount Pleasant Church give as the seventh item on the agenda: "Agreed for Br James W Parker to exercise a public gift."[1] James felt called to preach, and the church had given him permission to do so.

A month after James became a lay preacher, he began hearing rumors that two children had been brought in to Fort Gibson in northeastern Indian Territory. He knew that the rumors were true when he saw an article in a newspaper telling about the children. Three days before Christmas, in the worst part of winter, James again started toward Indian Territory. On January 15, 1843, he arrived at Fort Gibson, a military fort on the bank of the Grand River. The fort was surrounded by stagnant water and impenetrable canebrakes. Mosquitoes spread disease, and the death rate was unusually high. The log cabins built for the officers and dragoons were rotting and falling apart.[2]

James had high hopes of finding his grandson James Pratt Plummer and his nephew John Richard Parker. For once he was not disappointed. Two more of the five captives taken at Fort Parker had been liberated. The events that culminated in the deliverance of the two boys began when General

Zachary Taylor replaced General Matthew Arbuckle, who had commanded Fort Gibson for seventeen years. At the first opportunity, Taylor arranged a conference with a number of different Indian tribes and urged them to relinquish their American prisoners. The official correspondence stated that "much good was expected from the conference."[3]

The prediction proved accurate when three months later, on August 23, 1842, a group of Kickapoo Indians brought in James Pratt Plummer, whom they had purchased from the Comanches for four hundred dollars. The officers at the fort began teaching the boy English. On September 28 a Delaware Indian brought in John Richard Parker; they believed he was named Frederick Parker. James Pratt's language lessons were terminated because the two boys, "found much pleasure in each other's society as both spoke Comanche and it was difficult to induce either to attempt the English language." The officers considered sending one of the boys to Fort Smith in order to facilitate their schooling, but they took pity on the two and left them together.[4]

James's reunion with his grandson and nephew was an emotional experience. The two boys had been captured seven years before, when James Pratt had been sixteen months old and John six or seven years old:

> When the children were brought to me, although seven years had elapsed since I had seen them, and they had altered very much by growth, and from the ill usage of the Indians, I recognized in the features of my grandson, those of his mother, Mrs. Plummer; and my joy at rescuing him from Indian barbarity was not a little abated by the reminisences brought to mind by his striking resemblance of his mother. The sympathising officers of the garrison appeared to partake of the mingled feelings of joy and grief, it was beyond my power to restrain on the occasion.
>
> My grand son, learning that I had come after him, ran off, and went to the Dragoon encampment, about one mile from the Garrison. . . . Early the next morning Capt. Brown sent a Sergeant after my grandson. When he arrived, the Captain and some of the other officers joined with me in persuading him to go with me. After more than two hours conversation, we succeeded in making him understand how I was related to him, at which he appeared much astonished, and asked me if he had a mother. I told him he had not, as she had died. He then asked if he had a father. I told him he had, and if he would go with me he should see him. He then consented to accompany me.

It will be recollected that the children were very young when taken by the Indians, and consequently could now talk very little English. As I could not well understand them, nor they me, I was relieved from the pain of listening to their recital of the sufferings they had endured whilst among the Indians. The evidences, however, of the free exercise of savage barbarity, were visible upon the backs of these unfortunate children; for there was scarcely a place wherever the finger could be laid, without its covering a scar made by the lash. After these children became able to make themselves understood, their own recital of their sufferings would make any heart bleed.[5]

Once more James had to make his way back from Indian Territory to his home in Texas. He had little money, and it was the depth of winter. James placed the two boys on his horse and started out to walk eighty miles down the Arkansas River valley. Finally, James felt he could walk no farther, so he purchased a pony at Fort Smith. The three travelers had a rough journey because they were thinly clad, the weather was cold and wet, and the road was muddy and almost impassable in some places. Shortly after the three had crossed the Red River, one of their horses became stuck in the mud, and they labored for hours to get him out.

Finally the travelers arrived at Cincinnati, Texas, on the Trinity River, fifteen miles from Huntsville. News of their pending arrival had preceded them, and they were met in Cincinnati by James's wife Patsey and many other relatives and friends. James says of the reunion, "Joyous indeed was our meeting. I had now completed another tour of suffering; and grateful were my feelings to God on finding myself again with my family, and all in good health. The boys soon became attached to me and my family. They soon learned to speak English, and are now doing well."[6]

The chapter was not closed with the return of the two boys, however. An incident occurred that split the Parker and Plummer families forever. James refused to surrender James Pratt to his father, claiming that Plummer owed him the ransom money.

At this time L. T. M. Plummer was thirty-one years old, and he had remarried. Shortly after Rachel had died, he married Lizzie Lauderdale and was the father of two children by his second wife. He and his family were living in Montgomery County because of the continuing danger of Indians in the vicinity of Fort Parker. Although he had no slaves and no horses or cattle, Plummer was fairly prosperous, owning in Montgomery County two hundred acres worth seventy dollars and one town lot in Cincinnati, Texas, worth twenty-five dollars. In Robertson County he owned 3,317 acres valued at thirty-five dollars. That he was a respected citizen is shown by the fact that in 1836 he had been elected justice of the peace for the San Jacinto precinct near Huntsville.[7]

Just when it seemed that Plummer was recovering from the terrible tragedies that had occurred in his life, he had been forced to participate in the fiasco known as the Somervell Expedition. In mid-September of 1842, the Mexican army attacked San Antonio. President Sam Houston called up the county militia for active duty, and the draft was instituted in Montgomery County. L. T. M. enlisted on October 1, 1842, and became a member of the Montgomery County militia commanded by Colonel Joseph L. Bennett. By mid-October, a large portion of the Montgomery County men had assembled at Gonzales, where there was a considerable delay as the militiamen waited for the volunteers to arrive and for the organization of the expedition. After the volunteers arrived, the soldiers marched to San Antonio, and the Montgomery County men camped south of town in and around the partially destroyed San José Mission. The weather was unusually cold and rainy, and the soldiers were forced to live outdoors throughout November with insufficient shelter, food, or clothing. Since they received no rations from the government, they had to forage and "requisition" supplies from the people of San Antonio. The bumbling commander, General Alexander Somervell, was not respected by the men, and many thought he had been appointed because President Houston, who did not want all-out war with Mexico, desired the expedition to fail. In mid-November an unruly element of the expedition went to San Antonio, looted several homes, and reportedly raped a number of women. The other soldiers were appalled and disgusted. Also, most of the militiamen, unlike the volunteers, had little interest in the expedition and were anxious to return to their families and farms. According to pioneer historian John Henry Brown, who was a volunteer soldier under Captain Isaac N. Mitchell, "The greater portion of Bennett's militiamen, under various excuses and pretences, returned home." Another soldier stated, "Every one who wished to leave felt at liberty to do so." The men who remained marched to Laredo on the Rio Grande River where the inhabitants surrendered without a fight. Again some of the men looted the town. Much of the plunder was returned to the inhabitants, but Somervell had clearly lost control of his men. After the refusal of General Somervell to march into Mexico and attack the enemy, the men became increasingly rebellious, and on December 10, 1842, Somervell "paraded the

men and said, 'All who desired to return home could honorably do so.'"
The remaining men from Montgomery County returned home and were
spared the horrors of the ensuing Mier Expedition.[8]

Another conflict that L. T. M. had to deal with in 1842 was his disagree-
ment with his former father-in-law. James refused to return James Pratt to
his father. Perhaps he hoped to gain control of Rachel's part of L. T. M.'s
land grant. On the other hand, James always tried to gather his dwindling
family around him. He had petitioned the Montgomery County Court for
the guardianship of the three children of his brother Joseph Allen Parker,
who had died in Houston in 1840, and now perhaps he wanted to rear his
grandson who so closely resembled Rachel.[9]

Completely frustrated in his attempts to gain custody of his son,
L. T. M. wrote to President Houston, who sent a reply dated April 17, 1843,
at Washington-on-the-Brazos:

> Sir, Your communication in reference to the detention of your son by
> Mr. James W. Parker, came duly to hand. . . . In a case of this kind, the
> attempt to swindle a distressed father on account of his long lost child is
> in every way deserving of the severest reprehension. Though I had some
> reason to suspect the professions of Mr. Parker, yet, until this case was
> presented, I had not supposed him capable of practicing such scandalous
> fraud upon his kindred and connexions. . . . His pretensions about his
> liability for two hundred dollars, etc. are utterly groundless. You will,
> therefore, take your child home. Mr. Parker has not the shadow of right
> to detain him, and by so doing is not only laying himself under the im-
> putation of extreme brutality, but is subjecting himself to the penalties of
> the law.[10]

What happened next is not clear. According to family legend, James
Pratt was reared by his grandfather, James; records show, however, that
when Pratt was fourteen years old, he was not living with his father or his
grandfather but with his uncle by marriage, John Harrold. Rachel's older
sister Sarah Parker Nixon Thomas Harrold had died at the age of twenty-
nine, and her third husband had taken in James Pratt to live with him and
his family.[11]

James W. Parker's reputation suffered another blow on August 19, 1843. He
had continued to devote a great deal of time and energy to the Mount

Pleasant Church. In the minutes of the business meeting for August 2, the second item on the agenda is as follows: "Sister Tinsley persented sundy charges against Brother Parker motioned by Brother Lehr and seconded that the charges be taken up."[12]

Sixty-two-year-old Susanah Tinsley was the second wife of James Tinsley, a Revolutionary War veteran who had been born in Culpeper County, Virginia, a few miles from where Elder John Parker had lived. James Tinsley, Susanah, and their children had moved to Texas in 1837 and settled in Montgomery County. Susanah had been born in London and was much younger than her husband.[13] She had been one of the three members who had followed James Parker when he walked out of the business meeting on May 8, 1841, splitting the church into two factions. The charges recorded against James were:

ist for holding correspondence with suspicious charrecters

2d for aiding your sister in Law in getting a divorce

3d for saying you paid 1000 for the two children

4 for saying that you had paid out 8000 for Mrs. Plummer and the Two boys

5 you said in presence of Esqr Vesin [?] his wife and daughter that you had not kept a pistol in your hand in three months prior to your applying for a precept against N Y M

6t you said that you had a bill of sale for certain negroes that Bado run from Houston to your house and that they were your property

7th you joined in chat with L. Morgan which went to impeach the character of Susan Tinsley

The church's decision on the charges was written in the minute book under the date Sept 16, 1843, in a different handwriting: "Disowned the 17th rule of our own decorum by a motion made by Brothe C [illegible] seconded the charges against J W Parker were dropt and he was excluded for his lying disorderly conduct and abuse of the church in the present conference and the conference of [smudged] August last."

The church seemed to fall apart after James left. It limped along for a year, having few services and even fewer business meetings. The entry for June 15, 1844 is a poignant one: "Church met and in order—Brother Samuels Moderator. after divine Service proceded to business—Invited brothers and Sisters of our faith and order to take seet and send there friendly and opend the dore for the acception of members—none came forward."

Finally, the Mount Pleasant Church of the Regular United Baptist Faith and Order was disbanded on August 17, 1844, with the following words: "The church seeing her weakness and inability to travel it motioned and seconded that she be dissolved by lettering her members off carried . . . Adjourned in peace."[14]

In the midst of his problems with the church, James had heard of a young woman who had been purchased from the Comanches and taken to Jasper, Missouri. After hearing the description of the woman, James thought she might be Cynthia Ann, and he decided to go to Missouri. In an effort to raise money for the journey, he tried to sell some of his land for one-tenth of its value but was unsuccessful. The republic was nearly bankrupt, and there was little currency available. Finally in June, James decided to set out with only "a few dollars." He bade his family farewell, saying "that this would be the last journey I would go on in pursuit of the prisoner."

As James slowly made his way four hundred miles across rivers, over mountains and hills and plains, he found that people were glad to help him. He states that many of them "knew me well by character" and doubtless had heard of his seemingly endless search for the members of his family who had been captured eight years before. In fact, except for the extremely hot weather and the horseflies in Arkansas and Missouri, James enjoyed his "pleasant journey."

On August 5, 1844, he reached Jasper County, Missouri, in the plateau area of the Ozark Mountains. He soon ascertained that the young woman was not Cynthia Ann and for some reason decided that she was the daughter of a Mrs. Williams, who lived in Texas.[15] When he stated his intention to take her back to Texas with him, he was opposed by "one of the citizens" of Jasper County. James does not state what finally happened.

While in Jasper County, James heard about another white girl who was being held by a tribe of Kickapoo Indians. He traveled one hundred miles across the prairie to Westport, Missouri, which is now in the city limits of Kansas City. James presented his credentials, which included a passport from the "Executive of Texas," to Major Robert Cummins, whom James identifies as "the Indian Agent." The two men set out for Fort Leavenworth, thirty-five miles upriver. The officers at the fort helped the men locate the girl. James explains what happened: "We soon found the girl, who proved to be of the same nation of Indians, but having some white blood in her. They wished to pass her off as a white girl for the purpose of gain."

James went back downriver to Independence, a few miles from Westport, and placed an advertisement in the *Western Expositor* in which he offered a reward of five hundred dollars for Cynthia Ann or three hundred dollars for any other captive. In addition, James asked a Colonel Alvarier, whom James indentifies as the U.S. Minister to Santa Fe, to aid him in obtaining the release of Cynthia Ann.[16]

After doing all he could to locate his niece, James made his way to the home of his brother Nathaniel, who lived in Charleston, Illinois. He traveled across Missouri, taking time out to attend the yearly conference of the Mount Gilead Association near Quincy, and finally arrived at the home of his brother after traveling some 550 miles since his arrival in Missouri.[17]

In his narrative James says he remained some time in Charleston. He then makes an interesting observation: "It was here my friends again urged upon me to have my journal published." James had kept a journal, probably beginning shortly after the attack at Fort Parker, but it has been lost. At the beginning of the last chapter of his thirty-seven-page autobiography he makes the following statement: "In writing out the foregoing chapters, which cover the most interesting part of my narrative, it has been necessary to abridge as much as possible. In doing this, many interesting events and amusing anecdotes have unavoidably been omitted for want of space. To enter minutely into all the particulars, and to rehearse all that transpired in my journeyings in search of the prisoners, would occupy, at least, three hundred pages; the expense of printing which I am not able to bear."

After James had written his narrative, he traveled with Elder B. B. Piper to Louisville, Kentucky, where James published his autobiography in a volume that included the second version of Rachel's narrative. The title of the book is *Narrative of the Perilous Adventures, Miraculous Escapes and Sufferings of Rev. James W. Parker, during a Frontier Residence in Texas, of Fifteen Years; with an Impartial Geographical Description of the Climate, Soil, Timber, Water, &c., &c. &c. of Texas; Written by Himself. To Which Is Appended a Narrative of the Capture and Subsequent Sufferings of Mrs. Rachel Plummer, (His Daughter,) during a Captivity of Twenty-one Months among the Cumanche Indians, with a Sketch of Their Manners, Customs, Laws, &c.; with a Short Description of the Country over Which She Travelled Whilst with the Indians; Written by Herself.*[18]

The title is misleading since according to the dates in Rachel's 1838 narrative, she was held captive by the Comanches for thirteen months rather than twenty-one months. The last paragraph of James's narrative seems to indicate that in spite of everything, he was a deeply religious man: "Since I have been in Louisville, I have tried, under much affliction, to preach. I have also visited several of the neighboring churches—at New Albany, Sellersburg, Elk Creek, Buckrun, &c. I hope, through the mercy of Providence, soon to be in my home, where I shall endeavor to spend the remainder of my days in the faithful discharge of my duty to my God, my country and my family."

Some of James's adventures are difficult to believe. He realized this and included the following statement in the last chapter of his narrative:

> Another reason for omitting a detail of many of my sufferings and miraculous escapes, is, that I am confident few, if any, would believe them. The reader no doubt thinks that what I have already related of my sufferings is miraculous enough; but, could I retrace my life, and endure again my past sufferings, and make him an eyewitness to them, then he would agree with me, that what I have narrated is nothing, when compared with the awful reality. . . . My readers may feel some surprise that I always went on these tours alone. A moment's reflection will convince them of the propriety of my doing so. I was not permitted to take a sufficient number of men with me to fight the Indians, and my only hope was to steal the prisoners from the enemy. The fewer in company then, the less was the danger of my being discovered by the savages and killed.[19]

Although James's adventures do seem fantastic, they are no more so than those of other nineteenth-century pioneers, traders, and mountain men. James had been born in the wilderness in Georgia and had spent his whole life hunting and tracking wild animals. He was a many-faceted man with the determination, perseverance, and superhuman energy exhibited by many members of the Parker family.

$\prec\!\!\gg\!\!\gg$ CHAPTER 10 $\ll\!\!\ll\!\!\succ$

Called Home

J AMES RODE BACK to Texas. As he had promised his family,
he made no more trips in search of Cynthia Ann. In 1845, he moved
to what was then Houston County, and on May 3, 1845, he joined
Pilgrim Regular Predestinarian Baptist Church, the church founded
by Daniel in Illinois.[1]

Unlike James, through the years Daniel had spent almost all of his time
preaching, sometimes in the churches of the Union Regular Predestinarian
Association and often in homes when he was invited. Many stories have
been told about his ministry. Daniel's sermons usually lasted from two to
four hours. Before he began preaching, he would announce to the group
gathered before him that "if anyone had to leave in order to attend to their
animals, or just go, they were welcome to do so at any time during the
service." Unlike most of the Methodist services and some of the Baptist
services, Daniel's meetings were "quiet and orderly," although he was always "firm and aggressive" in the message he delivered.

A tenet of the Regular Baptists was that a minister should not accept
payment for his services. When asked about his refusal to accept any sort of
payment, Daniel would reply that "if people could afford to lose time to
hear him preach, he could afford to lose time preaching, and it would not
be right for him to accept money." Once when Daniel was preaching in a
home near San Augustine, a horse trader rode by and, seeing the horses
tied up in front of the house, stopped and went inside to inquire if anyone
would like to engage in a little horsetrading. Parker was preaching, and the
trader stayed to listen to the sermon. When Daniel had finished, the man
walked up to the pulpit and placed a silver dollar on it. Parker looked down
at the money, looked at the trader, and then walked away.

Another story illustrates Daniel's sense of humor. A delegation came to
him and asked him to preach to a group of people near the present site of

Rusk, Texas. Daniel named the day and time. On the appointed day he journeyed to within ten miles of the meeting place and stopped at a house to ask if he might spend the night. The inhabitants of the house refused him, saying that they were going into the settlement to hear Daniel Parker preach that night. Daniel did not tell the people who he was but rode on down the road, stopping at several other houses where he requested lodging for the night. At each house the inhabitants told him they were going to hear Daniel Parker preach. When he was almost at the settlement, one family agreed to let him stay with them on the condition that he attend the service. Daniel went along and sat down with his companions. The people in the gathering asked each other if anyone had seen Daniel Parker in the vicinity. No one had seen him. As they waited for the minister to appear, they passed the time making announcements. When the time arrived for Parker to preach, he stood up, walked to the pulpit, and delivered a sermon that lasted for four hours. He stayed two more days, preaching four hours each time.[2]

A setback in Daniel's battle against the missionary Baptists occurred in 1844. Bethel Church, which had been established in Sabine County in 1841, refused to join the Union Association of the Regular Baptist Faith and Order. Parker visited them and warned them that if they persisted in their present course, their constitution would be revoked. They defied him by voting to join another association even as he sat in their conference.[3]

Four months later, on December 3, 1844, the old warrior who had created his own lion's den died. On April 19, 1845, Pilgrim Church sought to honor Daniel, now that he had been "called home from the walls of Zion by his Great Heavenly Master," by commissioning his son John to write a biographical sketch, which they intended to publish in "some of the Religious Newspapers in the U.S." Also proposed were a monument and a memorial service to which leaders of the Regular Predestinarian Church would be invited from as far away as Indiana. What finally happened is not known, but the biographical sketch was written and a portion has survived. The manuscript is not signed.[4]

Pages 1–4 are mainly a paraphrase of Daniel Parker's autobiography, which had been published in the *Church Advocate*. Pages 5–8 are missing. Part of the information missing is a defense of Daniel against charges made against him by his enemies. Pages 9–11 describe Daniel's life in Texas, especially the formation of the Union Association. The biography writer describes Daniel's character:

He was never known (as we have knowledge of) to speak of an evil report of one of the members with out going to the accusd. and in the spirit of the Gospel laber with him. or them He was always reddy to forgive—when repentence seemd sinceer. He never urged week members to feed on strong meats.[5] He sharply reproved any brother or sister when he hird them speaking of the foibles of one of the members. he would leve his own concerns no matter how ergent the case might be. if he saw any probible difficulty riseing. whare he might stop it by his timely admonition. and cautions. He was always reddey to put the most faverable construction on the errors of his breathren. as long as thear was any hope of reclameing. he always cautiond young professors [of religion] not to go whare thare was temtations. never to mix with the world. to trade and trafic as little as posible He was never known to go among a set of profane men and reprove thear wickedness. he was allways reddy to supply the wants of the needy. as soon as he found thear need was such He was mild in his reproofs. but verry pointed his ever being reddy to fergive an error most generly brot sincerity in repentance. his penetrating judgement seldom failed him. in any mater of controversy. as to whare the falt lay. He was the [torn]st to honor the rich in prefferance to the poor. He never regarded riches as an honor. but a convenience An illgotten gain he ever abhord. and if a member failed to administer to the necesity of the poor (whare it was in thear power) he sharply reproved them if any treated a poor member with disrespect on account of his poverty he would not only reprove. but deal with them to exclusion if satisfaction was not obtained. no person was more attentive to the wants of the helpless.[6]

The biography writer continues by describing Daniel's death:

Some time in August he had undertaken to visit some churches—that he had assisted in constituting. nier Snow River, was taken sick and had to return. from which he never recoverd. He however was able to be about most of the time untell a few days prior to his disese—He told his friends as soon as he was taken sick that his time was at hand. His phisisians would tell him that his case was not bad. he would tell them that thay did not know. for (said he) my time is at hand that I must be offerd up. I do not the lest dread it. my master calls. I long to obey. I have fought the good fight. and Kept the faith. He earnstly prayd that the Lord would send some one to fill his place in the churches. He earnstly prayd that the out cast of Isreal might be brot in. that God would visit his people in mircy. to keep his church from the carrupting errors of the day. said that his mind had undergone no change since he commenced preaching. more than some facts appeard more plain than at first. said to the last of his existence that thear was but one true Gospel church. and that the Regular Predestinarian Baptist Church was that church. He lamented that thear was many of the deer Lambs of Jesus. who was blinded by the cunning craftiness of wicked men that lie in wait to deceve. He earnstly prayd that god would make duty plain before them. wean thear affections from fleshly temtations. Pray the Lord to send out more faithful laberers in to his vinyard. cautiond his breathren to always be ware of crveys. and the spirit of wickedness. to observe his former examples. & to take the word of God for the man of thear council.

He calmly arrangd all his wordly affairs with as much apparent unconcern as if he had been going on a journey. told his phisisian to use no harsh medicine. nor any thing but paliating medicine. The day prevous to his death. he said to the bystanders. it is indeed hard to die. if it was possible. or if it was the will of Heaven I would rather die easy (he suffered very much for several weeks before his death) but said he it is rite. on the night of his departure he appeard calm and serene. his suffering was not as intollerable as before. about 5 o'clock in the evening of the 3rd of Decem. He sweetly sunk in the arms of Death surrounded by many weeping friends. As the happy soul was leving its earthly tenament. to join its kindred spirits around his Heavinly fathers darling Throne of Glory. Oh Zion put on your Garments of Mourning. weep o yea mourner for us. in this fausw world. Weep all ye that have pleasantly sat under his shadow. Know ye not that a great man is falen in Isreal: Deerly beloved Brethren. let your hearts dictate for us. for our language cannot express our Grif. Oh close our beloved brother. our Father. Elder Daniel Parker sleep, the sleep of death. . . . his name is written in the he hearts of his breathren. Thear is his ephata written in capitol letters of indiscbrible Love that will waist but with the desolution of this mortal life . . . one strange occurrence here think worthy of remark as the breath left the boddy. He close his own eyes with his own hands and did not make even one dying struggle.[7]

Eccentric to the last, Daniel Parker the anti-missionary missionary was dead. He had wreaked havoc among the Baptists throughout the South, but all his life he had lovingly tended his "sheep," God's elect, founding an untold number of churches in Tennessee, Kentucky, Illinois, Indiana, Missouri, Louisiana, and Texas. In Texas he had founded at least nine churches.

Into his churches he had welcomed the poor, the enslaved, and the down-
trodden, and he had fought against slavery. He had tried to help the "Northern Indians" until the Edens massacre had turned him against them. As he
lay dying, perhaps he thought of God's words to the first Daniel: "Go thy
way Daniel for the words are closed up and sealed till the time of the end.
Many shall be purified, and made white, and tried; but the wicked shall do
wickedly; and none of the wicked shall understand. . . . But go thy way till
the end be: for thou shalt rest, and stand in thy lot at the end of the days."[8]

Shortly after Daniel Parker's death at the age of sixty-three, James W. Parker,
his forty-seven-year-old brother, moved to Houston County. On May 31,
1845, James was received by letter into the Pilgrim Regular Predestinarian
Baptist Church and immediately began to assume a leadership position in
it along with Daniel's son John.[9]

On October 4, 1845, the minutes of Pilgrim Church state that the "Mustang Peririe Church" near present-day Groesbeck requested that James W.
Parker be ordained so that he could become their pastor. In the meeting of
January, 1846, the records say that the members had unanimously agreed to
ordain James, and that they had requested that the ministers of Fort Houston, Sardis, and Bethlehem churches attend their next meeting in order to
assist in the ordination. It seemed that James, who in 1842 had been granted
permission to "exercise his public gift," was finally going to become the
minister of a church. Then the Pilgrim Church minutes of January 31, 1846,
cryptically tell the story of another defeat for James:

> 1st the church took up the refference relative to the ordination of Bro
> J W Parker Brother Hanks presented letters from our sisters Forthouston
> and Sardis refusing to comply with our petition for their helps at the
> time also A private letter from Br Biggs adviseing the church to Put off
> Brother Parkers ordination until after the next Union Association
> 2st agreed to lay it over until our Aprile meting
> 3d Brother J. W Parker informed the church that he had got angry
> and had even come verry near shooting a man The church After collect-
> ing all the information she was able on the subject says she is fully recosild
> with Bro Parker.[10]

James continued to hold a place of honor in the church, serving as moderator and as a "messenger" to the association meeting. On October 17,
1846, the Pilgrim Church made an attempt to repair James's tarnished repu-

tation. The third item on the agenda was: "Agreed that this church write and try to have appended to the minuets of our last association a peac inviting scrutiy in to the conduct of Bro J W Parker not that this church believes him guilty but that we believe the church has bin and continues to be unjustly implecated on his account as well we believe that Bro Parker['s] reputation has as unjustly bin assailed by those calling themselves Baptist and we believe Bro Parkers usefulness has greatly bin destroid by this unlawful course. Appointed Bro J W Parker to write the same and request him to report to morrow."[11]

Several pages are missing from the Pilgrim Church book, including the minutes for May and June of 1847. James is mentioned in the report for July 17, 1847: "Brother J W Parker says he had bin angry and is sorry that it become nessary for him to persue the course and hopes it will never be necessary for him to take the steps he did the church after hereing all she could says she is satisfide." The minutes of August 14, 1847, indicate that James had become embroiled in some sort of controversy with a man named Sam Stewart: "Brother Sam Stewart cald for a letter of dismission Referd until Sept Meting agreed to apoint 3 of our Body to go with Brother Stewart to labor with him for peace with Brother J W Parker."

The minutes of September 18, 1847, indicate that the controversy had been settled, but the problem of James's ordination again cropped up as the fifth item on the agenda for that date:

> Bro J W Parker informd the church that he had been informd that a report was in Circulation that the petitionary letter from Musstang Perary church praying for his Ministerial aid was not made by said Musstang Prarie church Bro Parker presented the certificate of Brother D Halmark and wife certifying that the said letter was the act of the church which produ[ce]d general satisfaction refer to certificate
>
> "we hereby certify that in the Month of September 1847 the Musstang Perare church made an order to send a petitionary letter to our Sister Pilgrim church praying for the ministerial aid of Bro J W Parker Bro Parker was then the Moderator of the church and Brother Isaac Parker clerk Protmn and Brother J W Parker consented to become the bearer of the letter this is facts which is known unto us as we was thare members and present and will testify the same when cald on."[12]

The entry in the Pilgrim minutes for November 20, 1847, recorded one of the low points in James's life: "Brother Mead produced a certificate from

Isaac Parker tha[t] he stated to Bro Mead that if Mustang Prarie church had cald for the ordination of Bro J W Parker he had no recollection of it but that it might have [been] done and sliped his memory the church is fully satisfied on the subject." James had claimed that he had been called to preach at Mustang Prairie Church and produced a letter to that effect, but the validity of the letter was questioned, and when James's brother Isaac, who held a high office in the church, was questioned about the alleged call, he said "he had no recollection of it." Shortly afterward, Isaac moved to Birdville near Fort Worth.

Four years passed. The second item on the agenda of the monthly business meeting for Pilgrim Church for February, 1851, was ominous: "Took up a charge against Brother J W Parker for using intoxicating spirits to too great an excess and Agreed to lay it over until next Meting Apointed Brthren A Bennett and Joseph kennedy a Committee to laber with Bro Parker and report at next Meting."[13]

The last time James W. Parker's name appears in the minutes of Pilgrim Church is in March of 1851: "Took up the refference relative to Brother J W Parker the Committee that was Apointed to Labor with Brother Parker reported as follows that tha went to Brother Parker and he denide the Charge to them as tha reported to the Church which report was receved and proced to exclude Brother Parker from amongst us." James W. Parker had been excommunicated.[14]

James's private life was a different story, a mixture of good and bad. After being a widower for several years, James had married Lavina Lackey Chaffin in 1847. Lavina had been born in Kentucky on April 19, 1808. She married Eli Chaffin, and they lived for a while in Clinton County, Illinois. In the early 1840s the Chaffins moved to Texas and settled on a 640-acre tract of land that lay in both Anderson and Houston counties. Eli died in 1845, and James and Lavina were married on April 27, 1847. Their only child, a son named Allen, died at an early age. The 1850 census for Houston County lists the members of James's household: James W. 54 (Predestinarian Baptist Minister with assets worth $10,000), Lavina A. 44, James W. 22, Frances M. 19, Martha M. 15, Catherine Nixon 12, and Nancy J. Thomas 7. The last two girls listed on the census were the children of James's oldest daughter Sarah, who had died in 1846. In spite of everything, James must have commanded a great deal of respect in Houston County because in 1852 he was elected justice of the peace.[15]

James was not fated to live a long life. In mid-1864, James W. Parker died at the age of sixty-seven. He had suffered through an incredibly hard life filled with turmoil and suffering. He had buried one wife and eight of his ten children. His only surviving children were his daughter Martha Crenshaw and his son James W. Parker. A memorial monument in the cemetery near Pilgrim Church contains no dates. The only inscription is "James W. Parker, Founder of Fort Parker."[16]

PART IV

CYNTHIA ANN

⋞⋟ CHAPTER 11 ⋞⋟

Miss Parker

I N 1840 NAUTDAH, whose name means "She carries herself with dignity and grace," was fourteen years old.[1] Taken from her home at the age of nine, she remembered the life she had led at Fort Parker. Nothing could erase from her mind the massacre, the screams, the blood, the terror when her mother placed her on the horse behind Peta Nocona. But her Anglo name lay hidden in the darkness of her subconscious mind— Cynthia Ann.

She must have remembered the wild ride through woods and across prairies into the eerie darkness until the triumphant warriors and their fierce women finally stopped in the cross timbers. What happened to Cynthia Ann that first night among the Indians will never be known. The Comanches were a capricious lot. Sometimes girl captives were raped and left beside the trail to die. If a young girl survived until the warriors returned to the main camp, the first few weeks were hard because she was often beaten and otherwise abused. As already described, if she proved to be tough and spirited, she might be adopted, and when she reached puberty, she would usually be married to her captor. Cynthia Ann was probably assigned the most elemental tasks at first—gathering wood, tending the fire, and watching the younger children.[2]

After Cynthia Ann's fabric dress had been removed or worn out, she would probably have been provided with a buckskin skirt and blouse or dress, leggings, and moccasins, the standard garb of the Comanche women and girls. Much later Cynthia Ann probably received a second dress. Possibly, she helped to make it by sewing two deer or antelope hides together, leaving a hole in the middle for her head. The hides from which these special dresses were made would have been carefully scraped and kneaded so that the skins were thin and soft. Long fringes decorated the sleeves and hem. Such dresses were ornamented with multicolored beads. The Indian women sewed with thread made from the muscles lying along the back-bone of a buffalo or deer. The sinew was dried and stored, and when a woman wanted to use it, she peeled off a narrow strip with her fingernail, moistened it in her mouth, rolled it with her fingers, and inserted it into the skin, using either a bone needle or an awl to make holes. Sometimes strips of buffalo hide were used instead of sinew. In cold weather leggings and beaded moccasins completed the ensemble. Comanche women wore bracelets and necklaces and painted their faces for special occasions. They lined their eyes with red or yellow, painted the inside of their ears red, and highlighted their cheeks with a red-orange circle or triangle. Sometimes they tattooed their faces and breasts.[3]

In 1846, ten years after the Fort Parker massacre, Cynthia Ann was seen by Texas Indian Agent Leonard Williams when he and ten other men were sent by U.S. Indian commissioners Pierce M. Butler and M. G. Lewis to try to induce the headmen of a large band of Comanches to attend a treaty conference then in progress on the upper reaches of the Brazos River. Williams was also told to purchase any captives held by the Comanches. What happened was reported in the *Clarksville Northern Standard* for May 25, 1846:

> Col. Leonard Williams, with a party of ten others was despatched to Pahauca's camp on the False Washita; on the 29th April he sent a runner to Gov. Butler, informing him of having found Miss Parker, and a yellow girl in the Comanche camp. The former was acquainted with Col. Williams in the early and happy days of her existence; during his stay she continued to weep incessantly. Twelve mules and two mule loads of merchandize were offered for her; but refused by the Indians, who say they will die rather than give her up. No situation can be depicted to our minds replete with half the horrors of that unfortunate young lady's. Our government should claim her with a strong hand, the sword should be made to avenge and to liberate. It is useless to talk of treating with those barbarians, until they are humbled by chastisement. The appearance of Col. Williams created considerable excitement among the Camanches. The young warriors laid a plan to murder him and his companions, which was overheard by a Mexican boy, (one of the many prisoners of that nation among the Indians,) who gave timely notice to Col. W., and he immediatley claimed the protection of Pahuace this chief with difficulty succeeded in pacifying and restraining his men.[4]

Two other mentions of Cynthia Ann appear in documents. The Indian commissioners Butler and Lewis wrote to the commissioner of Indian Affairs on August 8, 1846. Since the letter was sent only two months after the article about Cynthia Ann had appeared in the *Clarksville Northern Standard*, the incident mentioned by the commissioners is probably the same one:

> As to the ransom of white children who have been seized and de-tained in captivity, we have to remark, that we succeeded in rescuing one white child and three Mexicans. We heard of but three children of white parents, but it is said that there is a large number of Mexican children. One of the whites is a young man by the name of Lyons, who expressed an unwillingness to our runners to withdraw from his association. Of the other two, one is a girl about seventeen years old, and her brother, of the age of ten, known as the Parker children. They have been in captiv-ity of the Yam-pi-ric-coes, and were on the head of the Washita, where our runners saw them last. The young woman is claimed by one of the Camanches as his wife. From the influence of her alleged husband, or from her own inclination, she is unwilling to leave the people with whom she associates. The headmen seemed to aquiese in the propriety of her being surrendered, on an adequate sum in the way of ransom being paid. A large amount of goods and four or five hundred dollars were offered, but the offer was unavailing, as she would run off and hide herself to avoid those who went to ransom her. Measures, however, have been taken to secure both herself and brother. We were assured by the chief that he would take measures to have her delivered up to the authorities of the United States upon the next "fall of the leaves;" and if he would not yield to the inducements of the ransom money, he would exert forc-ible coercion.[5]

A year later, Robert S. Neighbors, who was Texas commissioner of In-dian Affairs, was still trying to implement the return of Cynthia Ann to her white relatives. On November 18, 1847, he wrote a report to the U.S. com-missioner of Indian Affairs that contained the following information:

> I would respectfully call the attention of the Commissioner to the fact, that the Comanches have yet in their possession one White pris-oner viz. a Miss Parker who was captured on the Brazos River in 1837. The friendly Chiefs have frequently promised to deliver her up, but have

not done so. She is with the Ten-na-wish band of Comanches, and with whom we hold little or no intercourse. They reside on the head waters of Red River. I have used all means in my power during the last summer to induce those Indians to bring her in, by offering large rewards, but am assured by the friendly Comanche Chiefs that I would have to use force to induce the party that has her to give her up. She is now about 18 years of age. It would be an act of humanity, if the Department could restore her to her friends, all other white prisoners have either died or been set at liberty—with the above exception. She is the only one I can hear of among the "Plains Tribes."[6]

Cynthia Ann had a number of reasons for wanting to stay with the Comanches. She had become completely acculturated, and she was married to Puhtocnocony, called Peta Nocona by the whites. Although Neighbors continued in his efforts to ransom Cynthia Ann, she evaded capture as she and her husband roamed about in the deep recesses of Comanchería.

By 1849, Cynthia Ann had been with the Comanches for thirteen years, some of the most turbulent and discouraging years that the lordly Comanches had ever experienced. Three disastrous defeats in battle had been dealt to the Penatekas, a band of Comanches with whom Cynthia Ann and her brother John were associated in 1847: the Council House Fight in San Antonio, the Battle of Plum Creek, and the fight on the Red Fork of the Colorado River. Other events that would hasten the Comanches' destruction were just over the horizon. From the south came more and more settlers greedily gobbling up the Comanche hunting grounds. The Indians bitterly hated the surveyors who came with "the thing that stole the land."[7] Another event, although it might have seemed unlikely to affect on the Comanches, brought destruction upon them: gold in California! The trickle of whites along the trails to the west swelled to a flood that nothing could stop. Over three thousand people traveled along the Canadian River route, which ran through the heart of Comanchería.[8]

Not only did the gold seekers hem in the northern Comanche bands and kill the game along the trails, but they also brought with them the most devastating enemy of the American Indian—disease. The Comanches had been hard hit in the smallpox epidemics of 1816 and 1839–40, but the cholera epidemic of 1849 wiped out half of the Comanches and their allies the Kiowas. Cholera struck suddenly. Violent diarrhea, vomiting, and sweating caused rapid dehydration and often death. As the summer heat beat down on the buffalo-hide tents, the Comanches watched with horror as their loved ones sickened and died, in some cases within two days. In desperation they fled from one campsite to another, leaving behind the dead and sometimes deserting the dying.[9]

After the death-dealing summer and the cold winter, a son was born to Cynthia Ann and Peta Nocona about 1849 on Elk Creek south of the Wichita Mountains.[10] He was Quanah, usually translated as "smell" or "fragrant." Quanah's explanation for the name was that he was born "in a bed of flowers."[11] During times of danger, Comanche women might give birth on the trail and then rejoin the caravan in a few hours, but in ordinary circumstances, preparations were made. First, if the woman did not have a lodge separate from the rest of the family, a new one was built, which might consist of brush if the weather were warm. Inside the lodge, the earth was softened and a hole was dug for a fire, which was used for heating stones, making steam, heating beverages, and burning sage. One or two stakes were driven into the ground for the woman to grasp when the pain became intense. She was attended by a midwife and several other women. As the birth progressed, hot stones were placed against the woman's back, and she was required to drink hot soup and hot water. She would usually lie on a bed but at times might walk around or squat over the hole and grasp the stakes. No men were allowed near unless the birth was especially difficult, in which case a medicine man was called in. Depending on his particular method of treatment, he might stroke the woman's abdomen, blow into her mouth, fan her with an eagle feather, or perform other rites.

When a child was born, the grandfather was called to the lodge to learn the sex of the child and then to announce the birth. If the child was a boy, the women inside would call, "It's your close friend." Girls were welcomed but were not as valued as boys. If the child was a girl, the midwife would simply announce, "It's a girl." The umbilical cord would then be wrapped and hung in a hackberry tree if one was available. If the cord was not disturbed before it rotted, it was believed that the child would have a long and happy life. The afterbirth was thrown into a creek or river, and the baby was bathed and wrapped in a robe made of rabbit skins. As soon as possible, the mother bathed in a running stream.[12]

A year or two after Quanah's birth, Cynthia Ann bore a second son, whom she named Peanuts. Usually Comanche children were named by elders of the tribe, but Quanah said that Peanuts was named "in childish remembrance of the good things that she [Cynthia Ann] had enjoyed around the fireside at Fort Parker before she was captured." Peanuts's unusual name and the fact that Quanah was possibly given the name "Fragrant" at birth seem to indicate that Cynthia Ann, who according to family legend was known as a "spirited squaw," and Peta Nocona, whose name means "He who travels alone and returns," may have chosen to defy Comanche custom and name their children themselves.[13]

At about this time, some white men again saw Cynthia Ann and her family. Captain Randolph B. Marcy, who explored the Red River in 1852, mentions Cynthia Ann and John in a report:

> There is at this time a white woman among the Middle Comanches, by the name of Parker, who, with her brother, was captured while they were young children, from their father's house in the western part of Texas. This woman has adopted all the habits and peculiarities of the Comanches; has an Indian husband and children, and cannot be persuaded to leave them. The brother of the woman, who had been ransomed by a trader and brought home to his relatives, was sent back by his mother for the purpose of endeavoring to prevail upon his sister to leave the Indians and return to her family; but he stated to me that on his arrival she refused to listen to the proposition, saying that her husband, children, and all that she held most dear, were with the Indians, and there she should remain.[14]

Lucy Parker desperately wanted her daughter to return to her, but Cynthia Ann had made the only decision that she could make and was doomed to suffer through one of the worst periods of Comanche history. Angered and frightened by the gradual reduction of their food supply and the ravage caused by the white man's diseases, the Comanches fought back with terrible fury. The Penatekas were a weakened and beaten people, but the Comanche tribes from the north filled the gap with long-range, lightning attacks. Now more often than not the Comanche forays were not just horse-stealing expeditions but murderous revenge raids on any whites within striking range.[15]

Probably at about this time Cynthia Ann and Peta Nocona became associated with the Quahadas, one of the northern bands of Comanches. According to family legend, Peta Nocona was originally a member of the Noconi tribe, who were middle Comanches, but he left the Noconis and joined the Quahadas as a chief. The evidence indicates that even though Peta Nocona and his wife and children lived with the Penatekas for a while, they left that band probably before the Penatekas settled on the reservation. Decimated by disease, defeated in battle, their hunting grounds appropriated by the Texans, about half of the Penatekas (430 persons) had moved to a reservation on the upper Brazos in 1855.[16]

Meanwhile in the valleys and canyons of the Canadian, Red, Pease, Washita, and Arkansas rivers, the northern Comanches, including the powerful Quahadas, sought to live the free and violent life they had always loved.

When Cynthia Ann became thirty years old in 1857, the stage was set for a new phase in the bloody Comanche-Texan struggle. Twelve years earlier in 1845, the Republic of Texas had been annexed by the United States, and a new group of men had entered the scene: U.S. soldiers, who had to learn how to combat the swarming, enraged Comanche warriors successfully. They began by building a line of forts along the frontier, just as the Spanish had done two hundred years before. This policy was not effective. Besides, in less than two years, a new line of forts had to be built because of the rapid advance of settlement.[17]

The winter of 1857–58 was a violent one along the Texas frontier, which snaked from Denison on the Red River to near Corpus Christi on the Gulf of Mexico. The frontiersmen were disgusted with the federal government, and finally on January 26, 1858, the Texas Legislature passed a bill authorizing Governor H. G. Runnels to call up an additional one hundred Texas Rangers. The senior captain chosen to lead the rangers was flamboyant politician, newspaper editor, and Indian fighter John Salmon Ford, also known as Rip Ford. Ford received his commission on January 28, 1858, and an official letter from Governor Runnels contained the following orders: "I impress upon you the necessity of action and energy. Follow any trail and all trails of hostile or suspected hostile Indians you may discover, and if possible, overtake and chastise them, if unfriendly."[18]

Ford stated his own attitude toward his assignment in his memoirs: "The intention was, from the beginning, to carry the war into the hunting grounds of the Comanches and their confederate tribes, to let their families hear the crack of Texas rifles and feel the disagreeable effects of hostile operations in their own camps. No one advocated any but a civilized mode of warfare. As far as the braves were concerned—the savages who had visited our frontier and slaughtered our people, regardless of age and sex—with them it was war to the knife."[19]

Men were quickly recruited and were warned against "galloping their horses in the streets and doing things calculated to demean themselves as rangers." Supplies, guns, and ammunition were purchased, placed in waterproof leather pouches, and loaded onto sixteen pack mules. The men left Austin in February and headed for the frontier, establishing a permanent camp on the Clear Fork of the Brazos near the Comanche and Brazos Indian reservations. After being joined by two other squads of rangers, the men prepared for the campaign. Ford states: "Drilling was done daily. The Indian drill was not neglected. Firing at targets on horseback at all gaits was practiced."[20]

Meanwhile, Shapley Prince Ross, the Indian agent on the Brazos Reservation, was recruiting reservation Indians to join the fighting force. Born in 1811 in Kentucky, Ross was another "old Indian fighter." Like Ford, he had served in the Texas Rangers under Jack Hays and had later commanded his own ranger company. When Ross set about recruiting reservation Indians to join the fighting force, he realized that the powerful old Anadarko chief José Casa María had not joined the group. Ross questioned him, and the chief explained that he had made a treaty with the Comanches and Creeks, and it would be dishonorable for him and his men to make war upon the Comanches without first notifying the Creeks of his intentions. Official notification involved returning to the Creeks some items María called "white wampum." María told Ross: "If I make war upon the Comanches without returning the white wampum to the Creeks, then I shall have Comanches and Creeks both to fight; it will be a violation of my promise." Ross gave María permission to send a messenger with the wampum to the Creeks. In a few days María announced, "I am ready now," and began "inducing" the warriors of his tribe to join the expedition.[21]

The Brazos Reservation Indians, who were Caddos, Tonkawas, Anadarkos, and Wacos, were eager to defeat the "wild Indians" because the reservation Indians were often blamed for depredations committed by non-reservation Indians. In addition, the Tonkawas and Comanches hated each other bitterly.[22]

Shortly before the Indian and white warriors departed for the deep recesses of Comanchería, Captain Ross suggested to the Indians "the propriety of getting up a war dance." The Indians were "delighted" at the prospect. In a letter to the secretary of state of Texas, Ford described the colorful event: "The war-dance was 'grand, gloomy, and peculiar.' Every participant had his own way in the matter; some sounded the fear-inspiring warwhoop; others crept along, cat-like, to pounce upon their astonished and demoralized foes; a squad would move up and attack an imaginary band of Comanches, and a shout of triumph would go up, loud enough to set a donkey's ears to ringing."[23]

The fighting force that headed toward the Red River on April 22, 1858, consisted of 102 Rangers and 113 Caddos, Tonkawas, Anadarkos, Wacos, Shawnees, Delawares, and Tahuacanos. Ford said of the men: "The command had a rather motley appearance. A number of Tonkawa Indians were on foot. They marched well." Two wagons were taken along. One was an ambulance provided for the "sick and wounded."[24]

The men crossed the Little Wichita, which runs through present Archer and Clay counties in Texas, and then the Big Wichita, now known simply as the Wichita River. Eight days into the journey, they reached the Red River. Ford said of the crossing: "The prospect of crossing was not encouraging. The stream was a succession of rivulets running between long beds of sand, dry in the middle. The wetted portion, not under water, was quicksand; in places it would quiver under the feet of the horses. The Indians told us a halt of a few minutes on one of these unstable spots would bog a horse almost irretrievably and endanger the safety of a man." Nevertheless, the crossing was made without incident, and then the men made their way alongside the river.[25]

In several days the command was deep into Indian country. Indians used as "advance guard," "flankers," and "spies" scoured the countryside for twenty miles in front and on each side of the company. The company left the Red River and traveled until they reached a stream they called the False Washita River. There they found a site where an estimated four hundred warriors had camped three or four days previously. They followed the trail of the Indians for a short while. On May 10, several Comanche arrowheads were found in a wounded buffalo, and the men knew that they were near a large encampment of Comanches. When the party reached the Santa Fe and Fort Smith road, in the distance they could see Comanches in the valley of the Canadian River. The aggressors were not observed by the Comanches, and from then on the ranger-Indian force kept to gullies and valleys.[26]

The next day the rangers and reservation Indians prepared to attack the Comanches. The braves were sent to the front and the right. Ford claimed the reason for this action was "to make the Comanches believe they had only Indians and bows and arrows to contend against." In the brilliant May sunshine, a strange pageant ensued. The whites had long known that there was a Comanche chief who wore into battle a breastplate of Spanish armor. Now he rode out to meet the reservation Indians. Ford describes the scene:

The head Comanche chief Po-bish-e-quash-o—Iron Jacket—sallied out to meet our Indians. He was a great medicine man, professed to blow arrows aside from their aim. He would move forward a short distance, describe a circle, and expel his breath from his mouth with great force. He was followed by warriors who trusted their safety in his armor. He was destined to fail: our Indians were armed mostly with Mississippi rifles and six-shooters; only a few had bows and arrows. The mail-clad and gorgeously-caparisoned Comanche chieftain moved in, seeming confident of being invulnerable. About six rifle shots rang on the air: the chief's horse jumped about six feet straight up and fell. Another barrage followed, and the Comanche medicine man was no more.[27]

George W. Paschal Jr., a young Texas Ranger whose mother was the daughter of a Cherokee chief, told a less romantic story. According to Paschal, Iron Jacket approached the attacking party "waving a small white cloth, about a yard square." In spite of the white flag, the rangers began shooting at him. He artfully dodged the "galling fire" for a few minutes, but was finally killed by a bullet from the rifle of Jim Pockmark, chief of the Anadarkos.[28]

Meanwhile, the rangers charged into the main camp with their guns blazing. The Comanches' bows and arrows were no match for the deadly Colt six-shooters and repeating rifles. Ford describes the battle: "The Comanches would occasionally halt and endeavor to make a stand; however, their efforts were unavailing. They were forced to yield the ground to our men in every instance. The din of the battle had rolled back from the river—the groans of the dying and the cries of the frightened women and children mingled with the reports of firearms and the shouts of the men as they rose from hill top, from thicket, and from ravine."[29]

Again, as in the battle on the Colorado and in the Council House Fight, women and children were killed along with the warriors. Ford tried to justify the slaughter: "It was not an easy matter to distinguish Indian warriors from squaws. The dress of the male and female does not differ greatly. The woman has a short buckskin tunic, wears her hair shorter, and her moccasins are somewhat different. A Ranger named Will Howard encountered a young brave about 17 or 18 years old. He was mounted on a good horse, and had three or four children with him. Howard fired, killed the youth and the horse. We annoyed him by telling that he killed a whole family. Some said it was a woman."[30]

One of the reservation Indians shot the second in command of the Comanches, and the battle seemed to be over, but there was another large encampment of Comanches three or four miles up the river, and they were hastening to help their comrades. According to legend, Cynthia Ann was in this encampment, and her husband Peta Nocona was the chief who led the second charge that day. Since each side feared the strength of the other, a ritual battle took place before the eyes of the spectators:

> With yells and menaces and every species of insulting gesture and language, they tried to excite the reserve Indians into some act of rashness by which they could profit. A scene was now enacted beggaring description. It reminded one of the rude and chivalrous days of knight-errantry. Shields and lances and bows and head dresses, prancing steeds and many minutiae were not wanting to compile the resemblance. And when the combatants rushed at each other with defiant shouts, nothing save the piercing report of the rifle varied the affair from a battlefield of the middle ages. Half an hour was spent in this without much damage to either party. A detachment of rangers was advanced to reinforce the friendly Indians, and the Comanches quitted the field, and the imposing pageant vanished from the view like a mimic battle upon the stage.

The rangers decided to charge the prancing Comanches, who quickly fled. The "run" lasted for about three miles, whereupon the rangers gave it up.[31]

The scene at the battleground was even more revolting than usual because of the ritual cannibalism of the Tonkawas. Ford states: "As we moved back through the Comanche camp, we saw the fine buffalo robes, the eatables, and the goods. The dead were lying around. Some of them were minus hands or feet. When we looked at the empty Tonk saddles we knew where they had gone. They had a feast soon after the fight."[32]

When Ford learned from a captured woman that Penateka chief Buffalo Hump had a large force twelve miles downriver, the ranger captain decided to return to the base camp. The final toll was two killed and three wounded in the ranger–reservation Indian ranks and seventy-six killed and "many wounded" in the Comanche camp and surrounding area. The rangers and reservation Indians returned home without incident, reaching their camp on the Brazos River on May 21. This battle broke up one of the Kotsoteka Comanche bands, probably the one that had been led by Iron Jacket.[33]

In addition, Major Earl Van Dorn of the U.S. Army followed up with two devastating attacks on Comanche bands in the same area. The people of one of the villages were apparently on their way to Fort Arbuckle to attend a treaty conference.[34]

<ᴈ̄⟩ CHAPTER 12 ᘐᔇ

The Hand of Savage Invasion

T HE SHERMANS WERE a typical pioneer family trying to improve their lives by homesteading a small farm in what was called
Stag Prairie on the western edge of Parker County. Some say that
Ezra Sherman was a greenhorn who did not even own a gun, but
others say he was overwhelmed by the swiftness of the attack. At any rate,
the Shermans were not prepared for the onslaught of marauding Comanches.[1]

About noon on a December day in 1860, Ezra and Martha Sherman and
their three young children were inside their log cabin seated around the
table. Outside a torrential rain was falling. A Comanche raiding party that
had been terrorizing the area was headed westward. Seeing the cabin, the
Indians stopped, dismounted, and entered. They shook hands with everyone and asked for something to eat. The Shermans "gave the Indians the
table." After the warriors had eaten, they suddenly became hostile and drove
the Shermans out into the rain. Ezra and Martha quickly started herding
their children toward the home of a neighbor, who lived half a mile away.
As they hurried as fast as they could on foot, they were suddenly overtaken
by the warriors, who took Martha Sherman. The frightened woman, in an
advanced stage of pregnancy, was driven back to the house by the braves,
who whipped her, lashing her face and beating her on the head. After
they had ransacked the house, the Indians grabbed Martha by the hair,
dragged her outside, stuck pins into her flesh, stripped off her clothing,
and raped her. Finally they scalped her, shot arrows into her, and left her
to die. The injured woman tried to drag herself to a muddy hole of water
nearby. She was found by her husband, who took her to a neighbors' house,
where the next day she gave birth to a dead child. She lived for four days,
telling and retelling her story to family and friends.[2]

As the Comanche raiding party headed to their stronghold in the broken country below the Staked Plains, they drove a huge herd of stolen

horses before them, which slowed their progress. Twenty-three-year-old Charles Goodnight, who lived on an outlying ranch, was told by neighbors that the Comanches were coming his way. Although he was young, Goodnight, who had grown up on the frontier, was tough and intelligent and destined to become one of the most famous and successful cattlemen of all time. The rain was falling in sheets as Goodnight jumped on his horse and rode to the neighboring ranches. With him he carried his long rifle with Matthew 6:33 engraved on the barrel: "Seek ye first the kingdom of God and his righteousness and all these things shall be added unto you." Goodnight alerted the families and asked the men to meet at daylight at Isaac Lynn's cabin on the upper Keechi Creek, where they might be able to "cut the Indians off."[3]

Eight men met at Lynn's ranch that morning. They headed west, and in spite of the rain that continued to fall, they found the Indians easy to track because of the large horse herd being driven. Goodnight and the others trailed the raiding party one hundred miles to the valley of the Pease River, a few miles from present-day Vernon. They finally decided that the Indians had already joined the main group, and eight men could not possibly defeat them, so they returned home and informed Captain Sul Ross of the Texas Rangers that they had trailed the Indians to the Pease River. Ross started making plans for a major expedition.[4]

The Sherman murder, the latest in a series of atrocities, was the last straw for the settlers in the Belknap, Palo Pinto, and Jacksboro area. Some forted up by joining together in the strongest and best protected log cabins. Others left the country in droves. An eyewitness described the exodus: "The most intense excitement and dire alarm pervades the whole country. Men, women, and children may be seen hurrying on horseback, on foot, and in sleighs to Camp Cooper and Weatherford; leaving behind their homes and property, unguarded and exposed to the ruthless hand of savage invasion. The entire settlement west of Weatherford have fled to the interior, and it . . . is left the extreme frontier post."[5]

At the same time, the men of the community, outraged by twenty-three murders in the past few months, decided to rid the country of the Comanches forever. A major expedition was planned. Good horses were needed, supplies were needed, and most important, men were needed— brave, experienced fighters, and lots of them. It was believed that the foe numbered anywhere from five hundred to two thousand deadly, intrepid adversaries. The brave selected their best horses and started winding up their family and business affairs in preparation for a long journey deep into

Indian country. They began preparing beef jerky and other food to take on the trip. Merchants in Weatherford and Palo Pinto, alarmed by the possible depopulation of the country, provided flour, coffee, and ammunition free of charge.[6]

J. H. Baker, who lived near Palo Pinto, rode into town on Saturday, December 1, 1860, and described the situation: "I have spent the day making ready to start on the Indian campaign. Quite a number of people in town today, some preparing to go on the expedition, some getting ready to leave the country, and some undecided about anything."[7]

Jonathan Hamilton Baker was brave, but he was by no means an experienced Indian fighter. In fact he had been in the Palo Pinto area only since the spring of 1858, but he had participated in the Reservation War in 1858–59. Trying to find his niche in the community, he bought a small ranch and started a school, which soon became successful. Baker faithfully kept a diary, and on July 13, 1860, he had taken stock of his life as indicated by the diary entry for that date:

> Another birthday has rolled around. Today I am 28 years old. Alas, how little have I accomplished, and how limited is my education. During the last year I have gone through a review of Rhetoric, Psychology, Physiology, Anatomy, Hygiene, Logic, and studied the second and third books of History of Europe, Asia, Africa, and read five volumes on teaching, containing 2,400 pages, besides a great deal of miscellaneous reading—school journals, newspapers, magazines, and at least one chapter in the Bible each day. I am now studying Chemistry, Algebra, and composition. I also keep up a course of reading on teaching. Have suceeded beyond my expectations in my teaching. . . . I have reduced the debt on my land to $300.

Baker was young and single, and with no hesitation decided to join the militia.[8]

Word about the expedition was spreading throughout the countryside by word of mouth and notices in the newspapers. Volunteers were instructed to meet at Loving's Valley on the border of Parker and Jack counties. On December 2, Baker gathered together his supplies and made his way to the camp. A holiday spirit was in the air, and at night the camp was noisy with laughter.[9]

The weather and the tempers turned nasty as a blue norther roared in on December 4, but by the afternoon the good cheer had been restored as the men lounged about "sleeping, joking, and training guns and pistols." Things looked even brighter when the provision wagon arrived "loaded with flour, [corn]meal, coffee, powder, lead, shot, caps, etc."[10]

December 5 found the men on the march again toward a mesquite valley in Young County about twenty-five miles east of Belknap. After the noon meal, the men organized the company. J. J. (Jack) Cureton was chosen as captain. Cureton was described by Charles Goodnight as "a splendid frontiersman and a fine man, an excellent Indian fighter, and a very popular commander." John M. Elkins said Cureton was as brave and cautious a man "as there was in the State of Texas." R. W. Pollard was chosen as first lieutenant, M. D. Sanders as second lieutenant, and Baker was chosen as first sergeant. The group was divided into nine squads with six men in each squad.[11]

While waiting for more men to join them, the volunteers had to move their campsite frequently so the horses would have good pasturage. The next day they lost their way while trying to find a good place to camp on the Brazos River. Amid much cursing, they camped on the west bank of the Brazos with poor grazing for the horses and the brackish Brazos River water for both man and beast. A Dr. Duling complained that "he would not care for himself but for his horse to travel all day and starve all night was too much for any horse to bear." Some of the men felt better after supper and a drink or two, and again there was much "whooping and yelling."[12]

A buffalo hunt on December 7 improved everybody's spirits and "camp no. 4" near California Creek was considered an improvement over the previous one. It was located in a little valley with good grass for the horses, but the only water was what Baker termed "sorry puddle-hole water." About nightfall, Captain Cureton came in with some recruits from Belknap. Another important addition to the group was rancher-lawyer William Mosely, who had been with Goodnight and the other men when they trailed the raiding party to the village on the Pease River. When Mosely told the volunteers that he thought there were about five hundred Indians in the village, they all knew that many more men were needed. The little army numbered less than one hundred men, though they were a dedicated and determined bunch. Volunteer John M. Elkins describes the feelings of the men: "Some might wonder if these ninety-six men would have actually followed an Indian trail that would lead them into a thousand or fifteen hundred warriors. I can answer that very emphatically now `yes, they would have followed any number where there was the slightest chance.' The majority of these men had lost some of their families or a friend, who was killed or carried away. Or they had just looked upon the mangled corpse, the scalped and bloody forms of whole families the victims of the ones they hoped to meet. Yes, these ninety-six men, if they could get no other to go, would have gone fearlessly into the midst of the many."[13]

Dispatches were immediately sent to Jacksboro and Palo Pinto and to Captain Ross at the ranger camp on Elm Creek a few miles from Belknap. Lawrence Sullivan Ross, or Sul, as he was called, had grown up on the frontier and had lived on the Brazos Indian Reservation from 1855 to 1858 while his father was Indian agent there. While home on vacation from Wesleyan University at Florence, Alabama, Ross had led 135 reservation Indians in the expedition against the Comanches led by Major Earl Van Dorn, which culminated in the battle at Wichita Village in 1858. Ross was seriously wounded but was nursed back to health by his Indian friends.[14]

In spite of the fact that Ross was only twenty-two years old, in 1859 he had been commissioned by Governor Sam Houston to form a ranger company. On September 11, 1860, Houston had written to Ross: "Upon the receipt of these orders you will proceed, without delay, to raise a company of mounted volunteers of Sixty men rank and file with three Lieutenants, four Sergeants and four Corporals for service in the neighborhood of Belknap. . . . You will guard the passes leading into the country, and should Indians get into the settlements, you will attack and if possible destroy them."[15]

The decision to send for Ross was not a popular one. Many of the men believed Ross was an Indian sympathizer because his father had been an Indian agent for a time. In fact, at a public barbecue on October 13, 1860, several resolutions were passed calling for Ross to "resign his captaincy and leave the frontier."[16]

Despite his unpopularity, Ross had no intention of resigning his commission. He had a sense of purpose, which he describes in a letter: "The necessity for vigorous measures soon became so pressing, however that I determined to make a desperate attempt to curb the insolence of these implacable hereditary enemies of Texas who were greatly emboldened by the small force left to confront them. I planned to accomplish this by following them into their fastnesses and carry the war into their own homes where this tribe, the most inveterate raiders on the border, retired with their captives and booty to their wild haunts amid the hills and valleys of the beautiful Canadian and Pease rivers."

Meanwhile, the volunteers had been waiting a week for reinforcements,

Lawrence Sullivan
Ross. Courtesy
George Barnard
Papers, the Texas
Collection, Baylor
University, Waco,
Texas.

and then Thursday, December 13 brought another cold norther and the
long-awaited Captain Sul Ross. Not only did he bring forty-seven rangers,
but he also brought twenty-three U.S. soldiers commanded by Sergeant
John W. Spangler, who had distinguished himself by killing six braves "in
personal combat" at the battle at Wichita Village. At this time the little
army consisting of citizen volunteers, Texas rangers, and U.S. soldiers numbered about 140 men, and they were finally ready for the hundred-mile
march to the Pease.[17]

Friday, December 14 was another bitterly cold day. At 8:30 A.M. the column formed up with scouts as an advance guard, the rangers and U.S.
soldiers next, and Captain Cureton with his company of volunteers bringing up the rear. Baker describes the march: "We marched in a northwest-
erly direction, over rather high, poor mesquite prairies, interspersed with
sharp ravines, and rocky points." At noon they ate "dinner" on "a branch of
the Little Wichita" River and several hours later camped on the "middle
fork of the Little Wichita."[18]

About twenty-five miles away in a Comanche village on a creek that flowed into the Pease River, a group of Comanche women toiled in the cold wind, hastily preparing food for the winter. As soon as the hunters killed buffalo, the women butchered the animals, brought the meat into camp, cut it into strips, and dried it on racks. They scraped the hides, removing bits of fat and flesh so the skins could be used for clothing and tents or could be traded for bullets, cooking utensils, and brightly colored cloth. The women prepared other food for the winter, such as pemmican and sausage. They also gathered hackberries and killed small animals, even skunks.

All the women were dressed in a similar manner and their hair was cropped below their ears. But one of the women was different. She had blue eyes.

The band was too close to the settlements, but little rain had fallen in the past year and the buffalo ranged far to the south looking for good grass. Soon the season the Comanches called "when the babies cry for food" would begin. Besides the bitter cold and howling winds on the Great Plains, hunger was a problem as food supplies ran low and were sometimes completely used up. In December of 1860 the Comanches and their Kiowa allies were already starving.[19]

On December 15 the volunteers, U.S. soldiers, and rangers spent another hard day marching northwest. Tension was building as they pushed farther and farther into Indian country. Ross described his feelings at about this time: "I pushed on although the unbroken silence was oppressive and seemed to repel our further advance as with some fearful presentiment."[20]

After a cold night, the men awoke to see the ground covered with frost. They traveled across "poor prairie uplands . . . [covered with] scrubby mesquite." Every once in a while they would cross a creek. Some of the crossings were difficult as the horses, mules, and men slipped and slid down steep banks to deep channels with boggy bottoms. The men pushed ahead until 2:40 P.M., when they reached the "Big Wichita," where they stopped, ate "dinner," and made "camp no. 10." The scouts found a mule and a horse they believed had been abandoned by the Indians on the last raid. After a lazy afternoon of "lounging about camp," hunting, and caring for the horses, the men turned in for another cold night.

On the morning of December 16, they were up earlier than usual. They crossed the Big Wichita and traveled in a northwest direction. To their left was a large herd of buffalo, estimated to be ten thousand in number. The men were riding leisurely along when suddenly some objects were spied on the horizon. Twelve men dashed toward them, eagerly anticipating bloody hand-to-hand combat to the death. Baker describes the action: "When the order was given the 6 went off at 'Gilpin' speed, followed by some 6 or 8 others and it was with great difficulty that the whole company was restrained from following the charge. All charged bravely, each vieing with the other, anxious to distinguish himself above the others and bring back a scalp. Just as the blow was about to be stricken that would crown their heads with glory, who can guess at the mortification of the men when it was discovered that the 'Indians' were buffalo hunters from Grayson County, the fun was all spoiled and the boys returned to the march on tired horses, and much disappointed."[21]

The morning of December 17 was not a happy one. The men awoke in a misting rain and the volunteers soon discovered that a number of the horses had strayed. The rangers and the U.S. soldiers, who seemed to have better methods of controlling their horses at night, led off at about 8:30 A.M. Baker and the other civilian volunteers who had not lost their horses soon followed. The men traveled northwest across poor land "without timber of value" until 11:00 A.M., when they reached the Pease River about twenty miles above its mouth. They stopped for the noon meal and decided to make "camp no. 12" since grass for the horses was available. Obtaining good water was a problem. Although the Pease was running at this point, the water in the river was salty and polluted with gypsum. A muddy pool was found a short distance from camp, but it had been so fouled by the buffalo that the water tasted of urine. The men and horses were forced to drink it because it was preferable to the salty "gyp water" of the Pease, which often caused diarrhea.[22]

That night more civilian volunteers arrived from Palo Pinto and Belknap, and the total force numbered about 170 men. Near the camp someone located the skin of a recently killed buffalo. Since all of the meat had been taken, the men surmised that it had been killed by Indians rather than by professional buffalo hunters, who took only the hide and perhaps a few choice portions of meat, such as the tongue or hump, leaving the rest to rot. Baker reported in his diary, "Other Indian signs are plentiful."

The men settled down for the night. The sky was cloudy, and the "lobo wolves," which hung around the buffalo herds waiting for a kill, were howling. Soon a thunderstorm poured rain on the men and horses. Sometime after midnight the guard came into the camp and reported that the thunder had stampeded the horses. The men sloshed about in the cold water and mud "amid the greatest confusion" and bitter complaining, but they found most of the horses and tied them to trees near the campfires.

As the men arose the next morning, they were consoled to see most of the horses standing around the camp, and the others were soon found. Nevertheless, morale could not have been at its peak in Captain Cureton's company. Some of the men had been in the field for more than three weeks, camping out in cold and rainy weather, drinking foul water, riding deep into Indian country through disturbing stillness during the day, and listening to the howling of wolves at night. The civilian volunteers watched their horses suffer as the animals tried to subsist on poor grass and worse water. The long marches through mesquite country and sometimes deep sand had taken their toll upon the animals, and by the end of each day most of them were exhausted.

Captain Cureton, realizing that an engagement with the enemy was not far off, decided to give his men a "small talk." He ordered them to "saddle up" and then to make "a hollow square." Cureton explained that the company needed better order and discipline. He asked who was willing to observe order and obey commands. All of the men "signified a willingness to comply." The frontiersman was quickly able to gain control over his men when it was necessary. Baker describes the scene: "The packs were put in the front and the company formed in regular next. All moved off in good order and the company presented a very imposing appearance." For fifteen miles, the rangers, U.S. soldiers, and civilian volunteers followed the treacherous Pease, crossing and recrossing it several times. Each time they followed the path of the buffalo because the river had quicksand, and the frontiersmen knew that it was safe to cross where the buffalo had crossed.[23]

A few miles up the river, a small group of Comanche women and children had broken away from the Indian village to go on an excursion to gather hackberries. The Indians relished the slightly sweet fruit and sometimes ate it on the spot, or they might take it home, remove the pulp, mix it with fat, roll it into balls, and roast the mixture on a stick. The women cut down a hackberry tree in order to gather all the berries.[24]

Downstream, the civilian volunteers spent an uncomfortable night on the south bank of the Pease in "camp no. 13." The water was "very bad," a cold north wind was blowing, most of the companies were out of meat, and the hunters failed to bring any in. The unusually large number of wolves prowling about had caused the civilian volunteers to camp in a straight line so that the campfires would serve as one line of defense against the wolves, and on the other side were the guards. The rangers and the U.S. soldiers were camped farther up on the north side of the river. The companies were separated so that the horses would have more grass.[25]

The next morning, December 19, every man knew that a bloody, hand-to-hand fight with a force much larger than theirs was imminent. As usual, the rangers and the U.S. soldiers got off earlier than the civilians. A heavy rain had soaked the guns, and the ammunition had to be "drawn" and the guns reloaded. Strayed horses again delayed Cureton's group. Goodnight explained simply that Ross, "having somewhat trained troops and consequently better disciplined men, got off ahead of us the next morning at daybreak."[26]

As Cureton's company was struggling to get off, Goodnight and Mosely, who were acting as advance scouts, found a pillowslip on the trail. Upon looking inside, they found a belt from a little girl's dress and a Bible with Martha Sherman's name on the flyleaf.[27]

Farther up the river, the women and children gathering hackberries had recently killed a skunk, skinned it, and eaten it for breakfast. Surely they could hear the noise of men and horses traveling up the river valley closer and closer to the village, and they must have dashed to their friends and relatives to warn them to run away as fast as they could.[28] The Indians had been gone only about ten minutes when Goodnight and Mosely discovered the campsite with the broken hackberry tree and a campfire with ashes still hot.[29]

Up ahead, the rangers and the U.S. soldiers were closing in on the village. Ross was sure Indians were near because a large number of buffalo ran toward the dragoons and rangers. Also, the air was filled with the screams of ravens, who smelled the blood and followed the Indian hunters as they slaughtered the buffalo. As Ross's command wound through the valley of the Pease, he would ride up to the top of one of the sandhills along the river bank to reconnoiter. On one of these hills he found the fresh tracks of four horses. He ran his horse southwest about a mile to a still higher hill, and to his great surprise, he saw below him only two hundred yards away a large Indian encampment. The village was not located on the river but on a creek that made a bend around a small hill.[30]

The Indians were frantically packing up all their belongings. The women could disassemble a lodge, lash it and all the other belongings to pack animals, pick up the children, and be ready to travel in a few minutes.[31] The blue-eyed woman had obeyed the command to move out and was riding north across a level, barren plain. She rode an excellent dark gray roan, and in her arms she carried her two-year-old daughter. As she fled, she searched for her two sons, aged eleven and nine. Unable to find them, she dashed back toward the creek, knowing she was risking her life and the life of her daughter.[32]

On the hill overlooking the village, Ross felt that he was undetected because of a cold, north wind that was whipping clouds of sand through the air. The ranger captain signaled his men to approach, and by the time they had arrived at his side, the Comanches were on the move. One of the rangers reported that Ross addressed his men with these words: "Boys, they are right over there and they are leaving now, going yon way. See that your guns, saddles and other equipment are in condition, for we've got to do our do at once. Mr. Stuart, you go back as hurriedly as you can till you meet Captain Cureton. Tell him the Indians are breaking camp and going off and we've got to attack, for if they get away we cannot overtake them on account of the condition of our horses."

Ross told Spangler, "You take your men and run around the end of that rough hill yonder. You can go around very well, for I see where they have been bringing the horse herd around it. As soon as you get to the end of the hill, you'll see the village all along up the creek. You encompass them there and keep them from crossing the river. When they see my men cross this rough ridge, they will attempt to cross at the mouth of the creek."[33]

Spangler yelled, "Let's go this way, boys," and headed for the hill. What happened next was a kind of mirror image of the Fort Parker massacre. The rangers and federal troops were the aggressors this time. They made an impressive sight strung out across the top of the hill. The men heard a piercing yell from the village below, indicating that the Comanches had seen them. Then the rangers and dragoons charged, galloping down the hill and across the boggy creek into the midst of the Indians.[34]

Benjamin Franklin Gholson was one of the rangers in the battle that day. He was only eighteen years old but had spent his entire life on the bloody Texas frontier. In later years, he told the story of that day over and over again.[35] Gholson said that the chief returned with a few warriors and tried to hold off the soldiers while the women and children escaped. Ross and others left out that detail, stating that the Indians fled in all directions as the rangers and soldiers galloped after them. Ross gives his version: "The attack was so sudden that a large number were killed before they could prepare for defense. They fled precipitately right into the arms of the sergeant and his twenty men. Here they met with a warm reception and finding themselves completely encompassed, every one fled his own way and was hotly pursued and hard pressed."[36] Goodnight, who did not arrive in time to participate in the action but witnessed it from a distance, told of the wanton massacre of Indian women by the rangers and U.S. soldiers: "The Rangers passed through the squaws, who were heavily loaded, and shot the Indians as they came to them. The Sergeant, on seeing this, fell in behind on the squaws, six or eight in number, who never got across the first bend of the creek they were so heavily loaded with meat, tent poles, and camp equipage that their horses could not run. We supposed they had about a thousand pounds of buffalo meat in various stages of curing. The Sergeant and his men killed every one of them, nearly in a pile."[37]

About fifteen dogs tried their best to defend their Indian masters. Their barking and growling added to the din of gunfire and screams of the wounded. Some of the dogs ran away, but others stayed until they were shot and killed.[38]

In a short while, all the rangers and soldiers had left the campsite and were chasing the individuals and groups fleeing in every direction. Frank Gholson reported that Ross shouted at him, "A lot of you men with the best horses go to them front Indians and try to stop them!"[39] Gholson dashed off and did not witness the rest of the rout at the Indian camp.

Captain Ross and ranger lieutenant Tom Kelliheir then charged off after what seemed to be three Indians: a chief riding double, and another Indian wrapped in a buffalo robe and riding a fleet, iron-gray horse. After pursuit of a mile or so, the two men caught up to the Indian on the gray horse. Ross drew his pistol to shoot when all of a sudden, the Indian stopped, held up a two-year-old child, and shouted, "Americano, Americano, Americano!"[40]

Ross shouted to Kelliheir, "Hold on to this captive!" The captain galloped full speed ahead and, aiming his pistol as well as he could, shot at the other fleeing pair. His aim was true. The Indian riding with the chief was shot in the back. Ross heard a piercing scream, and the wounded Indian fell from the horse, dragging the chief off also. The chief leaped to his feet. By this time Ross was almost on top of him. Arrows were whizzing about Ross's head as the chief released them in quick succession. One of the arrows hit Ross's horse, and the wounded animal began bucking wildly. Desperately holding onto the pommel of his saddle with his left hand, Ross kept firing his pistol, and one of the shots hit the chief in the elbow, making it impossible for him to draw his bow and defend himself. About this time, Ross's horse quieted somewhat, and the ranger captain fired two more shots that hit the Indian.[41]

Then the tall Indian, elaborately painted and garbed for the battle he had just lost, walked over to a lone mesquite tree growing on the prairie.

Wrapping his good arm around the tree, and leaning against it, he began to sing his death song.[42] Ross describes this in his courtly writing style:

> There was a plaintive melody in it which, under the circumstances, filled my heart with sorrow. He was a gigantic Indian, as graceful and handsome a warrior as ever rode to deadly lists; he fought with superb bravery and skill. Physically perfect, his body nude to the waist, was streaked fantastically with different colored pigments. His head dress consisted of two war eagles' plumes, one dyed vermillion, the other left in natural state, his head would have been conspicuous anywhere. Suspended from his neck by a massive chain, hung a disk or dice of beaten gold on which was rudely carved the figure of a tortoise. His arms encircled above the elbows with broad gold bands, his leggins of fawn skin were trimmed along the seams with a fringe of scalp locks as proof of his personal bravery, his moccasins had all sorts of grotesque designs worked in beads, his bearing was of great dignity.[43]

As the Indian sang, he seemed oblivious to everything around him. After a few minutes, Ross's Mexican cook, who was also the interpreter, rode up. Frank Gholson, who was off chasing a group of Indians down the Pease River and was not an eyewitness, heard the story later from Ross and others. Gholson gives an account of what happened next:

> When the Mexican came up Sull was afoot and the Indian was afoot and a hold of the sapling and there stood the Indian's horse. Sull asked the Mexican, "Who is he?" He said, "Well, he is Nacoma." We all knew him by reputation, but not by sight. Sull said, "Well, what is he talking about?" The Indian was not noticing them, was looking way off yonder and talking. "Oh!" he says, "the damn son of a bitch, he talk to his god." Sull says, "But what is he saying?" "Well, he says he wants his gekovah to give his token if he has done his duty as a chieftain, or ever failed his tribe, or failed or refused to do his duty any time in behalf of his tribe." Ross said, "But can you talk to him?" The Mexican said, yes. Ross said, "Tell him then if he will surrender he will not be shot any more."
> The Mexican broke loose talking to him in his own language. That was the first time, I suppose, that Nacoma noticed the Mexican. Quick as he spoke Nacoma turned and looked at the Mexican as much as to say, "Who is that talking my language?" I never knowed whether he recognized him or not.

So when the Mexican told him what the white captain had said, he looked at Sull then, looked back at Sull. Sull was standing there waiting for an answer. He said, "You tell the white captain when I am dead I will surrender but not before, and not to him," and that he was going to surrender to that other captain up there, his gekova. Then he made his motion to the other one and went right on talking to his gekova again.

Right when he made him that answer he turned loose that sapling, and he had a long spear with a china pole about nine feet long made fast at each end with a spear, which was sharp on each edge. The other end was made fast with a spanish knot to a buckskin lariat plaited from it, the other end around the horse's neck.

Just as he answered, both things were at the same time, he turned loose that sapling, and took his well arm and threw this spear at Sull that way. All Sull had to do was to be out of the way, beyond the end of the lariat. When Nacoma saw it didn't hit him, he just turned back to his sapling and went to talking again. Sull said to the Mexican, "This is the bravest man ever I saw. I can't shoot him any more!"[44]

Ross relates his feelings:

I could only look upon him with pity and admiration, for deplorable as was his situation with no possible chance of escape, his army utterly destroyed, his wife and child captives in his sight, he was undaunted by the fate that awaited him and preferred death to life. My Mexican servant begged to put him to death as his whole family had been massacred by this chief and he himself had suffered much torture at his hands and had been forced to run the gauntlet so I directed him to end his misery by a charge of buckshot from the gun he carried. Thus this brave savage who had been so long the scourge and terror of the Texas frontier passed into the land of shadows.[45]

Gholson continues his story: "Up came the Mexican's Mississippi rifle and he said with an oath, 'I can.' That Mexican shot him clear loose of that sapling. He just fell loose from it. Sull run up to him then, and he was lying on his back, and he looked up at him and breathed about three times and between breaths gritted his teeth like a wild hog [and died]."[46]

Ross picked up the chief's bow and arrow, headdress, shield, buffalo horns, and lance, which he planned to present to Governor Houston along with the scalps that had been taken as "trophies of war." The ranger captain remounted and rode back across the plain to where Lieutenant Kelliheir was guarding the woman and child. Kelliheir had "lung trouble" and on top of that was riding a high-strung horse. As the lieutenant coughed, tried to manage his skittish animal, and struggled to head off the dodging woman, he became furious. As Ross rode up, he shouted, "Captain, me ran me horse most to death and captured a damn squaw!"[47]

The ranger captain looked at the woman, whose face and hands were dirty from butchering and curing buffalo meat. Underneath the ample buffalo robe, she wore only "scanty garments." Her face and body were not painted, and her dress was torn.[48]

The woman looked at Ross with a "wild glare." Ross yelled, "Why, Tom, this is a white woman! Indians don't have blue eyes." Kelliheir yelled back, "Hell no! That ain't no white woman. Damn that squaw! If I have to worry with her any more I will shoot her!"[49]

Ross, still insisting that the woman was white, grabbed the bridle of her horse. About that time, the Mexican cook-interpreter, Antonio Martínez, rode up and Ross asked, "Who is she, Anton?" Martínez answered, "Oh! She is Nacoma's wife." "Well, who was she?" "I don't know. She was some white girl they raised."[50] Ross, Kelliheir, and Martínez restrained the woman as Martínez spoke to her in the Comanche language. The three men finally managed to quiet the frantic woman. Some of the men begged Ross to turn her loose and let her return to her adopted people, but Ross told them that "there were a number of white people in Texas who had lost children through capture by the Indians and that if this woman were turned loose every one of these people would feel that this was probably his child or relative."[51]

Taking the woman and child with him, Ross returned to the site of the Indian village, where some of the men were looting. The dead, mostly women, had been scalped except for one young man who had white features. The men had not scalped the young warrior, thinking he might be the son of the captured woman. Ross's men were bringing in thirty horses and mules they had found. The site of the Indian village was covered with a jumble of things, dropped and abandoned by the Indians in their frantic haste to escape. The men picked up what they fancied, "buffalo rugs, blankets, pack saddles, tents of dressed buffalo skins, meat, cooking vessels, axes, knives, tomahawks, tools for dressing skins, wooden bowls, mocasins, whetstones, leather bags filled with marrow out of bones and braines, little sacks of soup, sausages, guts stuffed with tallow and braines, and various other things."[52]

Ross noticed a Comanche boy about nine years old in the tall grass by the creek. The boy began to cry, thinking he was about to be killed. Ross put the boy behind him on his horse and went into the camp.[53]

Just then two men ran up, each carrying half of Nocona's scalp. They had scalped the corpse and then split the "trophy" so that each would have a "souvenir" to carry home.[54]

The woman asked Martínez if she could go back to where the body of her husband lay. Finding her more easily managed than she had been, Martínez explained to her that she would not be harmed if she did not resist. Then he took the woman back to where the corpses of the two Indians Ross had killed lay on the barren ground. The Indian who had been riding behind Nocona proved to be a girl about fifteen years old. Her buffalo robe and cropped hair had kept Ross from realizing she was a girl. Goodnight believed that she was "Nocona's second wife, a Spanish woman he had captured."

The rangers' captive dismounted, walked over to where the two bodies lay, bent over them, and began to moan and cry. But she was not allowed to pay her respects and express her grief for long. The men were impatient and did not have time to watch as she said good-bye to her loved ones. When the woman was asked to remount, she refused. A ranger who had ridden up took her baby and rode away, thinking she would follow. She seemed oblivious to what was happening, continuing to moan and cry. Finally the men grabbed her and put her on her horse as the Mexican explained to her that "she would make them kill her if she didn't come on."

They took the woman back to where the main battle had been fought. There she was allowed to walk among the dead. Over each body she uttered a prayer. She was stricken with grief when she came to the body of the young warrior who had white features. Martínez asked, "Who was he?" The woman replied, "He's my boy, and he's not my boy." She gave no further explanation.[55]

A new camp had been made in a cottonwood grove near the site of the main engagement. The rangers and the civilian volunteers were camped together. The woman with her child in her arms had been forced to ride away from the battle site. Goodnight describes the scene: "We all returned to a cottonwood grove along the river to camp, taking with us the captured woman and her infant in arms. We rode right over her dead companions. I thought then and still think how exceedingly cruel this was."[56]

After reaching the cottonwood grove, the woman was interrogated. Crying bitterly, she told Ross she did not remember her name or where she had been taken from, but she remembered the Indians taking and killing her sister. Civilian volunteer John M. Elkins later said: "She stated that her father was killed at the battle of some fort many years ago and that she and her brother were taken prisoners by the Indians; that her brother had died. She said that the recent raid that was so detrimental to the frontier was headed by her husband who was Chief Nocona and that on their return he had stopped by to join the hunting party when he was killed with the others by the men of Captain Ross and Sergeant Spangler." Other details that she gave convinced Ross that she was the "long lost Cynthia Ann Parker."[57]

She also told Ross that the Indians killed were part of a band who had been terrorizing the settlers recently. They had delivered the stolen horses to some other Indians, who had taken most of them to the main camp on the headwaters of the Canadian and Red rivers two hundred miles north. The raiders had intended to rest themselves and their horses and then pack up the meat and hides taken in their absence and take these to the main village, where four tribes had united in order to raid the frontier during the winter and spring. A group of thirty-five warriors planned to resume raiding in the settlements. Finally, the woman told Ross that the Indians were starving because the buffalo had been down so close to the settlements during the fall and winter.[58]

As night fell on the camp in the cottonwood grove, the woman continued to cry. Ross, thinking she was afraid that she and her daughter would be killed, instructed Martínez to tell her that "we recognized her as one of our own people and would not harm her." She became quiet and began to talk. She told Martínez that early that morning she and her two boys had heard the loud cry when the rangers were sighted and had fled with the other women and children. "After I had gone some distance, I missed both my boys. I came back in search of them, coming as near to the battle as I could. In this way I was caught. I'm greatly distressed about my boys, for I fear they are killed. They may be cut off to themselves or with other children and will freeze tonight, before some of the other Indians can find them tomorrow." She also told Martínez there was a large village up the river, and the Indians who had escaped would notify the other warriors, and they would return to attack the small group of whites.[59]

The captured Comanche boy was causing trouble. The rangers made him a bed, but he would not stay in it because it had been made by the white men. He kept going back to the big fire they had built, threatening his guards in Comanche, and saying "he wanted to freeze to death." Finally, several of the men stood the boy before the fire and wrapped a buffalo robe around him, hair side in. They tied a rope around the robe from top to bottom, shoved the boy down on the ground, and one of the men said, "Now, freeze if you can."[60]

It was a quiet time in the camp. A few people were sitting around the campfire. The woman was holding her child in her lap. She had gone through hell during the day, the same hell she had endured twenty-four years earlier as she watched her family and friends slaughtered and scalped. She had struggled valiantly to escape and rejoin her loved ones but once again found herself a captive held by a people whose ways she did not comprehend and who spoke a language she did not understand. She had been bullied, threatened, and interrogated, and now she was exhausted.

Jonathan Baker, a reserved, scholarly man and sometime Indian fighter, sat near her. He picked up a tiny moccasin and, noticing that the beadwork was especially beautiful, decided to keep it for a souvenir. Then he saw the woman looking intently at him. Glancing down at the feet of the Indian child, he saw that she had only one shoe. He held up the other, and the child toddled over, took the moccasin, put it on, and rushed back to her mother. The woman whose life had been one of almost ceaseless toil, who sat in rags with dirty face and hands, had taken the time to fashion for her daughter elaborate, beaded moccasins. As the men sat talking, they started to discuss the woman's identity. One remarked that "years ago a family by the name of Parker had been killed and a child Cynthia Ann Parker had been carried off."

Immediately the woman spoke: "Me Cynthia Ann." The intense interrogation had failed to bring back the memory of her name, or perhaps she did not care to reveal it to Ross, but when she heard it spoken, she responded. The men seated around the fire then knew that "the long lost Cynthia Ann Parker" had been recaptured. Captain Ross was not present, and the men did not tell him what Cynthia Ann had said.[61]

Later in the evening, there was "great rejoicing in camp . . . over the victory." The men sat for a long time by their campfires. Martínez started talking about what had caused his bitter hatred for Nocona. Gholson relates the story:

> When he was a small boy, his father was a ranchman in Mexico, not far from the Rio Grande. One morning his father and three more Mexicans were at the corral roping and catching a lot of horses, and his mother and the balance of his family was at the house. And there was a big bunch of Indians came around the corral, and it didn't take them long to kill the four Mexicans. Some of the Indians ran between them and the

house and circled around the corral. Well, they came to the house and his mother came out of the house and met him Nocoma, who was leading that charge, then a young man. She met him and plead with him in Spanish, in her language, not to kill the children and not to carry them off. There was another Mexican woman or two there. They killed the women, and carried off the children, him among them, and he saw Nacoma shoot his mother with a pistol when she was pleading with him. Nacoma kept him when they divided up the prisoners, and made a servant out of him. And that is the reason that he knew him and that woman, and knew what they called her, Palooch.[62]

Ross, Spangler, and the militia officers conferred that night. Ross and the dragoons planned to return immediately to Camp Cooper with the prisoners. The volunteers planned to "overtake the Indians or at least find out where they are."[63]

The next morning the cold wind of the norther had stopped blowing and the weather was pleasant. The Comanche boy was unrolled from his buffalo robe and ate a hearty breakfast. After breakfast some of Cureton's men went back to the Indian camp to collect the meat, buffalo robes, and other loot. Several of them located the trail of six or eight Indians. Upon following it, they came upon the body of one Indian. Baker recorded in his diary: "So Capt Ross was mistaken about all of the Indians. I think he was honestly mistaken, being deceived by the report of Serg't Spangler of the Dragoons. Who reported that his men killed a party of 7 Indians who ran in a different direction from where Ross and his men were engaged. We found only 1 killed at the place he designated, but we found the trail of 6 leaving this place, hence we concluded that Spangler lied and let his Indians get away. 7 all told, 4 squaws and 3 bucks are all of the dead Indians we have found."[64]

Cynthia Ann was encouraged to claim all of the horses and other property that had belonged to Nocona. She took her two horses, a dark bluish roan and a red and white paint horse. But refused to take anything else, saying that he had had two other wives and "she would take nothing unless she could have a division with them." She took her baby's clothes as well as her own but would not take the clothing of her two boys or any other clothing, explaining that "these belonged to the other children who were not there and that they might return to get them sometime." Cynthia Ann did not want to deprive the Indian children of any of their meager supply of clothing in the dead of winter, but her efforts to help the children were in vain. All of the clothing, buffalo robes, saddles, and other articles not ap-propriated by the soldiers, rangers, and civilians were burned.[65]

Dissatisfied with the fact that Ross had confiscated almost all the horses and disappointed that they had missed out on the fight with the Indians, Cureton and his men were determined to continue the pursuit. Baker ex-presses the feelings of the frontiersmen: "We very much wish to accom-plish something before we return."

A company of nine men went out scouting to try to discover the loca-tion of the main body of Indians. Baker and the others who stayed in camp had just about given up the scouts for lost when they returned on Decem-ber 24. Baker records in his diary: "They have discovered much fresh In-dian sign, north and west of us, and about 40 miles up this river (Pease) they found a very large trail going south; with every indication that there were 1,600 to 2000 Indians moving south with large bands of horses, to winter in a warmer climate."

On December 24, after the evening meal, Captain Cureton called all the men together and addressed them:

> Fellow soldiers we are generally of the opinion, from the report of the
> spies that we are too weak in our present condition to meet and vanquish
> the enemy. Permit me then, to give you my opinion as to the best means
> of procedure in this present crisis. I think it dangerous, and even fool-
> hardy, for a few men to undertake to follow these Indians that so over-
> whelmingly outnumber us. They will discover us by their spies, and when
> they realize how few we are in number, are sure to overpower and kill us.
> This would embolden the Indians and do us no good. My plan is for part
> of the men to go to the Wichita or Brazos, as many as feel they can stay,
> and wait on good grass and rest and graze their horses. The balance go
> into the settlements, get recruits, and fresh horses, and start as many
> men as possible from the lower settlements, and all unite in a general
> campaign. And be prepared for any emergency, and to kill as many of the
> "Red Devils" as possible, and take all of their horses from them. . . .
> When we depart I consider the company disbanded, and I do not wish
> any longer to be considered commander of it. . . . If I am with you on
> reorganizing, and am the choice of the company, I will serve you to the
> best of my ability.

A Mr. Wells was then called upon to speak: "It was understood that some 15 of the men were not going home. That they would stay in the upper reaches of the country, and follow the trails near their camping places. That they would spy out hunting parties of Indians, and clean them up. And in this way harrass the Indians until men would be brought into the field in sufficient numbers to whip the main body of Indians."

On December 25, 1860, Jonathan Baker wrote in his diary: "This morning about 9 o'clock the memorable retreat began." He told of the enormous number of buffalo robes the men carried home. He said they marched twenty-five miles and camped on Beaver Creek. He did not mention Christmas.[66]

CHAPTER 13

The Long-Lost Relative

C APTAIN SUL ROSS and Sergeant Spangler with their men and the three prisoners had left the camp on the Pease River six days before Cureton and his volunteers. After riding hard for four days, they arrived at Fort Belknap on December 22. Cynthia Ann tried in vain to escape from her captors so that she could return to her fatherless sons. Captive Indian women were sometimes allowed to escape. Their white captors knew that they were usually able to make their way back to their friends and family. But this captive was different. She was white, and Ross was convinced that she was Cynthia Ann Parker, the "white squaw," who was famous all over the frontier.[1]

Cynthia Ann and Prairie Flower were sent on to Camp Cooper with the U.S. soldiers, where the army wives could care for them.[2] Camp Cooper, located on a horseshoe bend in a narrow valley of the Clear Fork of the Brazos River, was composed of thirteen structures placed in the form of an "L." Six of the buildings were constructed of rough stone and oak boards, but the others were made of mud, tarpaulins, or pickets (poles placed upright with mud daubing in between). Some of the troops were housed in tents.[3]

Ross sent a messenger to Isaac Parker, Cynthia Ann's uncle.[4] The women at the camp gave Cynthia Ann some clothing. Gholson, who was at Camp Cooper at the time, describes the women's attempts to help her:

> There were at the camp some women, chiefly wives of officers, who became sorry for her and decided that they would do what they could to aid her to get back to civilization. They asked Kalahah [Kelliheir] to let them have her to keep a while. He was fearful of the result, but finally consented. The women took her out of the tent in which she was staying and took her up to one of their tents. They found enough clothes to

clothe her, had an old negro mammy prepare some hot water and wash her thoroughly, combed her hair and let her look at herself in a mirror. She submitted to all this willingly enough, apparently, until she got a good opportunity to get out the door of the place.

When this opportunity occurred she made a dive for the door and got past the negro mammy. It was about two or three hundred yards from there to her old tent and she struck out for it. Kalahah had stationed several men near by to act as guards to prevent her from escaping, but when we saw that she making for her tent we let her go. It was a race such as I have never seen before or since. In the lead was the squaw, jerking off clothes as she ran until she soon had on almost nothing; behind came the negro mammy frantically waving a cloth or something, two or three bewildered white women looked on and the squaw's little child, big enough to toddle around, following after, with nobody paying much attention to her. The squaw reached her tent and the next time she reappeared she had got rid of the remnants of her civilized garb and had somewhere raked up some more Comanche garments. This was the last time the women tried their hands at civilizing her.[5]

When Isaac Parker received the message from Ross, he started immediately for Belknap. Isaac was blue-eyed and blond with finely chiseled features. He had been elected sheriff, justice of the peace, and county treasurer in Illinois and had also made his mark in Texas. At this time Isaac, who was sixty-seven years old, lived with his wife Lucy at Birdville, a few miles west of the village of Fort Worth. They were prosperous and prominent members of the community and owned a large number of slaves. Except for two terms, Isaac had served Texas as a representative and senator almost continuously from 1836 until 1856. He was well known as a "stump speaker" who was "an orator of great power." Isaac had also served in Elisha Clapp's company of rangers during the Texas Revolution and had fought in a number of Indian battles, including the Battle of Village Creek in 1841. Settler John Lockhart said of him: "Isaac Parker was a member of the Texas congress when it sat at Washington [-on-the-Brazos], and was universally beloved for his kindness towards his fellows. So deep were the wounds caused by the murders of his brothers and family it saddened his after life so that he was scarcely ever seen to smile."[6]

Isaac set out in a "two horse hack." He first went to a relative named John Parker to ask John to accompany him to Fort Belknap since it was on the extreme edge of the frontier, and the Indians were raiding with alarm-

GENEALOGY 2
James W. Parker family

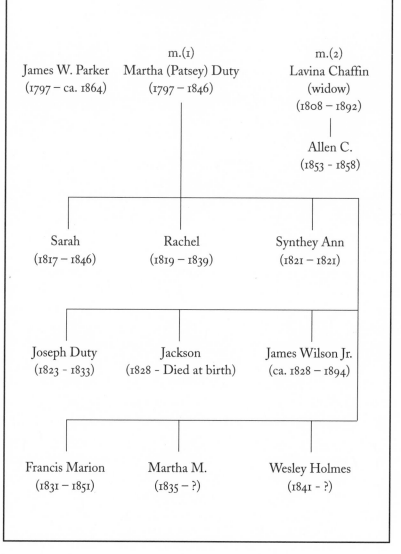

	m.(1)		m.(2)
James W. Parker	Martha (Patsey) Duty		Lavina Chaffin
(1797 – ca. 1864)	(1797 – 1846)		(widow)
			(1808 – 1892)

Allen C.
(1853 - 1858)

Sarah	Rachel	Synthey Ann
(1817 – 1846)	(1819 – 1839)	(1821 – 1821)

Joseph Duty	Jackson	James Wilson Jr.
(1823 - 1833)	(1828 - Died at birth)	(ca. 1828 – 1894)

Francis Marion	Martha M.	Wesley Holmes
(1831 – 1851)	(1835 – ?)	(1841 - ?)

Isaac Parker. Courtesy
Joseph E. Taulman
Collection, CN 04515,
the Center for
American History,
the University of
Texas at Austin.

ing frequency. John could not accompany him, but a neighbor named
A. B. Mason agreed to go. They made their way seventy miles to the vicinity of Fort Belknap, where they spent the night with the father of Francis
M. Peveler, one of the civilian volunteers who had fought at Pease River.
Francis's brother Louis Peveler and another cowboy offered to accompany
them on their journey because of the danger of Indian attack. The next
day the four men traveled twenty-five miles west to the ranger camp on
Elm Creek near present-day Throckmorton. Ross told Parker that he would
have to journey twenty miles south to Camp Cooper, where the woman
and child had been taken, and sent Antonio Martínez along with Parker
as an interpreter.[7]

They arrived at the camp at night. Isaac and his companions waited
until the following morning to call on the commanding officer. According
to Gholson, the men were taken to the tent where Cynthia Ann was held
captive: "She used a small pine box for a seat. The wind was blowing cold
from the north that morning. She was sitting on her box on the south side

of her tent crouched low, with her elbows on her knees and the palms of her hands on her jaws. When the men assembled she paid no attention whatever to them." Isaac's companion, A. B. Mason, related what happened at the interview. Mason said that when he and Isaac arrived at Camp Cooper, an interpreter was asked to question the captive woman and "cautiously" mention some minor details of the Fort Parker massacre in order to jar her memory. She listened but seemed lost in thought, except that every once in a while she was "convulsed by some powerful emotion." After a few moments, she gave the following account in "her beautiful language of intelligible signs and Comanche tongue."

I remember when I was a little girl, being a long time at a house, with a picket fence [the Fort Parker stockade] all around; one day some Indians came to the house, they had a white rag on a stick. My father went out to talk to them, they surrounded and killed him, then many other Indians came and fought at the house; several whites were killed; my mother and her four children were taken prisoners; in the evening mother and two of her children were retaken by a white man.

My cousin was taken with me and sold afterwards. My brother died among the Indians with the small pox; I lived with the Indians north of Santa Fe; have three children; two of them at home, and one with me; she is three years old; named Te-ish-put, (Prairie Flower).

All the Comanches got together in the fall come down to get horses; the friendly Reserve Indians always help to steal; Caddoes quit stealing with Comanches; Comanches and Caddoes fight now; friendly Comanches always come to help steal.

Take the horses to Santa Fe and Kansas and sell them to white men; some of them swaps to Mexico, all the Indians on sweet water fork Red River, the fourth prong on the south side above Big Witchita; think there is about five hundred; the little boy the Indians took was killed, before they came to me; he fought the Indians and did not like to go, and they killed him.[8]

Cynthia Ann told the men one more thing. When asked about the young warrior who had white blood, she told the men: "He was the son of another captive white girl who had been captured by the Comanches and had married an Indian."[9]

According to Mason's account, "when Col. P. requested the interpreter to ask her if she recollected her name, Cyntha Ann Parker, she arose before the question could be asked by him, and striking herself on the breast, exclaimed, 'me Cyntha Ann.'"[10]

Satisfied that the woman who sat before him was his niece, Parker decided to take her and Prairie Flower home with him. He was asked if he would like to take Martínez along so as to be able to communicate with Cynthia Ann, and he answered, "Yes, I would be glad to have him." Two rangers were also sent as guards on the dangerous return journey. The Parkers returned by way of Fort Belknap, where they spent two days and nights with the family of Francis Peveler. According to Peveler, Mrs. Peveler "had the woman and child cleaned up and provided them with a more presentable appearance to enter the white settlements." Prairie Flower played with the children on the ranch, and they "became devoted to her."[11]

The world that Cynthia Ann was entering was quite different from the one she had left twenty-four years earlier. In 1836 there were about fifteen thousand English-speaking people in Texas, and in 1860, according to the census records, there were more than six hundred thousand. At the time of the Fort Parker massacre, there were only three newspapers in Texas, but by 1860 there were seventy-one. In 1836 there were only a few wagon roads in the state, but in 1860, besides the thousands of miles of dirt roads, there were 272 miles of railroad tracks and plans for many more. Cynthia Ann's uncle Daniel would have been interested to know that there were over twenty thousand Baptists in the state, although the number of Predestinarian Baptists was only a small fraction of this. The racial and ethnic makeup of the state had changed greatly because earlier the population in the settled areas had consisted almost entirely of Anglos, Mexicans, and civilized Indians, but in 1860, 30 percent of the population were blacks, 4 percent were Germans, and most of the civilized Indians had been driven from the state. Log cabins and adobe houses still dotted the land, but frame structures far outnumbered them, and there were even some mansions. Several impressive homes in Austin, including the governor's mansion, had been designed by renowned architect Abner Cook.[12]

On the way to Birdville, Isaac, Cynthia Ann, Prairie Flower, and their companions traveled through Weatherford and then stopped off at Fort Worth. There, after much difficulty, Cynthia Ann was persuaded to have her picture taken with Prairie Flower. Word had spread about the recapture of Cynthia Ann, and she and Prairie Flower had become celebrities. According to Medora Robinson Turner, who was a child at the time, all the students were let out of school so that they could see the captives, who had been taken to Turner and Daggett's general store. Medora describes Cynthia Ann and

Cynthia Ann Parker and Prairie Flower. Courtesy Panhandle-Plains
Historical Museum, Canyon, Texas.

the scene that took place: "She stood on a large wooden box, she was bound
with rope, she was not dressed in Indian costume, but wore a torn calico
dress. Her hair was bronzed by the sun. Her face was tanned, and she made
a pathetic figure as she stood there, viewing the crowds that swarmed about
her. The tears were streaming down her face, and she was muttering in the

Indian language." The children asked the principal what she was saying, and he told them that she was asking to be taken back to her people.[13]

The next stop was Birdville, a tiny settlement situated on arid, rolling prairie, the type of land upon which Cynthia Ann had spent the last twenty-four years of her life. Isaac's home, located a few miles outside Birdville and a mile or two from the Trinity River, was a double log cabin with a dog run in the middle and a porch across the front. Inside was a stone fireplace. The house and simple furniture must have reminded Cynthia Ann of her family's tiny log cabin inside Fort Parker with its crude homemade bedstead, table, and stools.[14]

Cynthia Ann was not happy living with her uncle Isaac. She repeatedly tried to escape and had to be closely watched.[15] One of Isaac's neighbors, K. J. Pearson, wrote to his cousin John D. Floyd on February 3, 1861, and included in the midst of news of the secession convention, Indian problems, the hide business, and the weather was an account of Cynthia Ann's recapture and recognition of her name:

> I wrote to Lige something about Col. Parker having gone to Camp Cooper, in search of his niece who had been in captivity among the wild Comanche Indians since the 19th of May, 1836. He went and has come back. He found the woman to be his long-lost relative and here she is with her child, Go-Ish-Put (Prairie Flower) as pretty and sprightly a little girly, one or two years old, as you could wish to see. Cynthia Ann Parker was about nine years old when she was taken. Her brother was taken at the same time, but she says he died of smallpox long ago. She has almost entirely lost the English language and can speak nothing but the Comanche tongue. When Col. Parker went to where she was he told an interpreter that if she was the woman for whom he searched her name was Cynthia Ann. Before the interpreter had time to tell her this she exclaimed, striking herself on the breast, Cynthia Ann. Most evidently recollecting her name. She says she does not want to go back to the Indians because they whip too much.[16] She was the wife of a little chief and has two children yet with the Indians. She was with a party of Indians, when she was taken, that had been down into that country killing buffalo. Thirteen of them were killed in the fight which was a running one. . . . Last Sunday morning I saw her at her devotions which was truly a great novelty. She went out to a smooth place on the ground, cleaned it off very nicely and made a circle and a cross, on the cross she built a fire and burned some tobacco and cut a place on her breast and let blood

drop on the fire. She then lit her pipe and blowed smoke towards the sun and assumed an attitude of the most sincere devotion. She afterwards said through an interpreter that this was her prayer to her great spirit to enable her to understand and appreciate that these were her relatives and kindred she was among.[17]

One month after her recapture, Isaac took Cynthia Ann to Austin, where he planned to petition the legislature for a pension for her support and for the education of Prairie Flower. In 1860 and 1861 Texas was a hotbed of political discontent with Austin at its center. On November 6, 1860, the telegraph operators had broadcast the news: "Abraham Lincoln has been elected President of the United States." A few days later, the Texas flag was seen flying in many places, and there was talk of a second republic as masses all over the state were demanding secession. In Austin groups marched up and down Congress Avenue carrying torches and signs condemning Abraham Lincoln. On January 5, the secessionists staged a long parade that started at the capitol at midmorning and proceeded down Congress Avenue. At the head rode Rip Ford mounted on a white stallion, following him were carriages filled with ladies waving Lone Star flags, and bringing up the rear was a noisy group of men on horseback. In spite of the overwhelming demand for secession, Governor Sam Houston was adamantly opposed to it and refused to call a convention to decide whether the state should secede from the Union. Secessionists countered by calling their own convention. Houston was then forced to call in the legislature, which met on January 21. Although the men who crowded into the capitol were unruly, they listened respectfully as Houston delivered one of his greatest speeches. As usual he included an emotional appeal to his listeners: "A long struggle amid bloodshed and privation secured the liberty which has been our boast for three-quarters of a century. Wisdom, patriotism, and the noble concessions of great minds framed our Constitution. Long centuries of heroic strife attest the progress of freedom to their culminating point. Ere the work of centuries is undone, and freedom, shorn of her victorious garments, is started out once again on her weary pilgrimage, hoping to find, after centuries have passed away, another dwelling place, it is not unmanly to pause and at least endeavor to avert the calamity." In spite of Houston's efforts, the legislature approved the convention.[18]

Isaac Parker and Sam Houston had been good friends since the Battle of Horseshoe Bend in the War of 1812, where the two young men had fought against the Red Stick band of Creek Indians. Many years later,

Houston had sent Isaac as a representative to the United States to obtain support for the Texas Revolution. Now Houston was fighting another battle, one of the few that he lost. The secessionists poured into Austin in carriages and wagons and on horseback. They joined the continual demonstrations, which were creating havoc in the capitol. Into this turmoil rode Isaac, Cynthia Ann, and Prairie Flower. The torchlight processions may have reminded Cynthia Ann of the Comanche war dances held in the firelight before the braves went on the warpath.[19]

Having been in politics since 1838, Isaac Parker was well acquainted with influential people such as John Henry Brown, a newspaper editor and former state representative. Mrs. Brown and one of her friends took an interest in Cynthia Ann. They "dressed her neatly" and decided to take her and Prairie Flower to the capitol, where the secession convention was being held. The building must have been an impressive sight for Cynthia Ann. Located on a hill, it dominated the town. A broad avenue led up to its front doors. It was a three-story limestone structure that gleamed in the sunlight. Four marble Ionic columns supported a portico in front, and the edifice was capped with an impressive dome. Cynthia Ann and Prairie Flower were led up the broad stone steps to the second floor, where the secessionists were meeting in the Representative Hall. There they saw paintings, cornices, and massive tables. In the Representative Hall was a balcony, and the three ladies and the child climbed up its steps to seat themselves in the crowd. Down below on the floor, the representatives were debating some aspect of secession. All of a sudden Cynthia Ann grabbed up Prairie Flower and bolted for the door. She was captured once again. Then the ladies realized that Cynthia Ann thought that she was in an assemblage of chiefs who were deciding whether or not she should be put to death. They called to Mr. Brown, who was a member of the convention, and he succeeded in convincing her that everyone wished her well, and no one wanted to hurt her.[20]

While Cynthia Ann was in Austin, a newspaper reporter wrote of her:

Miss Cynthia Ann is now entirely unable to speak our language, and can converse only through an interpreter. She is now 34 or 35 years old, appears in good health, and has a very sprightly child about two years old. She is now in this city, and is being visited by very many. At first, after her recovery, she was afraid of being killed by her own countrymen, for the Comanches had her to think so. She believed the Comanches were the most numerous and powerful people in the world, and only now begins to learn that she had been deceived. She was aware that she was an Ameri-

Cynthia Ann Parker, unknown date. Courtesy Lawrence T. Jones III
Collection.

can. Her complexion is quite fair still, but her body and arms bear the
marks of being cruelly treated. The bill for the relief of this unfortunate
young woman, was referred to the Committee on the Judiciary.

The men of the legislature were generous to Isaac Parker's niece. She was
granted a pension of one hundred dollars a year for the next five years, for
the "support of said Cynthia Ann, and for the support and education of her
child, Topasannoh," as well as a league of land. Cynthia Ann's cousins Isaac

Duke Parker and Benjamin Parker were given title to the proposed land grant, which was "to be located, surveyed and patented as other land certificates upon any of the vacant and unappropriated public land of the state of Texas," to hold in trust for her since they were in effect considered to be guardians of a "minor."[21]

Since Cynthia Ann continued to be unhappy, her brother Silas Parker Jr. agreed to take her to live with him in Van Zandt County, and he was appointed her guardian on January 8, 1862. As Silas, Cynthia Ann, and Prairie Flower made their way east, with every step of the horse, Cynthia Ann and Prairie Flower moved farther away from their home on the plains, from the breaks and the mountains. The distance was greater, the land was unfamiliar, and escape would be harder, perhaps even impossible.

At last they reached Van Zandt County, and Silas took mother and daughter deep into the East Texas woods to his log cabin home to live with him, his wife Ann, and their three young children. Silas and his sister Orlena had both married members of the O'Quinn family. They had endured a hard childhood. After their father was killed at Fort Parker, their mother, Lucy, had to cope with the shocking death of her husband, the captivity of two of her children, a complete lack of money, and a probate case that dragged on from 1838 to 1843. Silas, Orlena, and possibly Lucy herself were cared for, clothed, and fed by Joshua Hadley for a long period of time. On May 11, 1943, in a letter to the court, Lucy mentions "the great inconvenience I labor under and my bad health at present." A short time later she petitioned the court to let her sell some land to pay off her debts and was then accused of being "about to squander said estate." During this time she married Thomas M. Strother on November 22, 1840, but divorced him after a short period of time. The estate was finally settled, and Lucy ended up with a league of land. She reportedly married two more times, first to a Mr. Usery and then to William W. Roberts. In 1850 Silas and Orlena were living with relatives Phebe and Adrian Anglin, and in 1852 Lucy died without seeing her beloved daughter Cynthia Ann returned to her white family.[22]

Silas was twenty-eight years old when Cynthia Ann and Prairie Flower went to live with him. A neighbor named Jordan W. Hobbs says of him:

About 1½ mile east of father['s home], as far back as we can remember, there lived a man named Silas Parker. He was a middleaged man in appearance, and like most men of those days of game hunting in the then wilderness of Van Zandt, Silas Parker usually carried along his old

shotgun so as to kill fat venison by the way. In talking, Silas Parker stut-
tered. Late in the fifties or just before the civil war, the news spread over
the thinly settled settlement that an Indian woman had come to live
with Silas Parker.... One thing we distinctly remember, she never mixed
with other people. We have no recollection of her ever being absent from
her Uncle's little log cabin by the big spring of water ... 27 miles west of
Tyler, 30 miles southeast from Wills Point, 16 miles southeast of Canton
and about 16 miles north, a little east of Athens."[23]

Cynthia Ann did not live with Silas and Ann very long. On April 1,
1862, Silas was mustered into the Confederate Army. Ann was left with
three young children and was pregnant with a fourth. She also had to constantly watch Cynthia Ann or she would walk off down the road "going
home, just going home." Ann would also try to prevent Cynthia Ann from
slashing her arms and breasts. One day Cynthia got hold of a butcher knife
and cut off almost all of her hair. It was too much for the young wife.[24]

Then Cynthia Ann and Prairie Flower went to live with Cynthia Ann's
younger sister Orlena, who was married to J. R. O'Quinn. The O'Quinns
lived a short distance from Silas on Slater's Creek near Asbury Chapel in a
heavily wooded area with small clearings here and there. A number of other
relatives lived in the same vicinity, including Cynthia Ann's aunt Phebe
Parker Anglin, who was married to Adrian Anglin. Cynthia Ann recognized Adrian as well as several others from her past. At first she and Prairie
Flower lived in the house with the O'Quinns, but since the cabin was
crowded and Cynthia Ann and Prairie Flower could not become accustomed to the food, the family built the two a separate house and started a
small farm for them, but Cynthia Ann did not till the soil.[25]

Adrian Anglin's daughter, Margaret, who had known Cynthia Ann before she was captured by the Comanches, spent a great deal of time with
her, and Cynthia Ann began to remember things from the distant past.
One day she revealed her painful memories of the Fort Parker massacre. A
relative named Tom W. Champion repeats Cynthia Ann's version of the
Fort Parker massacre:

> The whole earth was swarming with Indians and when they broke
> into the fort, Mrs. Parker and her three children and a Mrs. Rachel
> Plummer got out and started to leave. Cynthia Ann being the oldest, her
> mother gave her some money to carry in her apron. Mrs. Parker carried
> the baby. After they had gone some distance they saw the Indians com-

GENEALOGY 3
Silas M. Parker Family

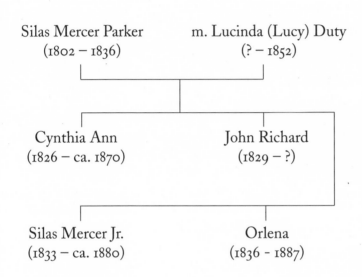

Silas Mercer Parker
(1802 – 1836)

m. Lucinda (Lucy) Duty
(? – 1852)

Cynthia Ann
(1826 – ca. 1870)

John Richard
(1829 – ?)

Silas Mercer Jr.
(1833 – ca. 1880)

Orlena
(1836 - 1887)

ing after them. Her mother told her to run out to one side and as she passed a certain bush to drop the money so the Indians would not notice it. They soon caught them and one took Cynthia Ann and the other took her brother, John, age 7 years, but did not molest her mother or the baby.

In those days ladies did not ride astride, and Cynthia Ann being raised very modest, the Indians had trouble getting her to ride the Indian's style. She said she would bite and scratch them, which would tickle them very much. As time passed she became more accustomed to the ways of the Indians. She said she had peeped through the wigwams several times and saw white men trying to ransom her out but she was forbidden to let them see her. She was taken by one band of Indians, and her brother by another.[26]

The Civil War was raging and times were hard in Texas. Many of the Parker, Anglin, and O'Quinn men went to war, and the women dragged out their old spinning wheels and looms and began to make clothing for themselves and for their loved ones on the front.[27] Cynthia Ann soon learned to spin, weave, and sew and was very good at it. She could tan a hide so that it was as soft as velvet, and soon people from all over the county were bringing her hides to tan. She was a hard worker and could chop wood as well as a man. Cynthia Ann "disliked a lazy person," and during those hard days while the men were away, the women worked far into the night. The women and children hunted for certain roots and herbs and gathered bark to be used for medicine. In the past the pioneers had relied upon the Indians to help them find remedies when no medicine was available. Perhaps Cynthia Ann knew plants and herbs that could be used for medicine. Cynthia Ann could speak English "when she wanted to," and she even learned to read and write, or perhaps she merely remembered what she had been taught before.[28]

Cynthia Ann still clung to her Indian customs. When a member of the family died, she would sing a plaintive mourning song and slash her body with a knife. The family would try to dissuade her from hurting herself but to no avail. One of the people she may have mourned was James Pratt Plummer. James Pratt had married twice (his first wife died) and was the father of four children. While serving in the Confederate Army, he died on November 17, 1862, in an army camp at Little Rock, Arkansas, of pneumonia brought on by typhoid fever. He was twenty-seven years old. Another cousin who died in the war was Ira Parker, Daniel's grandson.[29]

John Richard Parker, Cynthia Ann's brother, is also reported to have served in the Civil War as a civilian guide for John R. Baylor, lieutenant colonel of the 2nd Regiment of the Texas Mounted Rifles, who were originally charged with patrolling the road between Fort Clark and Fort Bliss. This story and others are unsubstantiated, and what actually happened to John in later life remains a mystery. The most widely circulated story is that John was unhappy with the whites and returned to live with the Comanches. While on a raid in Mexico, he became ill with smallpox and was abandoned by the Indians. A Mexican captive named Doña Juanita stayed with him and nursed him back to health. They married, and he became a rancher in Mexico, where he died in 1915. Cynthia Ann believed that John had died of smallpox before the Civil War began, as she revealed when she was interrogated at Pease River.[30]

Cynthia Ann's main problem seemed to be that she missed her sons and worried about them. The life of an orphan Comanche child was hard and would be especially so for her half-white sons. The family had promised that they would take her back to the tribe when the Civil War was over, and reportedly she lived on that hope.[31] Accounts vary about her adjustment. Champion reports: "Some think she was broken-hearted and never enjoyed life after she was parted from the Indians but this is a mistake in part. It is true that mother love for her Indian children would never die and memories of the wild and roving life of the Indians so vastly different to the white men's ways of living would cause her to fall into melancholy moods for a while, but this became less frequent as she became more accustomed to her environment." Antonio Hernández, who claimed to have been Ross's interpreter at Pease River, states in a letter to J. H. Beaty of Margaret, Texas, "After taking her to her brother and sister she became reconciled and remained with them." On the other hand, one of the neighbors remembered her sitting on the porch rocking Prairie Flower with tears rolling down her cheeks. But Cynthia Ann spent most of her time in the house trying to avoid the stares of the gawkers who would ride by the house trying to get a glimpse of the "white squaw."[32]

Champion describes Cynthia Ann's appearance: "She was a very pretty woman, about five feet, seven inches tall, weight 135 pounds, well built, beautiful blue eyes, light hair and a very fair and sunny disposition." T. J. Cates, a neighbor, says of her: "She looked to be stout and weighed about 140 pounds; well made. . . . She had a wild expression and would look down when people looked at her. . . . She was an open-hearted, good woman, and always ready to help somebody."[33] According to another family member, she was not difficult, just sad and mourning. Also, Cynthia Ann loved children.

Meanwhile, Prairie Flower was thriving. She played with the other children, and soon she was chattering in English more often than Comanche. Cates describes her: "Almost every Sunday my wife would carry the little Indian girl, Tecks Ann, visiting. She was pretty and smart and about three years old the last time we saw her." When Prairie Flower became old enough, she attended the school at Asbury Chapel and was an excellent student.[34]

Just as the Civil War was ending, Cynthia Ann was struck the final blow. Prairie Flower died of pneumonia caused by influenza in 1864. Still her family made no move to take her back to her sons. The O'Quinns moved to Anderson County near present-day Frankston and took Cynthia Ann with them. She lived six years longer. In 1870 she died "quietly," some said of influenza, others said of a broken heart. She was buried in Fosterville Cemetery near Frankston.[35]

Tom Champion gives his view of Cynthia Ann's life: "I don't think she ever knew but that her sons were killed and to hear her tell of the happy days of the Indian dances and see the excitement and pure joy which shown on her face, the memory of it, I am convinced that the white people did more harm by keeping her away from them than the Indians did by taking her at first."[36]

PART V

QUANAH

↤↦ CHAPTER 14 ↤↦

Thirsting for Glory

I N THE DISTANT REACHES of the Great Plains, a young boy was caught in a vast whirlpool that was drawing him closer and closer to its center, but he continued to struggle against the forces of white civilization.

Cynthia Ann's concern about her sons was justified. Because the buffalo herds were diminishing, and the rangers and soldiers had destroyed a large part of the food, homes, and clothing of the Comanches in the Battle of Pease River, some members of the band suffered greatly during the winter of 1860–61. Quanah later said: "As soon as the main body of Indians could get ready, they moved back north where they wintered from the Washita [River] to the Wichita mountains. They suffered much for provisions, as they were entirely north of the buffalo." After the death of Nocona, Quanah and Peanuts were cared for by Nocona's Indian wife, who had no children. The little family had no near relatives, and in Quanah's words, "We were often treated very cruelly as orphans of Indians only are treated."[1]

When Quanah was about thirteen years old, his Indian mother died, and his life became even harder. He says, "It then seemed to me I was left friendless. I often had to beg for food and clothes, and could scarcely get any one to make or mend my clothes. I at last learned that I was more cruelly treated than the other orphans on account of my white blood."[2] Horseback, who claimed to have been head chief of the Comanches for thirty-two years and may have been jealous of Quanah, said that the young orphan was called Quanah, which was interpreted as "stink" because of his white heritage.[3]

Quanah remembered other things from the distant past, such as the story his mother had told him about his birth. His tribe was at war with the Navajos in about 1849, and most of the men had gone to the Pecos River valley to fight. Cynthia Ann, who was about nineteen years old, was camped

on Elk Creek in the Wichita Mountains with the other women and children and the men who had not gone to war. Quanah describes his birthplace: "In Southwest Oklahoma, in the southwest part of Kiowa County, in
the beautiful Wichita Mountains, is a little creek hid away beneath the
swaying branches of the Post Oak and Elm which cluster [on] its banks
from one end to the other end for a few yards on either side. This is Elk
Creek and on the banks of which I (Quanah) Parker was born."[4]

Two or three weeks after Quanah's birth, the band heard that some Navajos were nearby, and most of the warriors rode away to fight. Fearing an
attack, the people who were left behind moved down the creek bed to a
secluded place. They often traveled in the water to keep the Navajos from
tracking them, but in spite of their precautions, sixteen Navajos discovered
their hiding place and captured two hundred horses. The men who were
left in the village pursued the Navajos, recaptured the horses, and killed
three of the enemy.

The victorious group sent a messenger back to camp, and when the
warriors returned, they were met by women singing and dancing. The first
woman to greet them was an old woman who was given three scalps, which
she attached to the top of a pole and carried back to camp, dancing and
singing a song of victory.

That night a four-day dance began. The star of the show was the old
woman with the scalp pole, who danced alone with the trophies dangling
from the top of the pole. Four-week-old Quanah was attending his first
victory dance.[5]

Quanah remembered other things from the time when his father was
alive and before his mother was recaptured. As a young boy he killed small
game for his family—trapping small birds and shooting fish with his bow
and arrow—but food was scarce because the Texans were pushing into the
Comanches' hunting grounds. Quanah often went to bed hungry. Once
when he was seven or eight years old, a guest had been invited to eat. From
her meager larder Cynthia Ann had prepared some sausage-like meat, which
she had made into several large balls and one small one. She told Quanah
that they were having a guest for dinner and that he should "act nice and
not eat too much." The visitor arrived, and everybody sat down to eat.
Quanah was given a small piece of the meat, which he quickly devoured.
He watched attentively as the visitor slowly ate his large piece of meat.
When the visitor finished and reached for a second portion, the boy told
the man that he should not have two big pieces while Quanah had only one
little one. The visitor gave Quanah the piece of meat, but it was so large

that Quanah could not eat it all. After the visitor had left, Cynthia Ann and Nocona crammed the meat into Quanah's mouth, forcing him to eat the rest of it. Quanah said, "I never spoke that way to a visitor any more."[6]

There were the good times. When Quanah was about nine years old, his people were camped on the Arkansas River. In the early part of the spring about three hundred of them, mostly women and children, decided to go to Santa Fe to trade. Quanah was given a spotted pony for the journey. Underground springs had loosened the soil in the riverbed, creating quicksand that could easily swallow a horse and rider. One day as the Comanches crossed the Arkansas River, Quanah's pony became bogged in the sand. Since Quanah was unwilling to abandon his mount, both were about to go under when a young man arrived who quickly threw a rope around the pony's neck and pulled the two out.

Everyone was dressed in buckskin and buffalo skins. The children wore deerskin tunics fringed on the sleeves and around the bottom. Little pieces of metal were attached to the fringe and to their moccasins so that they jingled as they walked or rode along. The young men acted as scouts, carefully surveying the countryside in all directions.[7]

One day as the travelers were eating their noon meal in a little canyon a short distance from the trail, the scouts rode into camp and reported that the Comanches were being followed by a group of soldiers with about 150 wagons. The braves quickly prepared to fight. Smearing their faces and bodies with paint, they donned their headdresses and other finery, gathered up their shields, bows, arrows, butcher knives, tomahawks, and lances and rode out to meet the government caravan. As the warriors approached, the soldiers raised a white flag. Knowing the white flag meant peace, the warriors shook hands with the soldiers. The leader told the Comanche warriors that they were friends and were sent by the White Father to help them. The soldiers then pulled hundreds of sacks out of the wagons and gave them to the Indians. The soldiers rode away but camped nearby. In a short while, the women and children cautiously crept out of the canyon to inspect the gifts from the White Father. The Indians opened the sacks and found salt, meat, flour, beans, and sugar, but fearing that the food was poisoned, they poured everything on the ground and kept the sacks to use in making clothing. The children were forbidden to touch anything, but Quanah stuck his finger into some sugar and licked it. He liked it, but Cynthia Ann would not let him eat much of it.

That night the soldiers were camped nearby, and the Indians visited them. Sometimes in this type of situation articles were traded, and often the women and children begged for sweets. Fearing trouble if the soldiers found out that Cynthia Ann was a white woman, Nocona painted her black and told her to keep away from the soldiers. The next day the soldiers and the Comanches remained in camp, but the following day the soldiers packed up and headed west. They promised to supply the Comanches with provisions if they would travel with the wagons. Quanah did not say whether or not the band accepted the offer.[8]

Finally the Comanche band reached Santa Fe and set up their lodges outside the town. The Comanches had traded in Santa Fe for many years. Although the town was now a part of the United States, it had changed little since the summer of 1837 when Rachel Plummer had wearily ridden through the narrow streets and into the square. Most of the same houses, churches, and shops were still standing, their crumbling adobe walls again in need of repair and a coat of whitewash. The Governor's Palace still faced the square, and on the southeast corner of the plaza was the home converted into a hotel where Rachel had stayed with the Donohos until they all fled to Missouri during the riots in the summer of 1837. Cynthia Ann did not see the impressive churches or Palacio del Gobierno because Nocona again smeared her face with smut and instructed her to stay out of sight.[9]

At one time when Nocona went to the square to trade, he obtained a watermelon. He took it to the camp and showed it to his family. It was the first one Quanah had seen. He tasted a little of it and enjoyed it very much. He says of the experience, "The more I ate of it the more I wanted."[10]

According to Quanah, while the Comanches were camped outside Santa Fe, Cynthia Ann gave birth to her second son, whom she named Peanuts. Quanah explains the name, "My mother named him Peanuts because of a childish remembrance of the good things she had enjoyed around the fireside at Fort Parker before she was captured by the Indians. A few names like this and an occasional visit to the Indian encampment by white traders was all that prevented my mother from forgetting her people entirely." Quanah must have confused the birth of Peanuts with that of Prairie Flower, who was born at about this time.[11] Quanah also states that Nocona had three wives, "one Indian, one Mexican, and one white woman, my mother."

Quanah had another vivid memory of his childhood. He was about twelve years old, and the Comanches were attending a peace conference. Quanah and some of his friends were practicing shooting their bows and arrows a short distance from the meeting. An old white man approached them and began talking to Quanah, who was distinguishable because of his gray eyes. The man asked if Quanah's mother had called him Quanah. When he said yes, the man asked to see his arms. Quanah rolled up his sleeves and showed the man a scar in the form of a cross, caused by a smallpox vaccination. The man then asked Quanah if his mother was a white woman. Quanah told him that she was and refused to talk further with the white man, but when the man left, he gave the boy a note and a small white flag, telling Quanah that "if my people ever went to battle with the white folks and I were in danger, for me to raise that flag and my little brother and I would not be harmed. He told me to give the note to the person who captured me, and I would be cared for." Quanah tore the note to pieces, threw them to the ground, and gave the flag to his girlfriend.[12]

When Quanah was about fifteen, he decided to go on the warpath. He says: "It was my father's wish, that I should go to war at an early age. My father had taught me not to be afraid of work or flee from an enemy." A friend of Nocona's gave Quanah the equipment he needed, "such as bow and arrows and a tomahawk."[13]

About thirty braves rode out of the camp near the Santa Fe Trail in southwestern Kansas. Their destination was San Antonio, which Quanah called Fort Sam Houston. They rode across the Staked Plains and then the Edwards Plateau until they reached a place in the Hill Country about three days' journey by foot from San Antonio. They found a secluded area, un-saddled their horses, hobbled them, and proceeded on foot. It was night when they approached San Antonio. They came to the house of a white man. No one was at home, but in a cornfield they found three horses, which they stole.

They continued moving south for about four miles until they came to four houses, where they stole fifteen more horses, and then camped for the night. At daybreak they killed a cow and ate some of the meat for breakfast. Climbing a hill, the braves watched all day to see if they were being fol-lowed. They saw no one, so the next night they captured more than twenty horses and returned to the same camp, where they spent the night. At about nine o'clock the next morning, they saw two men driving a cart down the road. They hid in the brush and, as the men approached, ambushed them. Between them the white men had only one pistol, and the Comanches easily killed and scalped them. Quanah and the others spent the rest of the day on the same hill watching to see if they were being pursued. In the evening they spied a group of horsemen following their trail. As soon as night fell, the warriors headed north, keeping in the wooded areas. After three days of "forced marching," the braves reached the place where they had left their horses and saddles. Retracing their steps, they returned home with their two scalps and the large herd of stolen horses. Their victorious return was celebrated with a huge war dance.

A week later, another war party rode out. This time Quanah was acting as squire to the chief. Sixty warriors left their camp in western Oklahoma headed for New Mexico. Crossing the High Plains, they turned south, traveling along the Pecos River and then the Peñasco River in southwestern New Mexico.

One day the Comanches came upon a lone Mexican traveling in a wagon drawn by two oxen. They killed and scalped him, took his meager provisions, demolished the wagon, and turned the oxen loose since they were too thin to eat. Then they traveled farther south and camped on the Peñasco River. The next day they followed the river until they came to a place that Quanah called Fort Peñasco. They climbed to the top of a hill and watched the fort for two days. Seeing no one, they decided to head for Fort Stanton, sixty miles north in the Sacramento Mountains.

While the Comanches were lying hidden in the mountains north of Fort Stanton, they saw a company of cavalry headed north. The soldiers halted, made camp, and sent three men to guard a herd of sixty gray mules and three horses while they grazed about three miles from camp. The Comanches swooped down and captured the herd, but the three soldiers escaped and alerted the main company.

The Indians tried to escape but were hampered by the large herd of livestock, and since the mules could not move fast, the braves were soon overtaken by the soldiers. The chief instructed Quanah and three other men to drive the herd into the mountains while the other fifty-seven warriors held off the soldiers. The Indians stationed themselves in a pass between two mountains and hid behind rocks and trees to fire upon the soldiers. The Comanches and soldiers fought for two hours with no casualties on either side. Since night was coming on, the soldiers retreated back to camp. The braves traveled northeast all night through the mountains and by daylight had reached the edge of the plains, stopping just long enough to eat some raw buffalo meat for breakfast in a canyon in the foothills.

They traveled on the plains all day and into the night, and when they finally stopped, men, horses, and mules were exhausted. The braves camped in a large circle with the mules and horses in the center. Everyone slept so soundly that by morning the mules and horses had walked out of the circle and were grazing as much as half a mile from the camp. It was well past sunup by the time the men gathered up the horses and mules, ate a breakfast of buffalo meat, and continued on their way. At noon they arrived at a waterhole that Quanah called Lost Lake. The tired braves rested and feasted on fish and ducks until the next day, when they headed toward home again. They reached the village in a few days, and another war dance was held. This one lasted for two or three days.[14]

Quanah and his friends were not the only Indians who were raiding, and as the years passed, the situation worsened. In 1867 a spring military campaign against the Plains Indians had proved a dismal failure. Nathaniel G. Taylor, commissioner of Indian Affairs, summarized in his annual report for the year of 1868 what had happened: "On the 19th of April, 1867, a military command burned the peaceful village of the Cheyennes on Pawnee Fork, Western Kansas, who had been at peace with us since the treaty of 1865, on the Arkansas, and were on lands assigned to them by that treaty. The Cheyennes flew to arms and the war of 1867 followed, in which we lost over 300 soldiers and citizens, several millions in expenses and an immense amount of public and private property, and killed it is believed six Indians and no more."[15]

After three months of bloodshed, the government leaders decided to try negotiation, and on July 20, 1867, Congress passed an act establishing the Indian Peace Commission. The original members of the commission were Nathaniel G. Taylor, commissioner of Indian Affairs; John B. Henderson, chairman of the Senate Commission on Indian Affairs; Generals William T. Sherman, William S. Harney, and Alfred H. Terry; and civilians John B. Sanborn of Minnesota and Samuel F. Tappan of Colorado.[16]

In August of 1867 the commissioners met in St. Louis and decided that the Plains Indians must be removed from the area of the "great roads of the Plains" and placed on reservations. The next step was to assemble as many representatives of the tribes as possible in one place and convince the Indians to sign a treaty.[17]

The place decided upon was a site on Medicine Lodge Creek in Kansas near where the Kiowas often held their annual medicine dance. The council grounds were situated in a valley surrounded by timber with good camping places to accommodate a large number of people and with plenty of grass for the vast horse herds of the Indians. When the commissioners arrived, some of the Indians had encamped a few days earlier and were going about their daily business. The men were talking or gambling, and the women were bringing in wood and water, sewing, cooking, or working on buffalo hides, and one woman was delousing her child. When the Indians became hungry, they would go to a large black kettle boiling on a campfire and, using a wooden spoon, eat out of the pot. After most of the Indians had arrived, a correspondent named Soloman T. Bulkley wrote this description for his readers back in New York City: "Five thousand Indians have assembled . . . in their glory of paint, rags, deerskin leggings, vermin-covered blankets, and dirty bodies, never washed except by the rains of heaven."[18]

After some preliminary ceremonies, the first general council began on October 19, 1867. One of the many reporters covering the council was Welsh-born Henry Morton Stanley, who later became famous for finding Dr. David Livingstone in Africa and greeting him with the words, "Dr. Livingstone, I presume?" Stanley was an accomplished journalist who took shorthand. He describes the setting for the council:

> A great clearing had been made in the centre of a grove of tall elms
> for the convenience of the grand council. Logs had been arranged so as
> to seat the principal chiefs of the Southern nations, and tables had been
> erected for the accommodation of the various correspondents. In front
> of these tables were the seats ranged in a semicircle for the Commis-
> sioners. Facing the Commissioners were a few of the most select chiefs
> of the different tribes. Beyond all were the ponies of the chiefs, forming
> a splendid background to the scene. Over the space allotted to the Com-
> missioners and the press were placed a few branches as a shelter from
> the sun.[19]

Quanah was about eighteen years old when he attended the council. Because of his youth, he would not have been included in the semicircle of chiefs, but he may have been one of the young men who sat on their horses or lounged on the ground a short distance away. Stanley continues his description: "At 10 A.M. the council was opened by Fishermore, the lusty crier of the Kiowa nation, who with a loud voice counseled the tribes to do right above all things."[20]

The first speaker was Senator Henderson, chairman of the Senate Commission on Indian Affairs. Henderson gave a long speech, saying in part:

> Our friends of the Cheyenne, Comanche, Apache, Kiowa, and Arapa-
> hoe nations, the Government of the United States and the Great Father
> has sent seven Commissioners to come here and have a talk with you.
> Two years ago the Government entered into a treaty with you at the
> mouth of the Little Arkansas, and we hoped then that there would be no
> war between us. . . . At present we have only to say that we are greatly

rejoiced to see our red brethren so well disposed towards peace. We are especially glad because we as individuals would give them all the comforts of civilisation, religion, and wealth, and now we are authorised by the Great Father to provide for them comfortable homes upon our richest agricultural lands. We are authorised to build for the Indian schoolhouses and churches, and provide teachers to educate his children. We can furnish him with agricultural implements to work, and domestic cattle, sheep, and hogs to stock his farm. We now cease, and shall wait to hear what you have to say, and after we have heard it, we will tell you the road to go.

The next man to speak was Satanta, chief of the Kiowas. Satanta had a folding chair upon which he sat, and before he began to speak, he put his hands in the loose dirt on the ground and rubbed sand over them to clean them. Then he went to each man and shook his hand. Impressive in appearance, he was a gifted orator, skillful in delivery and eloquent in his choice of words. He addressed the gathering: "The Commissioners have come from afar to listen to our grievances. My heart is glad, and I shall hide nothing from you." As usual, Satanta denied all wrongdoing:

> The Cheyennes are those who have been fighting with you. They did it in broad daylight, so that all could see them. . . . All the land south of the Arkansas [River] belongs to the Kiowas and Comanches, and I don't want to give away any of it. I love the land and the buffalo, and will not part with any. I want you to understand also that the Kiowas don't want to fight, and have not been fighting since we made the treaty. I hear a good deal of fine talk from these gentlemen, but they never do what they say. I don't want any of these medicine homes built in the country; I want the papooses brought up just exactly as I am. . . . I have told you the truth. I have no little lies hid about me, but I don't know how it is with the Commissioners; are they as clear as I am? A long time ago this land belonged to our fathers, but when I go up to the river I see a camp of soldiers, and they are cutting my wood down, or killing my buffalo. I don't like that, and when I see it my heart feels like bursting with sorrow. I have spoken.

Ten Bears, chief of the Yamparika Comanches, was then asked to speak. He declined, telling the commissioners: "Of myself I have no wisdom, but I expect to get some from you; it will go right down my throat."

Silver Brooch, chief of the Penateka Comanches, calmly delivered a scathing speech against the white man and his reservations:

> I have come away from down south to see and hear you. A long time ago the Penekdaty Comanches were the strongest band in the nation. The Great Father sent a big chief down to us, and promised medicines, houses, and many other things. A great, great many years have gone by, but those things have never come. My band is dwindling away fast. My young men are a scoff and a byword among the other nations. I shall wait till next spring to see if these things shall be given to us; if they are not, I and my young men will return to our wild brothers to live on the prairie. I have tried the life the Great Father told me to follow. He told me my young men would become strong, but every spring their numbers are less. I am tired of it. Do what you have promised us, and all will be well. I have said it.[21]

On the second day the council began shortly before noon. Twelve Osage chiefs who had recently arrived shook hands with everybody and sat down. Ten Bears then spoke:

> There is one thing which is not good in your speeches; that is, building us medicine houses. We don't want any. I want to live and die as I was brought up. I love the open prairie, and I wish you would not insist on putting us on a reservation. We prefer to roam over the prairie when we want to do so. If the Texans were kept from our country, then we might live upon a reserve, but this country is so small we cannot live upon it. The best of my lands the Texans have taken, and I am left to shift as I can best do. If you have any good words from the Great Father I shall be happy to hear them.

Satanta spoke next. After Satanta's speech, he and Ten Bears became embroiled in a heated argument, and Satanta stalked off. The warrior spectators, many of whom were drunk, joined in the altercation, creating a great deal of confusion. Satanta eventually returned, and he and Ten Bears continued to argue. Order was finally restored. According to correspondent Milton Reynolds, the bad temper of the Indians was caused by their growing realization that they would no longer be allowed to roam freely over the plains.

The last speech of the day was delivered by Senator Henderson, who at last got down to basics:

We say to you that the buffalo will not last for ever. They are now becoming few, and you must know it. When that day comes, the Indian must change the road his father trod, or he must suffer, and probably die. We tell you that to change will make you better. We wish you to live, and we will now offer you the way. . . . We are your best friends, and now, before all the good lands are taken by whites, we wish to set aside a part of them for your exclusive home. On that home we will build you a house to hold the goods we send you; and when you become hungry and naked, you can go there and be fed and clothed. To that home we will send a physician to live with you and heal your wounds, and take care of you when you are sick. There we will also send you a blacksmith to shoe your ponies, so that they will not get lame. We will send you a farmer to show your people how to grow corn and wheat, and we will send you a mill to make for you meal and flour.

Every year we will send to the warehouse a suit of clothing for each of your men, women, and children, so that they will not suffer from the cold. We do not ask you to cease hunting the buffalo. You may roam over the broad plains south of the Arkansas River, and hunt the buffalo as you have done in years past, but you must have a place you can call your own. . . . We propose to make that home on the Red River and around the Wichita mountains, and we have prepared papers for that purpose. Tomorrow morning, at nine o'clock, we want your chiefs and head men to meet us at our camp and sign the papers.[22]

The following morning, October 21, 1867, the Kiowa and Comanche chiefs made their marks on the treaty. The Comanches were Ten Bears, Painted Lips, Silver Brooch, Standing Feather, Gap in the Woods, Horseback, Wolf's Name, Little Horn, Iron Mountain, and Dog Fat. Quanah gives his opinion of the council: "I was at the Medicine Lodge Council. I had been on the warpath against the Navajo and met a small village of Cheyenne who told us the soldiers were coming with beeves, sugar, coffee, and other things and were going to have a big council. I went and heard it. There were many soldiers there. The council was an unusual one, a great many rows. The soldier chief said, 'Here are two propositions. You can live on the Arkansas and fight or move down to the Wichita Mountains and I will help you but you must remember one thing and hold fast to it and that is you must stop going on the warpath. Which one will you choose? All the chiefs chose to move down here.'"[23]

The 1867 Treaties of Medicine Lodge did not solve the conflict between the Indians and the whites, and a year later the infamous Battle of the Washita was perpetrated by the whites. In November of 1868, thousands of Comanches, Cheyennes, Kiowas, Arapahos, and Apaches were camped along the banks of the Washita River for more than twelve miles.[24] General Philip Sheridan, who supposedly remarked, "The only good Indians I ever saw were dead," which was later paraphrased to "the only good Indian is a dead Indian," decided that Black Kettle's village of Cheyennes needed to be annihilated. Black Kettle was trying to "follow the white man's road" but could not restrain his young men from raiding. Black Kettle had learned of the proposed attack and had gone with another Cheyenne chief and two Arapaho chiefs one hundred miles down the valley of the Washita to Fort Cobb to talk to General William B. Hazen. Black Kettle asked for permission to move his 180 lodges to a location near Fort Cobb or Fort Sill. Refused on both counts, he was told that if he kept his young men from raiding, his village would not be attacked. The Cheyenne and Arapaho leaders were issued sugar, coffee, and tobacco, and sent away. In spite of his promise to Black Kettle, Hazen knew that in a few days, Lieutenant Colonel George Armstrong Custer's troops would descend on the Cheyenne village.[25]

Sheridan was supported by his superior General Sherman, who wrote: "As brave men and as the soldiers of a government which has exhausted its peace efforts, we, in the performance of a most unpleasant duty, accept the war begun by our enemies, and hereby resolve to make its end final. If it results in the utter annihilation of these Indians it is but the result of what they have been warned again and again, and for which they seem fully prepared. I will say nothing and do nothing to restrain our troops from doing what they deem proper on the spot, and will allow no mere vague general charges of cruelty and inhumanity to tie their hands."

By November 27, 1868, the U.S. troops had located the Indian encampment on the Washita River and had prepared for an attack. The night was bitterly cold as the soldiers waited for the sun to light the way for the attack. In the dim light of dawn, the soldiers could see about forty white lodges in among the trees in a broad valley. Custer had decided on the same plan that he would later use at the Battle of the Little Big Horn—to divide the regiment and surround the village. The soldiers mounted their horses and the regimental band struck up an old song called "Garry Owen." Yelling and cursing and brandishing pistols, the soldiers charged into the snow-covered valley. One of the soldiers describes the scene: "On rushed these surging cavalcades from all directions, a mass of Uncle Sam's cavalry thirsting for glory."

Caught unawares, the Indians rushed out of their lodges with guns and bows in hand, but the cavalry were already upon them, charging between the lodges, shooting and slashing, and within ten minutes the village was taken. Small groups of Indians who had managed to escape fired at the soldiers from ravines and from behind trees. Most of these Indians were soon killed. Custer reported 103 fighting men killed, but other records indicate that only eleven warriors were killed, and the rest were women, children, and old men. Elderly Black Kettle and his wife were both slain. An eyewitness describes the camp and the surrounding area: "The battle is over and the field covered with dead animals and savages, muddy and smeared, and lying upon each other in holes and ditches. The field resembles a vast slaughter pen."

About ten o'clock, Custer noticed warriors on top of the hills near the valley. At the time he was busy supervising his men as they rounded up fifty-three prisoners, tallied up the loot, and then burned the village. More than eight hundred horses were slaughtered at Custer's command.

Noon approached. A squad of sixteen men led by Maj. Joel H. Elliot was missing. They had last been seen riding down the river in pursuit of a group of escaping Indians. Elliot had shouted as he rode away, "Here goes for a brevet or a coffin!" As the day wore on, the white men noticed that the Arapahos and the Cheyennes who had escaped had been joined by Comanches and Kiowas, and an ever increasing circle of warriors surrounded the valley. Skirmishes occurred from time to time. One of the soldiers had discovered that there were other villages upriver containing possibly thousands of inhabitants. Even though Major Elliot and his men were still missing, Custer ordered the soldiers and prisoners to mount their horses and prepare to depart. In a brilliant move, he ordered his command to line up in full formation, and with flags waving and the band playing "Ain't I Glad to Get out of the Wilderness," the troops marched straight toward the Indian villages. Custer's bluff worked, and the warriors soon dispersed as they rushed to protect their women and children. Under the cover of darkness, the soldiers doubled back and wearily started toward Camp Supply. In later years Custer was severely criticized for failing to ascertain the whereabouts of Elliot and his men, who as it turned out had been slaughtered and mutilated by Arapahos. Custer explained: "As it was not lacking but an hour of night, we had to make an effort to get rid of the Indians, who still loitered in strong force in the hills."[26]

Quanah gives his version of the events subsequent to the initial attack: "When we heard of the fight, all of our men hurried to the scene, but General Custer retreated when he saw so many of us coming. We did not get close enough to fight him. After several skirmishes without results, we returned to our camp and moved out on the plains and into the mountains near Santa Fe."[27]

At about this time, Quanah decided to follow the ancient path of the Comanche warrior, the Comanche War Trail to Mexico. He describes the preliminaries: "Tohausen was holding the pipe and we went to war in Chihuahua on the other side of the big river (Rio Grande). There were nine of us all riding mules. That was a long way to go and a horse soon gets tired so we rode mules."[28] The leader of the group was not a Comanche but a Kiowa. Described as "Quiet and unboastful," Tohausen was the nephew of the Great Tohausen, principal chief of the Kiowas for many years.[29]

The nine men set out from a Kiowa village located at the Antelope Hills on the Canadian River near the border of Texas and Oklahoma. The warriors headed southwest past the headwaters of the Red River, which Quanah called Big Sandy River, and made their way through the breaks up over the Caprock and onto the Staked Plains, which Quanah referred to as the "high flat country." As the mules strained to take the last step up the trail, suddenly the endless expanse of the Staked Plains lay before the eyes of the nine men—nothing but blue sky and grass billowing in the wind. Perhaps the wild flowers were blooming, presenting an endless sea of yellow, white, blue, and pink. The Indians knew every spring, pond, and lake on the Plains, but some of these watering places were seasonal, and others disappeared during an especially dry season, making the trip across the plains always a hazardous one. On this particular trip lack of water was a problem. On two separate occasions the men and the slowly plodding mules went without water for two days.[30]

Quanah does not give details of his route after he and the other men ascended to the High Plains, but they probably followed the main path of the ancient Comanche War Trail because of the water usually available at day-long intervals. After making their way across the Staked Plains for several days, the men would have descended at either Yellow House Canyon or Blanco Canyon near present-day Lubbock. The trail at this point was composed of a number of small trails that ran east of the Caprock for over one hundred miles, connecting the waterholes at points like those the whites called Tobacco Creek, Mooar's Draw, and Gholson Spring. A favorite stop on the trail was Big Spring, located in a canyon between steep walls of rock. The next waterhole was at Mustang Springs northeast of Midland. After that a long, grueling, often waterless two-day ride across the Chihuahuan Desert brought the raiders to the thousands of acres of sand now known as the Monahans Sandhills. Even in the shifting sands, the Comanches could identify certain places where they could always find water standing in pools or a few feet below the surface.[31]

The next important landmark on the trail was Horsehead Crossing on the Pecos River. Much of the lower Pecos valley was bounded on both sides by steep, towering cliffs, and the river had quicksand in some places and swift currents in others. One of the few places where the river could be crossed was Horsehead Crossing about twenty miles northwest of present day Girvin, Texas. Often Indian raiders returning from Mexico would push their horse herds unmercifully in order to elude any possible pursuers. The thirsty animals would drink the salty water of the Pecos, and some would die on the banks of the river from saline poisoning, while others would perish in the treacherous quicksand. Their skulls lined the shore, giving the crossing its name. For hundreds of years the next stop on the route to Mexico was Comanche Springs, the name given to half a dozen springs that poured forth thousands of gallons of water a day into a stream in a valley lined with trees and covered with lush grass and wildflowers. Quanah and his fellow warriors would not have the pleasure of spending several days in this valley because near the spring stood Fort Stockton, built in 1859, and within its confines were hundreds of U.S. soldiers. Never again would Indian raiders enjoy the icy waters of Comanche Springs.[32]

Quanah gives few details of the journey, saying only: "We traveled for a month. We did not go fast on account of the mules, and sometimes when we struck a good camp we remained in it 4 or 5 days until the mules got rested until finally we reached an Apache camp (Mescalero) and remained there for some time."[33]

The Mescaleros were a band of Apaches who lived in the mountains in West Texas, southern New Mexico, and northern Mexico. In 1856 they had been placed on a reservation in New Mexico, but some had escaped and returned to their mountain camps. Although for many years the Comanches had warred with the Mescaleros, an alliance had been established long before Quanah and the eight other men rode into the Mescalero camp. Since the Mescaleros occupied some of the mountainous area through which the War Trail passed, an alliance was certainly important to the raiders.[34]

This was probably the time when an important event occurred in

Quanah's life: he was introduced to peyote. The peyote ceremony was impressive. Enclosed in a large tepee filled with smoke from burning sage, the men sat all night, occasionally chewing peyote buttons, and dreaming strange dreams until the rising of the sun. A friend of Quanah's told the story of the young man's first experience with the drug:

> Quanah once eat one hundred. He did not know about mescal. He heard of it. He counted one hundred in the lodge in front of him and said to the mescal, "I hear about you. Maybe you make me see some medicine. I eat one hundred. If you do not help me make some medicine, I not eat your flesh any more." He gave them to the others to chew soft for him and to pray for him and he eat one hundred and he saw a man standing in front of him dressed in buckskin, yellow buckskin with a feather in his hair very pretty, and he looked at the man and saw that it was himself, and he heard the Mescal say. "Look at him, Quanah. I make him chief. He not afraid of me. I make him lead the people." He not chief at that time. Only poor weak man.[35]

Leaving the Mescalero camp to make their attack, Tohausen and his men proceeded along the portion of the Comanche War Trail that ran to Chihuahua. The trail forked north of Fort Stockton at Horse Mountain and ran for miles through the Chihuahuan Desert. One branch crossed the Rio Grande at the San Carlos Ford near present Lajitas, and the other crossed the big river at Paso del Chisos below the Chisos Mountains. These two branches ran through what is now known as the Big Bend. So called because of a sharp bend in the Rio Grande River, the area is an amazing compilation of different types of geological formations—mountains, canyons, flats, mesas, basins, rifts, uplifts, dikes, remains of volcanoes, lava beds, sheer stratified cliffs, and tall eroded standing rocks called hoodoos. According to an Indian legend, the Great Creator made the Earth, and when he was through, he took all the mountains and rocks left over and dumped them into the Big Bend.[36]

The Paso del Chisos route of the Comanche War Trail was spectacular. From Horse Mountain, the route ran south, crawling for miles across arid lands covered with tall tobosa grass. Springs created pools in deep, sandy creek beds lined with willows and cottonwoods.[37] The trail led through Persimmon Gap, where water could be found at Bone Spring, across grassy Tornillo Flat, and then east of the Chisos Mountains to water at Glenn Spring, an enormous spring in a valley tangled with willows and cattail rushes. The Paso del Chisos crossing of the Rio Grande was in a valley just west of Mariscal Mountain, where the river bottom was lined with natural flagstones, and the river was usually only four or five feet deep.[38]

The western fork of the War Trail ran to present-day Lajitas across a forbidding desert. In spite of the desolation, the Comanches could find an occasional spring as they followed the narrow valleys of Maravilla and Terlingua creeks. The hills around the creek beds provided a scene of strange beauty with alternating bands of white, blue, green, and purple clay.[39]

After Quanah and the eight other men crossed the Rio Grande, things started happening fast. Quanah describes the Chihuahua raid:

> Then we went on the warpath across the Rio Grande until we came near some high mountains when the leader said, "hobble the mules and turn them loose here. Put your saddles and robes on this tree.... We will go up on that mountain tonight."
>
> And the next morning at daylight we could see all around, there were streams running out of the mountains. Many white men's horses used this valley. Outside of the foothills was covered with cattle. We slept up there all day, and that night we went to look for horses. We were not trying to kill a man only looking for horses. As we travelled along we saw a light and crept up to it. It was a white man's house and we could hear the children talking. Tohausen said, "You stay here until I come back. I am going to look for horses." After a long time he came back, and said, "There are no horses there." Then we went looking for horses but did not find any and pretty soon Tohausen said, "We must go up in a mountain. It is pretty near daylight." So we went up on a mountain tired out.
>
> We kept going on that way for ten nights. Where the white man's houses are thick, they keep the horses hidden and they are hard to find. On the 10th night we found some horses and were saved. We started back traveling on the horses and one day we killed a calf. We had had nothing to eat for two days and everybody was hungry. We made a fire in a small creek bed and were turning the meat before the flames. Everybody hungry and watching the meat when someone looked up and said "Here come some Mexicans." There were 4 Mexicans coming who had not seen us yet. We threw the meat and the fire into the creek and Tohausen said, "Hide well in the brush and do not kill these men unless they find us. If they find us, kill them all and do not let one get away, for

we are here in the midst of these houses, and if one gets away and gives the alarm, the Mexicans will surround us and kill us all." We had a Mexican captive with us who understood their conversation. They were laughing and joking. We kept hidden until they rode off in a different direction without seeing us and we were saved.

We rode on until we got the mules and saddles and traveled back until we met a big Mescalero and Quahada Comanche camp where we stayed, for our mules were played out and our moccasins worn out. Here we met with another Kiowa warparty who told us the Kiowa village had moved to the forks of Wolf and Beaver Creeks when they started south.

One day our leader said, "I am going on the warpath into Mexico again. What are you going to do? Say plainly what your heart is. I am going to look for more horses." I and two other men said, "We are going back to the Kiowa village," so we started back across the Staked Plains. When we came to the head of Red River my mule played out, so I couldn't do anything with him. His ears lopped down and I put him away (abandoned him) and came on foot. The mules of the other two men were thin and only able to travel slowly. One day their ears lopped down and the others said to me, "You go on foot to the next creek and see if you see any signs."

I went on then to Salt Fork, that place the Kiowas often went to get salt at a salt spring where I looked for tracks. I saw some old horse tracks and I said, "these were made by a warparty." I next went over to Walnut Creek (North Fork of Red River) beyond the end of the mountains and looked for tracks but did not find any. There I waited for the other two men and we slept there that night.

Next day when the morning star was rising, I got up and the other two men said, "You go over toward the Washita and look for tracks on little creek this side and we will go on slower and will join you there." Then I went over a divide on to the head of a little creek that runs into the Washita. I went over on little creek and looked back but nobody came. I went to sleep and look again. Next morning nobody came. Maybe they passed by in the night or maybe they have lost their mules. I will go over to Washita. There I saw some people. They had no lodges but had horses, and I couldn't tell what people they were, so I crept down the bed of the stream until I could hear their talk and they were talking Kiowa. Then I spoke to them and they were astonished to see me and said, "You left a long time ago on the warpath and now you have come back." I said,

"Where is the Kiowa village?" and they replied, "You walk on foot down the river and you will get there before the sun goes down." And they packed their horses and we found a large village and my own lodge was with theirs.[40]

Quanah had risked his life on the Comanche War Trail and had returned with no horses—without even the mule he had ridden. The days of the Comanche War Trail were almost over.

⊰⊱ CHAPTER 15 ⊰⊱

It Was Quanah

DURING HIS LIFE Quanah was allied not only with the Kiowas and Mescaleros but also with several different bands of Comanches: the Penatekas and possibly the Noconis when he was a child and, as he grew older, the Quahadas and the Kotsotekas. As pressure from the whites increased and the number of Comanches steadily declined, the bands were merging. Quanah describes two battles he participated in after the Battle of the Washita. In both battles he fought as part of bands which were composed mostly of Kotsotekas and Quahadas. Evidently, Quanah spent most of his time between 1868 and 1872 with the bands of Mowway and Parraocoom.

After the Battle of the Washita, the Plains Indians were becoming more and more alarmed. Some did as they had agreed in the 1867 Treaties of Medicine Lodge—ceased their depredations and took up residence on the reservations—but others continued to raid. Mowway expressed his opinion about reservations: "When the Indians in here are treated better than we are outside, it will be time enough to come in." To compound the problem, the Indians on the reservation failed to receive the food, supplies, and other goods and services promised to them at Medicine Lodge because of Congress's delay in passing the bill authorizing the expenditures. On July 20, 1868, eight months after the signing of the treaties, Congress finally approved an appropriation of five hundred thousand dollars. Meanwhile, the Indians on the reservations were destitute, and others had left to resume their nomadic lives.

Another blow for the Comanches was the Battle of Soldier Spring on December 25, 1868. A band of Noconi Comanches camped near the western end of the Wichita Mountains were defeated by two hundred soldiers. Although no Indians were killed, sixty lodges and several tons of buffalo meat as well as a number of cooking utensils, weapons, and buffalo robes

Mowway, Comanche chief. Courtesy the Smithsonian Institution.

were burned or thrown into a pond. Even the girls' buckskin dolls and doll clothes were thrown into the flames. The principal chief of this band was Horseback, who was trying to follow the white man's road. At the time of the attack, he was probably at Fort Cobb.[1]

General Sheridan's winter campaign was having an effect, and in January of 1869, several weeks after the Battle of Soldier Springs, the Quahadas and some of the Kotsotekas sent a message to the commander at Fort Bascom in eastern New Mexico stating that they wanted to surrender to Colonel

George W. Getty in Santa Fe. Colonel Getty replied that they had to report in at Fort Cobb in Indian Territory, just like everybody else. The
Quahada and Kotsoteka leaders were probably hoping to get a reservation
in the plains area of eastern New Mexico, which was the western portion of
their hunting grounds. When Mowway and a number of other leaders
showed up at Fort Bascom they were instructed to report to Colonel Getty
in Santa Fe. After a March 6, 1869, conference in Santa Fe, the chiefs became alarmed and attempted to escape, but they were captured and transported to Fort Cobb.[2]

While the older men were trying to cope with a changing world, the
young men were still following the old ways, trying to steal horses so that
they could obtain wives, increase their economic and social status, and aug-
ment their prestige as warriors. In the summer of 1869, Quanah in a company of sixty-three Indians and "some Mexicans" left Santa Fe, New Mexico,
in order to raid in southwest Texas. Quanah gives a lengthy account of his
adventures. The Indians and Mexicans wound through the mountains surrounding Santa Fe and headed across the plains in the blazing heat of summer. After traveling for a number of days, they reached the Concho River.
Riding in the river valley, they came to within two miles of Fort Concho,
where they noticed a camp of cowboys. Quanah and his friends hid themselves in the rocks and bushes and waited until dark. Then in the moonlight the braves stampeded the horses, which fled in every direction. The
raiders captured only the fat horses, letting the lean ones go. The cowboys
fired shots into the darkness but hit no one.

The band continued south, traveling by night on a well-worn trail that
led to Mexico. The next night they reached a point about fifty miles west of
San Antonio, where they camped.

The warriors then headed southeast looking for prey. They found a lone
man driving an ox team and shot him with guns they had obtained in Santa
Fe. The sound of the shots aroused the neighbors, who quickly rounded up
a group of thirty men to chase Quanah and his companions. Since the
white men had long-range guns, the raiders quickly fled. Quanah purposely
fell behind and, turning his horse, hid in the bushes beside the trail. As two
of the pursuers rode by, he wheeled his horse out of the bushes and plunged
his spear into one of the men and then the other, killing both. Most of the
braves had stopped to watch what Quanah was going to do. When they
saw his success, they regrouped and charged the Texans, who were forced
to dismount and take cover behind some rocks. After a short gun battle,
the warriors ran out of ammunition and gave up the fight. They returned to

a river that Quanah called the San Salvador River, probably the San Saba River, and held a war council. The leaders were so impressed with Quanah's bravery that he was made a war chief.

At this place the band divided and some of the men went home. Quanah, covered with glory and full of his new power, stayed to lead a raiding party into the Hill Country between San Antonio and present-day San Angelo. Quanah's men tried to avoid being followed by crossing a stream they called Stony Creek. After being joined by another group of raiders, they made their way through the rough, brushy country by riding in the creek bed, which had high bluffs on each side. Feeling they were safe, the men made camp for the night in a secluded spot near the creek. In the morning as they were preparing their breakfast, the air was suddenly filled with gunfire. Everyone fled except Quanah, his cousin, and a third warrior who hid in the bushes. Quanah and the third warrior started to pursue the soldiers while Quanah's cousin stayed behind because his horse was worn out. Soon the two overtook a cavalryman who had fallen behind. The soldier panicked and raced toward a bluff, which his horse proved unable to climb. Then he jumped from his horse and desperately tried to claw his way up the bluff. Quanah shouted to the other Indian, who still had some arrows, "Shoot him! Shoot him!" The Indian shot an arrow into the soldier, killing him instantly.

The warriors regrouped and continued to pursue the soldiers, who dismounted and took cover behind some rocks. When the soldiers started to fire, the braves, unable to return the gunfire, retreated and started for home. They traveled until noon, when Quanah spied some soldiers. From his scouts he later learned that the soldiers had been following them for several days. The warriors hurriedly retreated and traveled until midnight, when they stopped to sleep in a grove of trees on a creek. As Quanah unsaddled his horse and was placing his saddle on the ground for his pillow, one of his men crept up to him and whispered, "There's a soldier asleep under that tree over there." No one would volunteer to investigate, so Quanah crawled as silently as he could through the darkness. What he found was a large chunk of wood from a fallen tree.

The next morning the men rose early and stealthily continued their journey, passing near Fort Concho during the day. That night, in spite of great danger this posed, the men built a fire and smoked. In order to conceal the flames, they stretched blankets around the fire. Before lying down to sleep, Quanah said, "In the morning, when it is time to get up, don't let me call you a second time." When Quanah saw the morning star rise, he cried,

"Wake up," but there was no response. He called twice more, then went back to sleep himself.

When the men finally awoke, the band resumed the homeward journey, driving their extra horses in front of them as they made their way through the mountains. They did not know that death lay ahead. Quanah explains: "All of a sudden, we looked and could not see the horses for the blue smoke from the soldier's guns. All the loose horses disappeared, and we were pursued by five soldiers. We were soon scattered, and I came upon my cousin defending two braves on a pony that was almost given out. I helped him rout the soldiers and save our friends, but shortly after my cousin was killed."

Quanah procured a fresh horse for one of his men, and then the braves scattered in all directions, making it difficult for the soldiers to follow. The soldiers gave up the hunt, and Quanah had made another successful escape. Quanah says of the rest of the trip: "In a few days, we were all at home in Sante Fe. We moved our camp north several days journey into the mountains for fear the soldiers would attack us if we stayed in Santa Fe."[3] Quanah and his men had put up a good fight against the U.S. troops, but soon they would confront a much more dangerous foe, No-finger Chief.

In February of 1871, Colonel Ranald Slidell Mackenzie rode into Fort Concho and assumed command of the 4th Cavalry. Mackenzie was in many ways a strange man. Taciturn, strict, and demanding, he was not an easy man under whom to serve. Wounded six times in the Civil War, he was often in pain, especially when he was in the field in rainy, cold weather. High-strung, he slept little during a campaign and became more than usually irascible. He had lost two fingers on his right hand, and the Indians called him Bad Hand or No-finger Chief. Reportedly his fairness, unselfishness, sincere concern for his men, and brilliance as a tactician caused his men to hold him in the highest respect.

Mackenzie was born into a military family but one that had a blighted past. His father, Alexander Slidell Mackenzie, was captain of the ship *Somers* when he heard talk of a mutiny. Captain Mackenzie hanged three men, one of whom was the son of the secretary of war. Captain Mackenzie was court-martialed and acquitted, but his reputation was ruined.

Ranald Mackenzie attended West Point and graduated first in a class of twenty-eight. He performed brilliantly in the Civil War and was promoted to brigadier general at the age of twenty-four. President Ulysses S. Grant said of him: "I regarded Mackenzie as the most promising young officer in

Ranald Slidell
Mackenzie in the
1870s. Courtesy West-
ern History Collec-
tion, University of
Oklahoma Libraries.

the army." After the war was over, as was customary, Mackenzie's rank was
reduced and he became captain of engineers in the regular army, but by
1867 he had once again risen quickly to the rank of colonel. When he assumed command at Fort Concho, he was thirty years old. An unusually
handsome man, he was five feet, nine inches tall and had gray eyes and
thick, brown hair. He never married, and President Grant said of him: "In
social and garrison life he was modest and retiring but dignified, affable,
and courteous."[4]

When Mackenzie arrived at Fort Concho, the Indian situation was deplorable. The Quaker Peace Policy instituted by President Grant was not
working. Many tribes lived and farmed in Indian Territory, which included
almost all of the land in present-day Oklahoma, but some of the Plains
Indians were not ready to give up their old life. Raiding parties, and even
whole bands, slipped away back into their favorite camps in the fertile valleys of the canyons that cut into the plains. There they resumed their hunting and raiding, and the raids were more frequent and vicious than ever
before because of the Indians' resentment, frustration, and anger.

One band of Comanches had not signed the Treaties of Medicine Lodge and had never gone into the reservation. The Quahadas, renowned for their ferocity and skill as warriors, continued to inhabit their spectacularly beautiful campsites in the far western reaches of Comanchería.

In May of 1871, two of the principal Kiowa chiefs, Satanta and Big Tree, were arrested and imprisoned, but two of the largest bands of Comanches, those of Mowway and Parraocoom, were still at large, actively raiding on the Texas frontier. An August expedition led by Mackenzie against the Kiowas under Kicking Bird was a failure because the chief returned to the reservation and delivered up forty-one horses and mules, and Mackenzie was summarily ordered to cease his pursuit of the Kiowas.[5] Mackenzie still had high hopes for a major autumn expedition into the Comanche strongholds in the canyons on the headwaters of the Brazos River. In September of 1871, Mackenzie assembled his troops at the ruins of old Camp Cooper, where Cynthia Ann Parker had been held after her recapture. Eleven years earlier, it had been a substantial place with neat structures of pickets and stone. Having been abandoned for ten years, the camp was in ruins, but the site was still beautiful, trees lining the banks of the Brazos with its clear water untainted by gypsum and salt.[6]

By October 3, 1871, all the preparations for the expedition had been completed, and six hundred soldiers, twenty-five Tonkawa scouts, an immense wagon train, and one hundred pack mules pulled out of the camp. As the men rode, they sang the verses of their old regimental song, "Come home, John, don't stay long; Come home soon to your own Chick-a-biddy!" The scouts were following the usual procedure as described by Robert G. Carter in his memoirs: "The Indian scouts, our faithful Tonks, under Lieutenant P. M. Boehm, were far in advance, well fanned out, combing the country for trails, with a selected advance guard in close support if necessary, and to guard against surprise."[7]

The command rode west-northwest, deep into the heart of Comanchería. The troops passed through what is presently Stamford in northern Jones County, traveled close to the thirty-third parallel until they could see the Double Mountain in the distance, and then camped for the night.[8]

The next day, the men started moving early in the morning, bearing to the northwest. After crossing the Double Mountain Fork of the Brazos River, the command camped in present-day Stonewall County near Cottonwood Springs on Tonk Creek.[9] The column moved out early the next morning, still moving northwest toward the breaks of the Staked Plains. The shallow Salt Fork of the Brazos was easily crossed, and the column made good time traveling over rolling country with sparse vegetation, mostly mesquite and cactus. Finally, the soldiers reached the broken country on the edge of the Staked Plains, with its solitary mesas and hills scarred by erosion.[10]

The soldiers established camp on Duck Creek, which originated near present-day Spur. Believing the enemy to be near, Mackenzie wanted to make a night march and surprise the Comanches before they could escape. When night fell, the Tonkawa scouts were told to go out scouting singly to find the Comanche village. They at first refused because they were afraid that without soldiers accompanying them, they would be mistaken for hostiles and accidentally shot by some of the men of the command. "After much persuasion," they set out in the darkness.

Hour after hour Mackenzie and the men waited, but the Tonkawas did not return. The sun rose and set and still there was no sign of the scouts. Impatient and fearing that his prey was escaping, Mackenzie ordered a night march. The night was cloudy without any light from the moon or stars, and in the inky blackness, the men struggled up and down ravines until they found themselves in a box canyon facing a high rock wall. After several hours of struggling through gullies trying to find a way around, they gave up and made camp where they stood. The soldiers rose before daylight and in the first light found a way around the steep cliff. For five hours they struggled through ravines and up and down rocky hills. At nine thirty in the morning they reached the Freshwater Fork of the Brazos, now known as White River, and made camp.[11]

During the day, as the Tonkawas were coming back from their scout, they suddenly ran upon four Comanche spies who were watching the camp. The Tonkawas chased the spies, but the Comanches had better horses and soon escaped into the hills.[12]

Cohayyah was one of the Comanches in Parraocoom's band. He describes the preliminary phase of the conflict: "When I was a young man on the prairie we had fights. Once we were camped on White River near Quitaque, when our scouts reported that the soldiers were coming."[13] When Parraocoom's band of Comanches prepared themselves for battle, the chief would gallop among the lodges shouting for every boy twelve years old or older to arm himself and get ready to fight. Then he would instruct all women who did not have babies to care for also to get ready to fight. The older men and women and the women with babies were ordered to pack up everything and start moving to a prearranged destination. Warriors who had guns were placed in one company and those who had only bows and arrows were placed in another. The braves practiced their maneuvers, circling, charging, and retreating. They also practiced their riding skills, such as holding onto a horse's side while firing under the neck.[14]

Back at Mackenzie's camp, the Tonkawas had arrived and reported that they had found what they believed to be the trail to the Comanche village. At three o'clock in the afternoon, Mackenzie ordered the men to pack up and get ready to move. The men started up the twenty-five-mile-long Blanco Canyon, which was not a deep chasm but rather a broad, fertile valley with bluffs that were lower and not as spectacular as those in the more northerly canyons. The command camped about one hundred yards from the river in a "pocket valley" with high bluffs on one side and the river with its quicksand on the other.[15]

The men sat around the fires for a while discussing the events of the day. Then all lay down to sleep except the few who were on guard duty. Shortly before midnight, the quiet was shattered by a piercing yell, half a dozen gunshots, and then the terrifying whoops of hundreds of Comanche warriors. Quanah was leading an attack on Mackenzie's command.[16]

In later years, exaggerating the numbers somewhat, Quanah said: "Had big war. I fought General MacKenzie. He had 2000 men. I had 450 men. I use this knife. I see little further perhaps eight miles, lots soldiers coming. I say, 'Hold on—no go over there. Maybe we go at night. Maybe stampede soldiers' horses first.' I got my men around in circle and tell them, 'Holler.' I gathered maybe 350 United States horses that night."[17]

As the soldiers began firing upon the Indians, the flashes from their guns revealed that the bluffs were covered with Comanche warriors. The officers shouted at their commands, "Get to your horses! Every man to his lariat! Stand by your horses!" The frightened animals went into a frenzy, which Carter describes as one of the most terrifying experiences of his life:

> The horses and mules, nearly six hundred in number, could be seen rearing, jumping, plunging, running and snorting, with a strength that terror and brute frenzy alone can inspire. They trembled and groaned in their crazed fright, until they went down on their knees, straining all the time to free themselves from their lariats. As they plunged and became inextricably intermingled and more and more tangled up, the lariats could be heard snapping and cracking like the reports of pistols. Iron picket pins were hurtling, swishing and whistling, more dangerous than bullets. Men, crouching as they ran, vainly endeavored to seize the pins as they whirled and tore through the air, only to be dragged and thrown among the heels of the horses with hands lacerated and burnt by the ropes running rapidly through their fingers.[18]

The stolen horses and the victorious Indians galloped off into the night, and as Carter says, "The yells of the retreating Indians from the distance came back on the midnight air with a peculiar, taunting ring, telling all too plainly that the Quahadas, Quanah's wild band of Comanches, had been among us."[19] About seventy of the most valuable horses and mules had been stolen, among them Mackenzie's "gray pacer" and another fine horse that belonged to Mackenzie's adjutant. Cohayyah's description of the horse raid is succinct: "At night we ran off their horses; we got a lot of them."[20] Cohayyah also describes what was happening in the Indian camp:

[We] saw soldiers coming from the south. Parraocoom was leader. We were camping at White River [near] 2 peaks called Quitaque. We had our scout who came in and reported a big herd of soldiers coming. Parraocoom began to talk loud, saying, 'Get all your good fast horses up.' Everyone did so. We went. Parraocoom was a great big fellow with curly hair. Parraocoom said, 'When I was a young man, I meet things straight ahead. I want you people to do the same. Be brave.' Quite a lot of medicine men among us. Two men riding horses (medicine men) went out with Parraocoom. Then came back. The medicine man's name was Quitawowoqui. No one would listen to commands until Parraocoom gave the word.[21]

Back in Mackenzie's camp, Carter was checking the outlying guard stations. He rode across the Freshwater Fork, about four feet deep at that point, and made his way through the brush up to the edge of a bluff. When the men stationed there told Carter which way the Indians had gone, he recrossed the stream and rode to the top of a hill where another small squad of men were stationed. There he was joined by Captain E. M. Heyl and Lieutenant W. C. Hemphill, both of whom were accompanied by a few men. Although it was still dark, the soldiers could see about twelve Comanches driving a group of stolen horses. Without hesitation, the men galloped down the hill. They gained on the Indians and opened fire when the Indians suddenly disappeared into a ravine. The braves soon reappeared on the other side and made for a bluff Carter could see in the light of dawn. The soldiers followed, but the ravine was difficult to cross. The horses had to jump over a shelf, land safely in the ravine, and then scramble up the other side. Both Carter and Heyl had good horses, so they were soon on the other side of the ravine, but only twelve of the enlisted men followed the officers. The soldiers galloped across the valley toward the bluffs, and when they reached a high spot, they were horrified to see before them hundreds of Indians, who instantly let out war whoops and raced toward the stunned soldiers. The soldiers had been led into a trap.

Carter realized the soldiers could not make it back to the ravine because their horses were exhausted. He decided the troopers should dismount and fire at the Indians while trying to retreat to the ravine, all the while hoping that Mackenzie, who was about two miles away, would hear the gunfire and come to the rescue. Carter shouted his plan to Captain Heyl, who seemed dazed. Heyl, following Carter's lead, yelled to his men, "Deploy out on the run, men, and give them your carbines!" The fourteen men formed a long line on the prairie, and lying down in the grass began a "deliberate and steady fire." The Comanches, who were approaching in a headlong rush, slowed down and began to circle. Carter describes the scene that met the eyes of his desperate party:

> They were naked to the waist; were arrayed in all their war paint and trinkets, with head dresses or warbonnets of fur or feathers fantastically ornamented. Their ponies, especially the white, cream, dun, and claybanks, were striped and otherwise artistically painted and decorated with gaudy stripes of flannel and calico. Bells were jingling, feathers waving, and with jubilant, discordant yells that would have put to blush any Confederate brigade of the Civil war, and uttering taunting shouts, they pressed on to what they surely considered to be their legitimate prey. Mingled with the shouts, whoops, and yells of the warriors could be distinctly heard the strident screeching and higher-keyed piercing screams of the squaws, far in rear of the moving circles, which rose above the general din and hub-bub now rending the air. In the midst of the circling ponies we could see what appeared to be two standard bearers, but upon their nearer approach we discovered them to be two scalp poles gaily decorated with long scalp locks, probably of women, with feathers and pieces of bright metal attached which flashed in the morning light. There were also other flashes seen along their line which I afterward ascertained were small pieces of mirrors held in the hand and used as signals in the alternate advances and retreats, deployments and concentrations, in place of tactical commands. These were carried by the principal warriors or sub-chiefs, acting, I supposed, as file closers, squad leaders, etc. They had no squad, platoon, or company line formations, and no two, three, or four Indians were seen at any time to come together or bunch. While a general line was maintained at all times, it was always a line of right and

left hand circling, individual warriors with varying radii, expanding and contracting into longer or shorter lines, advancing or retreating during these tactical maneuvers.[22]

The fourteen U.S. soldiers were deployed in a long line across the valley. Carter's five men were dependable and steady, some of the best in the command, but Captain Heyl's troopers were untested in battle. Heyl and his men had horses that were in better shape than those of the men in Carter's group. Suddenly, one of Carter's men yelled, "Lieutenant, look over there, quick; they are running out!" Captain Heyl on his magnificent black horse was leading the fleeing soldiers. The Comanches were overjoyed, and a group of warriors quickly charged Carter and his five men, who found bullets and arrows flying all around them.

Carter then decided upon a new plan. The six men would all mount and, while still firing at the Indians, would slowly make their way back to the ravine. The soldiers crouched down on their horses and were making rapid progress, holding the Indians in check by the deadly fire from their guns. A Private Downey was wounded in the hand but continued to fire, felling a brave who had moved in for the kill. As the soldiers neared the ravine, Carter shouted, "Now, men, unlock your magazines, bunch your shots, pump it into them, and make a dash for your lives! It is all we can do!"[23]

In the face of the concentrated gunfire, the Comanches dropped back in confusion. The soldiers had galloped to within a short distance of the ravine when Private Seander Gregg, who was about fifteen yards behind Carter, screamed, "Lieutenant, my horse is giving out!" Turning his head to look, Carter saw the horse falter and then saw a group of Comanches surround Gregg. The leader of the group was striking:

> A large and powerfully built chief led the bunch, on a coal-black racing pony. Leaning forward upon his mane, his heels nervously working in the animal's side, with six-shooters poised in air, he seemed the incarnation of savage brutal joy. His face was smeared with black war paint, which gave his features a satanic look. A large, cruel mouth added to his ferocious appearance. A full-length head-dress or war bonnet of eagle's feathers, spreading out as he rode, and descending from his forehead, over and back, to his pony's tail, almost swept the ground. Large brass hoops were in his ears; he was naked to his waist, wearing simply leggins, moccasins and a breechclout. A necklace of bear's claws hung about his neck. His scalp lock was carefully braided in with otter fur, and tied with

bright red flannel. His horse's bridle was profusely ornamented with bits
of silver, and red flannel was also braided in his mane and tail, but being
black, he was not painted. Bells jingled as he rode at headlong speed,
followed by the leading warriors, all eager to out-strip him in the race. It
was Quanah, principal war chief of the Quahadas.[24]

Carter stopped and ordered the other four men to do the same. He tried
to help Gregg by shooting at Quanah with a pistol, but the chief was riding
back and forth using Gregg as a shield. Carter yelled, "Use your carbine!"
Gregg tried, but, weak with fright, he did not pull the lever hard enough,
and the cartridge jammed. Then Carter shouted, "Pull your six shooter!"
As Gregg reached for the weapon, Quanah put a pistol to Gregg's head and
pulled the trigger.

Cohayyah gives his version of the skirmish:

> When we made a charge, the soldiers commenced to fire. The bullets
> came toward us like the roar of a sling whirling through the air. Some of
> the soldiers were dismounted, some mounted. They were about 250 yards
> away. I was riding one horse and was trying to catch another. One of my
> friend's horses was shot while we were trying to change horses. We had
> one army gray horse, which we were leading, and my friend mounted it.
> None of us got hit. The medicine man must have been very powerful.
> We had great faith in him. . . . The colored men got behind. Some
> Comanche shot one off a horse. There were quite a few colored soldiers.
> They scalped this man. The scalp was no good, but we had a big celebra-
> tion dance over it anyway. The Texas soldiers' chief was No-Finger chief.
> I saw him that day and also later the next day.[25]

Carter and his four men expected to be surrounded and killed by the
forty warriors who had ridden to within a few yards of them, but suddenly
Quanah wheeled his horse and headed for the bluffs with his men close
behind him. Turning his head, Carter saw the reason for Quanah's retreat.
Lieutenant Boehm had heard the shots and with his Tonkawa scouts and
some other soldiers had come to the rescue of Carter and his companions.
Boehm shouted to Carter, "Bob, you take the left and I'll take the right of
the line. Let's push them now. Mackenzie is right in our rear."[26]

Carter describes the scene that was before his eyes, "In the rear of the
Indian lines could be seen the squaws now bring up led ponies, keeping up
their shrill, discordant screeching and screaming, and at the base of the

butte, or low mountain, the savages were spread out, and circling here and there, looked like a swarm of angry bees." Then began a confrontation that Carter calls "one grand, but rather dangerous, circus." Each of the Comanche warriors began circling, making an individual circle within a large ever-moving front line. The Tonkawa scouts also started the circling motion, and occasionally one would dart out toward the Comanches. A Comanche would dash out also. The two would fire their guns, miss, and both race back to their front line. The circling continued for quite a while. Carter describes the women's contribution: "Occasionally a warrior could be seen to stagger as though about to fall; again, a pony was shot and fell, but instantly the wounded savage was hurried to the rear to be cared for by the squaws, who also brought up an extra pony, to remount the one whose animal had been shot, not forgetting to keep up their ear-splitting scream-ing, horrible screeching, and noisy exhibition of courage." The Comanches retreated slowly. Carter and a few others rode up a bluff from which sharp-shooters were firing at the soldiers below. On the steep path Carter's horse stumbled, crushing the lieutenant's leg against a rock. Finally the Indian lines broke, and the warriors scattered, disappearing into the hills and brush along the side of the canyon and then up over the rim onto the Staked Plains. The soldiers, riding on jaded horses, were unable to pursue the Comanches any farther. As was their custom, the Comanches had brought along fresh horses and were constantly able to replace worn-out mounts.[27]

Quanah gives his version of the battle: "Next morning they come up my trail. I ready to fight. I use this knife. Come up my trail lot men. Way ahead of it, maybe fifty or sixty men. I tell my men stand up behind hill, holler, shoot and run. I run to one side and use this knife. I came up right side and killed man sergeant and scalp."[28]

The soldiers dismounted, posted guards, and bivouacked for a few hours. Private Gregg was buried near the corner of a butte where a shadow fell in the afternoon. The ceremony was simple, and rocks were piled on the grave to prevent wolves from digging up the body.

At 2:30 P.M. the Tonkawas reported that they had found the trail of the main village. The weary men, some of whom were on foot, plodded unhap-pily up the canyon until nightfall, when they camped. During the night Mackenzie made the decision to send the dismounted men back to the supply camp on Duck Creek and to continue to pursue the Comanche village.

That morning, the column made its way up the canyon in pursuit of the Comanche village. Even though the Comanches had a head start of a day or more, Mackenzie reasoned that soldiers with pack horses could move faster than Indians encumbered with the elderly, the sick, and the very young as well as lodges, cooking equipment, and other paraphernalia.[29]

Late in the afternoon, the Tonkawas found where the Comanches had spent the night. The scouts continued to follow the trail up the canyon until they became confused because the Comanches had crisscrossed their tracks a number of times. Finally the Tonkawas concluded that the Comanches had somehow managed to double back, so the weary troops retraced their steps and made camp where they had found the traces of the Comanche campsite. In the morning the Tonkawas set out again to try to find the trail. Soon they signaled from the rim of the canyon. The soldiers struggled through ravines, over boulders, and up the steep bluff until they finally climbed over the rim of the canyon. There they saw the Staked Plains: "As far as the eye could reach, not a bush or tree, a twig or stone, not an object of any kind or a living thing, was in sight." Out of the sheltering canyon, the men noticed that the wind was cold, and dark clouds were blowing across the sky. A norther was coming in, and the soldiers were dressed in thin, summer uniforms. The troopers slowly rode along through the short, dry grass of the plains, following the droppings of the Comanches' horse herd. Then the Tonkawas signaled that they had found where the Comanches had descended back into the canyon, and in single file the horses and riders slipped and slid back down into the valley. There the men found a confusion of paths leading in all directions, but the cunning Tonkawas soon discovered one leading up the bluff on the other side of the valley. After again struggling up the steep rock wall, the soldiers found a clear, broad trail. The Comanches' desperate attempts to confuse the soldiers had failed; the Tonkawas had accomplished what the soldiers could never have done alone.

The fleeing Comanches were trying to protect themselves and their families, but their defeat seemed inevitable; the unencumbered soldiers rode easily over the level plains. Then all of a sudden the temperature began to drop rapidly. A cold wind burned faces and hands and pierced the thin uniforms. Comanche warriors appeared on the horizon. They circled on the left and right of the column, trying to check its rapid approach to their wives and children. The soldiers were undeterred in their pursuit. The Tonkawas grabbed their favorite horses, hastily painted themselves and their mounts, and pranced along the edge of the column. In the late afternoon, the soldiers began to notice lodge poles, iron and stone tools, firewood, lodges, and even puppies abandoned beside the trail. Then the moving village could be seen in the distance. The swarming warriors came closer and closer. Night began to fall and freezing rain and snow filled the howling wind. The soldiers expected at any minute to hear Mackenzie shout, "Trot! Gallop! Charge!" But the order never came, and the moving Comanche village only a mile or two away disappeared like a phantom village into the night.[30]

The soldiers were confused, and the Comanches were as well. Cohayyah says: "The soldiers kept on going and didn't pay any attention to us. They didn't shoot at us or bother us, but kept on going. That kept up until night. Some of us ran real close to them, but they paid no attention. We wondered why they wouldn't fight. Maybe they wanted to make peace." The Comanche band then traveled to the Double Mountain area where Mowway was camped. There they had a big celebration.[31]

Did Mackenzie fear that his men with their exhausted horses and insufficient clothing would suffer defeat, or did he visualize the massacre of the women and children who were so desperately trying to escape? Later Mackenzie would be forced to cause the slaughter he had avoided on October 12, 1871. The Comanches had escaped, but only for a little while.

The soldiers suffered through the night. Someone wrapped a buffalo robe around Mackenzie as he sat shivering under a makeshift tarpaulin covering. He had no overcoat and was suffering intensely from the cold because of his old wounds. By morning the norther had blown over, and the sun was shining again. A half-hearted attempt was made to follow the trail of the Comanches, but the command was in bad shape. Morale was low, the horses were worn out and suffering from lack of water, food was running out, and the nearest post to the west was Fort Sumner in New Mexico, 140 miles away. Mackenzie decided to turn back. The next day the column began to return over their old route. They silently marched across the Staked Plains for several days until they descended again into Blanco Canyon. Suddenly they heard the cry, "Indians! Indians!" The Tonkawas had surprised two lone Comanche braves who had been scouting the old trail of the soldiers through the canyon. Greatly outnumbered, the two Comanches were forced to dismount and take cover in a ravine. Lieutenant Boehm and the Tonkawas were trying to flush them out when Mackenzie, who had rushed over to supervise the operation, was struck by an arrow. The point was buried to the bone in his right thigh. Mackenzie had acquired his seventh and final wound in the service of his country.

Both the Comanche braves were shot and killed. Upon examining the bodies, Carter saw that one of the Comanches had been shot in the hand, but his bloody bowstring indicated that he had continued to draw his bow although he must have been in excruciating pain. The troopers camped for the night. The "savage" Tonkawas shot bullets into the bodies, scalped the two men, and cut a piece of skin from the breast of each of them. The "civilized" whites "decapitated the dead Quahadas, and placing the heads in some gunny sacks, brought them back to be boiled out for future scientific knowledge." The headless bodies were left for the wolves, which devoured them in the night.[32]

The troopers made their way back down Blanco Canyon to a site near the location of their fight with the Comanche braves. There Mackenzie allowed them to rest for a few days. Unwilling to give up the pursuit of the Comanches, Mackenzie took his troops and started toward the headwaters of the Pease River, where he thought the band might have gone, but his wound was so painful that he was forced to leave Captain Clarence Mauck in command and return to Duck Creek on October 29, 1871.

Several days later, Mackenzie was sitting in his tent plagued by his painful wound and exasperated by the failure of the expedition. Rain had fallen during the day, and a number of horses and mules had died from exhaustion. Mackenzie was in an unusually foul mood, and the surgeon assigned to the command, Dr. J. R. Gregory, decided to play a practical joke on him. Gregory went to Mackenzie's tent and, bustling with professionalism, removed the bandages from Mackenzie's wound, examined it closely, and told the general that "it was very inflamed, and unless he controlled his irritability, he would be impelled to amputate . . ." Gregory never finished his sentence because Mackenzie grabbed his walking stick and chased Gregory out of the tent.[33]

The fall campaign of 1871 had been a failure, and Colonel Ranald Slidell Mackenzie did not like failure.

❧ CHAPTER 16 ❧

So Many Soldiers

I N THE SUMMER of 1872 Mackenzie made another expedition into the canyons along the edge of the Staked Plains. The troops were mustered at Fort Richardson and then set out along the trail across California and Paint creeks and the Salt Fork of the Brazos, finally establishing a supply camp on the Freshwater Fork of the Brazos near the site of the previous year's battle at Blanco Canyon. They marched across the plains to Fort Sumner and Fort Bascom in New Mexico and then back to the supply camp without encountering any Indians.[1]

The bleeding frontier was clamoring for relief. The editor of the Gainesville *Gazette* chided Mackenzie for his apparent ineffectiveness:

> When Gen. Augur took charge of the Department, and issued the order to his officers to chastise Indians whenever they came into Texas, we had great faith that Colonel McKenzie would teach the Indians a lesson they would not soon forget for all time to come, and have anxiously waited to hear a good report of his command but in vain. The Indians are committing more depredations in Texas to-day than when Gen. Augur issued the order. We know nothing of the plan of the Indian campaign, but we know that Col. McKenzie extends but little protection to the frontier people in either life or property. If the Col. "means business," we would like to know that he was up to it.

Earlier in the year Mackenzie had captured a Comanchero named Polonio Ortiz, who claimed that the Comanches always camped either on the North Fork of the Red River or in Palo Duro Canyon, and Mackenzie intended to check out both places. Mackenzie wrote to the assistant adjutant general: "I have the honor to report that my command consisting of companies 'A.' 'D.' 'F.' 'I.' and 'L.' 4th Cavalry and 'I.' 24th Infantry, in all twelve officers and two hundred and seventy two enlisted men, with two Acting Assistant Surgeons, left camp on the Fresh Fork of the Brazos River, Texas on the 21st day of September and moved to the Salt Fork of Red River at a point about longitude 101.30' [near present-day Clarendon] without anything specially worthy of notice."[2]

Leaving the supply wagons guarded by five officers and fifty-seven enlisted men, Mackenzie led seven officers, two hundred and fifty enlisted men, and nine Tonkawa scouts toward McClelland's Creek twenty miles to the northeast. On September 29, the command struck the south fork of the creek about four miles above the forks of its two branches. As the command marched down the creek bed for two miles, the Tonkawas discovered two trails, one made by two horses and another made by a single mule. The scouts soon lost the trails, and Mackenzie called a halt until the Tonkawas could find them again. Captain Wirt Davis noticed that grapevines grew in the trees along the creek and, knowing the fruit was a favorite food of the Indians, he dismounted, examined the area, and found mule tracks and grapes scattered on the ground. Following a trail of grapes that had fallen from the packs of the Indians, the column left the creek bed and rode rapidly about twelve miles north across rolling grassland toward the North Fork of the Red River. The command suddenly came to a gully that led them to the North Fork.[3]

Sergeant John B. Charlton, who was in command of a squad of four men, describes what happened next: "After a ride of about half a mile we came to a 'draw' and looking down toward [the North Fork of] the Red River we saw we had plenty to do. Hundreds of horses were in view and were between us and the camp but we could see both plainly. The herders were trying to rush the horses into camp to mount the warriors. I was Junior Sergeant that day and was in charge of the rear column of 'F' Troop. When we reached the edge of the camp we received the order 'Right Front into line!' This threw me on the right of the company. I had in my set of fours Privates Rankin, Beals, Kelly and Dorst."[4]

Cohayyah describes what had happened before to the battle: "Mow-way not there. He was with the Peace People. The Chief in command of that village was killed, also his wife. Kaiwoatche was a young man. Another chief was Patchohionaiky. Kaiwoatche went out to look around. The Tonkaways and white soldiers saw him. He was riding a mule. But he got away. The soldiers came upon them [the village] almost at once. So many soldiers, 250."[5]

The most detailed account from a soldier's point of view is given by

Lieutenant William A. Thompson: "The charge was made in echelon, troops in columns of four. The General rode by the side of the commanding officer of 'A' Troop, which was the base troop. When the troop was near the center of the camp and parallel with a small ridge thickly covered with high grass, about ten or fifteen yards off, about seventy-five Indians raised in line and gave the troop a volley, but fortunately, and what will be the case in nine times out of ten, with very little damage, as the volley was high. Like all close Indian fighting it then became general and more or less individual."[6]

Sergeant Charlton describes the hand-to-hand combat: "The hottest part of the fight took place on our immediate front. . . . Rankin was shot in the stomach. . . . Dorst was shot through the neck and died at once, strangled by his own life blood. Kelly also was shot through the neck and died three days later. Beals was shot through the thigh with an arrow. I, alone, came off unscathed, but *I got the Indian who shot Kelly and Dorst.*"[7]

Lieutenant Thompson describes the terrible slaughter in a ravine:

The commanding officer of 'A' Troop cut off and enclosed about eighty warriors in a crescent-shaped ravine, through which ran a good sized brook. About the center was a deep pool some twenty-five or thirty feet long and eight or ten feet wide. When the troop was deployed the flanks commanded the exit of both the lower and upper portion of this ravine. The fighting was close and desperate; the Indians charged the line twice, but were driven back with great slaughter. As fast as the Indians were killed their bodies were thrown into this deep pool, from the fact that almost all Indians have a perfect horror and dread of being scalped after death, as they do not want to appear in the 'Happy Hunting Grounds' scalpless. This particular portion of the fight can best be pictured by imagining a troop of men in line on a stage firing into a crowded theater pit.[8]

Mackenzie's terse description was included in an official report written on October 12, 1872: "After a brisk fight of about half an hour the village was entirely carried, resistance to any extent being made at only one point, where three companies 'A.' 'F.' and 'L.' were engaged from time to time. 'F.' company being engaged from the commencement to the close more continuously than any other. 'D.' being sent after horses and 'I.' having attacked handsomely on the right, charged mounted through a small village somewhat detached and pursuing retreating Indians did not rejoin the main command till it was nearly dark."[9]

Cohayyah gives his version of the fight: "The young men went out to fight. One of my brothers was killed. Lots wounded. Had to kill soldiers with arrows because they were in gullies. The fight lasted until sun almost down. Women folks [hid] on creek. Lots of women came out of timber with their hands in the air and surrendered. Their husbands had got scared and left."[10]

The number of Indian dead is unknown. Mackenzie reported "twenty three Indian men whose bodies fell into our hands and one mortally wounded." Around October 10, 1872, a number of Comanches and Kiowas at Fort Sill reported to Major Schofield that twelve Indian men, twelve Indian women, and two Mexicans had been killed. According to Lieutenant Thompson, in later years the "Twa-ha-da chiefs" said that fifty-two members of the tribe had perished, a number of whom had been thrown into the pool.[11]

Clinton L. Smith, a captive who had been adopted by the Comanches, describes the carnage: "It seems that the soldiers tried to make a massacre of the attack, for they killed squaws, babies, warriors, and old white headed men. . . . The troops captured all of our horses, several thousand, and moved down the creek about ten miles, and we returned to the scene of battle and picked up all of the wounded. This little creek was of running water with deep holes from fifty to seventy-five yards long. Long grass grew along the edges of the stream and hung over the water. Many of the Indians escaped by jumping into the water and hiding under the overhanging grass. So many were killed and wounded in the water that it was red from hole to hole with blood."[12]

In his official report Mackenzie wrote that some of the prisoners who were very old or who were too badly wounded to be moved were left in the camp. Among the captured were eight Mexicans, seven of whom were women. Mackenzie wrote of them, "practically they have become Indians." Shortly after sundown, the soldiers with their prisoners moved two miles into some sandhills and made a "dry camp."[13]

The soldiers placed the herd of three thousand captured horses and mules in a large depression in the prairie, where Lieutenant Boehm and his nine Tonkawa scouts were assigned to guard them. That night a number of Comanche warriors began to circle the camp, screaming and firing a few shots. They gradually increased their circle until it included the horse herd. The raiders managed to stampede most of the horses, which they drove away into the darkness.[14]

Cohayyah reports: "One of the chiefs came up [to the lower village] and said, 'They got all our horses.' We fixed our horses' tails again. We came up at night. The women were under close guard and could not look up. We got all our own horses back and some of the soldiers' too. Also got some mules. Colored soldiers were holding the horses. They got scared and let them loose and we got them."[15]

The next day the command and the prisoners started across the prairie to their camp on the Salt Fork of the Red River. The captives were "herded like cattle" for eighteen miles to the place where camp was made for the night. There the prisoners were confined in a "corral" made by placing the supply wagons in a large circle.[16]

Again the Comanche braves waited until dark and by whooping and shooting managed to stampede and recapture some more horses and mules. In the morning all that was left of the herd of three thousand animals were fifty horses and nine mules. Carter states: "No effort after that was ever made to hold a herd of wild captured Indian ponies. *They were all shot.*"[17]

On October 1, 1872, Mackenzie and his men reached their camp on the Salt Fork of the Red River, where the wagon train had been left. The Indian braves gave up their pursuit and rode off with the horse herd into the breaks and canyons. Cohayyah describes the hard life of the survivors: "The Comanches have to get up early, eat quick and be alert." Quanah states: "While most of our men were away from our camp hunting buffalo, some soldiers came upon our camp . . . and captured a great many women and children and destroyed our tents and winter provisions. This was in the early part of winter and we could scarcely get enough food to keep us alive that winter."[18]

On October 2, the soldiers and the prisoners started the long march back to the supply camp on the Freshwater Fork of the Brazos, deep in Blanco Canyon. The prisoners were given horses, but no saddles were available so they rode bareback. The caravan headed south, retracing the route the soldiers had taken earlier along the eastern edge of the Staked Plains. Supplies ran low, and the soldiers and prisoners were given only one meal a day. Of the prisoners one man and seven women and children died on the march, as Mackenzie reported, "some of them from injuries received in the fight. All such [injuries] were accidental and they have had the best care possible, but the surgeon cannot make them follow his instructions." Five days later, after having traveled one hundred miles, they reached the supply camp. Mackenzie let everybody rest for a week and then sent the men back to their respective posts.[19]

The captives were placed in the care of Troops D and I, and all set out for Fort Concho, 160 miles away. All the prisoners were forced to make the trip, even a seriously wounded man and a young woman in the advanced stages of pregnancy. The trail lay across a vast prairie cut through with ravines, and as the wagon carrying the wounded and the pregnant woman jolted in and out of the gulches, the seriously wounded man died. According to Carter, who escorted the captives, "He was found bolt upright, stiff and immovable, against the side board, after being 24 hours on the way." The young woman gave birth. She arrived at Fort Concho in good condition, but the baby died.[20]

When the prisoners reached Fort Concho on October 21, the horses and mules were turned out of their stable and corral, and the Comanches took up residence. The stable was a huge rectangular stone building that had an attached corral with high stone walls. The Comanches had plenty of room inside and outside and were fed well, each receiving a daily ration of eighteen ounces of flour, twenty ounces of beef, two ounces of pork, and half an ounce of salt. Henry Taylor, a rancher who supplied the beef for the prisoners, reports: "Some of the women cooked the meat by holding it on a stick over the fire, but many others ate it raw." Rice, soap, coffee, tea, sugar, and medicine were also issued. Some of the prisoners began to get fat.[21]

As usual, the nearby townspeople came to observe the captured Indians, as did a number of officers' wives and children. Carter describes the scene: "All of our ladies with most of the children went to visit the prisoners in the corrals, much to the delight and profit of the Indians, who not only received presents of food and candy but had the privilege of holding the little white papooses in their arms, stroking our baby's long, light blonde hair and always exclaiming 'bueno!' 'Mucho bueno!!'—which was generally their most enthusiastic expression for the superlative whenever anything especially pleased them or appealed to their strongest emotions."[22]

Mary Lewis, a pioneer who lived near the fort, remembered another incident: "One of the women escaped by climbing over the wall of the corral, even though broken glass was scattered over the top." Mary also remembered hearing strange sounds on the prairie at night, cries of the owl and coyote, that sounded like signals from the free Comanches to the prisoners in the stable. Some soldiers gave presents of "bright trinkets" and sunbonnets to the prisoners. The captives were delighted with the trinkets but rejected the sunbonnets.[23]

Meanwhile, Parraocoom and the Comanches on the North Fork who had not been killed or captured made their way to the reservation at Fort Sill, arriving in less than a week.[24] The headmen reported to the office of

Mowway's village in 1872–73 when he and his band moved to Fort Sill to wait
for the release of the women and children captured by Mackenzie. Courtesy
the Smithsonian Institution.

the Indian agent, Quaker Laurie Tatum. Tatum was a good-hearted, practical man who was doing his best to carry out the orders of the government as
well as take care of his charges. When the chiefs arrived, Tatum was busy in
the annuity room. As he walked over to his office, he prayed for the Lord's
guidance. Tatum shook hands with the chiefs: "I told them that I was glad to
see them, and that I had been waiting to see them for three years and now
hoped we should all be friends." The chiefs told Tatum that they had fought
a battle with the soldiers and had been beaten. They said that they wanted to
be friends and would do what Tatum told them. They would "remain on the
reservation, send their children to school and do the best they could at farming," but first they demanded that Tatum return the prisoners who were being held at Fort Concho. Tatum told them that "they had some of my children that I had been trying for three years to obtain. Before I would talk to
them about their women and children, they must deliver to me all the white
children they had." In a few days, the Comanches brought in Clinton Smith
as well as a nine-year-old boy named John Valentin Moxie. The two boys
told Tatum about two other white captives, and in this manner Tatum eventually obtained the release of nineteen captives of the Quahada Comanches.[25]

Quanah briefly describes this part of Comanche history: "Some of our
men went to the agent at Anadarko [Fort Sill] and asked him to help them
get the women and children that had been captured. The agent's name was
Tatum. He was a good man and soon got the women and children, but our
people had to give the agent some white children they held as captives."[26]

One or even two of Quanah's wives may have been among the captive women.[27] Although it is difficult to piece together the story of Quanah's life, according to scanty family records he took two wives in 1872. In 1959 Baldwin Parker, one of Quanah's sons, told an interviewer about Quanah's first wife: "Her name was Tohayea. She was a Mescalero Apache, and was given to Quanah by her father, Apache chief Old Wolf, in 1872. He had met her in Mescalero, and had got her in exchange for five mules. They lived together about one year when Tohayea told Quanah, 'I can never belong to the Comanches.'" Quanah sent her back to her people.[28]

Also according to family records, Quanah took another wife in 1872, Weakeah, daughter of Penateka subchief Old Bear.[29] Quanah told the story of their courtship to Eugene Elliot White, a special Indian agent to the Kiowa-Comanche reservation from October 19, 1887, to September, 1888. White visited Quanah on a number of occasions, and during long evenings around the campfire, Quanah told White the story of his courtship of Weakeah.[30]

In 1872, Quanah was about twenty-three years old and Weakeah was about thirteen.[31] They thought of themselves as "just friends." One night a young warrior named Tannap appeared near Old Bear's lodge dressed in his finest clothes, which were bedecked with beads and small mirrors. He began to play his reed flute. Three nights later he stationed himself closer to the lodge and again played his plaintive songs. Two nights later he became bolder: "Spreading his blanket on the grass in front of Old Bear's tepee, and seating himself on it, he looked straight at the doorway and played softly all the love songs of the tribe."[32]

Weakeah "showed not her face to her wooer." When the sun rose the next morning, Tannap's father Eckitoacup appeared at the door of Old Bear's lodge. Old Bear exited his lodge and sat down with Eckitoacup on some buffalo skins under the brush arbor in front of the lodge. For a long time the two men talked in low tones, and the result of the conversation was that Eckitoacup offered ten horses for Weakeah. Knowing that Weakeah disliked Tannap, Old Bear did not give a definite answer.

That night Quanah and Weakeah met. She told Quanah what had happened and begged him to give Old Bear ten horses himself. Even though "calamities in war" had made Quanah poor, and he owned but one horse, he was determined to get the rest. He went to all his friends, and by the next afternoon, he drove ten horses to the lodge of Old Bear. There he learned that Eckitoacup, hearing of Quanah's plan, had raised the offer to twenty horses and had been promptly accepted by Old Bear. Quanah walked into Old Bear's tent and found Weakeah in tears, lying at her mother's feet. In "two sleeps" Tannap would come to take Weakeah to his lodge.

Quanah returned to his friends and asked them to help Weakeah to escape. The young warriors agreed to help, and the next night the plan would be put into action. That night Weakeah managed to meet Quanah outside Old Bear's lodge, and she enthusiastically agreed to the scheme. Although elopement was common among the Plains Indians, it was not without its dangers. The lovers were sometimes pursued, and if caught, one or both might be killed.

The next night at about eleven o'clock, Quanah went to Old Bear's lodge with a friend. Weakeah had sneaked out and was waiting. The three crept to the outskirts of the village, where twenty-one of Quanah's friends waited. Horses were being held in readiness for them, and they all rode out into the night. The band kept up a fast pace for seven hours. At dawn they stopped, ate a breakfast of dried buffalo meat, and allowed their horses to graze for a few hours. When the group resumed their journey, they scattered like quail with plans to meet at a designated place at nightfall. After resting for a few hours, they resumed their journey and traveled until the sun came up. By this time Quanah's band had reached Texas and "dared not travel any more in daylight." When night fell, they changed their course, split into couples, and again traveled all night. After several nights they met at Double Mountain, where they rested for several days to restore the strength of their horses. Then they split up again and headed south, traveling "from high point to high point until they came to a river, probably one of the branches of the Concho. There they established a camp, and in Quanah's words, "went to stealin' horses."[33] Adopted Comanche Herman Lehmann, says of the fugitives: "Another band which had just run away from Fort Sill joined us. This band was under Quanah Parker. Others came from different quarters until we became about three hundred strong."[34]

Quanah and his friends stayed in that region for over a year and, in Quanah's words, "just stole horses all over Texas." From time to time the young warriors would go to the reservation to visit their girlfriends and return with them and with other Indians. After about a year Quanah's band numbered "several hundred," according to his estimate.[35]

Eventually Eckitoacup learned where Quanah was and, gathering together his friends, went to punish him. Eckitoacup and his men located the band, and both sides lined up for battle. Seeing the great number of warriors that Quanah commanded, Eckitoacup decided to parley. Each side sent four men to negotiate. The delegates sat and smoked and talked for a long time, finally deciding that Quanah should pay Eckitoacup nineteen horses, "the pick of Quanah's herd." Quanah cheerfully agreed, bragging that "he knew a ranch where he could get nineteen others just as good in a few hours."[36]

Ella Cox Lutz, granddaughter of Weakeah, tells a slightly different story of the courtship of Quanah and Weakeah:

> There were many smiling glances for this young Chief, but his choice was Weakeah, the daughter of Yellow Bear [sic]. She had been promised by her father to her older sister's husband, in accordance with tribal law. They were to be married in a few days. Quanah made a decision. He hid near the stream and waited for Weakeah to come for water, and told her of his plans. Through the night Weakeah quietly loosened the stobs of the tepee near her bed and silently slipped out to meet Quanah. They joined a group of young men and a lady, riding at night and sleeping during the day until they reached a safe place.
>
> Quanah and his band were gone from the Comanche camps for almost a year. During this time some of the men had returned to get wives. The band had a large herd of fine horses. Soon after returning to the Comanche camp, Quanah and Weakeah became the proud parents of a daughter whom they named Nahnacuh. Nahnacuh was born in 1873.[37]

According to these family stories, Quanah may have had one or two wives at the time of Mackenzie's raid at the North Fork of the Red River, and they could have been among the captives held at Fort Concho during the winter of 1872–73. On January 12, 1873, five women captives, relatives of Noconi chief Horseback, were released because of his success in obtaining the release of white and Mexican captives as well as in recovering a large number of stolen horses and mules. On the journey from Fort Concho one of the women died. The other four were reunited with Horseback and his family. One of the women told about the battle at the North Fork and their capture, saying that they had been well treated and well fed and had had no work assigned to them, "not even to bring water or provide wood."[38]

The Indian agent Laurie Tatum took the opportunity to admonish the Comanches about their treatment of captives, especially white women, "always being much abused, and often suffering death as the result of it." According to Quaker teacher Thomas C. Battey, Horseback "acknowledged the truthfullness of the contrast, owning that he knew that the white man had a better heart than the red man, and he wanted to live in friendship with him."[39]

In April, orders were issued for the release of the remaining captives, and preparations for the journey began. Two or three nights before the date of departure, five women escaped from the stockade. The other prisoners, exactly one hundred in all, were loaded into wagons and started on their long journey to Fort Sill. The spring rains set in, and the captives and their escort of twenty-one soldiers led by Captain Robert McClermont had to slosh through mud and swim their horses and wagons across swollen rivers and creeks. They had a treacherous journey of three hundred miles along a "dim trail" that ran through a number of frontier villages. Many of the people on the frontier hated all Indians, even defenseless captive women and children. As the caravan neared Jacksboro, Texas, McClermont received word that a drunken mob of one thousand people awaited the arrival of the captives. McClermont sent the others along a back road and drove his wagon, or ambulance as it was then called, into town. There he sat for a long time as if waiting for the arrival of the caravan. After McClermont had given the captives enough time to be out of reach of the mob, he announced that he was going back to see what had delayed the wagon train. He rejoined the caravan as the drunken rabble waited for the victims who never came.[40]

The wagon train was on the road for seventeen days. At noon on June 10, 1873, several Comanches were loitering around the commissary at Fort Sill, complaining about the fact that the captive women and children had not arrived. They believed that they had been deceived. Just then the wagons appeared at the top of a hill. Battey describes what happened next: "They were at once recognized by them, and the ominous gloom which had hung as a dark cloud upon their countenances was at once dispelled, and a joyful expression took its place as the whole party, accompanied by an interpreter, set off at full speed to meet them. The change in feeling was complete, affecting not the Indians alone, but the employees at the Agency, and all the white people around. The news of their arrival was carried to the Comanche camps about as soon as horse-flesh was capable of doing it."[41]

The next day hundreds of Comanches showed up at the agency. There were tears and hugs as the Indians greeted the women and children they feared had been killed or mistreated. The captives reported having "been well fed and kindly treated." According to Battey, two of the soldiers "were brought in in irons for having offered abuse to the prisoners." The Indians in their joy repeatedly stated that "now they are strengthened to walk in that good, white road Washington is making for them." In a brief ceremony each of the Comanche chiefs went up to Captain McClermont, took his hand, and expressed gratitude. Some of the chiefs gave McClermont what Tatum called "a warm Comanche hug." One of the chiefs told McClermont that "he would always respect a white soldier for his sake." McClermont took the opportunity to make a speech, saying that "to-day, for the first time in his life, he had taken the hand of an Indian in friendship; But that, having so taken their hand, he should never expect to meet a Comanche on any other ground; that he should report to the 'big war chief' what he had seen and heard to-day, and tell him that the Comanches were enemies no more."[42]

The five women who had escaped from Fort Concho two days before the wagon train left for Fort Sill arrived on June 12. They had traveled on foot, crossed rain-swollen rivers, and lived on the animals they could catch and plants they could find, and it had taken them only four days longer than the wagon train.[43]

⋘ CHAPTER 17 ⋙

Blood upon the Land

D URING THE TWO YEARS after the surrender of Parraocoom and Mowway in October of 1872, Quanah along with many of the other Comanche young men spent most of their time raiding in Texas and New Mexico. But the settlers were pushing north and west, and the soldiers had found most of the waterholes and hideouts of the Indians. The Comanches were desperate because, as Comanche captive Herman Lehmann says, "We knew we could not remain long where we were, for the whites would hunt us down, and we believed that for every one we killed, seven would come to take his place."[1]

The spring of 1874 marked a turning point in the history of the Comanches. As the season progressed and the horses became fat and strong on the new grass, the young men grew restless and began to ride out of the reservation and back to their old life of hunting and raiding. Many were burning with desire for revenge because in the winter before, thirty Kiowas and Comanches had been killed. One of the bloodiest battles occurred on February 5, 1874, when a large group of Comanches and Kiowas who were returning from a raid in Mexico were intercepted by some soldiers of the 4th Cavalry led by Lieutenant George Buell. Eleven of the Indians were killed. One of Quanah's relatives was killed, and Quanah and others believed that the Tonkawa scouts had practiced their usual ritual and had eaten parts of the bodies of the slain.[2] Other Indian casualties included the uncle of Comanche medicine man Isatai and both the favorite son and a nephew of Kiowa chief Lone Wolf. In addition, as the spring rains fell heavy and hard, supply wagons bogged down and got stuck on the muddy roads, and the agents were forced to issue half rations to the hungry tribes. The Plains Indians on the reservations in Indian Territory became more than usually impudent and unruly.[3]

Most disturbing to the Indians was the slaughter of the buffalo at an unprecedented rate because of the invention of powerful repeating rifles, the construction of railroads into the plains, and the discovery of new uses for buffalo hides. The Indians grieved over the slaughter of the great animals, often saying, "They are our cattle, our money. Why do you wish to destroy them? They are all we possess." The buffalo were also an essential part of the spiritual well-being of the Comanches, a part of their religion.[4]

Two other causes of the increasing unrest were the theft of the Indians' livestock by whites and the conception that "Washington" was making unreasonable demands. According to Quaker missionary Thomas Battey, early in 1873 a Penateka warrior killed his father, and the warrior and two other young men ran away to Texas and started raiding. These three men were joined by two other young men and two women. On October 8, 1873, the Indian commissioner called for a council in his office and admonished the chiefs for the young people's deeds, reminding them that they had agreed that "when their women and children were returned to them, that henceforth they would keep the peace with the whites, and not raid any more in Texas. They had violated their pledge, raided, stolen horses, and committed murders there [in Texas], and now they must give him five of the guilty persons; giving them until the next morning to make their answer."[5]

As agreed, the Comanche chiefs returned to the council room the next morning and made their reply: "They could agree to all the terms demanded of them except the giving up of the five guilty young men, which they could not do unless the commissioner would give the names of the men he wanted, which he did not do. They then offered to restore all the horses and mules they had stolen, but this was a new road which they could not accept."[6]

The commissioner became angry and called the chiefs cowards. The chiefs replied that "they could not give him the five men, and if he wanted them, there were soldiers at the fort, and their young men were there,—take them himself, and he would have them if that was what he wanted. However, they wished it understood that they were anxious to maintain friendly relations with Washington, and would make one more proposition."[7]

The Comanche chief Cheevers proposed that Indian scouts should accompany a squad of soldiers and go into the "raiding district" of Texas to search for the guilty parties. The proposition was accepted. Soon troops and scouts made their way to Texas, where they had thirty days to capture the raiders. Meanwhile, some white men from Texas stole about two hundred horses and mules from the Indians. Thirty-seven animals were recovered and one of the thieves was arrested. Out on the plains, the warriors and scouts were unsuccessful in their search for the raiders. On November 30,

1873, the Indian agent received a telegram in which he was directed to tell the Comanches that they had ten days in which to turn over the raiders. Otherwise, their rations and annuities would be cut off, and the matter would be turned over to the military authorities. Quaker teacher Thomas Battey, who was a witness to these events, wrote in his diary: "Thus are the clouds gathering, which may ere long rain blood upon this land. May they be dispelled, is the prayer of my soul."[8]

On December 1, 1873, many Comanches reported to the agency, and the contents of the telegram were explained to them. Battey wrote in his journal: "It is not probable that they [the Comanches] will make any effort to arrest the men as that would be likely to produce war among themselves, and this despatch is looked upon by many of them as equivalent to a declaration of war against them." Battey went on to note that all the chiefs but two had tried to keep their young men from raiding, and the government proposed to punish the innocent with the guilty.

As predicted, the Comanches did consider the telegram to be a declaration of war; most of them left the reservation and fled to the plains. Several days later, the agent received another telegram, which ordered "a continuation of rations until further orders." The Indians drifted back into the reservation, but the damage had been done. The Comanches and Kiowas were furious and more frustrated than ever.[9]

It had become evident that the Quaker Peace Policy was a failure, and the members of Congress began discussing the possibility of turning the reservations over to the military. In one last effort to make the policy a success, the Quakers gathered together a group of commissioners to go to the various tribes to try to reason with them. Among the representatives was James E. Rhoads, who went to Indian Territory to beg the Indians to stop raiding. On April 5, 1874, he spoke at the Wichita Agency to an assembly that included a delegation of Comanches. The Indian chiefs replied that "they had heard the good talk their friends had given them,—that they thoroughly understood it; they were sorry Washington's heart got tired so quick; they did not get tired of trying to keep their foolish young men from raiding; that they had not entirely succeeded, but they did not raid nearly so much as formerly; they were encouraged to continue trying. They thought Washington ought to be more patient, and not let his heart get tired so quick." Several days later at the Kiowa Agency, a few Comanche chiefs and young warriors came into the office. One of the young men defiantly addressed the Quaker representatives, saying that "it mattered not what the chiefs said in council with the whites; they, the young men, were the warriors, and should not listen to them or anyone else; they should do as they pleased. Washington might be a big chief among white people, but he was not their chief, and had nothing to do with them, and that they should not be controlled by him."[10]

The stage was set for Isatai, medicine man and prophet. Isatai, whose name when translated means wolf vulva (he was also known as Quenatosavit or "White Eagle" at one point in his life), was a young, untried warrior, not even married. In May of 1874 he began his career as messiah to the desperate but undefeated Comanches, who put a great deal of faith in medicine men provided they could prove themselves. Especially important was the ability of the medicine man to protect warriors from injury when they went into battle. Isatai had not yet demonstrated that ability, but he seemed to have other extraordinary powers that were widely reported.[11]

Battey recorded in his journal what the Comanches on the reservation were saying about the powers of Isatai:

> He claims that he has raised the dead to life. He is reported to have raised from his stomach nearly a wagonload of cartridges at one time, in the presence of several Comanches. He then swallowed them again, informing the Comanches that they need not fear the expenditure of ammunition in carrying on a war against the whites, as he can supply all their needs in that line. He can make medicine which will render it impossible for a Comanche to be killed, even though he stand just before the muzzles of the white man's guns. He ascends above the clouds far beyond the sun—the home of the Great Spirit, with whom he has often conversed. He has done these things in open daylight, in the presence of many Comanches, remaining in the sky over night, and coming back next day; he had been known to do this four times.[12]

The cunning Isatai also declared that a comet that had appeared would disappear five days later, adding that after the disappearance of the comet, a drought would occur. When all of these natural phenomena occurred exactly as he had said, he became known among the Indians as a man of great power. People believed he "had power to control the elements, to send wind, lightning, thunder, rain, and hail upon his enemies, and in no respect is he inferior to the Great Spirit."[13]

Armed with this impressive power, Isatai called for a sun dance or medicine dance to be held in May at the junction of Elk Creek and the North Fork of the Red River. The Comanches of all bands were "ordered" by

Isatai, Quahada
medicine man.
Courtesy Pan-
handle-Plains
Historical Museum
Research Center,
Canyon, Texas.

Isatai to attend. Cheyennes and Arapahos also flocked to the valley near
the spot where Quanah had been born some twenty-five years earlier. A
Comanche woman named Querherbitty was present and later told her
grandson Joe Attocknie of a "gathering of mounted Comanches, both men
and women, following the directions [of Isatai]. The Comanches were gathered around a tall pole set into the ground. The top of the pole was in the
form of a cross. At his signal, the mounted Comanches started singing and
revolving around the cross. . . . The people nearest the center pole walked
their horses slow. Those farther out from the center had to ride faster. A
very dense dust cloud was raised as the riders at the very edge of the revolving mass had to whip and run their horses that much faster than those
nearer the center of the singing revolving throng."[14]

Mexican traders from Sante Fe sold whiskey to the members of the
assembly, and drunkenness reigned. The headmen and aspiring young war-

riors attended a "great smoker." The elders, seated in a large circle with many concentric rings of men of lesser importance surrounding them, slowly passed the pipe, each taking several puffs. For days they talked endlessly, and always they discussed the question, "When and where do we attack the Tai-bos (whites)?" One onlooker reported, "They have a great many hearts, would make their minds up at night for one thing and get up in the morning entirely changed." According to three Comanches named Timbo, Yellowfish, and Poafebitty, some of the men wanted to "exterminate" the Tonkawas first because they had reportedly eaten dead Comanches after a recent skirmish in Texas. Since most of the elders felt that the soldiers were expecting an attack on the Tonkawas, this plan was vetoed. Next Quanah spoke. He suggested to the assembly that everyone join together for an attack on Adobe Walls, an abandoned trading post on the Canadian River that had recently been reoccupied by traders and buffalo hunters. According to the Comanche informants, "This suggestion was met with instant and universal enthusiasm."[15]

As the martial character of the sun dance became increasingly apparent, a number of anti-war Comanches decided to leave. The pro-war element tried to detain the pacifists, even threatening to kill them. Mahseet, a Penateka Comanche, prepared to leave. Some Comanche warriors, members of the Little Horse soldier society, tore down Mahseet's lodge and seized his horse herd. Mahseet pleaded, "I am too old for any more war, I have too many children, but still I am being subjected to this authority." When Esahabit, a Penateka chief, demanded the return of the horses, a young warrior beat him severely with a whip. At this point Quanah, who according to Joe Attocknie was "the war party leader, and who was a member of the Little Horses," hurried to the scene and told the warriors that the horses should be turned over to Esahabit, who took them and drove them away. A number of Comanches did manage to escape from the assemblage, among them Horseback's band of Noconis, most of the Penatekas, and many of the Yamparikas.[16]

The sun dance wound itself down sometime in May, and the Quahada Comanches and their allies started to prepare seriously for war. Battey reports that on June 6, 1874, the hostile element of Comanches and Cheyennes "are hanging around the place where the Kiowa medicine dance will occur, in order to draw some of their young men into the measure, and so involve the Kiowas equally with themselves in the trouble consequent thereon." Isatai and Quanah started riding from one Indian camp to another recruiting warriors for the war against the whites. Since both the young men had relatives who had recently been killed by whites, they used the ancient custom of revenge as their motive for war. Quanah describes his efforts at recruiting men:

> A long time ago I had a friend who was killed by the Tonkaways at Double Mountain Texas. That made me feel bad. We grew up together. Went on warpath together. That made me feel very sorry. That man, Tonkaways kill him. Make my heart hot and I want to make it even. That time I little big man, pretty young man but know how to fight pretty good. I work one month. I go to Noconie Comanches camp on head of Cache Creek. Call in everybody. I tell him about my friend kill him Texas. I fill pipe. I tell that man, "You want to smoke?" He take pipe, smoke it, I give it to another man. He say "I not want to smoke." If he smoke pipe, he go on warpath. He not hang back. God kill him he afraid.[17]

Quanah next went to the Quahadas and Kiowas on Elk Creek. Iseeo, a Kiowa warrior, describes what happened there:

> Quanah had a nephew killed in Texas. He was a good looking young man, and Quanah was going about giving the pipe. We heard he was coming to the Kiowa. We saw somebody coming on the prairie crying one day and we said, "There he is, Quanah!" [He was] bringing a pipe. It was the custom to cry in these cases for the dead man unavenged. Quanah came into the village and asked, "Where is the chief's lodge?" I pointed out my uncle's lodge to him. He went to the left of the door all around the outside of the lodge, entered and sat down in the back of the lodge. Soon my uncle came in and called in all his young men, and I went in and sat down with them. Quanah said, "My nephew was killed by the white people. His body is lying on the ground in Texas. I want to get even. I am coming looking for you. I give you the pipe to smoke." Everybody heard him. All the young men watched to see if the chief smoked the pipe. If he was afraid of that pipe, they would not smoke it. If he was not afraid, everybody that wanted to go to war would smoke it with him.
>
> The chief said, "I am not afraid of that pipe, but hold up. Wait until all the old men hear about it. If they say good, I will smoke it." Quanah said, "All right. I will go talk to the old men." But they all were afraid of that pipe. A big Cheyenne village was higher up the creek, and Quanah went up there.[18]

Quanah had better luck at the Cheyenne camp. The Cheyennes were having a sun dance on the headwaters of the Washita River. George Bent, the half-Cheyenne son of a prominent trader, describes what happened:

> The sun dance had just come to an end, at the close of a fine June day, when a long line of warriors were seen riding toward the Cheyenne village. They were Comanches, with a few Kiowas, magnificently arrayed in war rigs and splendidly mounted, the Comanches at this time being very rich in fine horses. In a long line the visiting warriors rode inside and outside the great Cheyenne camp circle, chanting war songs, their war bonnets tossing in the breeze. Isatai rode at the end of the long line, making appeals, in Comanche, for the Cheyennes to join the war party, promising them much plunder when they wiped out the hunters at Adobe Walls, who as was well known, had loads of supplies. "My medicine is strong," he chanted, "and the hunters' bullets will not harm us."[19]

Quanah gives his version of the story:

> Then I go to Cheyennes. Lots 'em smoke pipe. Cheyenne camp up on Washita near [where] Fort Elliott [was later built], where Washita forks, with round hill between. Lots Comanche there, Otter Belt, He Bear [Parraocoom], Tabananica, and old man White Wolf there. A big village. Camps in different places and they ask me, "When you go warpath?" and I say, "Maybe tomorrow, maybe next day." Have dance at night. Big Horse [soldier society] dance here. Little Horse dance over there. Fox Quirt dance over there.[20] And I hear somebody, "Quanah, old men want to see you over here," and I see old man Otter Belt and White Wolf and lots old men, and they said, "You pretty good fight[er], Quanah, but you not know everything. We think you take pipe first against white buffalo killers. You kill white men. Make your heart feel good. After that you come back. Take all young men, go to Texas Warpath." Then I say to Otter Belt and He Bear, "You take pipe yourself. After that I take all young men, and go warpath Texas" and they say, "All right." Esati make big talk that time. "God tell me we going kill lots white men. I stop the bullets in gun. Bullets not penetrate shirts. We kill them just like old woman. God told me truth." Before that pretty good medicine Esati. He sit down away listen. God talk to him, "Maybe so fifty miles over there, little creek I see white soldiers. We go kill them." Pretty soon true. This time he listen what God tell him.[21]

Quanah Parker dressed in his war regalia. Courtesy the Smithsonian Institution.

Poafebitty and five or six other Indians report on this phase of the story: "Quanah first spoke about going out on the expedition before Isatai arrived at gathering. Isatai arrived and said he had power or medicine to prevent enemies guns from going off. So they gave him the leadership. Parraocoom was there. He died after they returned from the 'Dobe Walls fight."[22]

The list of Cheyenne war chiefs who joined Quanah was impressive. Old Man Horse says of them: "Setainte (White Bear), White Shield, Bird Bow, Howling Wolf, Lone Wolf. Quanah came up to Setainte's tepee, had big smoke and persuaded him to join. Pagotogoodle in it. Quite a bunch."[23]

Cohayyah speaks of the Quahada leaders: "Kaiwotche in command. Quanah was not in command. He was too young. He was never a recognized war chief. Essehabeet was one of the principal chiefs. Another chief was Taihayyahtai. Also Mahway."[24]

In spite of Cohayyah's opinion of Quanah's lack of a leadership role, others considered him to be the principal leader in the Battle of Adobe Walls. In later years the Kiowas referred to Adobe Walls as "the place where Quanah led his confederates." The combined force of Quahadas, Cheyennes, Arapahos, and a few Kiowas, whom Iseeo calls, "six or seven foolish Kiowas," rode to a campsite near present-day Mobeetie in the Texas Panhandle. The warriors camped and seven scouts were sent to look for "white men's houses on Canadian." The men were gone all night. Quanah continues with the story:

> Next day a man watching from little hill call out, "Here they come," and we run out and see scout circle 4 times to the right and we know they find houses. Then women and everybody make long line in front of the village. Old man Black Beard in the middle. Then seven scouts come up in single file in front. Old man Black Beard, he say, "Tell the truth. What did you see?" and the 1st scout say, "I tell you true. I see four or five log houses. I see horses moving around," and all seven scouts say the same thing. Black Beard say, "All right. Pretty soon we kill a white man. Everybody saddle up. Take your warbonnets and shields." Then we start out about 11 A.M. Stop about 4 P.M. Put saddles and blankets in trees and hobble extra ponies. Make medicine, paint faces, put on warbonnets, then travel in column fours until cross Canadian sundown. Keep along until pretty near a red hill near a little creek where houses were. We walk all the time. Hear trot a long way off.[25]

Yellowfish gives his version through an interpreter: "We shot some buffalo back over there [northwest behind the high bluff] the day before, and stopped and cooked them. Then we rested that night on the south side of the river."[26]

According to Quanah, someone complained that he wanted to sleep for a while so the head chief decided to camp for the night. "He Bear say, 'Dismount. Hold lariats in hand. I call you, mount again.' Some go to sleep. Some smoke tobacco and talk." The stage was set for the Battle of Adobe Walls, which marked the beginning of the end of freedom for Quanah and the Quahadas.[27]

June of 1874 was exceptionally hot, and as Isatai had predicted, a drought had descended on the land. In some places, swarms of locusts scoured the plains eating every green thing in sight. Several miles up the Canadian River valley from the Indian campsite, twenty-eight men and one woman were winding up the activities of the day. Most were professional buffalo hunters and skinners drawn to the grassy meadow in the Canadian River valley by greedy lust for gold and blood lust for the excitement of the hunt. Adobe Walls was an embryonic frontier town, a short row of sod and picket buildings running in a line from southeast to northwest.[28] Had things turned out differently, another row of buildings would have been erected on the other side with a dusty main street in between. This settlement was not the first in the area. Thirty-five years earlier, a trading post had been erected of adobe bricks, but hostile Indians had forced the whites to flee. In 1874 the ruins of the first post were still standing.[29]

J. Wright Mooar, one of the founders of the second Adobe Walls, gives his account of how the second village got started: "A supply merchant in Dodge, by the name of A. C. Myers, said if Mooar Bros. and Lane and Wheeler could stay down there all winter and hunt he could put a store there for all the hunters to come to; so he bought a large stock of goods and several outfits and located on the Canadian river. . . . Charles Rath, a competitor for the hunter's trade, followed with a stock of supplies; James Hanrahan with a saloon and Tom O'Keefe, a blacksmith, also soon followed. I moved over to the new town with the hunter's outfit and made one trip south of the Canadian for hides. John W. Mooar took our freight teams and hauled supplies from Dodge City for the new stores."[30]

There were four establishments in all. The southernmost one was the Rath and Company store, which was a sod building. A portion of it had been partitioned off to create a kitchen used to cook for the men at Adobe

Walls. The food service was provided by Rath and Company employees Hannah and William Olds, and a small room in the southwest corner of the structure served as a bedroom for the couple. The rest of the space was used as a salesroom.[31]

A short distance away was a saloon, also constructed of sod. The establishment had a doorway at each end, at least one window, and a number of loopholes that could be used to fire at attacking Indians. The sod roof was supported by a cottonwood ridgepole running the length of the building. Northwest of the saloon was a blacksmith shop built of pickets. A nearby creek bed had provided the cottonwood trees for the construction.[32]

Moving on along the "main street" of Adobe Walls, a person would encounter the west wall of a large picket corral built to discourage Indians from stealing the horses and to serve as a sort of crude fortress in case of attack. Round bastions were built on three corners, crude miniature turrets similar to those of a medieval castle. Within the corral were three picket structures: a stable, an eating hall in the southwest corner, and in the northeast corner stood the Myers and Leonard store. Seth Hathaway, one of the hunters at Adobe Walls, describes the inside: "It was in two rooms, the old and the new. In the new part was a counter across one side, behind which was kept the smaller stores, while in the old building was stacked flour, bacon, corn meal, horse feed, lead and other things for which the hunters found use and which Meyers traded for hides."[33]

Friday night, June 26, 1874, was hot and still in the valley of the Canadian River in the Texas Panhandle; the drought was in full force. The buffalo hunters and skinners who had come in from the lonely plains were ready for a good time. A number of them had gathered in Hanrahan's saloon. They must have talked about recent Indian attacks on isolated parties of buffalo hunters. Two weeks earlier, only fifteen miles from Adobe Walls, two men had been killed and horribly mutilated.[34] William (Billy) Dixon, only twenty-four years of age at the time but already a seasoned and tough frontiersman, described that night in the saloon:

> Several hunters had come in that day, and we planned to stay up late that night, celebrating our return to the range, telling stories about past experiences and joking about how much money we would have when the hunt was over. The night was sultry and we sat with open doors. . . . Outside could be heard at intervals the muffled sounds of the stock moving and stumbling around, or a picketed horse shaking himself as he paused in his hunt for the young grass. In the timber along Adobe Walls

Creek to the east owls were hooting. We paid no attention to these things, however, and, in our fancied security against all foes frolicked and had a general good time. Hanrahan did a thriving trade.

Hathaway says simply: "Some of the boys played cards, others talked about how many buffalo they had killed, and some kept busy swapping lies with one another."[35]

About midnight everyone went to bed. Most chose to sleep outside on the ground under the stars. Isaac and Jacob Scheidler, better known as Ike and Shorty, were teamsters. One of the two was ill with tuberculosis and the men had gone west in an attempt to improve his health. Ike and Shorty had chosen to sleep in one of their wagons, which was parked near the Myers and Leonard store. Shorty had come in the day before with a load of hides from a hunters' camp on Palo Duro Creek, and Ike had just delivered a load of merchandise to the Rath and Company store. The two men planned to return to Dodge City on June 27 with their two wagons loaded with hides. With them in the wagon was their black Newfoundland dog. Dixon also chose to sleep near his wagon, which was parked next to the black-smith shop. He got into his bed and placed his rifle beside him under his blanket to protect it from the dew.[36]

Everything was quiet until two o'clock in the morning, when the men in the saloon were awakened by a loud crack. They decided that the noise had been caused by the cracking of the ridgepole that ran the length of the saloon. The day before, an extra layer of sod had been placed on the top of the building because the roof was thought to be too thin to keep out the rain. Years later J. Wright Mooar claimed that a few days before the attack on Adobe Walls, Amos Chapman, a mixed-blood government scout and interpreter who often attended Cheyenne councils, had told Hanrahan the exact time of the Indian attack and Hanrahan or Dixon had fired a shot to arouse the men. Whatever the source of the noise, it served the purpose of waking up the men. Hanrahan ordered his employees Mike Welsh and Oscar Shepherd to climb onto the roof and remove some of the sod, and several other men went out to look for a piece of timber to prop up the ridgepole. Hanrahan provided free drinks for those who had helped, and they did not go back to bed, but the majority of the hunters did.[37]

Billy Dixon stayed up and just before dawn began to get his wagon ready for the hunt. Billy Ogg, a Hanrahan employee, went out to get some draft horses that were grazing a quarter of a mile to the southeast. In the pale light, Ogg spied the Indians in a long line in front of the creek. He turned on his heel and made a desperate run for the saloon. At about the same time, Dixon spied the Indians and yelled out, "Indians boys! Indians and lots of them!" Thinking the Indians were mainly after the stock, he grabbed his rifle and took time to tie his highly valued horse to the wagon. Dixon soon realized that the Indians were not just after the horses and, making a mad dash for Hanrahan's saloon, he arrived there shouting, "Let me in!" The men threw open the door, and Dixon ran inside. At about the same time, Ogg reached Hanrahan's saloon and fell to the ground exhausted. He pounded on the door, and the men let him in only moments before the Indians surrounded the buildings and attacked. The men sleeping outside grabbed their guns and dashed desperately toward the building nearest them. For some reason the Scheidler brothers stayed in their wagon.[38]

Nine men ended up in Hanrahan's. The youngest was twenty-year-old William Barclay "Bat" Masterson, who later became the famous sheriff of Dodge City. Eleven men defended Myers and Leonard's store. Except for the English-born proprietor Frederick J. Leonard, most were buffalo hunters and skinners.[39] Leonard had been sleeping in the corral when he heard shots that woke him up. The men in the store were apparently all sound asleep when the alarm was sounded, but fortunately for them blacksmith Thomas O'Keefe, who was sleeping outside, woke them up by kicking at the door and yelling, "Open up! Open up!"[40]

The weakest link in the chain of buildings was the northernmost edifice, the Rath and Company store. Only six men and one woman occupied this building, and none was a professional hunter.[41]

A few minutes after the alarm was sounded, hundreds of Indians were swarming around and even on top of the buildings. The occupants of each building started firing pistols through loopholes or chinks in the walls. Had they all been sound asleep when the attack occurred, the Battle of Adobe Walls would have been a very short one.[42]

The Indians had prepared for battle shortly before dawn in their camp downriver from Adobe Walls. Quanah tells what happened: "He Bear and Tabonanica call them. All mount again, travel until a little light. Pretty soon we make a line. All chiefs try to hold back young men. Go too fast. No good go too fast."[43] The Indians had lined up in the trees along Adobe Walls Creek. Isatai, wearing a headdress made of interwoven sage twigs, rode to a hill to the right of the long line so that he could watch the progress of the battle.[44] Yellowfish describes the events immediately preceding it: "We came on across [the Canadian River] the next morning, walking and leading our horses. Then when we were just a few hundred yards away we mounted and rode forward in long lines. The battle began just a few minutes before sun-up. I remember seeing a gun flash from the darkness surrounding the white men's shelters."[45]

Quanah continues the story: "Pretty soon they [the chiefs] call out, `All right. Go ahead!' We charge down on horses in wild charge. Threw up the dust."[46] Some of the Indians drove off a few of the horses and looted the wagons parked in the hide yards behind the stores. Others headed straight for the three buildings, believing themselves to be invincible because of the strong medicine of Isatai. Yellowfish talks about his medicine: "I didn't believe the guns of the whites could touch me. Our medicine man had fixed me up with plenty of medicine. I had on a feathered headdress and a robe made from the skin of a spotted calf, and I held a shield between me and the whites." With a wry smile he added, "Um . . . heap medicine."[47]

Timbo, who was also in the battle, had to try to survive without the protection of medicine. "The elders hadn't thought that I was old enough to fight and would not be called on to brave the white man's fire. But I was in the thick of it, riding with my band, the Log group. It was our boast that we stood like a log in battle. Yellowfish belonged to the Little Pony band. The Log fighters were led by Otter Belt, assisted by my father, Pari Kama. The Little Pony band was led by Smoking Mule assisted by Meesela. These groups had sixteen men each."[48]

Immediately the attackers were met by hot pistol fire from the saloon. The Indians and their horses soon began to fall. Quanah reports: "I saw men and horses roll over and over." Three men fell from their horses, one Comanche and two Cheyennes. The Comanche fell close to one of the buildings.[49]

The Scheidler brothers, trapped in their wagon only a few feet from the Rath and Company store, were the first white men to die. Timbo, tells what happened to the brothers: "Though there were Indians all around it, none of them knew that there was anyone in the wagon. Cheyenne, one of the best warriors in the band, rode up to the wagon and raised the wagon cover with his lance. Seeing the brothers, he spread the information, and the other warriors filled the wagon with deadly arrows." The Newfoundland dog fought so bravely that the Indians "scalped" him too, taking a strip of hide from his side.[50]

Meanwhile the Indians had broken window panes of the buildings and were using their horses as battering rams to try to break down the doors. Quanah tells of his attempts to get at the hated hunters: "Got on houses

with other Comanche and poked holes through to shoot." Yellowfish re-
calls: "Quanah . . . led the attack. [He] rode recklessly, as did all of the
tribesmen, up to the very door of one structure that stood partly open and
thrust his lance into the opening." Young braves, sick of the reservation and
desperate to prove themselves in battle, fell one by one. One young man
ran up to Rath's store, poked his revolver through a loophole and fired into
the building. He killed no one inside and was soon shot in the back. He lay
against the building, paralyzed, calling out to his father, who lay concealed
in a ravine to the south. The father answered, giving instructions to the
fallen warrior. One of the hunters went to the window and prepared to
shoot the boy. Seeing the man at the window, the boy turned his pistol on
himself and pulled the trigger.[51]

Another young boy, a Cheyenne named Horse Road, rode around the
buildings several times, verbally abusing the white men inside. Since he
was already wounded, he was determined to die bravely. In a last gesture of
bravado, he rode up to the door of one of the buildings and pounded on it
with his gun. He was soon shot and killed.[52]

The first half hour was the worst. The Indians charged around, desperate to get inside the structures. Clinging to one side of a horse and using
the mount as a shield, some warriors circled the buildings shooting arrows
or bullets under the horse's neck. Amid the den of whooping Indians, shouting men, and screaming horses could be heard the clear notes of a bugle. A
black man who had deserted from the army and joined the Indians was
giving the signal to rally. Yellowfish says of the bugler and his music, "His
calls were unnoticed by the Indians."[53]

Many of the Indian dead and wounded fell near the buildings. The warriors made heroic efforts to retrieve the fallen ones, believing the souls of
the dead would be denied entrance to the afterlife if their bodies had been
scalped or otherwise mutilated. Time and time again a warrior would ride
up to a dead or wounded man and either pull the victim up onto a horse or
drag him to safety. In one instance as two young braves were escaping, a
shot from the buffalo hunters broke the horse's leg. The horse, even though
it was bleeding and hobbling on three legs, carried the braves to safety.[54]

As the morning wore on, the Indians, finding that the deadly fire of the
buffalo hunters was "emptying too many saddles," started to take cover behind the corral, the wagons, and the stacks of buffalo hides. The bugler was
killed as he dashed from behind a wagon with a can of coffee and a sack of
sugar. Another warrior was killed as he tried to hide behind a stack of
buffalo hides. Finding that even this cover was useless in the face of the

powerful buffalo guns, the Indians retreated even farther away, many taking cover in the tall grass growing to the west of the buildings. But the Indians kept up a steady fire. At times they would fire a heavy volley, and a warrior would rise up out of the grass, run for short distance, and then fall down in the grass again.[55]

Another casualty that morning was Quanah. Wearing his long eagle-feather headdress, a sign of honor, Quanah fought bravely.[56] Sometime in the morning, he was four hundred yards from the buildings when his horse was shot and fell dead. Quanah was pitched headlong to the ground, and his gun flew through the air and landed some distance away. He took cover behind a buffalo carcass infested with rats. As he was crouching behind the rotting animal, he was struck by a ricocheting bullet. Quanah ran to a nearby plum thicket, where he was picked up by a mounted comrade. He was unable to use his arm for the rest of the day. In his autobiography Quanah barely mentions his injury, saying only, "That time I got shot in the side."[57]

In the terrible battle the animals suffered also. Some of the hunters' horses had been stampeded and stolen in the initial charge, but others had been wounded. As if seeking help from their masters, they drifted up to the buildings and stood there mute and bleeding until the Indians shot them.[58]

Withdrawing farther and farther away, the Indians learned the true power of the hunters and their guns. Even when the Indians thought they were out of range, a horse or a man would fall wounded or dead. Cohayyah explains: "Buffalo hunters had awful big range. Sometimes we wouldn't be thinking of it and they would kill our horses. Had telescopes on their guns. No wonder they could kill the buffalo!"[59]

Although the whites had superior weapons in the Battle of Adobe Walls, they were hard pressed in the first furious onslaught on the morning of June 27. Trapped in buildings stinking of sweat and human waste, they were suffocated by gunsmoke, deafened by the noise of gunfire, and filled with terror at the thought of death and mutilation—or, worse, torture. More than two hundred warriors swarmed everywhere. The sod buildings were impervious to bullets except through the windows, but Myers and Leonard's store was made of pickets, which the bullets could penetrate. Each of the men in this building made an individual barricade with sacks of flour and grain or anything else he could find. One of the men at Myers and Leonard's store remembers: "So close would they come that we planted our guns in their faces and against their bodies through the portholes."[60] At least the picket structure gave the inhabitants one advantage. They could knock out the mud chinking and have as many loopholes for firing as they wanted. The corral with its bastions at three corners was useless in the defense of the store. In fact, it was used by the Indians for cover as they fired at the whites. Billy Tyler and Fred Leonard ran out into the corral but quickly dashed back to the door of the store. Tyler turned back to shoot and was mortally wounded. He was dragged back into the store, where he died within the hour.[61]

The occupants of the Rath and Company store probably suffered the most. As noted, they were not hide men, and some were so frightened by the attack that they vomited. James Langdon reported that Hannah Olds fainted and, when she regained consciousness, tried to kill herself. On the other hand, Andy Johnson said that she helped her husband by handing him guns and ammunition. Johnson found his pistol to be his best defense in the heated fighting of the first five minutes. He fired every shot in the barrel even before he took time to pile barricades in front of the doors. He says of the situation: "There could be no organized resistance. . . . It was a case of every fellow look out for himself and 'get' as many Indians as possible."[62]

The occupants of Hanrahan's saloon were the most successful in their defense, but even they were not completely safe. As the battle progressed, it seemed to resemble a horrible shooting gallery where the Indians were like "sitting ducks." Dixon remembers: "At times the bullets poured in like hail and made us hug the sod walls like gophers when an owl is swooping past." Dixon remembers how he killed one of the warriors:

> Along about 10 o'clock, the Indians having fallen back to a safer distance from the buffalo-guns, some of us noticed a pony standing near the corner of a big stack of buffalo hides at the rear of Rath's building. We could see that an Indian behind the hides was holding the pony by the bridle, so we shot the pony and it fell dead. The pony was gaily decorated with red calico plaited in its mane. The falling of the pony left the Indian somewhat exposed to our fire, and the boys at Hanrahan's and Rath's opened upon him full blast. They certainly fogged him. No Indian ever danced a livelier jig. We kept him jumping like a flea back and forth behind the pile of hides. . . . I sized up what was going on behind the pile of buffalo hides, and took careful aim at the place where I thought the Indian was crouched. I shot through one corner of the hides. It looked to me as if that Indian jumped six feet straight up into the air, howling with pain. Evidently I had hit him. He ran zig-zag fashion for thirty or forty yards, howling at every jump, and dropped down in the tall grass.[63]

The Indians had been suffering a number of casualties from the guns of the hide men, but even now the warriors did not yet know the true strength of these weapons. The recently invented Sharps rifles were big guns, .50 caliber weapons that fired a long shell with a heavy load of powder. The hunters often loaded their own shells, so they knew exactly how far their bullets would go. They frequently engaged in shooting matches and fired at targets up to one thousand yards away. Not knowing what they were facing, a few Indians had ridden to what they thought was a safe distance and were holding a council. The hunters aimed carefully at the distant group and opened fire. According to Sam Smith, who was in the Rath and Company store: "One chief fell from his horse and the medicine man's horse was killed. This woke up the council."[64]

About noon the Indians had ceased charging and were firing on the buildings from various points. Since the men in the saloon were running out of ammunition, Hanrahan and Dixon decided to make a dash for Rath's store. Dixon describes their brave deed: "We peered cautiously outside to see if any Indians were ambushed where they could get a pot shot at us. The coast looked clear; so we crawled out of a window and hit the ground running and made a dash to Rath's in the fastest kind of time. The Indians saw us, however, before the boys could open the door, and opened at long range. The door framed a good target. I have no idea how many guns were cracking away at us, but I do know that bullets rattled round us like hail. Providence seemed to be looking after the boys at Adobe Walls that day, and we got inside without a scratch." The people at Rath's begged Dixon to stay at the store with them. They had no crack shots in their group, and they were doubly concerned because they were protecting Hannah Olds.[65]

As the afternoon wore on, the Indians fell farther back, as Dixon describes: "By 2 o'clock the Indians had fallen back to the foot of the hills and were firing only at intervals. They had divided their force, putting part on the west side and part on the east side of the buildings. Warriors were riding more or less constantly across the valley from one side to the other, which exposed them to our fire. So we began picking them off. They were soon riding in a much bigger circle, and out of range."[66]

When the Indians realized they had been defeated, they became incensed at Isatai. Isatai explained that his medicine had been broken when some Cheyennes had killed a skunk shortly before the attack, but as Quanah reports, the Cheyennes were "pretty mad" at Esati, asking "What's the matter you medicine, you 'polecat medicine'?" A Cheyenne named Hippy grabbed the bridle of Isatai's horse and was about to whip the medicine man because his medicine had failed and because they thought him a coward since he had refused to fight at Adobe Walls, but the other Cheyennes told Hippy, "Let him go."[67]

Quanah sums up the battle in a few words: "That pretty hard fight. From sunrise until 12 o'clock. Then we go back. . . . Get saddles and bridles and go back to village. . . . No use Indians fight Adobe."[68]

Frustrated, furious, the Indians broke into bands and surged across the plains, pillaging, murdering, and burning. Quanah tells what he did next. "Then I take all young men. Go warpath to Texas."[69]

At four o'clock the white men started venturing out of the buildings. Gruesome sights awaited them. Dixon found a dead warrior at the edge of the tall grass to the west of the buildings. "The object that I had seen crawling along the edge of the tall grass was . . . a dead Indian lying flat on his stomach. He was naked, save for a white breech-cloth. His six-shooter was in his belt. The Indian had been shot through the body, and one knee had been shattered. I could see the trail he had made by the blood on the grass. . . . He had crawled a quarter of a mile with shattered knee before I killed him."[70]

Near dusk the white men buried their dead. They wrapped the bodies in blankets and buried them in a single grave near the corral. The hunters added another horror to the scene when they decapitated and scalped eleven dead Indians and then placed the heads on the spikes of the gate to Myers and Leonard's corral.[71]

For days buffalo hunters who had been stranded on the plains streamed into Adobe Walls. Isolated bands of Indians were seen from time to time. The bodies of the Indians and horses were dragged some distance away from the living quarters and buried in a large pit. Seeking to reinforce the fortress, the men built small lookout towers on top of the two stores. William Olds was standing atop Rath's store in one of the towers when he saw a small group of Indians in the distance. He hurried down the ladder and in his haste accidentally pulled the trigger of his gun, shooting himself in the head. His head a mass of blood, he fell dead at his wife's feet.

Most of the hide men and traders fled to Dodge City during the first two weeks of July. The merchants hired a few buffalo hunters to stay at Adobe Walls to guard the buildings and kill any buffalo that were near. Not finding any buffalo, these men left on August 20, 1874, with an escort of soldiers.

A month or two later, the Indians had the last word. They recovered the bones of their dead, wrapped them in buffalo robes and blankets, and placed them on the south side of the Canadian River some distance above Adobe Walls. Then they ripped apart Rath's store and burned Myers and Leonard's store, the blacksmith shop, and the corral. Only the sod saloon was left standing. The second Adobe Walls was no more. The ruins were mute testimony to shattered dreams of wealth for the white men and freedom for the Indians.[72]

Fifty-five years later as Yellowfish stood on the site of the battle, he said, "We left Wild Horse one of our leaders on this battlefield. Our men died, some of them peacefully many years later, thinking they were in the right. We are all brothers under one nation, and we would like to do honor here to our own braves as well as our white brothers. It is right. I have spoken."[73]

ᦂᐤ CHAPTER 18 ᐤᦂ

I Lived Free

THE BATTLE OF ADOBE WALLS and other depredations in Texas, Kansas, Colorado, New Mexico, and Indian Territory caused the government of the United States to take decisive action against the Plains Indians. On July 15, 1874, General William Tecumseh Sherman sent General Philip Sheridan the following telegram: "Don't you think it would be well to order the 6th and 10th Cavalry to converge on Fort Sill and settle this matter at once, and prevent the Indians from turning towards Texas—as they naturally will—to get even, especially if they have got the worst of it thus far. Each detachment could follow some fresh trail, and word could be sent the friendly Indians in advance to collect for safety at Fort Sill. The hostiles should be stripped of all horses, mules, etc. Unless something is done now, the rascals will merely rest awhile and start afresh." President Ulysses S. Grant's five-year-long peace policy was canceled, and on July 25, 1874, the United States was officially at war.[1]

An operation was planned in which thousands of soldiers would crisscross the canyons and breaks of the Texas Panhandle, where most of the hostiles were thought to be hiding. In a report, Brigadier General C. C. Augur describes the operation: "Colonel Mackenzie, with one column, was to operate from his old supply-camp on the fresh fork of the Brazos, and to draw his supplies from Fort Griffin, distant a hundred and twenty miles. Lieutenant Colonel Davidson, Tenth Cavalry, with another column, was to operate west from Fort Sill, drawing his supplies from that post; Lieutenant Colonel Buell, Eleventh Infantry, with still another column, to operate between the two, with a supply-camp near to where the Wanderer's Creek empties into Red River. This arrangement has been carried into effect and these columns are now in the field." In addition, Colonel Nelson A. Miles was moving south from Camp Supply, and Major William Price from Fort Bascom, New Mexico.[2]

The Indians at the agencies were informed that all who intended to stay within the reservation were required to enroll and report for roll call every day. If they were found outside the boundaries, they would be attacked. After the deadline, all Indians who came to the agency would be disarmed and would be considered prisoners of war. By the end of September, 1,370 Indians had enrolled at Fort Sill: 479 Comanches, 585 Kiowas, and 306 Kiowa Apaches.[3]

On August 30, 1874, Colonel Miles tracked five hundred warriors, mostly Cheyennes, to a site near Palo Duro Canyon. A running battle ensued, but most of the Indians escaped. Then Miles sent Captain Wyllys Lyman with thirty-six wagons to the Canadian River to pick up some supplies. On September 9, Lyman and his men were ambushed by several hundred Kiowas and Comanches. The battle lasted three days, but then the Indians gradually drifted off in small groups when they saw that a large number of soldiers were congregating in the vicinity.[4]

On September 10, Miles, feeling the need to send some dispatches to Camp Supply, decided to send Billy Dixon and Amos Chapman, who had hired on as scouts. Miles offered Dixon and Chapman a large escort, but they declined, taking only four soldiers and an interpreter, because they believed they had a better chance to get through with a small detachment. The men left at eight in the evening and, traveling all night, reached the vicinity of the Lyman wagon train fight. Not knowing about the fight, at sunrise they were surprised to see one hundred Indians not far away. The Indians attacked, and after a devastating first few minutes, Dixon and his companions managed to take cover in a buffalo wallow, a slight indentation in the prairie. The whites held off the Indians all day until the warriors gave up the attack. One soldier was killed and all the others except Dixon were wounded. The survivors were not rescued until September 13.[5]

At about the same time as the soldiers and scouts were trapped in the buffalo wallow, Major Price, who had marched with a detachment of soldiers from Fort Bascom in New Mexico, ran into a force of about one hundred Comanche and Kiowa warriors. The Indians fought bravely for one and one half hours until their women and children could escape, and then they withdrew.[6]

Miles and Price joined forces and sent out small expeditions to comb the area around Palo Duro and Tule canyons, and in mid-September, Davidson's troops joined the effort to flush the Indians from their hiding places. The drought and intense heat of summer had been replaced by heavy and frequent rains, which turned the plains into a vast sea of mud; the

Indians called the last months of the Red River War "the Wrinkled Hand Chase." The operations of Miles, Price, and Davidson had driven several hundred Kiowas, Comanches, and Cheyennes into the inner reaches of the vast and spectacular Palo Duro Canyon, and there on September 28, 1874, the most important battle of the Red River War was fought by the troops under General Ranald Mackenzie. At dawn Mackenzie and his men slipped and slid down a steep path into the canyon and attacked a large group of Indians who had abandoned their lodges and were fleeing up the sides of the canyon. The fight lasted a few minutes, and only four bodies were found at the time, but later the Indians stated that fifty or sixty people had been killed. Two hundred lodges were destroyed, and over a thousand horses and mules were slaughtered. Although most of the Indians escaped, many were on foot, their homes and winter food supply had been destroyed, and soon the punishing northers would whistle across the plains.

Sherman was disappointed in the outcome of the Palo Duro battle and complained to Sheridan: "I wish the troops had managed to kill more bucks, but when they are disarmed & unhorsed and collected on their Reservation under military surveillance they will likely behave themselves for a time, at least until the Quakers manipulate them a while longer." Other important actions occurred in October, when Buell and his forces chased a large group of Kiowas and Cheyennes up the Salt Fork of the Red River and succeeded in destroying over four hundred lodges, and in November, when Miles attacked and routed a large Cheyenne village near McClelland Creek.[7]

As the Red River War raged in the canyons and river bottoms on the edge of the Staked Plains, Quanah and his band for the most part remained aloof, far to the south. After the defeat at Adobe Walls, Quanah and his followers had ridden to the east, driving the horse herd of the buffalo hunters before them. The next day Quanah and his men and several Kiowas split off from the group and headed southeast. Quanah describes what happened next:

> Several days after that, we found a little settlement just east of the Wichita Mountains. We attacked it early one morning, killed seven persons, burned the houses and captured several horses. Turning homeward, we went southwest through Texas and got several horses from a ranch and killed two cows for meat. Leaving there still going toward home, we traveled several days. One day about noon, a friendly Kiowa, who had been at the Anadarko Agency, came to where we were stopped for din-

ner and told us that a large number of soldiers were after us. We hurried on home and there learned that our friends who had left us in Western Oklahoma had been attacked by soldiers and a great many of them were killed and several captured.[8]

As the summer passed, Quanah and his companions heard that their allies were surrendering. Back at Fort Sill some of Quanah's former allies disclosed that the Quahadas were camped on the stream that had carved out Yellowhouse Canyon. Mackenzie and his troops checked out the report but did not find the band there on October 31. Mackenzie continued to pursue the elusive Quahadas throughout the winter. Finally realizing that they were far to the south, he recommended that the commander of the Department of Texas, General C. C. Augur, send out troops from Fort Concho to scour the Pecos River valley and the Guadalupe Mountains. Mackenzie continued traveling to the south as far as present-day Gail, Texas, where he and his troops were snowed in. While there, he received a message from General Sheridan informing him that the Red River War was over and that he was ordered to proceed to Fort Sill, where he would be in charge of the Comanche-Kiowa and Cheyenne-Arapaho reservations.[9]

Quanah describes what was happening in the Indian camp: "Having several hundred good horses, we kept a good watch for the approach of the enemy and when we would learn that they were coming in our direction we would quickly move. Several of my men, with our families, kept up that kind of tactics all that winter and until the next summer. During that time we were almost continually going, as the soldiers were after us and many times they were almost upon us."[10]

More Comanches surrendered. Before Mackenzie's arrival at Fort Sill on March 16, 1875, Lieutenant Colonel J. W. Davidson sent scouts to parley with some Comanches who were still out. The scouts were successful, and on April 18, three chiefs arrived at Fort Sill and surrendered, 170 persons and seven hundred horses. In the past, Quanah had been closely associated with two of the chiefs, Mowway and Wild Horse.[11]

Mackenzie then decided to lure in the last of the Quahadas. Some Indians at Fort Sill had told him a large band was camped on a stream that ran out of the Caprock on the west side of present-day Post, Texas. The men chosen for the dangerous mission were three Comanches, Wild Horse, Habbywake, and Toviah; and two white men, Sergeant John B. Charlton, who had fought in the battle at Blanco Canyon; and Dr. Jacob J. Sturm.[12] Sturm was a self-educated physician and the post interpreter.

He had married a Caddo woman and at times lived with that tribe. Charlton described Sturm as a "half-breed interpreter" named Storms: "His first name I've forgotten if I ever knew it. He was an old bear hunter who lived somewhere on the Washita." Although the other Indians had surrendered unconditionally, Mackenzie offered terms to the last holdouts. Charlton tells the substance of the verbal message that Sturm was charged with delivering to the head chief of the Quahadas: "If Mow-wi and his band will come into Fort Sill and surrender, giving up arms and ammunition, he would be made comfortable and be taken care of by the Government. Would be, in a manner, free as long as they gave no trouble, but if they would not come in that he (General MacKenzie) would follow him until his band was exterminated."[13]

The emissaries started on their journey on April 23, 1875, traveling west from Fort Sill and camping the first night on Cache Creek, which the guides called Tozopassa Honovit. The second camp was made on what the Quahadas called Buogcervis Honovit or Turkey Creek, five miles from present-day Altus, Oklahoma. When the men arose in the morning, they heard the loud, raucous cry of a raven that was flying around the camp, and later in the day the men encountered immense herds of buffalo. The Indian guide told Dr. Sturm, "Our morning visitor the Raven, never lies and is a good friend to the red man, always letting him know when he is in the neighborhood of Buffalo." Veering to the southwest, the men crossed the Red River. Sturm describes the river in his journal: "In place of finding water, we found only a great broad bed of sand, that did not seem to have been saturated with water in twelve months. Indian name Peoppassa Neovit or dry river."[14]

Three days later the men reached the Pease River, which the Comanches called Acumacup Neovit or Buffalo Tongue River because of a legend in which a Comanche hunter killed a number of bison, removed their tongues, buried them in the ground, and then held a buffalo dance during which all the people feasted on the tongues.[15] It was also called Wahpit Honovit or Cedar River. This too the men found to be completely dry, but the guides knew where they were going, and in the evening the party made camp on a creek fed by a stream of clear water with a pool that held perch and other fish. The Comanche name was Hokene Honovit or Pit Creek.[16]

On April 29, the delegation stopped at noon at "a large creek of good water."[17] As the men lounged in the shade, they did not feel at peace, for as Sturm says, "Here we feel uneasy seeing many Buffalo running in every direction which is some indication that Indians are near us." Their fears

were justified when late in the afternoon they found the fresh trail of Indians. Reversing their direction and traveling north along the lower edge of
the Staked Plains until nightfall, they reached the camp of Quahada chief
Black Beard with his band of fifty people. Sturm describes the encounter
with Black Beard and his band: "He received us very kindly. After a hearty
supper on Buffalo meat and a smoke which is always a preliminary to an
'Indian talk' I proceeded to tell him that I brought a message from General
MacKenzie the great Warchief of the white soldiers at Fort Sill, asking him
to come in and surrender himself and his people to the Military Authority
of the United States to which he readily assented saying that he was tired
of war and anxious for peace and he advised me to proceed to the main
camp as soon as possible which he said was about 'Two sleeps' distance.
. . . Black beard made me a present of a Mule giving me the choice of all he
had he is a jovial good fellow and treated us with utmost kindness."[18]

Leaving Black Beard's camp about noon, the emissaries traveled fast
and at nightfall camped in Blanco Canyon on Tosah Honovit, now called
the White River. The next day the Comanche guide led the group up a
steep bluff and onto the Staked Plains. In the late afternoon the men descended into Yellowhouse Canyon and camped on Tahtemareie or Traders'
Creek.[19]

After a hard day's travel of thirty-five miles, the men camped on Sand
Creek near present-day Post, Texas, where they found "the poorest grass
and most unpalatable water we had on the trip." They were disappointed
because according to Mackenzie's information, this was the location of the
main Quahada camp.[20]

Resuming their journey, the messengers traveled over the Staked Plains
until they sighted the Quahada camp on one of the creeks that flowed out of
the Caprock near present-day Gail.[21] Sturm describes what happened next:

> On our arrival in camp the Indians rode up from every direction to
> see who we were and finding we were peace messengers they invited us
> to alight from our horses, which were taken care of by the squaws while
> we were escorted to a large tent by the men. Here we divided our to-
> bacco, coffee, and sugar with them which pleased them immensely hav-
> ing none of the luxuries for a long time. After they had drunk some
> coffee we proceded to their counsil house after the usual preliminary
> smoking I delivered the message sent out to them by Col. McKenzie,
> with which they seemed well pleased. They however would not give us a
> definite answer as some of their principal men were out of camp and all

must have time to deliberate so arrangements were made to meet again tommorow when a final answer would be given—the most of them seem willing to come in, to give up the best horses and all the mules but wishing to retain the great bulk of their Ponies. I told them that I could make no terms with them and that they had to make up their mind to surrender unconditionaly to General McKenzie. After the talk was over I was invited to the tent of their great medicine man Isahtite with whom I had a big talk. He told me that he would go with me and that all his people must go. He is a very young man but has a good deal of influence among his people. He stated that about thirty men of the tribe were on a Buffalo Hunt, but were expected in camp tommorrow.[22]

The next day the negotiations continued:

We are again in counsel to day and Quinah a young man of much influence with his people made a speech in favor of coming in here. The medicine man then told his people they must all prepare to come in to Fort Sill and as his authority seems to be absolute they all agreed to start tommorrow. . . . The medicine man says he is no chief but admits that he has much influence over his people and that they will do what he tells them. He further states that he has not acquired his influence by being a warrior and what influence he has he acquired by kind treatment of his people, never abusing them. He says he has a big heart, loves everybody and every living thing that he never gets mad or strikes even a beast. We shall start tomorrow for Black Beard's camp from which point I expect to dispatch messengers to Fort Sill to inform General MacKenzie of the entire success of my trip.[23]

The following morning the Comanches headed toward Fort Sill accompanied by the emissaries. Sturm describes their departure: "We broke camp this morning and all are on the move in the direction of Black Beard's camp. Isahtite has written his letter which represents one white man and three Indians coming in his camp and his people running out to meet them. He states that when the Buffalo Hunters see this letter they will know that messengers from Sill have visited their camp and brought 'good words' and that they are all on their way to this place. The letter was written on a piece of Buffalo skin and stuck on a pole."[24]

Sergeant Charlton, writing years later, remembers the three days in the Quahada camp differently: "On reaching there [the camp] they took our arms, ammunition, horses, etc., away from us and placed the four of us in a tepee with sufficient guards around us to keep us secure." Charlton told how the chief called in all the men of his band for a meeting. "This continued until the third day. In the meantime we were treated well; had plenty to eat and were not molested. I don't deny the strain was beginning to be felt, by all of us. Our fate, should they refuse to go in with us, we tried hard not to think about. On the third day, when our nerves were most tense, suddenly we heard a yelling followed by more shouts. I caught Storms by the arm and asked him what it all meant. He wasn't sure himself but told me he thought it was 'all right.'" Sturm was correct. Soon the chief and all the other Indians came over to the men and told them that they would accept the terms of surrender. "Then followed a tiresome time of handshaking and overdone manifestations of friendship, etc."[25]

Several Comanches also gave accounts of the surrender. Yellowfish and some others said: "Six in party who went out to persuade the Quohadas to come in. It was SW. of Sill, south of White river 8–10 day trip. South of Quitaque. Perhaps at southern end of cap rock. Nayweah (a gap) is name of creek. River that comes through a gap. A great cedar bluff on the north side of it. I was with the Quohada band. Isatai was the chief, Quanah there but he was not the big chief."[26]

An unidentified Comanche informant added: "[We] were way out in Texas. Message came through two white men. Were camped on creek having horse races. Some fellows on hill [gave the alarm]. [We] began to get ready for battle. Message was that Washington wanted us to come back, that the country was getting smaller. We would have to settle down. Some of us would have to be jailed. Headmen got together (Quanah, Isatai) and decided to come back."[27]

Sturm describes the first leg of the journey as the emissaries and the Quahadas set out for Fort Sill: "Leaving the low ground we climbed by the Indians route to the high plains starting over them in a northeasterly direction. The caravan soon strung out for miles affording a most beautiful aspect on this great plain."[28]

The travelers moved in a leisurely fashion across the edge of the Staked Plains, descending into a canyon or ravine when they wanted to camp or rest for a while. Many of the people had horses that were poor and weak, so everyone had to travel slowly. The trip was filled with nostalgia. As the Indians traveled, they hunted buffalo, antelope, and wild horses. They feasted on fresh meat and a plant they roasted in rock-lined pits. One night they decided to hold a dance. Sturm explains: "The Indians are having a big dance tonight and make it to be the last Medicine dance they ever expect to have [on] these broad Plains. They say that they will abandon their roving life and try to learn to live as white people do."[29]

Finally descending from the Staked Plains and veering to the east, the caravan camped on an unnamed creek a few miles south of present-day Matador. Sturm felt sorry for his charges as they made their last trek across their homeland: "I know these Indians bid adieu to these their old haunts with many regrets some offered pretty stern resistance to going in and I can not much blame them for it. . . . They have given up their old haunts, leaving their great vaste plains to go down to live in the lower ground and learn the ways virtues and vices of their white brothers."[30]

The Indians took time out to play: chasing chaparral hens and riding full speed clinging to the side of an old wagon they had found. Twenty miles from the Red River the Indians camped near present-day Quanah, Texas. Several messengers from Fort Sill arrived and were received in the traditional Comanche manner: "The whole camp on hearing of their coming assembled and formed a half circle and received them with drums beating, singing and shouting and the messengers on reaching the circle rode inside then galloped out. This was done three or four times and then they rode to the middle of the circle and said they had brought good news, which was received with shouts. They then went to an arbor and after a general smoke told the news which was all well received with hah's and approving grunts."[31]

Sturm sent Comanche messengers to Mackenzie with a letter. The missive contained information about Isatai: "I hope Esatite will be well received as he had been mainly instrumental in bringing his people in. . . . I have stayed at his lodge and he has treated me with the kindness of a brother."[32] Quanah was chosen as one of the two messengers, probably because he was leader of one of the bands. Quanah and his companion arrived at Fort Sill on May 13. There on May 19 with the help of Colonel Mackenzie, Quanah wrote a letter to his white relatives inquiring about his mother and sister.[33]

By May 21, the caravan was camped on the south bank of the Red River. After several days' delay caused by rainy weather and swollen creeks, the white men and the Indians slowly made their way to Fort Sill. There the Indians surrendered, one hundred warriors, and three hundred women, children, and old men. They turned over their considerable combined wealth of fourteen hundred horses. Sturm explains what happened: "According to appointment about noon of the 2nd of June the Indians were met by the

Troops and quietly surrendered themselves and their arms, and were escorted by the troops to Fort Sill. Arriving there they marched to their place
of confinement and all the warriors were put under guard. The old men
and the squaws proceeded to their appointed camping ground and quietly
encamped. Their horses and mules were turned over to the Troops and here
ended my labor in bringing the Quah-de-res band of Comanches from the
Staked Plains their former home into the Indian Reservation." Among
those who came into Fort Sill were Quanah's sixteen-year-old wife Weakeah
and her two-year-old daughter Nauhmahkuh.[34]

Quanah speaks of the surrender of the Quahada band: "And after I found
that we could not get any more help from our friends and that the soldiers
would not cease chasing us, and that my number was getting smaller all the
time, I decided to go to Fort Sill and give up, which I did June 2, 1875. I
surrendered to Col. R. S. Mackenzie. At the time of my surrender, I was
chief of the Nocones, Cohoites, Chochetakers and Comanche Indians;
which position I have held ever since."[35]

According to family legend, before Quanah made his decision to surrender, he went to the top of a mesa to meditate. He was willing to fight to
the death but he did not want to lead his people to annihilation. He remembered his mother, who had learned to live in another culture. Quanah
had started to pray to the Great Spirit when he saw a lobo wolf that howled
at him and then trotted off in the direction of Fort Sill. Next an eagle
appeared, dived at Quanah several times, and flew toward Fort Sill. Quanah,
whose real name was said to be Eagle, took these incidents as signs that he
should convince his people to surrender.[36]

As the years passed, Quanah gradually gained power and influence. He
became a judge, the leader of the Native American Church, and principal
chief of the Comanches. Quanah was a survivor, smart, tough, and resil-
ient, and he always took care of his people and his family. He had a total of
eight wives and twenty-two children. Hugh R. Scott, who conducted a
number of interviews with Quanah, relates some of the complications aris-
ing. Indian Commissioner Thomas J. Morgan had promised to build
Quanah a house. But Morgan backed down on his promise when he learned
that Quanah had seven wives at that time. When Morgan's decision and
the reason for it were reported to Quanah, he replied that "a man with
seven wives needed a house much more than a man with only one."

Morgan decided to force the issue. Quanah made a trip to Washington
to discuss the matter. He tried to explain his position, saying: "A long time

Quanah Parker and Andrew Jackson Houston. Courtesy Panhandle-Plains
Historical Museum Research Center, Canyon, Texas.

ago I lived free among the buffalo on the Staked Plains and had as many wives as I wanted, according to the laws of my people. I used to go to war in Texas and Mexico. You wanted me to stop fighting and sent messages all the time: 'You stop, Quanah. You come here. You sit down, Quanah.' You did not say anything then, 'How many wives you got, Quanah.' Now I come and sit down as you want. You talk about wives; which one I throw away? You pick him? You little girl, you go 'way; you got no papa—you pick him? You little fellow, you go 'way; you got no pappa—you pick him?"[37]

Quanah kept his wives and children. He obtained his spacious two-story house, not from Morgan but from the cattlemen to whom he leased land, and on the roof he painted stars so that he would have insignia like those on the uniforms of the white generals.

Quanah had loved his mother dearly, and in 1910 he petitioned to have her remains and those of Prairie Flower moved to a graveyard on the reservation near his home. When Cynthia Ann was reinterred, he spoke at her grave in English. His words show how her influence had helped him to become the great leader that he was: "Forty years ago my mother died. She captured by Comanches, nine years old. Love Indian and wild life so well no want to go back to white folks. All same people anyway, God say. I love my mother. I like white people. Got great heart. I want my people follow after white way, get educate, know work, make living when payments stop. I tell 'em they got to know pick cotton, plow corn. I want them know white man's God." The Comanches followed Quanah's advice, and this was his greatest accomplishment. Quanah ended his speech with these words, "Comanche may die today, tomorrow, ten years. When end comes then they all be together again. I want see my mother again then."[38]

Two months later on February 23, 1911, Quanah Parker died, great-grandson of Elder John Parker, great-nephew of Daniel and James W. Parker, cousin of Rachel Parker Plummer, and son of Cynthia Ann Parker and Peta Nocona. Blood had been shed on the land by whites and Indians alike, but finally the blood of the two races was mingled in one man— Quanah Parker, the last chief of the Comanches.

NOTES

CHAPTER I. A POOR SINNER

1. J. A. (Joseph Albert) Dickson, untitled manuscript, privately owned, ca. 1907–1909, 7.
2. John Parker, Pension Application, National Archives, Washington, D.C.; Charles Edward Parker, Elder John Parker [title of document], Sargent Papers, Illinois State Historical Library, Springfield, Illinois; Guy W. Small, "The Life of Daniel Parker," master's thesis, East Texas Baptist College, Marshall, 1954, 1. Several genealogical studies have been conducted indicating that Elder John Parker was the descendant of Deacon Thomas Parker (1607–ca. 1683), who in 1635 sailed from London to New England with a group of Puritans who settled in Massachusetts, but the proof is not conclusive. Helen G. Reagan, *The Reagan-Parker Family Genealogy*, 264–70.
3. In 1776 Culpeper County consisted of the present-day counties of Culpeper, Madison, and Rappahannock. George B. Everton, Sr., ed., *The Handy Book for Genealogists*, 7th ed., 305–306.
4. Garnett Ryland, *The Baptists of Virginia, 1699–1926*, 37.
5. David Benedict, *A General History of the Baptist Denomination in America, and Other Parts of the World*, 2:305–306.
6. Robert Baylor Semple, *History of the Baptists in Virginia*, 29–41, 233, 238.
7. John Parker, Pension Application; John Parker, Military Record, National Archives, Washington, D.C.
8. Claudine McCallay Dollar, *The Gardner, Kendrick, Forgey, Parker, Gage-McComas Families*, 314, 321; Charles E. Parker, Elder John Parker; May Reagan Mathes, Daughters of the American Revolution Application, Palestine Public Library, Palestine, Texas.
9. Dollar, *Gardner, Kendrick Families*, 321; Reagan, *Reagan-Parker Genealogy*, 271.
10. John Parker, Military Record. This document was signed by John Parker.
11. John Parker, Military Record; Dollar, *Gardner, Kendrick Families*, 342.
12. Daniel Parker, "A Short History of the Life and Progress of the Editor," *Church Advocate* 2 (1831): 261–62.
13. Ibid., 259–63.
14. Rufus Babcock, ed., *Forty Years of Pioneer Life*, xxxiii–xxxiv; William Warren Sweet, *Religion in the Development of American Culture, 1765–1840*, 134–37.
15. Robert William Mondy devotes a chapter to frontier fights in *Pioneers and Preachers: Stories of the Old Frontier*, 107–27.
16. James Ewing, *A Treasury of Tennessee Tales*, 32–39.
17. James Ross, *Life and Times of Elder Reuben Ross*, 129–30; Parker, "Short History," 261–63.
18. Ross, *Life and Times*, 131–32.

19. Parker, "Short History," 263–64.
20. Ibid., 266–67.
21. Ross, *Life and Times*, 66.
22. Babcock, ed., *Forty Years*, 25–26.
23. Ryland, *Baptists of Virginia*, 35–36.
24. Parker, "Short History," 267.
25. Herman A. Norton, *Religion in Tennessee*, 12.
26. Daniel Parker family Bible records, privately owned.
27. Parker, "Short History," 268.

CHAPTER 2. THE WRONG ROAD

1. Parker, "Short History," 268.
2. Dollar, *Gardner, Kendrick Families*, 342–47; Reagan, *Reagan-Parker Genealogy*, 292–93; Joe Bailey Parker, Family Group Sheets, privately owned.
3. Sweet, *Religion in American Culture*, 111; William Warren Sweet, *Religion on the American Frontier: The Baptists, 1783–1830*, 21–22.
4. Ross, *Life and Times*, 90; John F. Cady, *The Origin and Development of the Missionary Baptist Church in Indiana*, 23; Sweet, *Religion in American Culture*, 110–11.
5. Ross, *Life and Times*, 76.
6. John Carr, *Early Times in Middle Tennessee*, 29.
7. Ross, *Life and Times*, 76.
8. Parker, "Short History," 268.
9. A. W. Putnam, *History of Middle Tennessee; or Life and Times of Gen. James Robertson*, 397 (drawing); J. Woolridge, ed., *History of Nashville Tennessee*, 94.
10. Parker, "Short History," 268; John Parker, Pension Application; C. J. Puetz, *Tennessee County Maps*, 29. Jill K. Garrett states on p. 126 of *Historical Sketches of Dickson County, Tennessee* that "John Parker, Sr., in 1810 received 640 acres on Parker's Creek, then known as Parker's fork of Turnbull Creek, bounded by Joseph Vos' west boundary line. *(Tennessee Land Grants, Book C.)* Early settlers were James Tidwell, Moses Parker, Isiah Tidwell, and Levin Dickson."
11. Ross, *Life and Times*, 106.
12. *The Goodspeed Histories of Montgomery, Robertson, Humphreys, Stewart, Dickson, Cheatham, Houston Counties of Tennessee*, 923–24.
13. Corlew, *History of Dickson County*, 48. Turnbull Baptist Church still exists and is Dickson County's oldest church.
14. Parker Genealogy Chart; Turnbull Primitive Baptist Church Minutes of the Session and List of Members, vol. 1, 1806–1818 (the title was added at a later date), Tennessee State Library and Archives, Nashville, Tennessee, microfilm. Water stains have made some of the names illegible, but most can still be read:

MENS NAMES
Daniel Parker Jun. [Elder John's son]
Joseph Hubbs
Moses Parker [Born in South Carolina. Arrived in Dickson county before
    Elder John and like Elder John had sons named John and Daniel.]
John Hall
Daniel Parker Eldest [Moses' son]

Aaron Parker Eldest Dismissed
John Parker Jun Excmed [Moses' son]

WOMENS NAMES
Sary Hubbard Dismist
Molly Hall Dismist by Leter
Sary Parker Junn
Hannah Parker
Mary Ross Dismist
Sary Parker Sen
Ruth Parker dead

15. Ross, *Life and Times,* 326.
16. Turnbull Baptist Church Minutes.
17. Parker, "Short History," 269–70.
18. A recently built, small white frame church named Old Hopewell Missionary Baptist Church now occupies the site, but ancient gravestones, their inscriptions obscured by time, stand in the small cemetery in the churchyard. Personal observation of the author in July of 1986.
19. Parker, "Short History," 270.
20. Sweet, *Religion in American Culture,* 111–12.
21. Parker, "Short History," 274. A handwritten original deed in the Joseph E. Taulman Papers in the Center for American History in Austin, Texas, describes Daniel's new home: "a certain tract or parcel of land situate lying and Being in the County of sumner and state of Tennessee on both sides of the Caney fork of Drake's Creek of Barren [County] containing Two Hundred fifteen Acres begining at a black oak on William Browns heit [?] corner runing North one Hundred and sixty six poles then west to Leonard Browns Northeast corner, the[n] south along Browns line to the Center of the spring then down the spring branch to a small hickory then south and to two small Hickorys on the north side of the Creek nearly oposite the spring thence up the said creek or the meanders thereof to a poplar and spanish oak on the south side of the Creek at the mouth of a hollow thence south fifty six poles to a small white oak saplin ten poles East of Leonard Browns northeast Corner then East to the Begining." Deed of Sale from Edward Given to Daniel Parker, Jan. 22, 1811. See also Puetz, *Tennessee County Maps,* 29.
22. Parker, "Short History," 274–76.
23. John Bond, *History of the Baptist Concord Association of Middle Tennessee and North Alabama,* 27–28.
24. Ibid., 28–29.
25. Ross, *Life and Times,* 145.
26. Parker, "Short History," 270–71.
27. Ibid., 272.
28. Ibid., 271.
29. Small, "Life of Daniel Parker," 1.
30. Parker, "Short History," 272.
31. Biographical Sketch of Daniel Parker, Center for American History, Austin, Texas, 2. Daniel Parker's son John agreed to write the biographical sketch, but the manuscript is not signed.

32. Biographical Sketch of Daniel Parker, 3–4.
33. Ibid., 4.
34. Parker, "Short History," 273–74.
35. Biographical Sketch of Daniel Parker, 4.
36. Ibid.; Parker, "Short History," 273.
37. Biographical Sketch of Daniel Parker, 4.
38. Benedict, *General History*, 2:224; Bond, *History*, 25.
39. Bond, *History*, 24.
40. Parker, "Short History," 276.
41. Ibid., 276–77.
42. Bond, *History*, 25–27; Parker, "Short History," 277.
43. Parker, "Short History," 277.

CHAPTER 3. PLAIN AND UNPOLISHED— THE DIAMOND IN THE ROUGH STATE

1. Parker, "Short History," 277.
2. Ibid.
3. Dollar, *Gardner, Kendrick Families*, 342–49; Reagan, *Reagan-Parker Genealogy*, 292–357; Parker, Family Group Sheets; James W. Parker, *Narrative of the Perilous Adventures, Miraculous Escapes and Sufferings of Rev. James W. Parker [and] the Capture and Subsequent Sufferings of Mrs. Rachel Plummer*, 5. "In 1811, fighting broke out with the tribes along the Upper Mississippi, and the territorial militia was mustered. In terms of men killed and battles fought, the Indian War in Missouri was insignificant. It was serious mainly because it coincided with the War of 1812, in which England partly directed the activities of her Indian allies." Writers Program, *Missouri*, 46.
4. Reagan, *Reagan-Parker Genealogy*, 292; Dollar, *Gardner, Kendrick Families*, 343.
5. Parker, Family Group Sheets; Parker, "Short History," 277–78.
6. William S. Speer, ed., *The Encyclopedia of the New West*, 290; Charles E. Parker, Elder John Parker.
7. Edward P. Brand, *Illinois Baptists: A History*, 60.
8. Christiana Holmes Tillson, *A Woman's Story of Pioneer Illinois*, 25. See also Elihu Benjamin Washburne, *Sketch of Edward Coles, Second Governor of Illinois, and the Slavery Struggle of 1823–4*, 69.
9. William Henry Perrin, ed., *History of Crawford and Clark Counties*, 127–29, 133.
10. Robert P. Howard, *Illinois: A History of the Prairie State*, 3–4.
11. Ibid., 2.
12. Perrin, ed., *History of Clark and Crawford Counties*, 127–28.
13. Ibid., 133, 134. Milk sickness was later found to be caused by drinking milk from cows that had eaten snakeroot or rayless goldenrod. The victim often died. Sylvia Van Voast Ferris and Eleanor Sellers Hoppe, *Scalpels and Sabers*, 66. Abraham Lincoln's mother is thought to have died from milk sickness. For many years the lives of the Lincolns and the Parkers were parallel, and they were surely acquainted. The two families had lived in adjacent counties in Virginia during the time of the Revolutionary War. Later, Crawford County, Illinois, which was the home of most of Elder John Parker's clan from 1817 to 1833, was only sixty miles from Spencer County, Indiana, where Abraham Lincoln and his family lived from 1816 to 1830. Both families were Predestinarian Baptists.

14. Tillson, *A Woman's Story*, 28.

15. Howard, *Illinois*, 113.

16. Perrin, ed., *History of Crawford and Clark Counties*, 134.

17. Joseph E. Taulman Papers, various documents, 1821–41, Center for American History, Austin, Texas.

18. Parker, "Short History," 275.

19. Donald E. Tingley, "Illinois Days of Daniel Parker, Texas Colonizer," *Journal of the Illinois State Historical Society* 51 (1958): 391–92.

20. Reagan, *Reagan-Parker Genealogy*, 272; Myldred Stebbins to Jo Ella Exley, letter, Aug. 20, 1987; Billie Price, "Elder John Parker and His Family," *Roadrunner* (Chaparral Genealogical Society, Tomball, Texas), 10 (1984): 203; William Henry Perrin et al., comps., *The History of Coles County Illinois*, 290–91.

21. Perrin, ed., *History of Crawford and Clark Counties*, 137; Tingley, "Illinois Days," 392.

22. Theodore Calvin Pease, ed., *Illinois Election Returns, 1818–1848*, vol. 18 of *Collections of the Illinois State Historical Library*, 196; Brand, *Illinois Baptists*, 59; Howard, *Illinois*, 120.

23. Tingley, "Illinois Days," 392. The Illinois and Michigan Canal was completed in 1848. Newton Bateman and Paul Selby, eds., *Biographical and Memorial Edition of the Historical Encyclopedia of Illinois*, 1:287. Abraham Lincoln, who first served in the Illinois legislature in 1834, also promoted the building of a canal system and, like Daniel, was opposed to slavery.

24. Washburne, *Sketch of Edward Coles*, 70–71; Tingley, "Illinois Days," 393.

25. Edward P. Brand, *Illinois Baptists*, 81; Washburne, *Sketch of Edward Coles*, 90–91, 98.

26. Daniel Parker et al., "To the People of the State of Illinois," *Illinois Intelligencer*, Mar. 8, 1823, 1.

27. Washburne, *Sketch of Edward Coles*, 137.

28. Thomas Ford, *A History of Illinois from its Commencement as a State in 1818 to 1847*, 1:62–63.

29. Brand, *Illinois Baptists*, 83; Washburne, *Sketch of Edward Coles*, 134.

30. Perrin, ed. *History of Crawford and Clark Counties*, 89–90.

31. Brand, *Illinois Baptists*, 61–62, 144; Babcock, ed., *Forty Years*, 81, 94, 156.

32. Babcock, ed., *Forty Years*, 65, 68.

33. See Holy Bible, King James Version, 1 Chronicles 16:10–12 and Genesis 25:18. Cady, *Origin and Development*, 36; Daniel Parker, "For the Intelligencer," *Illinois Intelligencer*, Dec. 7, 1822, 1.

34. Babcock, ed., *Forty Years*, 157.

35. Brand, *Illinois Baptists*, 76–77.

36. Cady, *Origin and Development*, 38–40; Harlow Lindley, ed., *Indiana as Seen by Early Travelers*, 181.

37. Parker, "Short History," 276.

38. Daniel Parker, *A Public Address to the Baptist Society and Friends of Religion in General on the Principle and Practice of Foreign Missions for the United States of America*, 8–9.

39. Brand, *Illinois Baptists*, 69.

40. John Mason Peck, "Historical Sketches of the Baptist Denomination in Indiana, Illinois, and Missouri," *Baptist Memorial and Monthly Chronicle* 1 (1842): 198. Eds. R. Babcock and J. O. Choules. New York: John R. Bigelow, n.d.

41. Babcock, ed., *Forty Years*, 149–50.

42. Daniel Parker, *Views on the Two Seeds*, 3–7. According to Baptist historian Max Lee, "Parker's doctrine of the two seeds . . . . was an attempt by Parker to soften Calvin's double-edged predestination, exempt God from the charge of foreordaining any of his creation to condemnation, and place the responsibility for condemnation on the unrepentant sinner." Lee, "Daniel Parker: Politician, Baptist, and Anti-Missionary," *Texas Baptist History* 6 (1986): 3–4. Noted Baptist authority John F. Cady disagrees, stating that Parker insisted that "God's children would be saved and those of the Devil irrevocably lost, and no amount of missionary activity could alter their fate one way or the other." Cady, "The Religious Environment of Lincoln's Youth," *Indiana Magazine of History* 37 (1941): 26.

43. Brand, *Illinois Baptists*, 145.

44. Parker, "Short History," 280.

45. Ibid., 280–81.

46. Small, "Life of Daniel Parker," 19–20.

47. Brand, *Illinois Baptists*, 160.

48. Parker, "Short History," 282.

49. Pease, ed., *Illinois Election Returns*, 1:261.

50. Parker, "Short History," 282.

51. Brand, *Illinois Baptists*, 77, 114–15; John F. Cady, in "The Religious Environment of Lincoln's Youth," pp. 20–30, postulates that Abraham Lincoln's antipathy to established religion was caused by the in-fighting of the Predestinarian Baptists, which he witnessed during his youth. Young Lincoln is said to have mimicked the pastors he heard preach in his parents' home church, Little Pigeon Baptist Church. Daniel may have been one of those he mocked since Daniel sometimes preached in the Little Pigeon neighborhood.

52. Parker, "Short History," 285.

53. Perrin, ed., *History of Crawford and Clark Counties*, 141.

54. Speer, ed., *Encyclopedia of the New West*, 290.

55. Ben J. Parker, "Early Times in Texas and History of the Parker Family," *Palestine Daily Herald*, Feb. 12, 1935.

56. "Records of an Early Texas Baptist Church, 1833–1847," *Quarterly of the Texas State Historical Association* 11 (1907–1908): 89, 91.

57. Gifford E. White, ed., *1840 Citizens of Texas*, vol. 3: *Land Grants*, 218; Villamae Williams, ed., *Stephen F. Austin's Register of Families*, 30. Flora May Starr Miller, *The House of Starr*, 7. The home of John and Susannah Starr still stands near Palestine, Texas. It was built in 1856 in the Late Greek Revival style. The fireplaces are made of hand-cut sandstone. Claude Dooley and Betty Dooley, eds., *Why Stop? A Guide to Texas Historical Roadside Markers*, 2nd ed., 378. Mary and Jesse Kendrick had two sons and eight daughters who lived to maturity. During the Campbellite Movement, both sons left the Baptist Church and became Church of Christ ministers. According to one of her sons, Mary Parker Kendrick also "boldly declared her faith in the cause of reformation." Dollar, *Gardner, Kendrick Families*, 228–30, 292–312, 343.

58. Daniel Parker family Bible records; Parker, "Short History," 259.

59. Knox County Marriages, Book A, Knox County Courthouse, Vincennes, Indiana, 63; Richard Duty, will, Jan. 4, 1822, Knox County Wills, Book A, Knox County Courthouse, Vincennes, Indiana, 133–35.

60. Parker, "Early Times"; Carl L. Greenwood to Joseph E. Taulman, letter,

Sept. 11, 1931, Joseph E. Taulman Papers, Center for American History, Austin, Texas; Gifford E. White, ed., *1840 Citizens of Texas*, vol. 3: *Land Grants*, 218; Gifford E. White, ed., *The First Settlers of Houston County, Texas*, 7–8; Gifford E. White, ed., *Character Certificates in the General Land Office of Texas*, 139–40; "Records of an Early Texas Baptist Church," 92; Hulen M. Greenwood, *Garrison Greenwood: Ancestors and Descendants*, not paginated.

61. Parker, "Early Times"; Biographical Sketch of Daniel Parker, 10.

62. "Records of an Early Texas Baptist Church," 92; Greenwood to Taulman, Sept. 11, 1931. Betty Harkness Land, "Off to Texas," *Searcher* (Southern California Genealogical Society) 20 (1983): 38–39. A brilliant astronomical display took place on and around November 13, 1833, when the earth passed through the Leonid meteor shower.

63. Land, "Off to Texas," 39.

64. "Holland Creek," Ron C. Tyler, ed., *New Handbook of Texas*.

65. Greenwood to Taulman, letter, Sept. 11, 1931. The log cabin was expanded and eventually became the Fanthorp Inn, which has been restored and is now the center of the Fanthorp Inn State Historic District.

66. Parker, "Early Times"; Daniel Parker, typescript copy of will, Apr. 12, 1844, Palestine Public Library, Palestine, Texas.

CHAPTER 4. FATHER, FORGIVE THEM

1. According to Joe Bailey Parker's Family Group Sheets, Rachel and L. T. M. were married on March 28, 1833, with no place given. When L. T. M. applied for a land grant, he gave his date of entry into Texas as 1832. White, *1840 Citizens*, 3:227. On May 22, 1834, L. T. M. applied for admission into the Austin and Williams Colony, giving his age as twenty-two. He stated that his wife's name was Rachel and that she was sixteen years old. Malcomb D. McLean, *Papers Concerning Robertson's Colony in Texas*, 8:248. L. T. M. may have been related to the Hollands who had settled near the present-day town of Anderson. Family historian Jewel Peters York stated in a privately owned biographical sketch of L. T. M. Plummer: "Luther Thomas Martin Plummer was born in Carolina County, Maryland, in 1811. Son of Thomas Plummer and Margaret Holland. He had three brothers, James Pratt, Philemon Holland and Edgar. Also one sister Mary. Following his brother Philemon to Illinois, Crawford County, he met the Parker family in the early 1830's and went with them to Limestone County, Texas at present Fort Parker. He married Rachel Parker." On April 1, 1835, L. T. M. received a league of land in Robertson's Colony. McLean, *Papers Concerning Robertson's Colony*, 10:26, 160. In 1867, L. T. M. was a staunch Methodist who was planning to attend a district meeting. L. T. M. Plummer to My Dear Nephews, letter, Nov. 2, 1867, Plummer family papers, privately owned.

2. Reagan, *Reagan-Parker Genealogy*, 293; Parker, Family Group Sheets; Parker, *Perilous Adventures*, 5–6.

3. Speer, ed., *Encyclopedia of the New West*, 290.

4. U.S. Department of the Census, Bureau of the Census, *Fifth Census of the United States, 1830, Conway County, Arkansas Territory;* James W. Parker to Stephen F. Austin, letter, June 29, 1832, Austin Papers, vol. 2, unpublished, mentioned in Calendar, Center for American History, Austin, Texas.

5. Parker, *Perilous Adventures*, 6; White, *1840 Citizens*, 3:218.
6. Parker, *Perilous Adventures*, 6. According to the account written by Josiah Wilbarger's brother, John Wesley Wilbarger, as Josiah lay wounded, his deceased sister appeared to him in a dream and told him to remain where he was, and he would be rescued. That same night, a neighbor's wife dreamed she saw Josiah "naked, scalped, and wounded" but alive. She convinced her husband and others to return to the scene of the battle, where they found Josiah still alive. After he was rescued, he never fully recovered from his wounds, but he lived for eleven years. Wilbarger, *Indian Depredations in Texas*, 7–14; "Wilbarger, Josiah," Tyler, ed., *New Handbook*.
7. McLean, *Papers Concerning Robertson's Colony*, 10:26, 47, 155–60; Parker, *Perilous Adventures*, 7.
8. Plummer to My Dear Nephews, letter, Nov. 2, 1867.
9. Eugene C. Barker, ed., "Journal of the Permanent Council (October 11–27, 1835)," *Quarterly of the Texas State Historical Association* 7 (1904): 260; *Biographical Directory of the Texan Conventions and Congresses, 1832–1845*, 148–49; Eugene C. Barker, *The Life of Stephen F. Austin, Founder of Texas, 1793–1836*, 370–94.
10. "Consultation," Tyler, ed., *New Handbook*; Barker, *Life of Stephen F. Austin*, 420–21; Paul D. Lack, *The Texas Revolutionary Experience*, 38–52.
11. Rupert N. Richardson, *Texas: The Lone Star State*, 2nd ed., 89.
12. John J. Linn, *Reminiscences of Fifty Years in Texas*, 112–13.
13. Anson Jones, *Memoranda and Official Correspondence Relating to the Republic of Texas, Its History and Annexation*, 13; Herbert Gambrell, *Anson Jones: The Last President of Texas*, 53.
14. Linn, *Reminiscences*, 283; Barker, ed., "Journal," 260–61; Harold J. Weiss, "The Texas Rangers Revisited: Old Themes and New Viewpoints," *Southwestern Historical Quarterly* 97 (1994): 621–28.
15. Barker, ed., "Journal," 261–62; *Telegraph and Texas Register*, Oct. 26, 1835.
16. Eugene C. Barker, "The Texan Declaration for Taking up Arms against Mexico," *Quarterly of the Texas State Historical Association* 15 (1912): 176, 178; "Declaration of Nov. 1, 1835," Tyler, ed., *New Handbook*.
17. Lewis W. Newton and Herbert P. Gambrell, *A Social and Political History of Texas*, 154. See also Barker, *Life of Stephen F. Austin*, 419–20 and Louis J. Wortham, *A History of Texas from Wilderness to Commonwealth*, 2:375–77.
18. "Declaration of Nov. 1, 1835," Tyler, ed., *New Handbook*.
19. "Santa Anna, Antonio López de," Tyler, ed., *New Handbook*; Wilfrid Hardy Callcott, *Santa Anna: The Story of an Engima Who Once Was Mexico*, 4, 81, 131, 139; Seymour V. Connor, "The Battle of San Jacinto," in *Battles of Texas*, Seymour V. Connor et al., 71; Margaret Swett Henson, "Politics and the Treatment of the Mexican Prisoners after the Battle of San Jacinto," *Southwestern Historical Quarterly* 44 (1990): 192.
20. Lucy A. Erath, ed., "Memoirs of Major George Bernard Erath," pt. 1, *Southwestern Historical Quarterly* 26 (1923): 233; Small, "The Life of Daniel Parker," 44–51; "Convention of 1836," Tyler, ed., *New Handbook*.
21. "Runaway Scrape," Tyler, ed., *New Handbook*; Ann Raney Coleman, *Victorian Lady on the Frontier of Texas: The Journal of Ann Raney Coleman*, 83–89; Dilue Rose Harris, "The Reminiscences of Mrs. Dilue Harris," *Quarterly of the Texas State Historical Association* 4 (1900): 162–67; Noah Smithwick, *The Evolution of a State*, 90–91; Lack, *Texas Revolutionary Experience*, 224–28.

22. The following list is in the Texas State Library, General Land Office Muster Roll Book, Austin, Texas:

Capt. Eli Seals List of Rangers Jan. 1st 1836
Joseph A. Parker
A. Anglin
S. Bates
LTM Plummer
Richard Duty
Robert B. Frost
F. Holland
J. W. Parker
L. D. Nixon
B. Parker

23. McLean, *Papers Concerning Robertson's Colony,* 13:337; Comptroller of Public Accounts, Audited Military Claims #2823, James W. Parker, Texas State Library, Austin, Texas; Ray A. Walter, *A History of Limestone County,* 14.

24. The San Antonio Road crossed the Trinity River near where Highway 21 crosses today. Jesse Wallace Williams, *Old Texas Trails,* 179; "Old San Antonio Road," and "Robbins's Ferry," Tyler, ed., *New Handbook;* J. (John) W. Baker, *A History of Robertson County, Texas,* 345; D. W. (DeWitt Clinton) Baker, ed., *A Texas Scrap-Book,* 198. See Mrs. A. D. Gentry, "The Runaway Scrape," for a firsthand account of the flight of the refugees from Fort Houston and Fort Brown, which were near Fort Parker. *Frontier Times* 4, no. 6 (1927): 9–12.

25. Parker, *Perilous Adventures,* 85. The Robertson treaty is mentioned in the memoirs of Joel W. Robinson in McLean, *Papers Concerning Robertson's Colony* 10:393–94.

26. Walter, *History of Limestone County,* 13–14; John Holland Jenkins, *Recollections of Early Texas,* 23–25; John Henry Brown, *Indian Wars and Pioneers of Texas,* 26; "Coleman, Robert M." and "Moore, John Henry," Tyler, ed., *New Handbook;* Wilbarger, *Indian Depredations,* 218–19; McLean, *Papers Concerning Robertson's Colony,* 10:47.

27. Walter, *History of Limestone County,* 13.

28. Ibid., 14; Hans Peter Nielsen Gammel, ed., *Laws of Texas,* 1:526–28; Muster Roll [of] Silas M. Parker, General Land Office Muster Roll Book, Texas State Library, Austin, Texas.

Joseph A. Parker	Discharged	Jan. 25
C. M. Tinnin	Died	Dec. 26
Abram Anglin	Discharged	Jan. 25
Silas Bates	"	"
F. Hollands	"	Jan. 25
L. D. Nixon	"	Jan. 25
Catfish a Cherokee Indian served 30 days		

29. Daniel Parker Jr., statement, June 18, 1836, John R. Price Papers, Center for American History, Austin, Texas; McLean, *Papers Concerning Robertson's Colony,* 12:551–52, 13:206–16, 313; Thomas W. Kavanagh, *Comanche Political His-*

tory: An Ethnohistorical Perspective, 249–50. As recorded in Dorman H. Winfrey and James M. Day, *The Indian Papers of Texas and the Southwest, 1825–1916,* 1:13–17, 50–52, a treaty was made with the Cherokees and "associated bands" on February 23, 1836, and on May 29, 1838, a treaty was made with the Comanches. See also Kavanagh, *Comanche Political History,* 249–50.

30. F. Todd Smith, *The Caddo Indians: Tribes at the Convergence of Empires, 1542–1854,* 127–30.

31. Comptroller of Public Accounts, Audited Military Claims #2823, James W. Parker, Texas State Library; Parker, *Perilous Adventures,* 9.

32. Robert M. Hayes, *It Really Happened in East Texas,* 121–22.

33. Walter, *History of Limestone County,* 14; Tom W. Champion, "To the *Review,*" *Athens Review,* Oct. 4, ca. 1935, reprinted in "Capture and Life of Cynthia Ann Parker," *Palestine Herald Press,* June 6, 1937. See also Dan Parker Sr., Additional Details on Parkers Fort Massacre, Joseph E. Taulman Papers, Center for American History, Austin, Texas, 2–4; Daniel Parker Jr., statement, June 18, 1836, John R. Price Papers, Center for American History, Austin, Texas; Joseph E. Taulman and Araminta McClellan Taulman, The Fort Parker Massacre and Its Aftermath, Joseph E. Taulman Papers, Center for American History, Austin, Texas. Fort Houston was the closest settlement to Fort Parker. See "Fort Houston," Tyler, ed., *New Handbook,* and Edna McDonald Wylie, "The Fort Houston Settlement," master's thesis, Sam Houston State Teacher's College, Huntsville, Texas, 1958.

34. Dollar, *Gardner, Kendrick Families,* 342–49; Parker, Family Group Sheets; Richard Duty, will, Jan. 4, 1822, Knox County Indiana Wills, Book A: 133–35, Knox County Courthouse, Vincennes, Indiana. At least four of the seven women at Fort Parker at the time of the attack were descendants of Richard Duty, and "Granny Parker," wife of Elder John, was his widow. The persons listed in Richard Duty's will recorded in Knox County, Indiana, in 1822 are his wife Sally and his children mentioned in the following order: Nancy Harvy, Amy Stokes, John Duty [deceased], Polly Baldwin, Sally Ann Duty, Rachel McChord, Patsey Parker, Sarah Ann Duty [probably the same as Sally Ann Duty above], Thomas Duty, Elisabeth Duty, William Duty, Richard Duty, Henry [?] Duty, Sussannah Duty, and Catherine Duty. In Crawford County Marriages, 1817–1874, Book C: 14, Crawford County Courthouse, Palestine, Illinois, is recorded the marriage of Elizabeth Duty to James Abbett on Oct. 17, 1831, but I have not found a record of a Duty-Kellogg marriage.

35. Rachel Plummer, *Rachael Plummer's Narrative of Twenty One Months Servitude as a Prisoner among the Commanchee Indians,* 7; Rachel Plummer, *Narrative of the Capture and Subsequent Sufferings of Mrs. Rachel Plummer,* 6. In a signed statement Daniel Parker Jr. made on June 18, 1836, he states that Lucy Parker, "Told us That She was Very Confident it was Cadow Indians who took her Prisoner, Indians she had seen before, Very darke Couler." In another statement on the same day, he states: "I do Certify That an Indian known by the name of Jinie Jim, who spoke Inglish Plain, Told me some few days before the taking of the Navisot Fort, that there was five hundred Indians imbodied up near the Cross timbers on Trinity river, amongst whome were some or a nomber of Cadows. . . . That the 500 Waryers had, to his know[ledge] started and was then on their way to the Navisot Fort to distroy it." Daniel Parker Jr., statement, John R. Price Papers, Center for American History, Austin, Texas.

36. This account of the Fort Parker Massacre is based on the following eye-witness accounts: Plummer, *Narrative of Twenty One Months Servitude* (hereafter cited as *Narrative 1838*), 5–8; Rachel Plummer, *Narrative of the Capture* (hereafter cited as *Narrative 1844*), 2–4; Abram Anglin in Baker, ed., *Scrap-Book*, 198–200; James W. Parker, *Perilous Adventures*, 9–12; Cynthia Ann Parker in "The White Captive," *Civilian and Gazette* (Galveston), Feb. 5, 1861, 3.

37. Plummer, *Narrative 1838*, 6–7; Plummer, *Narrative 1844*, 4.

38. Plummer, *Narrative 1844*, 4; Plummer, *Narrative 1838*, 7.

39. Plummer, *Narrative 1838*, 7; Plummer, *Narrative 1844*, 4.

40. Dolly Webster, *A Narrative of the Captivity and Suffering of Dolly Webster among the Camanche Indians in Texas*, 10. Carl Coke Rister, ed., *Comanche Bondage: Beales's Settlement and Sarah Ann Horn's Narrative*, 127–39, 144–45, 150–54.

41. Plummer, *Narrative 1838*, 7–8; Plummer, *Narrative 1844*, 5.

42. Plummer, *Narrative 1844*, 4.

43. Baker, ed., *Scrap-Book*, 199; Parker, *Perilous Adventures*, 12.

44. Baker, ed., *Scrap-Book*, 199.

45. Ibid.

46. Ibid.

47. Parker, *Perilous Adventures*, 12–13.

48. Ibid.

49. Ibid., 14.

50. Ibid.

51. Ibid., 12.

CHAPTER 5. VENGEANCE IS MINE

1. Plummer, *Narrative 1838*, 8; See "Cross Timbers," Tyler, ed., *New Handbook*.

2. Plummer, *Narrative 1844*, 5–6; Plummer, *Narrative 1838*, 9.

3. Parker, *Perilous Adventures*, 14–15; G. M. Crittenden Papers, privately owned.

4. Ibid., 15–16. James intended to take the bones back to Illinois for burial. According to family legend, the bones were stored in the loft of James's smokehouse in Grimes County until they were destroyed when the smokehouse accidentally burned down. Dan Parker, Sr., Add Parker Massacre Story, Joseph E. Taulman Papers, Center for American History, Austin, Texas, 1–3; Taulman and Taulman, Fort Parker Massacre, 10–11.

5. Parker, *Perilous Adventures*, 16.

6. Ibid.

7. Ibid., 17; Walker County Genealogical Society and Walker County Historical Commission, *Walker County, Texas: A History*, 4–5; James W. Parker, Sr., Deed of Sale to James W. Parker, Jr., Nov. 11, 1851, Deed Book D: 11–12, Anderson County, Texas.

8. Llerena Friend, *Sam Houston: The Great Designer*, 73.

9. Parker, *Perilous Adventures*, 17.

10. Ibid., 18; "Robbins, Nathaniel," Tyler, ed., *New Handbook*; Friend, *Sam Houston*, 59.

11. Parker, *Perilous Adventures*, 18.

12. Ibid., 18–19.

13. Ibid., 5–6.

14. Ibid., 19. The only information that I have been able to find about what happened

to Elizabeth Kellogg after her rescue is that she died sometime before March 19, 1861. "The Legislature: Editorial Correspondence of the Gal. News, Mar. 19, 1861," *Standard* (Clarksville, Texas), Apr. 6, 1861, 3.

15. Parker, *Perilous Adventures*, 19; Graham Landrum and Allan Smith, *An Illustrated History of Grayson County, Texas*, 3, 8; "Coffee's Station," Tyler, ed., *New Handbook*.

16. Rister, *Comanche Bondage*, 162; "Coffee, Holland," Tyler, ed., *New Handbook*; Landrum and Smith, *History of Grayson County*, 1–5; Wilbarger, *Indian Depredations*, 17–18, 394–95. William P. Zuber, who lived in Montgomery County at the same time as James Parker did, said of Coffee: "Coffee or men connected with him, bought horses from the Indians which they had stolen in Texas, drove them to more distant localities, and sold them for a profit. This trade encouraged the Indians to increase their thefts in Texas, and, incidentally, to increase their murders." William Physick Zuber, *My Eighty Years in Texas*, 107. About July 27, 1842, James W. Parker informed a writer for the Houston newspaper *Telegraph and Texas Register* that he had heard from "several respectable persons" that "early in the spring several Commanches and other hostile Indians, came to those posts and requested the traders to send word to the Texian government, and inform it that they were desirous to treat for peace. The traders, however, believing that if peace should be established between these tribes and the Texians that their trade would be broken up, told the Indians that the Texians would not listen to their overtures; but were determined to wage a war of extermination against them. This so exasperated the Indians, that they returned to their tribes and determined to renew hostilities." The caption for the article was "Indian Traders."

17. Landrum and Smith, *History of Grayson County*, 1; Arrell Morgan Gibson, *Oklahoma: A History of Five Centuries*, 28.

18. Landrum and Smith, *History of Grayson County*, 3. A detailed description of a trading post is given in, W. H. Clift, "Warren's Trading Post," *Chronicles of Oklahoma* 2 (1924): 129–40. A replica of a typical trading post has been constructed at the Museum of the Great Plains in Lawton, Oklahoma.

19. Parker, *Perilous Adventures*, 19–24.

20. Fanny Kelly, *Narrative of My Captivity among the Sioux Indians*, 79–80; Rister, *Comanche Bondage*, 136, 144; Z. N. Morrell, *Flowers and Fruits in the Wilderness or Forty-Six Years in Texas and Two Winters in Honduras*, 65; Linn, *Reminiscences*, 341–42.

21. Rister, *Comanche Bondage*, 152; George Catlin, *Letters and Notes on the Manners, Customs, and Conditions of North American Indians*, 2:74, plate 165. Richard Irving Dodge, *Our Wild Indians: Thirty-Three Years' Personal Experience among the Red Men of the Great West*, 524–29.

22. Ernest Wallace and Adamson Hoebel, *The Comanches: Lords of the South Plains*, 141, 241, 259, 261–64, 271; Stanley Noyes, *Los Comanches*, 69–73; Rister, *Comanche Bondage*, 183.

23. Dodge, *Our Wild Indians*, 530; Randolph B. Marcy, *Adventure on Red River*, 169; Robert S. Neighbors, "The Nauni or Comanches of Texas; Their Traits and Beliefs, and their Divisions and Intertribal Relations" in *Information Respecting the History, Condition, and Prospects of the Indian Tribes of the United States*, ed., Henry R. Schoolcraft, 2:132; Noyes, *Los Comanches*, 90–92.

24. Rister, *Comanche Bondage*, 128; Wallace and Hoebel, *Comanches*, 15, 112–13.

25. Plummer, *Narrative 1844*, 7.

26. Carl Coke Rister, *Border Captives*, 4–6.

27. Plummer, *Narrative 1844*, 7; Plummer, *Narrative 1838*, 9–10.

28. Plummer, *Narrative 1838*, 10.

29. Ibid.

30. Ibid., 10–11.

31. According to Henderson Yoakum, in the spring of 1837 the Mexicans had sent a number of agents among the various Indian tribes to induce them to make war against the Texans. Yoakum, *History of Texas*, 2:227. See also Morris W. Foster, *Being Comanche*, 72.

32. Plummer, *Narrative 1838*, 11.

33. Ibid., 11–12; Plummer, *Narrative 1844*, 17–18.

34. Plummer, *Narrative 1844*, 13–17.

35. Ibid., 18–20.

36. Ibid., 19–20.

37. Ibid., 22–23.

38. Ibid., 23.

39. Parker, *Perilous Adventures*, 24.

40. Francis R. Lubbock, *Six Decades in Texas*, 36.

41. Sam Houston to Daniel Parker, letter, Feb. 13, 1837, Joseph E. Taulman Papers, Center for American History, Austin, Texas. A copy in Amelia W. Williams and Eugene C. Barker, eds., *The Writings of Sam Houston, 1813–1863*, 2:53–54, differs slightly from the original. A letter written on Sep. 8, 1836, from Sam Houston to Daniel Parker helps to explain the Feb. 13 letter. Houston had "authorized and directed" Daniel to "erect a Fort or Block House, and place a Flat [ferry] in the Trinity river above the Cumanche Crossing." Williams and Barker, *Writings of Sam Houston*, 1:446.

42. Parker, *Perilous Adventures*, 24–28.

43. Mattie Austin Hatcher, *Letters of an Early American Traveller: Mary Austin Holley. Her Life and Her Works, 1784–1846*, 70.

44. Andrew Forest Muir, ed., *Texas in 1837*, 29, 36.

45. John H. (Holmes) Jenkins, *Audubon and Texas*, 4; Friend, *Sam Houston*, 87.

46. Parker, *Perilous Adventures*, 28; Williams and Barker, eds., *Writings of Sam Houston*, 4:32.

47. Parker, *Perilous Adventures*, 29; "Montague, Daniel," Tyler, ed., *New Handbook*.

48. Parker, *Perilous Adventures*, 29–31.

CHAPTER 6. HOW CHECKERED ARE THE WAYS OF PROVIDENCE

1. Plummer, *Narrative 1844*, 24.

2. Ibid., Josiah Gregg, *Commerce of the Prairies*, 257.

3. Plummer, *Narrative 1844*, 24–26.

4. Ibid., 24, 26; Plummer, *Narrative 1838*, 14; Gregg, *Commerce*, 260n 9.

5. Writers' Program, *New Mexico*, 187–88; Gregg, *Commerce*, 77; Thomas James, *Three Years among the Indians and Mexicans*, 147; Plummer, *Narrative 1838*, 15; Marian Meyer, *Mary Donoho: New First Lady of the Santa Fe Trail*, 39; Ralph Emerson Twitchell, *Old Santa Fe: The Story of New Mexico's Ancient Capital*, 228.

6. Meyer, *Mary Donoho*, 38–39, 51–61; John E. Sunder, ed., *Matt Field on the Santa Fe Trail*, 202–205; Susan Magoffin, *Down the Santa Fe Trail and into Mexico: The Diary of Susan Shelby Magoffin, 1846–1847*, 103–104; Brown, *Indian Wars*, 28–37; Rister, *Comanche Bondage*, 98–198.

7. Brown, *Indian Wars*, 36–37; Marian Meyer, "First U.S. Woman Arrives in Santa Fe," *Journal North* (Albuquerque newspaper), June 24, 1987, 6; Meyer, *Mary Donoho*, 22–25; "Donoho, William," in *The Handbook of Texas*, ed. Walter P. Webb and H. Bailey Carroll; Plummer, *Narrative 1844*, 26.

8. Writers' Program, *New Mexico*, 187.

9. Gregg, *Commerce*, 103; F. (Francis) Stanley, *Ciudad Santa Fe: Mexican Rule 1821–1846*, 2:84, 127–28, 143; James, *Three Years*, 147; *Old Santa Fe Today*, 13; Henry Inman, *The Old Santa Fe Trail: The Story of a Great Highway*, 13–14.

10. Ralph Emerson Twitchell, *The Leading Facts of New Mexican History*, 2:147; Inman, *Old Santa Fe Trail*, 16–17; Writers' Program, *New Mexico*, 194–95.

11. Stanley, *Ciudad Santa Fe*, 2: 87–92; *Old Santa Fe Today*, 49; L. Bradford Price, *Spanish Mission Churches of New Mexico*, 126–33; Sunder, ed., *Matt Field*, 202; Inman, *Old Santa Fe Trail*, 18–19. The altar screen is now in the Church of Cristo Rey in Santa Fe. See picture on p. 147 of Writers' Program, *New Mexico*.

12. Inman, *Old Santa Fe Trail*, 14–15; Gregg, *Commerce*, 103; Twitchell, *Old Santa Fe*, 237n.

13. James, *Three Years*, 154–55; Magoffin, *Down the Santa Fe Trail*, 103, 114, 118–24, 145, 150; Gregg, *Commerce*, 151–54, 167–71, 180; Sunder, ed., *Matt Field*, 237–40.

14. Plummer, *Narrative 1838*, 15; Plummer, *Narrative 1844*, 26.

15. As long before as 1680, Santa Fe had been taken over by Pueblo Indians rebelling against their Spanish masters.

16. Writers' Program, *New Mexico*, 71. Gregg, *Commerce*, 91–92.

17. Firsthand accounts of the rebellion in Rio Arriba can be found in Janet Lecompte, *Rebellion in Rio Arriba, 1837*, 90–119, 152–55.

18. Gregg, *Commerce*, 91–92; Lecompte, *Rebellion*, 7–21.

19. Stanley, *Ciudad Santa Fe*, 2: 128; Gregg, *Commerce*, 92–93; Brown, *Indian Wars*, 36–37; Meyer, *Mary Donoho*, 16.

20. Lecompte, *Rebellion*, 21–34; Gregg, *Commerce*, 93; Meyer, *Mary Donoho*, 42–43; Rister, *Comanche Bondage*, 172.

21. Gregg, *Commerce*, 93; Lecompte, *Rebellion*, 34; Meyer, *Mary Donoho*, 42–43; Plummer, *Narrative 1844*, 26.

22. Lecompte, *Rebellion*, 35–39, 118; Meyer, *Mary Donoho*, 43; Gregg, *Commerce*, 94.

23. William Donoho returned to Santa Fe in 1838 to tie up his business affairs. Meyer, *Mary Donoho*, 14, 73.

24. Gregg, *Commerce*, 24.

25. Ibid., 35–36.

26. Ibid., 217n.

27. Jack D. Rittenhouse, *The Santa Fe Trail: A Historical Bibliography*, 16. See also the picture opposite p. 26 in Gregg, *Commerce*.

28. James Josiah Webb, *Adventures in the Santa Fe Trade*, 79.

29. Sunder, ed., *Matt Field*, 251–55; Webb, *Adventures*, 74–77; Writers' Program, *New Mexico*, 234–36; Magoffin, *Down the Santa Fe Trail*, 91–95.

30. Rittenhouse, *Santa Fe Trail*, 16; Henry Pickering Walker, *The Wagonmasters: High Plains Freighting from the Earliest Days of the Santa Fe Trail to 1880*, 27; Plummer, *Narrative 1844*, 26–27.

31. Gregg, *Commerce*, 217n. A group of traders that may have included the Donoho party left Santa Fe on August 12, 1837, arriving in Independence shortly before October 2. Lecompte, *Rebellion*, 119–20.

32. R. L. Duffus, *The Santa Fe Trail*, 102–106. Twitchell, *Leading Facts*, 2:139–40n.

33. Plummer, *Narrative 1844*, 27; Pearl Wilcox, *Jackson County History*, 201; Sunder, ed., *Matt Field*, 61–65.

34. Meyer, *Mary Donoho*, 70; Plummer, *Narrative 1838*, 15; Plummer, *Narrative 1844*, 27.

35. "Notice," *Telegraph and Texas Register*, Jan. 20, 1838; Plummer, *Narrative 1844*, 27; Plummer, *Narrative 1838*, 15. Mrs. Horn and Mrs. Harris both died soon after their arrival in Missouri. Brown, *Indian Wars*, 36.

36. Plummer, *Narrative 1838*, 15; Plummer, *Narrative 1844*, 27.

37. Plummer, *Narrative 1844*, 27. The travelers probably passed through Clarksville, Texas, because the Donohos settled in Clarksville in the fall of 1839 and opened a hotel that became one of the most popular ones in the area. Meyer, *Mary Donoho*, 76–80, 87–89; Meyer, "First Woman," 6; Pat B. Clark, *The History of Clarksville and Old Red River County*, 100.

38. Plummer, *Narrative 1844*, 27; Plummer, *Narrative 1838*, 15.

39. *Telegraph and Texas Register*, Mar. 3, 1838.

40. Parker, *Perilous Adventures*, 31; Plummer, *Narrative 1838*, 15.

CHAPTER 7. THE TONGUE OF SLANDER

1. Gulick, ed., *Lamar Papers*, 2:493–95; Leon Sanders, ed., "A Letter from East Hamilton, Texas," *East Texas Historical Journal* 28, no. 2 (1990): 47; Alexander Horton, *A. Horton: Patriot of the Republic of Texas*, 35–38; C. L. Sonnichsen, *Ten Texas Feuds*, 11–57; Joseph F. Combs, *Legends of the Pineys*, 1–20; "Regulator-Moderator War," Tyler, ed. *New Handbook*. "Counterfeiting" referred not only to money but also to fraudulent land certificates.

2. Smithwick, *Evolution of a State*, 61.

3. McLean, ed., *Papers Concerning Robertson's Colony*, 10:404; Lucy A. Erath, ed., "Memoirs of Major George Bernard Erath," pt. 1, *Southwestern Historical Quarterly* 26 (1923): 22; Parker, *Perilous Adventures*, 85.

4. Parker, *Perilous Adventures*, 17; Walker County Genealogical Society and Walker County Historical Commission, *Walker County, Texas*, 4–5; Mary Davis, "Early History of Montgomery," *Herald* (Montgomery County Genealogical and Historical Society) 11 (1988): 139; Gustav Dresel, *Gustav Dresel's Houston Journal*, 67; William Harley Gandy, "A History of Montgomery County, Texas," master's thesis, University of Houston, Houston, Texas, 1952, 7, 191; W. N. Martin, "A History of Montgomery," master's thesis, Sam Houston State Teachers College, Huntsville, Texas, 1950, 48, 73.

5. Joseph William Schmitz, *Texas Culture in the Days of the Republic, 1836–1846*, 45–46; William Ransom Hogan, *The Texas Republic: A Social and Economic History*, 45–52; Mary Reid, "Fashions of the Republic," *Southwestern Historical Quarterly* 45 (1941–42): 244–54; Betty J. Mills, *Calico Chronicle*, 17–45; Gilbert Cuthbertson, "Sam Houston's Neighbors," *Texana* 9 (1971): 260–61; "Evans, Moses," Tyler, ed. *New Handbook*.

6. James W. Parker vs. William W. Shepperd, Case 25, Montgomery County District Court Minutes, 1839–41, Walker County Courthouse, Huntsville, Texas;

James W. Parker vs. William W. Shepperd, Montgomery County, Texas (Republic), Court Proceedings, 1826 to 1868, Woodson Research Center, Fondren Library, Rice University, Houston, Texas. Although the court ruled in favor of James, he was awarded only his costs of $189.12; moreover, the case was dismissed in the spring of 1840 because James had failed to provide security for court costs.

7. Gulick, ed., *Lamar Papers*, 2:493–95.

8. Eric Lee Blair, *Early History of Grimes County*, 95; A. J. (Andrew Jackson) Sowell, *Early Settlers and Indian Fighters of Southwest Texas*, 43.

9. Sowell, *Early Settlers*, 43–44.

10. Gulick, ed., *Lamar Papers*, 2:494.

11. Plummer to My Dear Nephews, letter, Nov. 2, 1867. At the time of his death in 1839, Joseph Allen Parker owned over 10,000 acres of land according to the declaration of his son George Washington Parker. Joseph A. Parker Estate, Harris County Probate Records, May 1869, Harris County Courthouse, Houston, Texas; Plummer, *Narrative 1838*, 3.

12. Harris County Historical Society, *Houston: A Nation's Capital, 1837–1839*, 98; David G. McComb, *Houston: The Bayou City*, 70. Marj Gurasich, *History of Harris County Sheriff's Department, 1837–1983*, 8.

13. Plummer, *Narrative 1844*, 1.

14. James W. Parker, *Defence of James W. Parker against Slanderous Accusations Preferred against Him*, 3–7.

15. Parker, *Perilous Adventures*, 31–32; Plummer to My Dear Nephews, letter, Nov. 2, 1867; Parker, Family Group Sheets.

16. Heddenberg and Vedder vs. James W. Parker, loose papers, 1839, Harris County Courthouse Annex, Houston, Texas.

17. Reagan, *Reagan-Parker Genealogy*, 293; Parker, Family Group Sheets; Millie Gray, *The Diary of Millie Gray, 1832–1840*, 132–33. According to the city sexton of Houston, 299 people died (most but not all from yellow fever) from July 24, 1839, to December 3, 1839, which was about one-twelfth of the population. McComb, *Houston*, 88.

18. Davis, "Early History," 138; Montgomery County Commissioner's Court Records, Walker County Courthouse, Huntsville, Texas; James W. Parker vs. Bloodsoe and Gay, Case 57, Montgomery County District Court Minutes, 1839–41, Walker County Courthouse, Huntsville, Texas; White, *1840 Citizens*, 1:23, 92; Gifford E. White, ed., *1840 Citizens of Texas*, vol. 2: *Tax Rolls*, 111; U.S. Department of Commerce, Bureau of the Census, *Seventh Census of the United States, 1850*, Montgomery County, Texas.

19. James W. Parker vs. Bloodsoe and Gay, Case 57.

20. William Bollaert, *William Bollaert's Texas*, 281; James W. Parker vs. Bloodsoe and Gay, Case 57.

21. James W. Parker vs. Stephens and Wilson, Case 52, Montgomery County District Court Minutes, 1839–41, Walker County Courthouse, Huntsville, Texas.

CHAPTER 8. THE HOUSE OF GOD

1. Gifford White, ed., *The 1840 Census of the Republic of Texas*, 115.

2. *Republic of Texas, 5 Cong., 1 Sess., 1840–1841, House Journal*, 133.

3. The site is in the Sam Houston National Forest near Huntsville; Church Book [Mount Pleasant Church of the Regular United Baptist Faith and Order], San

Jacinto Museum of History, Houston, Texas, July 25, 1838–Aug. 8, 1840; Walker County Historical Society and Walker County Historical Commission, *Walker County, Texas: A History,* 675.

4. Church Book [Mount Pleasant], July 10, 1839, Aug. 10, 1839, May 7, 1840, June 13, 1840, Aug. 4, 1840.

5. Ibid., July 11, 1840.

6. "Records of an Early Texas Baptist Church," 99–100, 103.

7. "Cherokee War," Tyler, ed., *New Handbook;* Dianna Everett, *The Texas Cherokees,* 86–96; Winfrey and Day, *Indian Papers of Texas,* 1:14–17; Paul N. Spellman, *Forgotten Texas Leader: Hugh McLeod and the Texan Santa Fe Expedition,* 29–31.

8. James T. DeShields, *Border Wars of Texas,* 213–14; "Killough Massacre," "Cherokee War," "Cordova Rebellion," and "Kickapoo Indians," Tyler, ed., *New Handbook;* Everett, *Texas Cherokees,* 96; Ray A. Stephens, "The Killough Massacre," *Texana* 7 (1969): 322–27; Wilbarger, *Indian Depredations,* 620–22; Hattie Seale Joplin, "When Cherokee War Whoops Rang through Texas," *Frontier Times* 8 (July 1931): 471–75; Dooley and Dooley, eds., *Why Stop?* 252–53; Arrell Morgan Gibson, *The Kickapoos: Lords of the Middle Border,* 155.

9. Everett, *Texas Cherokees,* 96; Gulick, ed., *Lamar Papers,* 2:265–67, 464–65; Gibson, *The Kickapoos,* 155–56; J. H. Greenwood, "J. H. Greenwood, Early Texas Pioneer," *Frontier Times* 2, no. 4 (1925): 22; "Rusk, Thomas Jefferson," Tyler, ed., *New Handbook;* Stephen L. Moore, *Taming Texas: Captain William T. Sadler's Lone Star Service,* 113, 120–30.

10. Brown, *Indian Wars,* 57; Greenwood, "J. H. Greenwood, Early Texas Pioneer," 20–23; Small, "Life of Daniel Parker," 53; Gulick, ed., *Lamar Papers,* 2:263–65, 464–65; Moore, *Taming Texas,* 131–42; Edens Family Association, *The Edens Adventure: A Brief History of the Edens Family in America,* 33–41; McLean, *Papers Concerning Robertson's Colony,* 17:260–61; Houston County Historical Commission, *History of Houston County, Texas 1687–1979,* 12–13.

11. "Parker, Daniel," Tyler, ed., *New Handbook;* Ernest Wallace et al., eds., *Documents of Texas History,* 2nd ed., 102; Small, "Life of Daniel Parker," 51–52.

12. Small, "Life of Daniel Parker," 70; Church Book [Mount Pleasant], Aug. 8, 1840.

13. Church Book [Mount Pleasant], Feb. 13, 1841, Apr. 17, 1841, May 8, 1841.

14. Parker, *Perilous Adventures,* 33.

15. Gibson, *History of Oklahoma,* 52–54; Mattie Lloyd Wooten, *Women Tell the Story of the Southwest,* 48; Parker, *Perilous Adventures,* 20.

16. Parker, *Perilous Adventures,* 33–35.

17. Church Book [Mount Pleasant], Oct. 8, 1841.

CHAPTER 9. SUNDRY CHARGES

1. Church Book [Mount Pleasant], Aug. 15, 1841–Nov. 17, 1842; Nick Malavis, "Equality under the Lord's Law: The Disciplinary Process in Texas Baptist Churches, 1833–1870," *East Texas Historical Journal* 31 (1993): 14, 21.

2. Parker, *Perilous Adventures,* 35–36; Grant Foreman, *Pioneer Days in the Early Southwest,* 63, 289; Grant Foreman, "The Centennial of Fort Gibson," *Chronicles of Oklahoma* 2 (1924): 121–22; Jack K. Bauer, *Zachary Taylor: Soldier, Planter, Statesman of the Old West,* 99.

3. Parker, *Perilous Adventures,* 36; Foreman, *Pioneer Days,* 284.

4. Foreman, *Pioneer Days,* 285.

5. Parker, *Perilous Adventures,* 36–37.

6. Ibid., 37.

7. Jewel Peters York, genealogical charts, Plummer family papers, privately owned; Montgomery County Tax Rolls, microfilm roll #01, Clayton Genealogical Library, Houston, Texas; Montgomery County Genealogical and Historical Society, *Montgomery County History,* 25.

8. Joseph Milton Nance, *Attack and Counterattack: The Texas-Mexican Frontier, 1842,* 409–13, 428–536, 625; Zuber, *Eighty Years in Texas,* 106–16; Gandy, "Montgomery County," 120–24; John Henry Brown, *History of Texas from 1685 to 1892,* 2:234–38; Sam W. Haynes, *Soldiers of Misfortune: The Somervell and Mier Expeditions,* 24–33, 39–65; Sterling Brown Hendricks, "The Somervell Expedition to the Rio Grande," *Southwestern Historical Quarterly* 23 (1919–20): 112–40; Joseph Milton Nance, *Dare-Devils All: The Texan Mier Expedition, 1842–1844,* 12.

9. Petition of James W. Parker for Guardianship over the minors of Joseph A. Parker, February Term, 1842, J. W. Parker File, Star of the Republic Museum, Washington, Texas. The petition reads as follows:

Republic of Texas
Montgumery County
    This petition of James W. Parker a citizen of Said county humbly represents to the Honorable Probate Couty of said county. that Joseph A. Parker died in the county of Harrison [Harris] 1839 Intestate and your petitioner petitiond the Honorable the probate Court of harris for the Guardianship of the Miner heirts of said J. A. Parker. your petitioner now had Elizabeth Parker and Lafeyet Parker in his possession James W. Parker Jr. one of the heirs is now in the possession of one Foster Bobo who refuses to give him up to your petitioner. Your petitioner thearfore prays that your Honor will appoint him Guardeen for the said Eliza agd Latssin and Layfeyet aged Eleven and James Washington aged nine years in this county. and he further prays your Honors order to Foster Bobo. to give up the said James Washington Parker Jr to your petioner and your petitioner as in duty will ever pray. Dated at Parkers Mill the 25th Feby—42 J W. Parker.

10. Williams and Barker, eds., *Writings of Sam Houston,* 4:180–81.

11. R. E. Plummer to Jo Ella Exley, interview, Sept. 21, 1986; U.S. Department of Commerce, Bureau of the Census, *Seventh Census of the United States, 1850, Houston County, Texas;* Parker Genealogy Chart, Huntsville Public Library, Huntsville, Texas.

12. Church Book [Mount Pleasant], Aug. 19, 1843.

13. *Texas and the American Revolution,* 60–63; Walker County Genealogical Society and Walker County Historical Commission, *Walker County, Texas,* 220–21.

14. Church Book [Mount Pleasant], Aug. 19, 1843–Aug. 17, 1844.

15. The young woman to whom James referred was possibly Elizabeth Williams, daughter of Owen and Polly Killough Williams. She had disappeared in the Killough Massacre. Stephens, "The Killough Massacre," 324.

16. Colonel Alvarier was probably Don Mañuel Alvarez, the American consul at Santa Fe.

17. Parker, *Perilous Adventures*, 39–41.
18. Ibid., 38, 41.
19. Ibid., 38–39, 41.

CHAPTER 10. CALLED HOME

1. "Records of an Early Baptist Church," 89, 150.
2. Small, "Life of Daniel Parker," 41–43.
3. "Records of an Early Baptist Church," 145–46.
4. Ibid., 149–50; Biographical Sketch of Daniel Parker, 15–16.
5. "Strong meats" probably refers to the following passage from the King James Version of the Bible: "Ye are of dull hearing. For when for the time ye ought to be teachers, ye have need that one teach you again which be the first principles of the oracles of God; and are become such as have need of milk, and not of strong meat." Hebrews 5:11–12.
6. Biographical Sketch of Daniel Parker, 11.
7. Ibid., 11–15.
8. John M. Carroll, *A History of Texas Baptists*, 49; Bible, King James Version, Daniel 12:9–10, 13.
9. "Records of an Early Baptist Church," 150.
10. Ibid., 152–53; Church Book [Mount Pleasant], Nov. 17, 1842.
11. "Records of an Early Baptist Church," 154, 156.
12. "Records of an Early Texas Baptist Church, 1833–1847," *Quarterly of the Texas State Historical Association* 12 (July 1908): 2–3.
13. Ibid., 3, 17.
14. Ibid., 17.
15. U.S. Department of Commerce, Bureau of the Census. *Seventh Census of the United States, 1850, Houston County, Texas;* Anderson County Genealogical Society, *Pioneer Families of Anderson County Prior to 1900,* 52; Parker, Family Group Sheets; Houston County Historical Commission, *Houston County (Texas) Cemeteries,* 3rd ed., 888; Reverse Index to Marriage Record, Anderson County Court House, Palestine, Texas; *Biographical Directory,* 149; Parker, *Perilous Adventures,* 6.
16. At the September, 1864, term of the Houston County Court, James's daughter Martha Crenshaw and her husband H. J. Crenshaw were named executors of his will. The will no longer exists because the courthouse was destroyed by fire. "Administrators' Notice," *Weekly Quid Nunc* (Palestine, Texas), Nov. 8, 1864, 2.

CHAPTER 11. MISS PARKER

1. Ella Cox Lutz, "Quanah Parker: The Last Comanche Chief," *Daughters of the American Revolution Magazine* 106 (1972): 154–55. Quanah Parker stated in an undated letter to Charles Goodnight that his father "Nocona . . . took her [Cynthia Ann] into captivity." Quanah Parker to Charles Goodnight, copy of undated letter, Bill Neeley Papers, Panhandle-Plains Historical Museum, Canyon, Texas.
2. Wallace and Hoebel, *Comanches,* 262.
3. Ibid., 77, 80, 84–86; Clark Wissler, *North American Indians of the Plains,* 50–52.

For a picture of two Comanche girls in 1834, see Catlin, *North American Indians*, plate 165, "Two Comanche girls, children of the chief."

4. *Northern Standard* (Clarksville, Texas), May 25, 1846, 2. See also Grant Foreman, "The Journal of Elijah Hicks," *Chronicles of Oklahoma* 13 (1935): 68–99; Grant Foreman, "The Texas Comanche Treaty of 1846," *Southwestern Historical Quarterly* 51 (1948): 316–32; Carl Henry Elam, "The Butler and Lewis Mission and Treaty of 1846," *West Texas Historical Association Year Book* 46 (1970): 72–100; Stan Hoig, *Jesse Chisholm: Ambassador of the Plains*, 74–81; "Williams, Leonard G.," Tyler, ed., *New Handbook*.

5. P. M. Butler and M. G. Lewis to the Hon. W. Medill Commissioner of Indian Affairs, letter, Aug. 8, 1846, *House Executive Documents No. 1*, 30th Congress, 2nd Session, p. 578.

6. Robert S. Neighbors to the Hon. W. Medill, Commissioner of Indian Affairs, report, Nov. 18, 1847, 30th Congress, 1st Session, Sen. Committee Report 171, 9, National Archives, Washington, D.C.

7. Rupert Norval Richardson, "Comanches," in *Indian Tribes of Texas*, Dorman H. Winfrey et al., 50.

8. Wallace and Hoebel, *Comanches*, 298–99.

9. Wallace and Hoebel, *Comanches*, 149, 298; W. (Wilbur) S. Nye, *Carbine and Lance*, 17; Kavanagh, *Comanche Political History*, 331–32; James Mooney, "Calendar History of the Kiowa Indians," in *Seventeenth Annual Report of the Bureau of American Ethnology to the Secretary of the Smithsonian Institution, 1895–96*, 1:274–75. Mooney estimated that one-third of the native inhabitants perished.

10. Quanah himself gives the date of his birth in an undated letter written to Charles Goodnight. "From the best information I have, I was born about 1850 on Elk Creek just below the Wichita Mountains." Quanah gave other dates as he grew older. In an article written by Charles Goodnight for the *Southwest Plainsman* in 1925 and later reprinted as "True Sketch of Quanah Parker's Life" in the *Frontier Times* in November, 1926, he stated: "As nearly as I can ascertain, he [Quanah] was born in the year 1846, in what is now Oklahoma, on the northwest branch of Cache Creek." In *Quanah Parker: Comanche Chief*, p. 7, William Hagan gives Quanah's birthdate as "about 1852," and includes a brief summary of his investigation. Quanah's birthplace is also problematical. In his autobiography, which was dictated to J. A. (Joseph Albert) Dickson about 1907–1909, Quanah gives his place of birth as "Elk Creek in the Wichita Mountains." Quanah is reported to have given other locations for his birth, such as Cedar Lake in Gaines County, Texas, which is recorded on a historical marker at the site. Wichita Falls, Texas, is given in John Henry Brown's *Indian Wars and Pioneers of Texas*. Brown states on p. 43: "Capt. Quanah Parker, [was] born, as he informed me, at Wichita Falls, in 1854." It is possible that Quanah became interested in genealogy as he grew older and through inquiries determined the location and approximate date of his birth, which he recorded in his autobiography and in his letter to Goodnight. After an extensive analysis of all the sources available, I have used 1849 as the date of Quanah's birth and Elk Creek as the location.

11. Goodnight, "True Sketch," 5. For more information, see note 4 to chapter 14.

12. Wallace and Hoebel, *Comanches*, 142–44.

13. Dickson, untitled manuscript, 10; Wallace and Hoebel, *Comanches*, 121–23; Wayne Parker, Quanah Parker Last Chief of the Kwahadi Obeys the Great

Spirit, Quanah Parker Collection, Panhandle-Plains Historical Museum, Canyon, Texas, 2.

14. Marcy, *Adventure on Red River*, 169.

15. Wallace and Hoebel, *Comanches*, 301–302.

16. Charles Goodnight, *Charles Goodnight's Indian Recollections*, 25–26; Wallace and Hoebel, *Comanches*, 301–302.

17. John Salmon Ford, *Rip Ford's Texas*, 221–22. Wallace and Hoebel, *Comanches*, 300–301; T. (Theodore) R. Fehrenbach, *Comanches: The Destruction of a People*, 398–403.

18. "Capt. Ford's Expedition against the Indians," *State Gazette* (Austin, Texas), May 22, 1858; Wallace and Hoebel, *Comanches*, 301; Richardson, *Comanche Barrier*, 229–32; W. (William) J. Hughes, *Rebellious Ranger*, 129–32; Ford, *Rip Ford's Texas*, 224.

19. Ford, *Rip Ford's Texas*, 225.

20. Ibid., 224–27; Hughes, *Rebellious Ranger*, 132–35.

21. Ford, *Rip Ford's Texas*, 227–28; Richardson, *Comanche Barrier*, 234–35; Hughes, *Rebellious Ranger*, 136; "Jose Maria" and "Ross, Shapely Prince," Tyler, ed., *New Handbook*.

22. Wallace and Hoebel, *Comanches*, 335; "Brazos Indian Reservation," and "Tonkawa Indians," Tyler, ed., *New Handbook*. See also W. W. (William Wilman) Newcomb, *The Indians of Texas*, 335, and George Klos, "'Our People Could Not Distinguish One Tribe from Another': The 1859 Expulsion of the Reserve Indians from Texas," *Southwestern Historical Quarterly* 97 (1994): 605–607.

23. Ford, *Rip Ford's Texas*, 228; Hughes, *Rebellious Ranger*, 136–37.

24. Ford, *Rip Ford's Texas*, 229, 231. The *State Gazette* (Austin, Texas), May 29, 1858, contains three firsthand accounts of the expedition, those of Captain John S. Ford, 2d Lieutenant A. Nelson, and R. C. (Ranger Robert Cotter). The reports of Ford and Nelson were reprints of their official reports to Governor H. R. Runnels. The titles were "Great Battle with the Indians!!! Official Reports of Capts. Ford and Nelson" and "The Indian Fight on the Wichita—Graphic Sketch."

25. Ford, *Rip Ford's Texas*, 229–30; Ford and Nelson "Great Battle"; [Cotter], "Indian Fight on the Wichita"; Hughes, *Rebellious Ranger*, 138–40.

26. Ford, *Rip Ford's Texas*, 231–32; Ford and Nelson, "Great Battle"; [Cotter], "Indian Fight on the Wichita"; Hughes, *Rebellious Ranger*, 140.

27. Ford, *Rip Ford's Texas*, 233.

28. Joseph B. Thoburn and Muriel H. Wright, *Oklahoma: A History of the State and Its People*, 1:71n; "Paschal, George Washington," in Webb and Carroll, eds., *Handbook of Texas;* "Pix, Sarah Ridge," Tyler, ed., *New Handbook;* Ford and Nelson, "Great Battle"; [Cotter], "Indian Fight on the Washita."

29. Ford, *Rip Ford's Texas*, 233–34; Ford and Nelson, "Great Battle"; [Cotter], "Indian Fight on the Washita"; Hughes, *Rebellious Ranger*, 143–44.

30. Ford, *Rip Ford's Texas*, 234.

31. Ibid., 234–35; DeShields, *Cynthia Ann Parker*, 34; Ford and Nelson, "Great Battle"; [Cotter], "Indian Fight on the Washita"; Hughes, *Rebellious Ranger*, 145–48.

32. Ford, *Rip Ford's Texas*, 236; Ford and Nelson, "Great Battle"; [Cotter], "Indian Fight on the Washita."

33. Ford, *Rip Ford's Texas,* 236; Klos "Our People," 606–607; Walter P. Webb, *The Texas Rangers,* 151–61; Ford and Nelson, "Great Battle"; [Cotter], "Indian Fight on the Wichita"; Richardson, *Comanche Barrier,* 231–38. For a recent study (1996), see Kavanagh, *Comanche Political History,* 365–67.

34. Richardson, *Comanche Barrier,* 238–42; Webb, *Texas Rangers,* 160–61; Nye, *Carbine and Lance,* 18–24; Harold B. Simpson, *Cry Comanche,* 107–18; Robert G. Hartje, *Van Dorn,* 60–74.

CHAPTER 12. THE HAND OF SAVAGE INVASION

1. Goodnight, *Indian Recollections,* 15; Rupert N. Richardson, "Cynthia Ann Parker," in *Women of Texas,* James M. Day et al., 82.

2. Goodnight, *Indian Recollections,* 15–16; John M. Elkins, *Indian Fighting on the Texas Frontier,* 30; "A Thrilling Narrative," *Galveston Weekly,* Feb. 5, 1861; Jonathan Hamilton Baker, Diary of Jonathan Hamilton Baker (1832–1918) of Palo Pinto County, Texas, 1858–1918. Secured from his daughter Elizabeth Baker, Seattle, Washington, 1932 through Judge E. B. Ritchie, Mineral Wells, by J. Evetts Haley, typescript copy, Center for American History, Austin, Texas. Nov. 28–29, 1860.

3. "Goodnight, Charles," Tyler, ed., *New Handbook;* Goodnight, *Indian Recollections,* 16. The rifle is on display at the Panhandle-Plains Historical Museum in Canyon, Texas.

4. Goodnight, *Indian Recollections,* 17–18; Bessie Ross Clarke, untitled manuscript, Texas Collection, Baylor University, Waco, Texas, 56.

5. Pauline Durett Robertson, *Panhandle Pilgrimage,* 67.

6. Ibid., 67; Baker, Diary, Nov. 30, Dec. 1, 1860; Elkins, *Indian Fighting,* 31.

7. Baker, Diary, Dec. 1, 1860.

8. Ibid., July 13, 1860.

9. Ibid., Dec. 2, 1860; Elkins, *Indian Fighting,* 31.

10. Baker, Diary, Dec. 4, 1860.

11. Jack Loftin, *Trails through Archer,* 61; Baker, Diary, Dec. 5, 1860; Elkins, *Indian Fighting,* 31. See also J. Marvin Hunter, *The Trail Drivers of Texas,* 788–92, and "Cureton, J. J. (Jack)," Tyler, ed., *New Handbook.*

12. Baker, Diary, Dec. 6, 1860.

13. Elkins, *Indian Fighting,* 31–32; Baker, Diary, Dec. 7, 1860.

14. Francis M. Peveler to J. Evetts Haley, interview, Oct. 14, 1932, Nita Stewart Haley Memorial Library and J. Evetts Haley History Center, Midland, Texas; "Ross, Lawrence Sullivan," Tyler, ed., *New Handbook;* Victor M. Rose, *Ross's Texas Brigade,* 158–59.

15. Williams and Barker, eds., *Writings of Sam Houston,* 8:139–40.

16. Elkins, *Indian Fighting,* 32; Baker, Diary, Oct. 13, 1860.

17. Baker, Diary, Dec. 8–13, 1860; M. L. Crimmins, "First Sergeant John W. Spangler," *West Texas Historical Association Year Book* 26 (1950): 72.

18. Baker, Diary, Dec. 14, 1860.

19. Ibid., Dec. 19, 1860; Wallace and Hoebel, *Comanches,* 70; "From the Frontier," *Dallas Herald,* Jan. 2, 1861, 1.

20. Clarke, untitled manuscript, 57.

21. Baker, Diary, Dec. 16, 1860.

22. Ibid., Dec. 16–17, 1860; B. F. [Benjamin Franklin] Gholson, Frank Gholson's Account of the Death of Nacona and Rescue of Cynthia Ann Parker, dictated

by Frank Gholson to Felix Williams about 1931, B. F. Gholson Reminiscences, Center for American History, Austin, Texas, 6–9.

23. Baker, Diary, Dec. 16–18, 1860; Gholson, Frank Gholson's Account, 7.

24. Goodnight, *Indian Recollections*, 20–21; Wallace and Hoebel, *Comanches*, 73; Gholson, Frank Gholson's Account, 7.

25. Baker, Diary, Dec. 18, 1860; Goodnight, *Indian Recollections*, 19; Gholson, Frank Gholson's Account, 9.

26. Goodnight, *Indian Recollections*, 19.

27. Baker, Diary, Dec. 19, 1860; Goodnight, *Indian Recollections*, 20–21.

28. Gholson, Frank Gholson's Account, 9; Goodnight, *Indian Recollections*, 21; Bailey Phelps, *They Loved the Land: Foard County History*, 7.

29. Elkins, *Indian Fighting*, 33; Goodnight, *Indian Recollections*, 20–21.

30. G. A. Holland, *History of Parker County and the Double Log Cabin*, 50; Clarke, untitled manuscript, 57; Gholson, Frank Gholson's Account, 10; Phelps, *They Loved the Land*, 7.

31. Wallace and Hoebel, *Comanches*, 86; Gholson, Frank Gholson's Account, 10.

32. B. F. [Benjamin Franklin] Gholson, Recollections of B. F. Gholson told to J. A. Rickard. Presented to the Library, University of Texas, by Professor Eugene C. Barker, Department of History, 1937, B. F. Gholson Reminiscences, Center for American History, Austin, Texas, 12–14; Goodnight, *Indian Recollections*, 23; Gholson, Frank Gholson's Account, 9–10.

33. Gholson, Frank Gholson's Account, 5.

34. Gholson, Recollections of B. F. Gholson, 6; Clarke, untitled manuscript, 57; Gholson, Frank Gholson's Account, 10–11.

35. Gholson, Frank Gholson's Account, 1; "Gholson, Benjamin Franklin," Tyler, ed., *New Handbook; Memorial and Biographical History of McLennan, Falls, Bell, and Coryell Counties, Texas*, 365–67; R. J. Gerald, "Benjamin Frankson Gholson, Texan," *Frontier Times* 4, no. 11 (1927): 46–51; "Married Seventy Years," *Frontier Times* 9 (1932): 366–67; "Captain Gholson Passes On," *Frontier Times* 9 (1932): 517.

36. Clarke, untitled manuscript, 58; Gholson, Frank Gholson's Account, 12; Phelps, *They Loved the Land*, 7.

37. Goodnight, *Indian Recollections*, 22; Phelps, *They Loved the Land*, 7.

38. Gholson, Frank Gholson's Account, 11.

39. Gholson, Recollections of B. F. Gholson, 6; Gholson, Frank Gholson's Account, 12–13.

40. Clarke, untitled manuscript, 58; Gholson, Frank Gholson's Account, 20.

41. Clarke, untitled manuscript, 58–59; Gholson, Frank Gholson's Account, 13–15.

42. Gholson, Frank Gholson's Account, 15. An example of a warrior's death song follows: "Oh sun you remain forever, but we Ko-eet-senko must die, Oh earth you remain forever, but we Ko-eet-senko must die." Nye, *Carbine and Lance*, 144.

43. Clarke, untitled manuscript, 59.

44. Gholson, Frank Gholson's Account, 15–17; Phelps, *They Loved the Land*, 7.

45. Clark, untitled manuscript, 60.

46. Gholson, Frank Gholson's Account, 17; Gholson, Recollections of B. F. Gholson, 27; Phelps, *They Loved the Land*, 7.

47. Clarke, untitled manuscript, 60–61; Holland, *Double Log Cabin*, 51.

48. Goodnight, *Indian Recollections*, 24; Clarke, untitled manuscript, 61; Dickson, untitled manuscript, 2; Gholson, Recollections of B. F. Gholson, 10.

49. Gholson, Frank Gholson's Account, 18–19; Gholson, Recollections of B. F. Gholson, 10; Clarke, untitled manuscript, 61.

50. Gholson, Frank Gholson's Account, 19; Gholson, Recollections of B. F. Gholson, 10.
51. Gholson, Frank Gholson's Account, 19; Gholson, Recollections of B. F. Gholson, 10.
52. Gholson, Recollections of B. F. Gholson, 11, 27; Baker, Diary, Dec. 19, 1860.
53. Clarke, untitled manuscript, 61. Ross named the boy Pease and took him to his home in Waco. Ross said of him: "He became an obedient member of my family." Gholson said of Pease: "Sull's father lived at Waco, and had several Negroes and put that Indian among them Negroes and was raised with them. He used the Indian as a cowboy as soon as he got big enough." Gholson, Recollections of B. F. Gholson, 21. Pease refused to return to the Comanches and died in 1887 in McLennan County. See also Lawrence T. Jones, "Cynthia Ann Parker and Pease Ross: The Forgotten Photographs," *Southwestern Historical Quarterly* 93 (1990): 381–84.
54. Gholson, Frank Gholson's Account, 19.
55. Ibid., 20; Goodnight, *Indian Recollections*, 22; Gholson, Recollections of B. F. Gholson, 27.
56. Goodnight, *Indian Recollections*, 23.
57. "From the Frontier," *Dallas Herald;* Elkins, *Indian Fighting* 34; Clarke, untitled manuscript, 61.
58. "From the Frontier," *Dallas Herald.*
59. Clarke, untitled manuscript, 61; Gholson, Recollections of B. F. Gholson, 12–13.
60. Gholson, Recollections of B. F. Gholson, 13.
61. Baker, Diary, Dec. 19, 1860. The shoe story was also related by Francis Peveler to J. Evetts Haley in an interview on Oct. 14, 1922.
62. Baker, Diary, Dec. 19, 1860; Gholson, Frank Gholson's Account, 18.
63. Baker, Diary, Dec. 19, 1860.
64. Ibid., Dec. 20, 1860. According to historian M. L. Crimmins, Lieutenant Robert E. Lee, who was in command of the Second Cavalry, wrote the following in his report on the Battle of Pease River: "He [Spangler] started with a part of Company H and a detachment of state troops from Camp Cooper in December, and marched north to Pease River, a tributary of Red River, where on the 19th he encountered a war-party of Comanches, and killed fourteen, wounded some, and captured three warriors and forty-five animals without loss or serious hurt to the victors." Lee referred to the battle as a "brilliant success" for Spangler. Crimmins, "First Sergeant John W. Spangler," 75.
65. Gholson, Recollections of B. F. Gholson, 14.
66. Baker, Diary, Dec. 24–25, 1860.

CHAPTER 13. THE LONG-LOST RELATIVE

1. "From the Frontier," *Dallas Herald;* Gholson, Recollections of B. F. Gholson, 15.
2. Clarke, untitled manuscript, 61.
3. Carl Coke Rister, *Robert E. Lee in Texas,* 57; Sallie Reynolds Matthews, *Interwoven,* 43.
4. Clarke, untitled manuscript, 62; Holland, *Double Log Cabin,* 51.
5. Gholson, Recollections of B. F. Gholson, 17–18.
6. Holland, *Double Log Cabin,* 46–47; *Biographical Directory,* 148–49; John Washington Lockhart, *Sixty Years on the Brazos,* 124; Speer, ed., *Encyclopedia*

of the New West, 291; "Parker, Isaac," Tyler, ed., *New Handbook;* Reagan, *Reagan-Parker Genealogy*, 317–18; Parker, Family Group Sheets.

7. Peveler to Haley, interview, Oct. 14, 1932; Holland, *Double Log Cabin*, 51; Clarke, untitled manuscript, 62; Gholson, Recollections of B. F. Gholson, 19.

8. "The White Captive," *Civilian and Gazette.* Mason's narrative was originally printed in the *White Man*, a frontier newspaper.

9. Gholson, Recollections of B. F. Gholson, 27.

10. "The White Captive," *Civilian and Gazette.*

11. Holland, *Double Log Cabin*, 51–52; Gholson, Recollections of B. F. Gholson, 23; Peveler to Haley, interview, Oct. 14, 1932.

12. Morrell, *Flowers and Fruits*, 218; Ronald C. Ellison, *Texas and Baptist Sunday Schools, 1829–1996*, 170; Marilyn McAdams Sibley, *Lone Stars and State Gazettes: Texas Newspapers before the Civil War*, 72; Llerena B. Friend, "The Texan of 1860," *Southwestern Historical Quarterly* 62 (1958): 2–5, 13.

13. Taulman and Taulman, The Fort Parker Massacre, 25; Thelma Ray, *The History of Birdville*, privately published, Haltom City Public Library, Haltom City, Texas, 22.

14. Holland, *Double Log Cabin*, 46–47. The cabin with some original furnishings is now in Log Cabin Village in Fort Worth, Texas. Terry G. Jordan, *Log Cabin Village*, 101–102.

15. Clarke, untitled manuscript, 62; Taulman and Taulman, The Fort Parker Massacre, 25.

16. See "The Legislature: Editorial Correspondence, *Standard.*"

17. K. (Kindred) J. Pearson to John D. Floyd, typescript copy of a letter, Feb. 3, 1861, Fort Sill Museum, Fort Sill, Oklahoma. Kindred J. Pearson, who was married to a Parker, was a saddle and harness maker in Birdville, Texas. He had come to Texas from Flat Creek, Bedford County, Tennessee, and was writing to his cousin who lived in Flat Creek. Kindred J. Pearson, undated biographical sketch by an anonymous author, privately owned.

18. Stephen B. Oates, "Texas under the Secessionists," *Southwestern Historical Quarterly* 67 (1963): 167–68; Williams and Barker, eds., *Writings of Sam Houston*, 8:248; "Secession" and "Secession Convention," Tyler, ed., *New Handbook.*

19. Oates, "Texas under the Secessionists," 169.

20. Brown, *Indian Wars*, 42; *Biographical Directory*, 148–49; "Brown, John Henry," Tyler, ed., *New Handbook;* Seymour V. Connor et al., *Capitols of Texas*, 121–36; Taulman and Taulman, The Fort Parker Massacre, 25.

21. "The Legislature: Editorial Correspondence, *Standard;*" Gammel, *Laws of Texas*, 5: 423–26. It is unknown what happened to the land grant. See Margaret Schmidt Hacker, *Cynthia Ann Parker: The Life and the Legend*, 38–39.

22. Silas M. Parker, deceased, Lucinda Parker, Admrx., Probate Case #35, Montgomery County Courthouse, Conroe, Texas; Montgomery County Genealogical and Historical Society, *Early Montgomery County, Texas Marriages Found in the "Black Boxes," 1838–1872*, 32; Joe Baily Parker, Family Group Sheets; Parker Genealogy Chart; Alex Harper to Jo Ella Exley, interview, March 2, 2001; U.S. Department of Commerce, Bureau of the Census, *Seventh Census of the United States, 1850, Anderson County, Texas.*

23. *Wills Point Chronicle*, December 8, 1910, Van Zandt County Genealogical Society, Canton, Texas.

24. Silas was given a special assignment. He was detailed as a teamster to Shreve-

port, La., by special order of General K. Smith. He remained there until the end of the war. "Silas Parker," 15th Infantry, *Texas Confederate Compiled Service Records,* P-Sm, M 323, microfilm roll 379, National Archives, 1960; U.S. Department of Commerce, Department of the Census, *Eighth Census of the United States, 1860, Van Zandt County, Texas;* Alex Harper to Jo Ella Exley, interview, March 2, 2001.

25. Champion, "To the Review"; "Where Was Cynthia Ann Parker Captured?" *Crowell Index,* Oct. 8, 1909; DeShields, *Cynthia Ann Parker,* 59; U.S. Department of Commerce, Bureau of the Census, *Eighth Census of the United States, 1860, Henderson County, Texas; Eighth Census of the United States, 1860, Van Zandt County, Texas.*

26. Champion, "To the Review."

27. Orlena's husband J. R. O'Quinn was mustered in to the Confederate army in February of 1862. He was detailed as a teamster and stayed in Texas during his service. "James Rufus O'Quinn," 6 Texas Cavalry (Stone's Regiment, 2 Cavalry), *Texas Confederate Compiled Service Records:* M–P, M 323, microfilm roll 40, National Archives, 1960.

28. Taulman and Taulman, Fort Parker Massacre, 25; Wentworth Manning, *Some History of Van Zandt County,* 85; Champion, "To the Review." Alex Harper to Jo Ella Exley, interview, March 2, 2001.

29. Champion, "To the Review"; Jewel Peters York, genealogical charts, Plummer family papers, privately owned; Jewel Peters York to R. E. Plummer Jr., letter, Apr., 1974, Plummer family papers, privately owned; "James P. Plummer," Muster Roll Abstract, Texas State Archives, Austin, Texas; Plummer, James Pratt, *Texas Confederate Compiled Service Records,* 15 Cavalry (2nd Reg., Johnson's Brigade) Mi-S, M323, microfilm roll 88, National Archives, 1960; "Ira Parker," *Texas Confederate Compiled Service Records,* 1st Infantry (2nd Infantry) Mo-Pe, M323, microfilm roll 253, National Archives, 1960. Pauline Buck Hohes, *A Centennial History of Anderson County, Texas,* 30.

30. Elkins, *Indian Fighting,* 34–35; "The Legislature: Editorial Correspondence, *Standard;"* Pearson to Floyd, letter, Feb. 3, 1861. "Parker, John," Tyler, ed., *New Handbook.* John's middle name, Richard, is given in the following document: Lucinda Parker, Admrx. of estate of Silas M. Parker, dec. To the Honl. Jesse Grimes, Judge of the Probate Court of Montgomery County, *Herald* (Montgomery County Genealogical and Historical Society) 11 (1988): 82, 100.

31. Eugene Graham O'Quinn, "Quanah—the Eagle: Half-White Comanche Chief," *Our Heritage* (Van Zandt County Genealogical Society, Canton, Texas) 2, no. 4 (1981): 20; "Where Was Cynthia Ann Parker Captured?" *Crowell Index;* DeShields, *Cynthia Ann Parker,* 59.

32. Champion, "To the Review"; Alex Harper to Jo Ella Exley, interview, March 2, 2001.

33. Champion, "To the Review"; Manning, *Some History,* 85; Alex Harper to Jo Ella Exley, interview, March 2, 2001.

34. Manning, *Some History,* 85; Champion, "To the Review"; "Says Cynthia Ann Parker Buried in Henderson [County]: Cousin of Quanah Parker Gives Out Interview Regarding Burial Place of Noted Woman," *Wills Point Chronicle,* Nov. 3, 1910.

35. Disenter[n]ment Permit. Texas State Department of Health, Bureau of Vital

Statistics, Austin, Texas. Charles A. Ott Collection, Fort Sill Museum, Fort Sill, Oklahoma; J. R. O'Quinn to Quanah Parker, letter, June 19, 1908, Quanah Parker Collection, Panhandle Plains Historical Museum, Canyon, Texas; O'Quinn, "Quanah—the Eagle," 23; "Where Was Cynthia Ann Parker Captured?" *Crowell Index;* "Says Cynthia Ann Parker Buried," *Wills Point Chronicle;* U.S. Department of Commerce, Bureau of the Census, *Ninth Census of the United States, 1870, Anderson County, Texas.*

36. Champion, "To the Review." According to G. A. Holland in *History of Parker County and the Double Log Cabin:* "Be it said to the credit of the State of Texas and to the honor of the Parker family that negotiations were being made to return her to the Indian wilds of the West when the declaration of War Between the States of the North and South interfered in the final consumation of their plans." 53–54.

CHAPTER 14. THIRSTING FOR GLORY

1. Goodnight, *Indian Recollections,* 28; "From the Frontier," *Dallas Herald;* Dickson, untitled manuscript, 12.
2. Dickson, untitled manuscript, 14–18.
3. Emmor J. Harston, *Comanche Land,* 156, 164, 184. Harston, who idolized Horseback, recorded what Horseback told him about the Comanches, much of which is erroneous. Some of the many meanings that have been given for "Quanah" are as follows: "heap good smell," in E. E. White, *Experiences of a Special Indian Agent,* 278; "fragrant," in Quanah Parker Lineage and Family of Quanah Parker; "stinking belly," in C. E. Campbell, "Down among the Red Men," *Kansas Historical Collections* 42 (1926–28): 633; "smell" or "odor" in Hugh Scott, *Some Memories of a Soldier,* 151; "perfume or possibly odor" in Goodnight, "True Sketch," 5; "sweet odor or bed of flowers," in Wayne Parker, *Quanah Parker Last Chief of the Kwahadi.* According to Lila Robinson and James Armagost in *Comanche Dictionary and Grammar, kwanaru* means "have odor, have bad odor, *modern* smell good" while *kwihnai* means "eagle," a bird considered to be sacred. According to family members, Quanah Parker's real name was Eagle, and Quanah was his nickname. Because of the similarity in sound, it is possible that Kwihnai or Eagle was changed to Kwanaru or "stinking" after the death of Quanah's parents, when he was shunned because of his mixed blood, and later the word took on a positive meaning because of Quanah's accomplishments. Quanah's third daughter, Wanada Parker Page, stated that 'Quanah' was not even the real name of her father; it was only a nickname. The name he was given by his parents was 'Cetah' or 'Chetah,' (The Eagle)." Eleanor Mitchell Traweek, *Of Such as These: A History of Motley County,* 13; Quanah Parker Lineage and Family of Quanah Parker. In May of 1875, Dr. Jacob J. Sturm gave Quanah's name as Quinah. Ernest Wallace, "The Journal of Ranald S. Mackenzie's Messenger to the Kwahadi Comanches," *Red River Valley Historical Review* 3 (1978): 237. A short time later, Ranald S. Mackenzie stated that Quanah's name was Citra. John Henry Brown, "Sequel to a Remarkable History," *Dallas Weekly Herald,* June 5, 1875.
4. Dickson, untitled manuscript, 7.
5. Ibid., 7–9.
6. Ibid. 15–16.

7. Ibid., 11. For a description of a Comanche village traveling, see Catlin, *Letters and Notes*, 2:64–65. See also plate 166, "Comanche moving camp; dog fight en route."

8. Dickson, untitled manuscript, 9–11. For a description of the military presence on the Santa Fe Trail during this period, see Leo E. Oliva, *Soldiers on the Santa Fe Trail*, 93–130.

9. Dickson, untitled manuscript, 10.

10. Ibid.

11. Ibid., 10–11.

12. Dickson, untitled manuscript, 13; Aubrey C. Birdsong, Reminiscences of Quanah Parker, 1965, Quanah Parker File, Fort Sill Museum, Fort Sill, Oklahoma. Smallpox vaccination had been provided to Muguara's band of Penateka Comanches as early as 1838. Frederic Leclerc, *Texas and Its Revolution*, 51–52. In 1864 a government physician was sent among the Plains Indians to vaccinate them against smallpox. James Mooney, "Calendar History of the Kiowa Indians," 1:177.

13. Dickson, untitled manuscript, 14.

14. Ibid., 14–18.

15. William H. Leckie, *Military Conquest of the Southern Plains*, 56n.

16. Henry M. Stanley, "A British Journalist Reports on the Medicine Lodge Peace Council of 1867," *Kansas Historical Quarterly* 33 (1967): 249; Leckie, *Military Conquest*, 58.

17. Leckie, *Military Conquest*, 59.

18. Alfred A. Taylor, "Medicine Lodge Peace Council," *Chronicles of Oklahoma* 2 (1924): 105; George Bird Grinnell, *The Fighting Cheyennes*, 273; Douglas C. Jones, *The Treaty at Medicine Lodge*, 32, 78–9; Carl Coke Rister, *Border Command*, 54.

19. Henry M. Stanley, *My Early Travels and Adventures in America and Asia*, 244; Jones, *Treaty*, 34–35; Stan Hoig, *The Battle of the Washita*, 29.

20. Stanley, *Travels*, 244.

21. Ibid., 247–50; Jones, *Treaty*, 112–17.

22. Stanley, *Travels*, 253–56; Jones, *Treaty*, 112–27; Hoig, *Battle*, 29.

23. Charles J. Kappler, *Indian Affairs: Laws and Treaties*, 2:982; Quanah Parker, Told in English & Signs & Comanche, Ledger Book 1:23, H. L. Scott Material, W. S. Nye Collection, Fort Sill Museum, Fort Sill, Oklahoma.

24. Evan S. Connell, *Son of the Morning Star*, 195.

25. Connell, *Son*, 175–76, 179–80; Dee Alexander Brown, *Bury My Heart at Wounded Knee*, 162; Leckie, *Military Conquest*, 91–92; Paul Andrew Hutton, *Phil Sheridan and His Army*, 56–59.

26. George Armstrong Custer, *My Life on the Plains*, 258; Connell, *Son*, 180–92; Brown, *Bury*, 164; Hoig, *Battle*, 124–43; Leckie, *Military Conquest*, 101–104; De B. Randolph Keim, *Sheridan's Troopers on the Borders*, 128, 141–51; Hutton, *Phil Sheridan*, 67–68, 71–72.

27. Dickson, untitled manuscript, 37. In an earlier interview with Hugh Scott, Quanah made what seems to be a contradictory statement: "That was when [ca. June, 1869] I first heard that the Cheyennes had been wiped out on Washita by white soldiers." Parker, Told in English & Signs, H. L. Scott Material, Ledger Book 1:27.

28. Parker, Told in English & Signs, H. L. Scott Material, Ledger Book 1:23.

29. Hugh Corwin, *The Kiowa Indians*, 25. See "Dohason," Tyler, ed. *New Handbook*.

30. Parker, Told in English & Signs, H. L. Scott Material, Ledger Book 1:23.

31. The following description of the Comanche War Trail was formulated from on-site observation as well as the following: "Comanche Trail" and "Big Spring," Tyler ed., *New Handbook;* Gunnar Brune, *Springs of Texas*, 1:144, 156, 237–38, 401, 462; T. N. Campbell and William T. Field, "Identification of Comanche Raiding Trails in Trans-Pecos Texas," *West Texas Historical Association Year Book* 44 (1968): 128, 144; Ralph A. Smith, "The Comanche Bridge between Oklahoma and Mexico, 1843–1844," *Chronicles of Oklahoma* 39 (1961): 54–69; Richardson, *Comanche Barrier*, 193–210; *Water, Oil, Sand and Sky*, 5–6; J. Evetts Haley, *Fort Concho and the Texas Frontier*, 2–5; Ron C. Tyler, *The Big Bend: A History of the Last Texas Frontier*, 65–66; Darwin Spearing, *Roadside Geology of Texas*, 291–321; Daniel J. Gelo, "'Comanche Land and Ever Has Been': A Native Geography of the Nineteenth-Century Comancheria," *Southwestern Historical Quarterly* 103 (2000): 273–307.

32. "Horsehead Crossing" and "Fort Stockton," Tyler ed., *New Handbook;* J. Evetts Haley, *Charles Goodnight: Cowman and Plainsman*, 129–34; Ray Miller, *Ray Miller's Texas Forts: A History and Guide*, 103–104; Haley, *Fort Concho*, 2–5; Smith, "Comanche Bridge," 54–69.

33. Parker, Told in English & Signs, H. L. Scott Material, Ledger Book 1:23.

34. "Apache," Tyler ed., *New Handbook;* C. L. Sonnichsen, *The Mescalero Apaches*, 88–91, 135. Plummer, *Narrative 1844*, 13. By the 1850s the Comanches and Mescaleros were allied in their raids on Mexico. George Archibald McCall, *New Mexico in 1850: A Military View*, 102–103. Rachel Plummer had mentioned that in 1836 or 1837 she had met the Ferbelows, another name for the Mescaleros.

35. Parker, Told in English & Signs, H. L. Scott Material, Ledger Book 1:85–86; Omer C. Stewart, *Peyote Religion: A History*, 34, 45–49, 57.

36. "Comanche Trail" and "Lajitas," Tyler, ed., *New Handbook;* Smith, "Comanche Bridge," 54–55; Campbell and Field, "Identification of Comanche Raiding Trails," 134; Tyler, *Big Bend*, 65–66; Spearing, *Roadside Geology*, 291–321. See also Ross A. Maxwell, *The Big Bend of the Rio Grande: A Guide to the Rocks, Landscape, Geologic History, and Settlers of the Big Bend National Park*, 8–92.

37. In *Springs of Texas* 1:84–88, published in 1981, Gunnar Brune listed sixty-one springs in Big Bend National Park and stated that there were other springs in the park. See also Kelly Fenstermaker, "Life on Tap," *Texas* (*Houston Chronicle Magazine*) Oct. 11, 1998, 8–12.

38. Maxwell, *Big Bend of the Rio Grande*, 37, 49–50; Roland H. Wauer, *Naturalists' Big Bend*, 36–41, 76–83, 89.

39. Arthur R. Gomez, *A Most Singular Country*, 1.

40. Parker, Told in English & Signs, H. L. Scott Material, Ledger Book 1:23–27.

CHAPTER 15. IT WAS QUANAH

1. Nye, *Carbine and Lance*, 46–48, 78–82, 159; Leckie, *Military Conquest*, 64–67.

2. Charles L. Kenner, *A History of New Mexican–Plains Indian Relations*, 182; Kavanagh, *Comanche Political History*, 422–23.

3. Dickson, untitled manuscript, 33–36.

4. U. [Ulysses] S. Grant, *Personal Memoirs of U. S. Grant*, 583; Ernest Wallace,

Ranald S. Mackenzie on the Texas Frontier, 7–15; Robert G. Carter, *On the Border with Mackenzie,* xii–xiii, 535–41; Charles M. Robinson, *Bad Hand: A Biography of General Ranald S. Mackenzie,* 49; Joseph H. Dorst, "Ranald Slidell Mackenzie," *Journal of the United States Cavalry Association* 10 (1897): 367–70, 372–73, 381–82; W. A. Thompson, "Scouting with Mackenzie," *Journal of the United States Cavalry Association* 10 (1897): 433; Michael D. Pierce, *The Most Promising Young Officer: A Life of Ranald Slidell Mackenzie,* 8–9, 67–79. Pierce gives evidence to support his view that Mackenzie had a good sense of humor and was much less stern than how he is usually portrayed.

5. Wallace, *Mackenzie,* 34–35, 40–45; Carter, *On the Border,* 105–48.

6. Wallace, *Mackenzie,* 45–46; Carter, *On the Border,* 157–58.

7. Carter, *On the Border,* 159; Wallace, *Mackenzie,* 46.

8. Wallace, *Mackenzie,* 47; "Double Mountain," Tyler, ed. *New Handbook; The Roads of Texas,* 47; Jack Flippin, "Legends of the Double Mountain," *Texas* (*Houston Chronicle* Magazine), Jan. 22, 1995, 8–10, 14; Gelo, "Comanche Land," 286–87. Double Mountain rises to a height of two thousand feet and is a well-known landmark in Stonewall County.

9. The springs were producing a small amount of water in 1997. See also Brune, *Springs of Texas,* 1:413

10. Carter, *On the Border,* 161; Carl Coke Rister, *Fort Griffin on the Texas Frontier,* 89; Wallace, *Mackenzie,* 47–48.

11. Carter, *On the Border,* 161–63; "Duck Creek," Tyler, ed. *New Handbook; The Roads of Texas,* 46; Wallace, *Mackenzie,* 48–49.

12. Carter, *On the Border,* 163.

13. Nye, *Carbine and Lance,* 151.

14. Clinton Smith, *The Boy Captives,* 103–104.

15. Carter, *On the Border,* 163–65; "Blanco Canyon," Tyler, ed., *New Handbook;* Dan Flores, *Caprock Canyonlands,* 45.

16. Carter, *On the Border,* 165, 167n; Nye, *Carbine and Lance,* 151.

17. Charles H. Sommer, *Quanah Parker: Last Chief of the Comanches,* 43.

18. Carter, *On the Border,* 165–66.

19. Ibid., 167.

20. Ibid.; Nye, *Carbine and Lance,* 151.

21. Cohayyah to W. S. Nye, 2nd interview, Mar. 18, 1835, notebook #16:30, W. S. Nye Collection, Fort Sill Museum, Fort Sill, Oklahoma.

22. Carter, *On the Border,* 168–73.

23. Ibid., 173–75.

24. Ibid., 176.

25. Carter, *On the Border,* 151; Cohayyah to W. S. Nye, Mar. 18, 1835, 32–33.

26. Carter, *On the Border,* 177–79.

27. Ibid., 179–82.

28. Sommer, *Quanah Parker,* 43.

29. Flores, *Canyonlands,* 45; Carter, *On the Border,* 186.

30. Carter, *On the Border,* 187–93.

31. Cohhayah to W. S. Nye, Mar. 18, 1835, 33.

32. Wallace, *Mackenzie,* 53; Edward S. Wallace, "General Ranald Slidell Mackenzie, Indian Fighting Cavalryman," *Southwestern Historical Quarterly* 56 (1953): 386–87; Carter, *On the Border,* 195–99.

33. Carter, *On the Border,* 200–203.

CHAPTER 16. SO MANY SOLDIERS

1. Wallace, *Mackenzie*, 66–73; Carter, *On the Border*, 376.
2. Ranald S. Mackenzie to Departmental Headquarters, letter, Oct. 12, 1872, 4546 1/2 AGO 1872, RG94, National Archives, Washington, D.C.; *Dallas Herald*, Aug. 10, 1872; Wallace, *Mackenzie*, 64, 68, 77, 78.
3. Nye, *Carbine and Lance*, 161; Mackenzie to Departmental Headquarters, letter, Oct. 12, 1872; Wallace, *Mackenzie*, 79; Carter, *On the Border*, 377; "Garza County," Tyler, ed., *New Handbook;* Robert G. Carter, *The Old Sergeant's Story*, 85.
4. Carter, *Old Sergeant's Story*, 85.
5. Cohayyah to W. S. Nye, interview, Mar. 17, 1935, notebook #18:18–20, W. S. Nye Collection, Fort Sill Museum, Fort Sill, Oklahoma.
6. Thompson, "Scouting," 430.
7. Carter, *Old Sergeant's Story*, 85; Carter, *On the Border*, 381.
8. Thompson, "Scouting," 431.
9. Mackenzie to Departmental Headquarters, Oct. 12, 1872.
10. Cohayyah to W. S. Nye, Mar. 17, 1935, 18–20; Carter, *On the Border*, 377–79.
11. Mackenzie to Departmental Headquarters, Oct. 12, 1872; G. W. Schofield, letter to Act. Asst. Adjt. Genl., Dept. of Texas, Oct. 10, 1872, National Archives, Washington, D.C.; Thompson, "Scouting," 431. See also Nye, *Carbine and Lance*, 62, and *Annual Report of the Commissioner of Indian Affairs to the Secretary of the Interior for the Year 1872*, 93–94.
12. Smith, *Boy Captives*, 128–29.
13. Mackenzie to Departmental Headquarters, Oct. 12, 1872; Carter, *Old Sergeant's Story*, 86; Carter, *On the Border*, 379–80.
14. Mackenzie to Departmental Headquarters, Oct. 12, 1872; Richardson, *Comanche Barrier*, 361–63; Carter, *Old Sergeant's Story*, 83–84, 86.
15. Cohayyah to W. S. Nye, Mar. 17, 1935, 20.
16. Smith, *Boy Captives*, 129–30.
17. Thompson, "Scouting," 431; Mackenzie to Departmental Headquarters, Oct. 12, 1872; Carter, *On the Border*, 378; Richardson, *Comanche Barrier*, 361–63.
18. Cohayyah to W. S. Nye, Mar. 17, 1935, 21; Dickson, untitled manuscript, 38; Wallace, *Mackenzie*, 83.
19. Wallace, *Mackenzie*, 83–84; Mackenzie to Departmental Headquarters, Oct. 12, 1872; Carter, *On the Border*, 382–83.
20. Wallace, *Mackenzie*, 83–84; Carter, *On the Border*, 383–89.
21. Wallace, *Mackenzie*, 84–85; "Wild as Coyotes," *Fort Concho Report* 17, no. 2 (1985): 22–23; "Over 100 Indians Held Prisoners of War," *Fort Concho Report* 12 (1980): 17; Nye, *Carbine and Lance*, 164.
22. Carter, *On the Border*, 409–10, 417.
23. "Over 100 Indians," 17.
24. Wallace, *Mackenzie*, 86.
25. Lawrie Tatum, *Our Red Brothers and the Peace Policy of President Ulysses S. Grant*, 135–54.
26. Dickson, untitled manuscript, 38; *Annual Report of the Commissioner of Indian Affairs to the Secretary of the Interior for the Year 1872*, 220.
27. Lieutenant Matthew Leeper Jr., son of a former Indian agent at Fort Cobb, recognized many of the prisoners and reported that there were thirty-four Kotsotekas, thirty Quahadas, eighteen Yamparikas, eleven Noconis, and nine

Penatekas. He did not give the names. A few of the names were recorded by
Laurie Tatum in a letter to Enoch Hoag on Dec. 9, 1872. Kavanagh, *Comanche
Political History*, 434, 513n. Polonio Ortiz, a captured Comanchero, had reported on October 10, 1872, to Adjutant John A. McKinney that he recognized
many of the captives as a part of a band with whom he had recently lived and
traded at "that part of Texas known as Mucha Que," which is a few miles east
of present-day Gail, Texas. Polonio Ortiz to Adjutant John A. McKinney,
statement, Oct. 10, 1872, National Archives, Washington, D.C.

28. Baldwin Parker to Morris Swett, interview, Aug. 24, 1959, Quanah Parker file
    compiled by Gillett Griswold, Fort Sill Museum, Fort Sill, Oklahoma.

29. Although Weakeah's father is usually given as Yellow Bear, three of Quanah's
    daughters—Wanada Page, Neda Birdsong, and Alice Purdy—said that his
    name was Old Bear, brother of Yellow Bear. Quanah Parker Lineage and Fam-
    ily of Quanah Parker, Fort Sill Museum, Fort Sill, Oklahoma.

30. White, *Experiences*, xxviii, 275–76.

31. Quanah Parker, Wife Weakeah and their Children, Fort Sill Museum, Fort
    Sill, Oklahoma.

32. White, *Experiences*, 278–79.

33. Ibid., 279–86.

34. Herman Lehmann, *Nine Years among the Indians, 1870–1879*, 108.

35. White, *Experiences*, 286. Goodnight, who probably obtained his information from
    Quanah, says that there were three hundred in the band. Charles Goodnight to
    J. Evetts Haley, interview, Nov. 18, 1926, Nita Stewart Haley Memorial
    Library and J. Evetts Haley History Center, Midland, Texas.

36. White, *Experiences*, 287–88.

37. Lutz, "Quanah Parker: The Last Comanche Chief," 154.

38. Thomas C. Battey, *The Life and Adventures of a Quaker among the Indians*, 112–13.

39. Ibid., 113.

40. Battey, *Life and Adventures*, 161–64; Carter, *On the Border*, 390–91; Dickson,
    untitled manuscript, 38.

41. Battey, *Life and Adventures*, 161–62.

42. Battey, *Life and Adventures*, 163–64; Tatum, *Our Red Brothers*, 168; Richardson,
    Comanche Barrier, 365.

43. Battey, *Life and Adventures*, 165.

CHAPTER 17. BLOOD UPON THE LAND

1. Lehmann, *Nine Years*, 153.

2. Nye, *Carbine and Lance*, 187; James M. Haworth to Enoch Hoag, letter, Mar.
   28, 1874, Indian Territory Miscellaneous, Kiowa and Comanche Papers, 1869–
   74, National Archives, Washington, D.C.; Parker, Told in English & Signs &
   Comanche, Ledger Book 1:14; Iseeo Account, H. S. Scott Material [title of
   notebook], W. S. Nye Collection, Fort Sill Museum, Fort Sill, Oklahoma,
   58–59; Kavanagh, *Comanche Political History*, 444; Philip H. Sheridan,
   "Record of Engagements with Hostile Indians in Texas 1868 to 1882," *West
   Texas Historical Association Year Book* 9 (1933): 101–18; Rupert N. Richardson,
   "The Comanche Indians at the Adobe Walls Fight," *Panhandle-Plains Historical Review* 4 (1931): 26. Quanah said "a friend" in Parker, Told in English
   and Signs, Ledger Book 1:14, but in Dickson, untitled manuscript, 38,

Quanah said "cousin." Iseeo said "nephew" in Iseeo Account, 58, but
Yellowfish said "uncle" and gave his name as Tekyatie (Traveled Till Daylight)
in Roy Riddle, "Indian Survivors of Adobe Walls Visit Site 65 Years after
Fight," *Amarillo Daily News,* Apr. 26, 1939, 13. See also T. Lindsay Baker and
Billy R. Harrison, *Adobe Walls: The History and Archeology of the 1874 Trading
Post,* 310*n* 16.

3. Nye, *Carbine and Lance,* 40, 187; James L. Haley, *The Buffalo War: The History of
the Red River Uprising of 1874,* 50; Richardson, *Comanche Barrier,* 371–72;
Kavanagh, *Comanche Political History,* 445.

4. Nye, *Carbine and Lance,* 187–88.

5. Battey, *Life and Adventures,* 205.

6. Ibid.

7. Ibid., 205–206.

8. Ibid., 206–12.

9. Battey, *Life and Adventures,* 206–12; Richardson, *Comanche Barrier,* 368–71;
Kavanagh, *Comanche Political History,* 440–43; Nye, *Carbine and Lance,* 175–82;
Campbell, "Down among the Red Men," 638–40.

10. Battey, *Life and Adventures,* 263–71.

11. Richardson, *Comanche Barrier,* 372–73; Kavanagh, *Comanche Political History,*
445; "Isatai," Tyler, ed., *New Handbook.*

12. Battey, *Life and Adventures,* 302–303.

13. Ibid., 303; Richardson, *Comanche Barrier,* 372–73; Donald F. Schofield, "W. M. D.
Lee, Indian Trader," *Panhandle-Plains Historical Review* 54 (1981): 51–52.

14. Nye, *Carbine and Lance,* 190; Kavanagh, *Comanche Political History,* 445–46; See
also William C. Meadows, *Kiowa, Apache, and Comanche Military Societies,* 318–23.

15. Nye, *Carbine and Lance,* 190; James M. Haworth to Enoch Hoag, letter, June 8,
1874, National Archives, Washington, D.C.; James M. Haworth to Smith, letter, Sept. 1, 1874, 43 Congress, 2nd Session, *House Executive Documents No. 1,*
Annual Report of War, National Archives, Washington, D.C., 40; Richardson,
Comanche Barrier, 374–75; Kavanagh, *Comanche Political History,* 446.

16. Richardson, *Comanche Barrier,* 375; Battey, *Life and Adventures,* 307–308; James
M. Haworth to Smith, letter, Sept 1, 1874; Kavanagh, *Comanche Political His-
tory,* 49–51. The Little Horses and Big Horses were Quahadas. Meadows,
Kiowa, Apache, and Comanche Military Societies, 279.

17. Parker, Told in English & Signs, Ledger Book 1:14; Battey, *Life and Adventures,*
308. See also Meadows, *Kiowa, Apache, and Comanche Military Societies,* 305–
307: Meadows interprets "friend" as "brother" in a military society.

18. Iseeo Account, 58–60.

19. George E. Hyde, *Life of George Bent Written from His Letters,* 358.

20. The Fox Quirt was a Penateka and Noconi military society. Meadows, *Kiowa,
Apache, and Comanche Military Societies,* 287.

21. Parker, Told in English & Signs, Ledger Book 1:14–15. See also Bernard
Mishkin, *Rank and Warfare among the Plains Indians,* 28–34.

22. Poafebitty, Frank, Yellowfish, Felix Cowens & several old women to W. S.
Nye, interview, notebook #9:18–19, W. S. Nye Collection, Fort Sill Museum,
Fort Sill, Oklahoma.

23. Old Man Horse to W. S. Nye, interview, notebook #16:19, W. S. Nye Collection, Fort Sill Museum, Fort Sill, Oklahoma.

24. Cohayyah to W. S. Nye, Mar. 18, 1935, 35.

25. Parker, Told in English and Signs, Ledger Book 1:15–16; James Mooney, "Calendar History of the Kiowa Indians," 1:203; Nye, *Carbine and Lance*, 190–91.

26. Riddle, "Indian Survivors," 13.

27. Parker, Told in English & Signs, Ledger Book 1:16.

28. See sketch on p. 131 of Baker and Harrison, *Adobe Walls.*

29. Baker and Harrison, *Adobe Walls*, 13–14; "Adobe Walls, Texas," Tyler, ed., *New Handbook.*

30. J. Wright Mooar, "Frontier Experiences of J. Wright Mooar," *West Texas Historical Association Year Book* 4 (1928): 89.

31. Baker and Harrison, *Adobe Walls*, 20, 157–58.

32. Ibid., 15, 22–23, 131, 163–66.

33. Seth Hathaway, "The Adventures of a Buffalo Hunter," *Frontier Times* 9 (1931): 130; Baker and Harrison, *Adobe Walls*, 18, 142, 145, 149–50, 153.

34. Baker and Harrison, *Adobe Walls*, 32, 50; William Dixon, *Life of "Billy" Dixon, Plainsman, Scout and Pioneer*, 145–47.

35. Dixon, *Life*, 153–54; Hathaway, "Adventures," 130.

36. Baker and Harrison, *Adobe Walls*, 60, 85; Dixon, *Life*, 155.

37. Baker and Harrison, *Adobe Walls*, 51–52, 58; Dixon, *Life*, 156–57; Haley, *Buffalo War*, 31; Hathaway, "Adventures," 130–31.

38. Baker and Harrison, *Adobe Walls*, 52; Dixon, *Life*, 157–60; Hathaway, "Adventures," 130–31.

39. One of the hunters, Dutch Henry Born, later became a noted horse thief, then a successful miner, and eventually a respected citizen of Colorado.

40. Dixon, *Life*, 115, 160; Baker and Harrison, *Adobe Walls*, 55, 76.

41. Baker and Harrison, *Adobe Walls*, 54, 82–85.

42. Dixon, *Life*, 161; Baker and Harrison, *Adobe Walls*, 52–57.

43. Parker, Told in English & Signs, Ledger Book 1:16; Baker and Harrison, *Adobe Walls*, 49.

44. Grinnell, *Fighting Cheyennes*, 323–24; Hyde, *Life of George Bent*, 359.

45. Riddle, "Indian Survivors," 13; Hathaway, "Adventures," 131.

46. Parker, Told in English and Signs, Ledger Book 1:16–17.

47. Riddle, "Indian Survivors," 1.

48. Ibid.

49. Baker and Harrison, *Adobe Walls*, 53; Parker, Told in English & Signs, Ledger Book 1:17; Grinnell, *Fighting Cheyennes*, 324; Hathaway, "Adventures," 131.

50. Baker and Harrison, *Adobe Walls*, 60–61; Riddle, "Indian Survivors," 13; Dixon, *Life*, 161; Hathaway, "Adventures," 131. In a Cheyenne painting on a buffalo hide, Quanah is pictured as spearing one of the Scheidler brothers. See Bill Neeley, *Quanah Parker and His People*, picture section following p. 177, and *The Mighty Chieftains*, 160–61.

51. Hyde, *Life of George Bent*, 360; Baker and Harrison, *Adobe Walls*, 61–62; Parker, Told in English and Signs, Ledger Book 1:17; Riddle, "Indian Survivors," 13.

52. Hyde, *Life of George Bent*, 360; Hathaway, "Adventures," 132.

53. Hyde, *Life of George Bent*, 360; Baker and Harrison, *Adobe Walls*, 68; Parker, Told in English and Signs, Ledger Book 1:17; Riddle, "Indian Survivors," 13; Dixon, *Life*, 163–64; Hathaway, "Adventures," 133.

54. Dixon, *Life*, 164–65; Wallace and Hoebel, *Comanches*, 189.

55. Dixon, *Life*, 161, 164–66; Baker and Harrison, *Adobe Walls*, 68–69; Hathaway, "Adventures," 133.

56. Parker, Told in English & Signs, Ledger Book 1:17. Quanah's war bonnet is now in the Panhandle-Plains Historical Museum in Canyon, Texas.

57. Parker, Told in English & Signs, Ledger Book 1:17; Dixon, *Life*, 186–87; Baker and Harrison, *Adobe Walls*, 63–64.

58. Dixon, *Life*, 175–76.

59. Cohayyah to W. S. Nye, Mar. 18, 1935, 34; Parker, Told in English & Signs, Ledger Book 1:17; Baker and Harrison, *Adobe Walls*, 64–65.

60. Baker and Harrison, *Adobe Walls*, 56; Hathaway, "Adventures," 131.

61. Dixon, *Life*, 164; Baker and Harrison, *Adobe Walls*, 56; Hathaway, "Adventures," 131.

62. Baker and Harrison, *Adobe Walls*, 54–55; Andrew Johnson, "The Fight at 'Dobe Walls,'" *Kansas City Star*, Aug. 6, 1911, 5A.

63. Dixon, *Life*, 165–66.

64. Baker and Harrison, *Adobe Walls*, 64–65; Dixon, *Life*, 167; G. Derek West, "The Battle of Adobe Walls," *Panhandle-Plains Historical Review* 36 (1963): 2.

65. Dixon, *Life*, 166–68.

66. Ibid., 170.

67. Grinnell, *Fighting Cheyennes*, 324; Parker, Told in English & Signs, Ledger Book 1:17; Donald J. Berthrong, *The Southern Cheyennes*, 386.

68. Parker, Told in English & Signs, Ledger Book 1:17; Mooney, "Calendar History of the Kiowa Indians," 1:203.

69. Parker, Told in English & Signs, Ledger Book 1:17.

70. Dixon, *Life*, 173; Baker and Harrison, *Adobe Walls*, 65.

71. Dixon, *Life*, 176; Baker and Harrison, *Adobe Walls*, 71, 97–98; Nelson A. Miles, *Personal Recollections and Observations of General Nelson A. Miles*, 1:163; J. T. Marshall, *The Miles Expedition of 1874–1875: An Eyewitness Account of the Red River War*, 5.

72. Baker and Harrison, *Adobe Walls*, 95–98, 107; Dixon, *Life*, 181–82; Iseeo Account, 58.

73. Riddle, "Indian Survivors," 13.

CHAPTER 18. I LIVED FREE

1. Haley, *Buffalo War*, 84–93, 99, 106; Joe F. Taylor, ed. "The Indian Campaign on the Staked Plains, 1874–1875," *Panhandle-Plains Historical Review* 34 (1961): 10. "Jones, John B.," Tyler, ed., *New Handbook;* Leckie, *Military Conquest*, 194–98.

2. General C. C. Augur to the Secretary of War, letter, *House Executive Document No. 1*, 43rd Congress, 2nd Session, *Annual Report of the Secretary of War, Annual Report of the Commissioner of Indian Affairs for 1874*, National Archives, Washington, D.C., 40; Nye, *Carbine and Lance*, 211; Harston, *Comanche Land*, 163; Hutton, *Phil Sheridan*, 248–89; Ernest Wallace, ed., *Ranald S. Mackenzie's Official Correspondence Relating to Texas*, 2:77–78.

3. Haley, *Buffalo War*, 106, 111; Nye, *Carbine and Lance*, 210; Leckie, *Military Conquest*, 199–200.

4. Haley, *Buffalo War*, 132–36, 153–58; Nye, *Carbine and Lance*, 215–19; Leckie, *Military Conquest*, 210–14; Hutton, *Phil Sheridan*, 252; Wallace, *Official Correspondence*, 2:112–24.

5. Haley, *Buffalo War*, 158–65; Dixon, *Life*, 199–220; Leckie, *Military Conquest*, 214–15; Miles, *Personal Recollections*, 173–74.

6. Haley, *Buffalo War*, 161–63; Leckie, *Military Conquest*, 216.

7. Leckie, *Military Conquest,* 217–24; Haley, *Buffalo War,* 176–83; Nye, *Carbine and Lance,* 221–24; Carter, *On the Border,* 488–95; Hutton, *Phil Sheridan,* 254.

8. Dickson, untitled manuscript, 39.

9. Wallace, *Mackenzie,* 155; Wallace, "Journal," 229.

10. Dickson, untitled manuscript, 39.

11. Wallace," Journal," 229–30; Kavanagh, *Comanche Political History,* 449–50; Nye, *Carbine and Lance,* 231.

12. Sturm did not include Charlton in his list of men who went to bring the Comanches in, but Carter and Nye believed that he had gone on the mission. Also Yellowfish said that there were "six in the party" and another Comanche informant mentioned "two white men."

13. Carter, *Old Sergeant's Story,* 113; Wallace, "Journal," 229.

14. Wallace, "Journal," 231; Gelo in "'Comanche Land and Ever Has Been,'" 288–89, confirms or gives "retranslations" of the Comanche names of the creeks and rivers that Sturm includes in his journal.

15. Wallace, "Journal," 233. The usual explanation of the name is that the South Pease River was a favorite trading spot and many "tongues" were spoken there. Charles Goodnight told J. Evetts Haley: "The greatest of the trading grounds was on the Tongue River, and from it came the origin of the name 'Las Lenguas,' meaning 'those tongues.' The Mexicans used that term to designate languages, but say 'tongue' instead of 'language.' It was necessary for the traders to be able to speak the Indian tongues." Interview, Nov. 18, 1926, Nita Stewart Haley Memorial Library and J. Evetts Haley History Center, Midland, Texas; "Pease River," Tyler, ed., *New Handbook.*

16. Wallace, "Journal," 233–34.

17. Today the springs that feed the creek still flow, and the name of the town near this place celebrates them. It is called Roaring Springs. Brune, *Springs of Texas,* 1:338; Traweek, *Of Such as These,* 48.

18. Wallace, "Journal," 234–35.

19. Ibid., 235.

20. Ibid., 236.

21. See Wallace, "Journal," notes 22 and 23. "Mosquito Creek" was probably Mesquite Creek, the upper reaches of which are crossed by Highway 1054 today. The place where the creek flows into the broken country below the Caprock is sheltered by high cliffs and would have been a good winter campsite.

22. Wallace, "Journal," 236–37.

23. Ibid., 237–38.

24. Ibid., 238.

25. Carter, *Old Sergeant's Story,* 114.

26. Poafebitty, Frank, Yellowfish, Felix Cowens, and several old women, interview with W. S. Nye, notebook, #9:18.

27. Unidentified informant to W. S. Nye, interview, notebook #11:39, W. S. Nye Collection, Fort Sill Museum, Fort Sill, Oklahoma.

28. Wallace, "Journal," 238.

29. Ibid., 239–41.

30. Ibid., 241.

31. Ibid., 243–44.

32. Ibid., 245.

33. Ibid.; Hagan, *Quanah Parker: Comanche Chief,* 15; Brown, "Sequel to a Remarkable History."

34. Wallace, "Journal," 246; Quanah Parker, Wife Weakeah and their Children (from information furnished by the children in 1936 and the addition of some dates and data from agency listings), Quanah Parker History File, GG [Gillett Griswold], Fort Sill Museum, Fort Sill, Oklahoma; Pierce, *The Most Promising Young Officer,* 167–68; Hagan, *United States–Comanche Relations,* 116–19; Robinson, *Bad Hand,* 184–85; Nye, *Carbine and Lance,* 235.

35. Dickson, untitled manuscript, 40. Although Quanah claimed to have been the principal chief at the time of the surrender, the information in Sturm's journal and Yellowfish's previous statement seems to indicate that Isatai was the headman. Isatai had established himself as a powerful medicine man, and even the debacle at Adobe Walls had not diminished his stature with Quanah and others. At Quanah's death in 1911, Isatai was one of the contenders for the position of head chief of the Comanches. "'Great Father' Calls the Comanche Leader," *Lawton Daily News,* Feb. 24, 1911, 1. See also Foster, *Being Comanche,* 89, 111–12, 188n 67, 189n 82. However, in the 1930s, William S. Nye wrote of Isatai: "Today the Comanches have forgotten and forgiven. They refer to Isatai as 'that comical fellow.'" Nye, *Carbine and Lance,* 191.

36. Parker, Quanah Parker Last Chief of the Kwahadi.

37. Scott, *Some Memories of a Soldier,* 151.

38. Clyde L. Jackson and Grace Jackson, *Quanah Parker: Last Chief of the Comanches,* 159; "'Great Father' Calls the Comanche Leader," 1; O'Quinn, "Quanah—the Eagle," 28; Hagan, *United States–Comanche Relations,* 293.

BIBLIOGRAPHY

MANUSCRIPTS AND ARCHIVAL SOURCES

Baker, Jonathan Hamilton. Diary of Jonathan Hamilton Baker (1832–1918) of Palo Pinto County, Texas, 1858–1918. Secured from his daughter Elizabeth Baker, Seattle, Wash., 1932 through Judge E. B. Ritchie, Mineral Wells, by J. Evetts Haley. Typescript copy. Center for American History, Austin, Tex.

Biographical Sketch of Daniel Parker. Center for American History, Austin, Tex.

Birdsong, Aubrey C. Reminiscences of Quanah Parker, 1965. Quanah Parker File, Fort Sill Museum, Fort Sill, Okla.

Capt. Eli Seals List of Rangers, Jan. 1st, 1836. General Land Office Muster Rolls. Texas State Library, Austin, Tex.

Church Book [Mount Pleasant Church of the Regular United Baptist Faith and Order]. San Jacinto Museum of History, Houston, Tex.

Clarke, Bessie Ross. Untitled manuscript. Texas Collection, Baylor University, Waco, Tex.

Cohayyah to W. S. Nye. Interview, Mar. 17, 1835. Notebook #18:14–21. W. S. Nye Collection, Fort Sill Museum, Fort Sill, Okla.

———. 2nd Interview, Mar. 18, 1835. Notebook #16:28–38. W. S. Nye Collection, Fort Sill Museum, Fort Sill, Okla.

Comptroller of Public Accounts, Audited Military Claims #2823, James W. Parker. Texas State Library, Austin, Tex.

Crawford County Marriages, 1817–74, Book C. Crawford County Courthouse, Palestine, Illinois.

Crittenden, G. M. Papers. Privately owned.

Daniel Parker family Bible records. Privately owned.

Dickson, J. A. Untitled manuscript. Privately owned, ca. 1907–1909.

Disinter[n]ment Permit. Texas State Department of Health, Bureau of Vital Statistics, Austin, Aug. 25, 1965. Bill Neeley Papers, Panhandle-Plains Historical Museum, Canyon.

Duty, Richard. Will, Jan. 4, 1822. Knox County Indiana Wills, Book A:133–35. Knox County Courthouse, Vincennes, Indiana.

Gholson, B. F. (Benjamin Franklin). Frank Gholson's Account of the Death of Nacona and Rescue of Cynthia Ann Parker, dictated by Frank Gholson to Felix Williams about 1931. B. F. Gholson Reminiscences, Center for American History, Austin, Tex.

———. Recollections of B. F. Gholson told to J. A. Rickard. Presented to the Library, University of Texas, by Professor Eugene C. Barker, Department of History, 1937. B. F. Gholson Reminiscences, Center for American History, Austin.

Given, Edward. Deed of Sale to Daniel Parker, Jan. 22, 1811. Joseph E. Taulman Papers, Center for American History, Austin, Tex.

Goodnight, Charles, to J. Evetts Haley. Interview, Nov. 18, 1926. Nita Stewart Haley Memorial Library and J. Evetts Haley History Center, Midland, Tex.

Greenwood, C. (Carl) L., to Joseph E. Taulman. Letter, Sept. 11, 1931. Joseph E. Taulman Papers, Center for American History, Austin, Tex.

Harper, Alex, to Jo Ella Exley. Interview, March 2, 2001.

Haworth, James M., to Enoch Hoag. Letter, June 8, 1874. National Archives, Washington, D.C.

———. Letter. Mar. 28, 1874. Indian Territory Miscellaneous, Kiowa and Comanche Papers, 1869–74. National Archives, Washington, D.C.

Heddenberg and Vedder vs. James W. Parker. Loose papers, 1839. Harris County Courthouse Annex, Houston, Tex.

Houston, Sam, to Daniel Parker. Letter, Feb. 13, 1837. Joseph E. Taulman Papers, Center for American History, Austin, Tex.

Iseeo Account. H. S. Scott Material [title of notebook]. W. S. Nye Collection, Fort Sill Museum, Fort Sill, Okla, 58–60.

Joseph A. Parker Estate. Probate Records, vol. D:269, 295; vol. O:380, vol. T:29. Harris County Courthouse, Houston, Tex.

Joseph E. Taulman Papers, 1821–41. Center for American History, Austin, Tex.

Kindred J. Pearson. Undated anonymous biographical sketch. Privately owned.

Knox County Marriages. Book A. Knox County Courthouse, Vincennes, Ind.

Mackenzie, Ranald S., to Departmental Headquarters. Letter, Oct. 12, 1872. 4546 1/2 AGO 1872, RG94, National Archives, Washington, D.C.

Mathes, May Reagan. Daughters of the American Revolution Application. Palestine Public Library, Palestine, Tex.

Montgomery County Commissioner's Court Records. Walker County Courthouse, Huntsville, Tex.

Muster Roll [of] Silas M. Parker. General Land Office Muster Roll Book. Texas State Library, Austin, Tex.

Neighbors, Robert S., to Hon. W. Medill, Commissioner of Indian Affairs. Report, Nov. 18, 1847. 30th Congress, 1st Session, Senate Committee Report 171: 9–10. National Archives, Washington, D.C.

Old Man Horse to W. S. Nye. Interview. Notebook #16:19–20. W. S. Nye Collection, Fort Sill Museum, Fort Sill, Okla.

O'Quinn, J. R., to Quanah Parker. Letter, June 19, 1908. Quanah

Ortiz, Polonio, to Adjutant John A. Mc Kinney. Statement, Oct. 10, 1872. National Archives, Washington, D.C.

Parker Collection, Panhandle-Plains Historical Museum, Canyon, Tex.

Parker, Baldwin, to Morris Swett. Interview, Aug. 24, 1959. Quanah Parker file compiled by Gillette Griswold, Fort Sill Museum, Fort Sill, Okla.

Parker, Charles Edward. Elder John Parker [title of document]. Sargent Papers, Illinois State Historical Library, Springfield.

Parker, Dan, Sr. Add Parker Massacre Story. Joseph E. Taulman Papers, Center for American History, Austin, Tex.

———. Additional Details on Parkers Fort Massacre. Joseph E. Taulman Papers, Center for American History, Austin, Tex.

———. Letter titled Genealogy Parker Family, June 13, 1987. Joseph E. Taulman Papers, Center for American History, Austin, Tex.

Parker, Daniel. Typescript copy of will, Apr. 12, 1844. Palestine Public Library, Palestine, Tex.

Parker, Daniel, Jr. Statement, June 18, 1836. John R. Price Papers, Center for American History, Austin, Tex.

Parker Genealogy Chart. Huntsville Public Library, Huntsville, Tex.

Parker, James W., Sr. Deed of Sale to James W. Parker, Jr., Nov. 11, 1851. Deed Book D, Anderson County, Tex.

Parker, James W., to Stephen F. Austin. Letter, June 29, 1832. Austin Papers, vol. 2, unpublished, mentioned in Calendar. Center for American History, Austin, Tex.

———. Petition of James W. Parker for guardianship over minors of Joseph A. Parker, February Term, 1842. J. W. Parker File, Star of the Republic Museum, Washington, Tex.

———.vs. Bloodsoe and Gay. Case 57, Montgomery County District Court Minutes, 1839–41. Walker County Courthouse, Huntsville, Tex.

———.vs. Stephens and Wilson. Case 52, Montgomery County District Court Minutes, 1839–41. Walker County Courthouse, Huntsville, Tex.

———.vs. William W. Sheppard. Case 25, Montgomery County District Court Minutes, 1839–41. Walker County Courthouse, Huntsville, Tex.

———. Montgomery County, Texas (Republic) Court Proceedings, 1826–68. Woodson Research Center, Fondren Library, Rice University, Houston, Tex.

Parker, Joe Bailey. Family Group Sheets. Privately owned.

Parker, John. Military Record. National Archives, Washington, D.C.

———. Pension Application. National Archives, Washington, D.C.

Parker, Quanah, to Charles Goodnight. Copy of undated letter. Bill Neeley Papers, Panhandle-Plains Historical Museum, Canyon, Tex.

———. Told in English & Signs & Comanche. Ledger Book 1:14–17. H. L. Scott Material, W. S. Nye Collection, Fort Sill Museum, Fort Sill, Okla.

Parker, Silas M., deceased, Lucinda Parker, Admrx. Probate Case # 35. Montgomery County Courthouse, Conroe, Texas.

Parker, Wayne. Quanah Parker Last Chief of the Kwahadi Obeys the Great Spirit. Quanah Parker Collection, Panhandle-Plains Historical Museum, Canyon, Tex.

Pearson, K. (Kindred) J., to John D. Floyd. Typescript copy of letter, Feb. 3, 1861. Fort Sill Museum, Fort Sill, Okla.

Peveler, Francis M., to J. Evetts Haley. Interview, Oct. 14, 1932. Nita Stewart Haley Memorial Library and J. Evetts Haley History Center, Midland, Tex.

Plummer, James P. (Pratt). Muster Roll Abstract. Texas State Library, Austin.

Plummer, L. T. M., to My Dear Nephews. Letter, Nov. 2, 1867. Plummer family papers, privately owned.

Plummer, R. E. to Jo Ella Exley. Interview, Sept. 21, 1986.

Poafebitty, Frank, Yellowfish, Felix Cowens, & several old women to W. S. Nye. Interview. Notebook #9:18–20. W. S. Nye Collection, Fort Sill Museum, Fort Sill, Okla.

Quanah Parker Lineage. Quanah Parker File, Fort Sill Museum, Fort Sill, Okla.

Quanah Parker, Wife Weckeah and their Children (from information furnished by the children in 1936 and the addition of some dates and data from agency listings). Quanah Parker History File, GG [Gillette Griswold]. Fort Sill Museum, Fort Sill, Okla.

Reverse Index to Marriage Record. Anderson County Courthouse, Palestine, Texas.

Schofield, G. W., to Asst. Adjt. Genl., Dept. of Texas. Letter, Oct. 10, 1872. National Archives, Washington, D.C.

Stebbins, Myldred, to Jo Ella Exley. Letter, Aug. 20, 1987.

Taulman, Joseph E., and Araminta McClelland Taulman. The Fort Parker Massacre and Its Aftermath. Joseph E. Taulman Papers, Center for American History, Austin, Tex.

Turnbull Primitive Baptist Church Vol. 1, 1806–1918, Minutes of the Session and List of Members [not the original title]. Tennessee State Library and Archives, Nashville.

Unidentified informant to W. S. Nye. Interview. Notebook #11:39. W. S. Nye Collection, Fort Sill Museum, Fort Sill, Okla.

York, Jewel Peters. Biographical sketch of L. T. M. Plummer. Plummer family papers, privately owned.

———. Genealogical charts. Plummer family papers, privately owned.

———.to R. E. Plummer Jr. Letter, Apr. 1, 1974. Plummer family papers, privately owned.

BOOKS AND ARTICLES

"Administrators' Notice." *Weekly Quid Nunc* (Palestine, Texas), November 8, 1864, 2.

Aldrich, Armistead A. *The History of Houston County, Texas.* San Antonio: Naylor Company, 1943.

Allen, Irene Taylor. *Saga of Anderson: The Proud Story of a Historic Texas Community.* New York: Greenwich Book Publishers, 1957.

Anderson County Genealogical Society. *Pioneer Families of Anderson County Prior to 1900.* N.p., ca. 1983.

Annual Report of the Commissioner of Indian Affairs to the Secretary of the Interior for the Year 1872. Washington, D.C.: Government Printing Office, 1872.

Augur, C. C., to the Secretary of War. *House Executive Document No. 1.* 43d Congress, 2d Session. Annual Report of the Secretary of War. *Annual Report of the Commissioner of Indian Affairs for 1874.* National Archives, Washington, D.C., 40.

Babcock, Rufus, ed. *Forty Years of Pioneer Life: Memoir of John Mason Peck D. D. Edited from his Journals and Correspondence.* Philadelphia: American Baptist Publication, 1864. Rpt., Carbondale: Southern Illinois University Press, 1965.

Baker, D. W. C. (De Witt Clinton). *A Texas Scrap-Book: Made Up of the History, Biography, and Miscellany of Texas and Its People.* New York: A. S. Barnes, 1875. Rpt., Austin: Texas State Historical Association, 1991.

Baker, J. (John) W. *A History of Robertson County, Texas.* Waco: Texian Press, 1971.

Baker, T. Lindsay, and Billy R. Harrison. *Adobe Walls: The History and Archaeology of the 1874 Trading Post.* College Station: Texas A&M University Press, 1986.

Barker, Eugene C., ed. "'Journal of the Permanent Council' (October 11–27, 1835)." *Quarterly of the Texas State Historical Association* 7 (1904): 249–78.

———. *The Life of Stephen F. Austin, Founder of Texas, 1794–1836: A Chapter in the Western Movement of the Anglo-American People.* Nashville: Cokesbury Press, 1926. Rpt., Austin: University of Texas Press, 1980.

———. "The Texan Declaration for Taking Up Arms against Mexico." *Quarterly of the Texas State Historical Association* 15 (1912): 173–85.

Bateman, Newton, and Paul Selby, eds. *Historical Encyclopedia of Illinois.* 2 vols. Chicago: Munsell Publishing Company, 1906.

Battey, Thomas C. *The Life and Adventures of a Quaker among the Indians.* Boston: Lee and Shepard, 1875. Rpt., Norman: University of Oklahoma Press, 1968.

Bauer, Jack K. *Zachary Taylor: Soldier, Planter, Statesman of the Old Southwest.* Baton Rouge: Louisiana State University Press, 1985.

Benedict, David. *A General History of the Baptist Denomination in America, and Other Parts of the World.* 2 vols. Boston: Manning and Loring, 1813. Rpt., Freeport, N.Y.: Books for Libraries Press, 1971.

Benner, Judith Ann. *Sul Ross: Soldier, Statesman, Educator.* College Station: Texas A&M University Press, 1983.

Berthrong, Donald J. *The Southern Cheyennes.* Norman: University of Oklahoma Press, 1963.

Biographical Directory of the Texan Conventions and Congresses, 1832–1845. Austin: Book Exchange, 1941. Rpt., San Augustine, Tex.: S. Malone Printer, 1986.

Blair, Eric Lee. *Early History of Grimes County.* Austin, Tex.: n.p., 1930.

Bollaert, William. *William Bollaert's Texas.* Norman: University of Oklahoma Press, 1956.

Bond, John. *History of the Baptist Concord Association of Middle Tennessee and North Alabama.* Nashville: Graves Marks and Company Printers, 1860.

Brand, Edward P. *Illinois Baptists: A History.* Bloomington, Ill.: Pantagraph Printing and Stationary Company, 1930.

Brown, Dee Alexander. *Bury My Heart at Wounded Knee.* New York: Hold, Rinehart and Winston, 1971.

Brown, John Henry. *History of Texas from 1685 to 1892.* 2 vols. St. Louis: L. E. Daniell, 1893. Rpt., Austin: State House Press, 1988.

———. *Indian Wars and Pioneers of Texas.* Austin: L. E. Daniell, 189?. Rpt., Austin: State House Press, 1988.

———. "Sequel to a Remarkable History." *Dallas Weekly Herald,* June 5, 1875.

Brune, Gunnar. *Springs of Texas.* Vol. 1. Fort Worth: Branch-Smith, 1981.

Butler, P. M., and M. G. Lewis to Com. of Indian Affairs. Letter, Aug. 8, 1846. *House Executive Document No. 1.* 30th Congress, 2d Session. Pp. 578–79.

Cady, John F. *The Origin and Development of the Missionary Baptist Church in Indiana.* Franklin, Ind.: Franklin College, 1942.

———. "The Religious Environment of Lincoln's Youth." *Indiana Magazine of History* 37 (1941): 16–30.

Callcott, Wilfrid Hardy. *Santa Anna: The Story of an Enigma Who Once Was Mexico.* Norman: University of Oklahoma Press, 1936.

Campbell, C. E. "Down among the Red Men." *Kansas Historical Collections* 17 (1926–28): 623–91.

Campbell, T. N., and William T. Field. "Identification of Comanche Raiding Trails in the Trans-Pecos Texas." *West Texas Historical Association Year Book* 44 (1968): 128–44.

"Capt. Ford's Expedition against the Indians." *State Gazette* (Austin, Tex.), May 22, 1858.

"Captain Gholson Passes On." *Frontier Times* 9 (1932): 517.

Carr, John. *Early Times in Middle Tennessee.* Nashville: Privately printed, 1857. Rpt., Nashville: Parthenon Press, 1958.

Carroll, J. (John) M. *A History of Texas Baptists.* Dallas: Baptist Standard Publishing Company, 1923.

Carroll, B. H. *The Genesis of American Anti-Missionism.* Louisville: Baptist Book Concern, 1902.

Carter, Robert G. *The Old Sergeant's Story: Fighting Indians and Bad Men in Texas from 1870 to 1876.* Privately printed, 1926. Rpt., Bryan, Tex.: J. M. Carroll and Company, 1982.

———. *On the Border with Mackenzie, or Winning West Texas from the Comanches.* Washington, D.C.: Eynon Printing Company, 1935. Rpt., New York: Antiquarian Press, 1961.

Catlin, George. *Letters and Notes on the Manners, Customs, and Conditions of North American Indians: Written during Eight Years' Travel (1832–1839) amongst the Wildest Tribes of Indians in North America.* 2 vols. London: Constable and Company, 1844. Rpt., New York: Dover Publications, 1973.

Champion, Tom W. "To the *Review*" *Athens Review,* Oct. 4, ca. 1935. Rpt., in "Capture and Life of Cynthia Ann Parker," *Palestine Herald Press,* June 6, 1937.

Clark, Pat B. *The History of Clarksville and Old Red River County.* Dallas: Mathis, Van Nort and Company, 1937.

Clarke, Mary Whatley. *The Palo Pinto Story.* Fort Worth: Manney Company, 1956.

Clift, W. H. "Warren's Trading Post." *Chronicles of Oklahoma* 2 (1924): 129–40.

Coleman, Ann Raney. *Victorian Lady on the Texas Frontier: The Journal of Ann Raney Coleman.* Ed. Richard King. Norman: University of Oklahoma Press, 1971.

Combs, Joseph F. *Legends of the Pineys.* San Antonio: Naylor Company, 1965.

Connell, Evan S. *Son of the Morning Star.* San Francisco: North Point Press, 1984.

Conner, Seymour V., et al. *Battles of Texas.* Waco: Texian Press, 1967. 53–75.

Conner, Seymour V., et al. *Capitols of Texas.* Waco: Texian Press, 1970.

Corlew, Robert Ewing. *A History of Dickson County, Tennessee.* Tennessee Historical Commission and Dickson County Historical Society, 1956.

Corwin, Hugh D. *Comanche and Kiowa Captives in Oklahoma and Texas.* Guthrie, Okla.: Privately printed, 1959.

———. *The Kiowa Indians: Their History and Life Stories.* Lawton, Okla.: n.p., 1958.

Crimmins, M. L. "First Sergeant John W. Spangler, Company H, Second United States Cavalry." *West Texas Historical Association Year Book* 26 (1950): 68–75.

Custer, George Armstrong. *My Life on the Plains, or Personal Experiences with Indians.* Norman: University of Oklahoma Press, 1962.

Cuthbertson, Gilbert. "Sam Houston's Neighbors: A Record of Early Montgomery County." *Texana* 9 (1971): 260–69.

Davis, Mary. "Early History of Montgomery." *Herald* (Montgomery County Genealogical and Historical Society) 11 (1988): 135–41.

DeShields, James T. *Border Wars of Texas.* Tioga, Tex.: Herald Company, 1912. Rpt., Austin: State House Press, 1993.

———. *Cynthia Ann Parker: The Story of Her Capture.* San Antonio: Naylor Company, 1934. Rpt., San Augustine, Tex.: S. Malone Printer, 1986.

Dixon, Olive K., ed. *Life of "Billy" Dixon: Plainsman, Scout and Pioneer.* Dallas: P. L. Turner Company, 1927. Rpt., Austin: State House Press, 1987.

Dodge, Richard Irving. *Our Wild Indians: Thirty-three Years' Personal Experience among the Red Men of the Great West.* A. D. Worthington and Company, 1882. Rpt., Williamstown, Mass.: Corner House Publishers, 1978.

Dollar, Claudine McCallay. *The Gardner, Kendrick, Forgey, Parker, Gage-McComas Families.* Blair, Okla.: Pioneer Publishing Company, 1983.

Dooley, Claude, and Betty Dooley, eds. *Why Stop? A Guide to Texas Historical Roadside Markers.* 2d ed. Houston: Lone Star Books, 1985.

Dorst, Joseph H. "Ranald Slidell Mackenzie." *Journal of the United States Cavalry Association* 10 (1897): 367–82.

Dresel, Gustav. *Gustav Dresel's Houston Journal: Adventures in North America and Texas, 1837–1841.* Austin: University of Texas Press, 1954.

Duffus, R. L. (Robert Luther). *The Santa Fe Trail.* New York: Longmans, Green and Company, 1930.

Edens Family Association. *The Edens Adventure: A Brief History of the Edens Family in America.* Wolfe City, Tex.: Henington Publishing Company, 1992.

Elam, Earl Henry. "The Butler and Lewis Mission and Treaty of 1846." *West Texas Historical Association Year Book* 46 (1970): 72–100.

Elkins, John M. *Indian Fighting on the Texas Frontier*. Amarillo: Russell and Cockrell, 1929.

Ellison, Ronald C. *Texas and Baptist Sunday Schools, 1929–1996*. Baptist General Convention of Texas, 1997.

Erath, Lucy A., ed. "Memoirs of Major George Bernard Erath," pt. 1. *Southwestern Historical Quarterly* 26 (1923): 207–33.

Everett, Dianna. *The Texas Cherokees: A People between Two Fires, 1819–1840*. Norman: University of Oklahoma Press, 1990.

Everton, George B., ed. *The Handy Book for Genealogists*. 7th ed. Logan, Utah: Everton Publishers, 1987.

Ewing, James. *A Treasury of Tennessee Tales*. Nashville: Rutledge Hill Press, 1985.

Fehrenbach, T. (Theodore) R. *Comanches: The Destruction of a People*. New York: Alfred A. Knopf, 1974.

Fenstermaker, Kelly. "Life on Tap." *Texas (Houston Chronicle* Magazine), October 11, 1998, 8–12.

Ferris, Sylvia Van Voast, and Eleanor Sellers Hoppe. *Scalpels and Sabers: Nineteenth Century Medicine in Texas*. Austin: Eakin Press, 1985.

Flippin, Jack. "Legends of the Double Mountain." *Texas (Houston Chronicle* Magazine), January 22, 1995, 8–10, 14.

Flores, Dan L. *Caprock Canyonlands*. Austin: University of Texas Press, 1990.

Ford, John Salmon. *Rip Ford's Texas*. Austin: University of Texas Press, 1963.

Ford, Thomas. *A History of Illinois, from Its Commencement as a State in 1818, to 1847*. 2 vols. Chicago: S. C. Griggs and Company, 1854. Rpt., Chicago: R. R. Donnelley, 1945.

Foreman, Grant. "The Centennial of Fort Gibson." *Chronicles of Oklahoma* 2 (1924): 119–28.

———. *Pioneer Days in the Early Southwest*. Cleveland: Arthur H. Clark Company, 1926.

———. "The Texas Comanche Treaty of 1846." *Southwestern Historical Quarterly* 51 (1948): 313–32.

———, ed. "The Journal of Elijah Hicks." *Chronicles of Oklahoma* 13 (1935): 68–99.

Foster, Morris W. *Being Comanche: A Social History of an American Indian Community*. Tucson: University of Arizona Press, 1991.

Friend, Llerena. *Sam Houston: The Great Designer*. Austin: University of Texas Press, 1969.

———. "The Texan of 1860." *Southwestern Historical Quarterly* 62 (1958): 1–17.

"From the Frontier." *Dallas Herald,* January 2, 1861, 1.

Gambrell, Herbert. *Anson Jones: The Last President of Texas*. Privately printed, 1947. Rpt., Austin: University of Texas Press, 1988.

Gammel, Hans Peter Nielson, ed. *The Laws of Texas, 1822–1897*. 10 vols. Austin: Gammel Book Company, 1898.

Gandy, William Harley. "A History of Montgomery County, Texas." Master's thesis, University of Houston, 1952.

Garrett, Jill K., ed. *Historical Sketches of Dickson County Tennessee*. Privately published, 1971.

Gelo, Daniel J. "'Comanche Land and Ever Has Been': A Native Geography of Nineteenth-Century Comancheria." *Southwestern Historical Quarterly* 103 (2000): 273–307.

Gentry, Mrs. A. D. "The Runaway Scrape." *Frontier Times* 4, no. 6 (1927): 46–51.

Gerald, R. J. "Benjamin Franklin Gholson, Texan." *Frontier Times* 4, no. 11 (1927): 46–51.

Gibson, Arrell Morgan. *The Kickapoos: Lords of the Middle Border.* Norman: University of Oklahoma Press, 1963.

———. *Oklahoma: A History of Five Centuries.* 2d ed. Norman: University of Oklahoma Press, 1981.

———. *The History of Oklahoma.* Norman: University of Oklahoma Press, 1984.

Gomez, Arthur R. *A Most Singular Country: A History of the Occupation in the Big Bend.* Salt Lake City: Brigham Young University, 1990.

Goodnight, Charles. *Charles Goodnight's Indian Recollections.* Amarillo, Tex.: Russell and Cockrell, 1928.

———. "My Recollections of the Buffalo Days." *Southwest Plainsman,* November 14, 1925.

———. "True Sketch of Quanah Parker's Life." *Frontier Times* 4, no. 2 (1926): 5–7.

Goodspeed's History of Tennessee. 1886. Rpt., as *The Goodspeed Histories of Montgomery, Robertson, Humphreys, Stewart, Dickson, Cheatham, Houston Counties of Tennessee.* Columbia, Tenn.: Woodward and Stinson Printing Company, 1972.

Grant, U. (Ulysses) S. *Personal Memoirs of U. S. Grant.* New York: World Publishing Company, 1967.

Gray, Millie. *The Diary of Millie Gray, 1832–1840.* Houston: Fletcher Young Publishing Company, 1967.

"Great Battle with the Indians!!! Official Reports of Capts. Ford and Nelson." *State Gazette* (Austin, Tex.), May 29, 1858.

"'Great Father' Calls the Comanche Leader." *Lawton Daily News,* February 24, 1922.

Greenwood, Hulen M. *Garrison Greenwood: Ancestors and Descendants.* Houston: H. M. Greenwood, 1986.

Gregg, Josiah. *Commerce of the Prairies.* Norman: University of Oklahoma Press, 1954.

Grinnell, George Bird. *The Fighting Cheyennes.* Norman: University of Oklahoma Press, 1956.

Gulick, Charles Adams, Jr., ed. *The Papers of Mirabeau Buonaparte Lamar.* 6 vols. Austin: Texas State Library, 1920–27. Rpt., Austin: Pemberton Press, 1968.

Gurasich, Marj. *History of Harris County Sheriff's Department, 1837–1983.* Houston: Harris County Sheriff's Deputies' Association, 1983.

Hacker, Margaret Schmidt. *Cynthia Ann Parker: The Life and the Legend.* El Paso: Texas Western Press, 1990.

Hagan, William T. "Quanah Parker." In *American Indian Leaders: Studies in Diversity,* ed. R. David Edmunds. Lincoln: University of Nebraska Press, 1980.

———. *Quanah Parker: Comanche Chief.* Norman: University of Oklahoma Press, 1993.

———. *United States–Comanche Relations: The Reservation Years.* New Haven: Yale University Press, 1976.

Haley, J. Evetts. *Charles Goodnight: Cowman and Plainsman.* Norman: University of Oklahoma Press, 1949.

———. *Fort Concho and the Texas Frontier.* San Angelo, Tex.: San Angelo Standard-Times, 1952.

Haley, James L. *The Buffalo War: The History of the Red River Indian Uprising of 1874.* Garden City, N.Y.: Doubleday and Company, 1976. Rpt., Norman: University of Oklahoma Press, 1985.

Harris County Historical Society. *Houston: A Nation's Capital, 1837–1839.* D. Armstrong Company, 1985.

Harris, Dilue Rose. "The Reminiscences of Mrs. Dilue Harris." *Quarterly of the Texas State Historical Association* 4 (1900): 85–127, 155–89; 7 (1904): 214–22.

Harston, J. Emmor. *Comanche Land.* San Antonio: Naylor Company, 1963.

Hartje, Robert G. *Van Dorn: The Life and Times of a Confederate General.* Nashville: Vanderbilt University Press, 1967.

Hatcher, Mattie Austin. *Letters of an Early American Traveller: Mary Austin Holley, Her Life and Her Works, 1784–1846.* Dallas: Southwest Press, 1933.

Hathaway, Seth. "The Adventures of a Buffalo Hunter." *Frontier Times* 9 (1931): 105–12, 129–35.

Haworth, James M., to Smith. Letter, September 1, 1874. *House Executive Document No. 1.* 43 Congress, 2d Session. Annual Report of Secretary of War. National Archives, Washington, D.C., 220.

Hayes, Robert M. *It Really Happened in East Texas.* Fort Worth: Branch Smith, 1971.

Haynes, Sam W. *Soldiers of Misfortune: The Somervell and Mier Expeditions.* Austin: University of Texas Press, 1990.

Hendricks, Sterling Brown. "The Somervell Expedition to the Rio Grande." *Southwestern Historical Quarterly* 23 (1919–20): 112–40.

Henson, Margaret Swett. "Politics and the Treatment of the Mexican Prisoners after the Battle of San Jacinto." *Southwestern Historical Quarterly* 94 (1990): 189–230.

Hogan, William Ransom. *The Texas Republic: A Social and Economic History.* Norman: University of Oklahoma Press, 1946.

Hohes, Pauline Buck. *A Centennial History of Anderson County, Texas.* San Antonio: Naylor Company, 1936.

Hoig, Stan. *The Battle of the Washita: The Sheridan-Custer Indian Campaign of 1967–69.* Garden City, N.Y.: Doubleday and Company, 1976.

———. *Jesse Chisholm: Ambassador of the Plains.* Niwot: University Press of Colorado, 1991.

Holland, G. A. (Gustavus Adolphus). *History of Parker County and the Double Log Cabin: Being a Brief Symposium of the Early History of Parker County, Together with Short Biographical Sketches of Early Settlers and Their Trials.* Weatherford, Tex.: Herald Publishing Company, 1937.

Holley, Mary Austin. *The Texas Diary, 1835–1838.* Austin: University of Texas Press, ca. 1965.

Horton, Alexander. *A. Horton: Patriot of the Republic of Texas.* San Augustine, Tex.: S. Malone Printer, 1984.

Houston County Historical Commission. *History of Houston County, Texas 1687–1979.* Tulsa, Okla.: Heritage Publishing Company, 1979.

———. *Houston County (Texas) Cemeteries.* 3d ed. Crockett, Tex.: 1987.

Howard, Robert P. *Illinois: A History of the Prairie State.* Grand Rapids, Mich.: William B. Eerdsman Publishing Company, 1972.

Hughes, W. (William) J. *Rebellious Ranger: Rip Ford and the Old Southwest.* Norman: University of Oklahoma Press, 1990.

Hunter, J. W. (John Marvin). *The Trail Drivers of Texas.* Cokesbury Press, 1925. Rpt., Austin: University of Texas Press, 1985.

Hutton, Paul Andrew. *Phil Sheridan and His Army.* Lincoln: University of Nebraska Press, 1985.

Hyde, George E. *Life of George Bent Written from His Letters.* Norman: University of Oklahoma Press, 1968.

"Indian Traders." *Telegraph and Texas Register* (Houston, Tex.), July 27, 1842.

Inman, Henry. *The Old Santa Fe Trail: The Story of a Great Highway.* New York: Macmillan Company, 1899.

Irion, Shannon, and Garrett Jenkins, eds. *Ever Thine Truly: Love Letters from Sam Houston to Anna Raquet.* Austin: Jenkins Garrett Press, 1975.

Jackson, Clyde L., and Grace Jackson. *Quanah Parker: Last Chief of the Comanches.* New York: Exposition Press, 1963.

James, Thomas. *Three Years among the Indians and Mexicans.* Chicago: R. R. Donnelley, 1953.

Jenkins, John Holland. *Recollections of Early Texas.* Austin: University of Texas Press, 1958.

Jenkins, John H. (Holmes). *Audubon and Texas.* Austin: Pemberton Press, 1965.

Johnson, Andrew. "The Fight at 'Dobe Walls.'" *Kansas City Star* (Kansas City, Mo.), August 6, 1911, sec. A, 5.

Jones, Anson. *Memoranda and Official Correspondence Relating to the Republic of Texas, Its History and Annexation.* New York: D. Appleton and Company, 1859. Rpt., Chicago: Rio Grande Press, 1966.

Jones, Douglas C. *The Treaty at Medicine Lodge.* Norman: University of Oklahoma Press, 1966.

Jones, Lawrence T. "Cynthia Ann Parker and Pease Ross: The Forgotten Photographs." *Southwestern Historical Quarterly* 93 (1990): 379–84.

Joplin, Hattie Seale. "When Cherokee War Whoops Rang through Texas." *Frontier Times* 8 (1931): 471–75.

Jordan, Terry G. *Log Cabin Village: A History and Guide.* (Austin): Texas State Historical Association, 1980.

"The Journal of Elija Hicks." *Chronicles of Oklahoma* 13 (1935): 68–99.

Kappler, Charles J. *Indian Affairs: Laws and Treaties.* 3 vols. Washington, D.C.: Government Printing Office, 1904.

Kavanagh, Thomas W. *Comanche Political History: An Ethnohistorical Perspective, 1706–1875.* Lincoln: University of Nebraska Press, 1996.

Keim, De B. *Sheridan's Troopers on the Border: A Winter Campaign on the Plains.* New York: George Routlege and Sons, 1885. Rpt., Freeport, N.Y.: Books for Libraries Press, 1970.

Kelly, Fanny. *Narrative of My Captivity among the Sioux Indians.* Hartford, Conn.: Mutual Publishing Company, 1871. Rpt., Secaucus, N.J.: Citadel Press, 1973.

Kenner, Charles L. *A History of New Mexican–Plains Indian Relations.* Norman: University of Oklahoma Press, 1969.

Klos, George. "'Our People Could Not Distinguish One Tribe from Another': The 1859 Expulsion of the Reserve Indians from Texas." *Southwestern Historical Quarterly* 97 (1994): 599–619.

Lack, Paul D. *The Texas Revolutionary Experience: A Political and Social History, 1835–1836.* College Station: Texas A&M University Press, 1992.

Land, Betty Harkness. "Off to Texas." *Searcher* (Southern California Genealogical Society) 20 (1983): 38–39.

Landrum, Graham, and Allan Smith. *An Illustrated History of Grayson County, Texas.* Fort Worth: Historical Publishers, 1967.

Leckie, William H. *The Military Conquest of the Southern Plains.* Norman: University of Oklahoma Press, 1963.

Leclerc, Frederic. *Texas and Its Revolution.* Trans. James L. Shepherd III. Houston: Anson Jones Press, 1950.

Lecompte, Janet. *Rebellion in Rio Arriba, 1837.* Albuquerque: University of New Mexico Press, ca. 1985.

Lee, Max. "Daniel Parker: Politician, Baptist, and Anti-Mission Missionary." *Texas Baptist History* 6 (1986): 1–9.

"The Legislature: Editorial Correspondence of the Gal. News, March 19, 1861." *Standard* (Clarksville, Tex.), April 6, 1861, 3.

Lindley, Harlow. *Indiana as Seen by Early Travelers.* Indianapolis: Indiana Historical Commission, 1916.

Linn, John J. *Reminiscences of Fifty Years in Texas.* New York: D and J Sadlier and Company, 1883. Rpt., Austin: State House Press, 1986.

Lockhart, John Washington. *Sixty Years on the Brazos: The Life and Letters of Dr. John Washington Lockhart, 1824–1900.* Waco: Texian Press, 1976.

Loftin, Jack. *Trails through Archer: A Centennial History, 1880–1980.* Burnet, Tex.: Eakin Publications, 1979.

Lubbock, Francis R. *Six Decades in Texas.* Austin: Pemberton Press, 1968.

Lutz, Ella Cox. "Quanah Parker: The Last Comanche Chief." *Daughters of the American Revolution Magazine* 106 (1972): 154–55.

Magoffin, Susan. *Down the Santa Fe Trail and into Mexico: The Diary of Susan Shelby Magoffin, 1846–1847.* New Haven: Yale University Press, 1926.

Malavis, Nick. "Equality under the Lord's Law: The Disciplinary Process in Texas Baptist Churches, 1833–1870." *East Texas Historical Journal* 31 (1993): 3–23.

Manning, Wentworth. *Some History of Van Zandt County.* Privately printed, 1919. Rpt., Winston-Salem, N.C.: Hunter Publishing Company, 1977.

Marcy, Randolph B. *Adventure on Red River: Report on the Exploration of the Headwaters of the Red River by Captain Randolph B. Marcy and Captain G. B. McClellan.* Norman: University of Oklahoma Press, 1837.

"Married Seventy Years." *Frontier Times* 9 (1932): 366–67.

Marshall, J. T. *The Miles Expedition of 1874–1875: An Eyewitness Account of the Red River War.* Austin: Encino Press, 1971.

Marshall, Thomas Maitland. "Commercial Aspects of the Texan Santa Fe Expedition." *Southwestern Historical Quarterly* 20 (1916–17): 242–59.

Martin, W. N. "A History of Montgomery." Master's thesis, Sam Houston State Teachers College, Huntsville, Tex., 1950.

Matthews, Sallie Reynolds. *Interwoven: A Pioneer Chronicle.* Austin: University of Texas Press, 1958.

Maverick, Mary Ann Adams. *Memoirs of Mary A. Maverick.* San Antonio: Alamo Printing Company, 1921. Rpt., Lincoln: University of Nebraska Press, 1989.

Maxwell, Ross A. *The Big Bend of the Rio Grande: A Guide to the Rocks, Landscape, Geologic History, and Settlers of the Area of Big Bend National Park.* Austin: Bureau of Economic Geology of the University of Texas at Austin, 1968.

McCall, George Archibald. *New Mexico in 1850: A Military View.* Norman: University of Oklahoma Press, 1968.

McComb, David G. *Houston: The Bayou City.* Austin: University of Texas Press, 1969.

McLean, Malcomb D. *Papers Concerning Robertson's Colony in Texas.* 18 vols. Arlington, Tex.: University of Texas at Arlington Press, 1974–93.

Meadows, William C. *Kiowa, Apache, and Comanche Military Societies.* Austin: University of Texas Press, 1999.

A Memorial and Biographical History of McLennan, Falls, Bell, and Coryell Counties, Texas. Chicago: Lewis Publishing Company, 1893. Rpt., St. Louis, Mo.: Ingmire Publications, 1984.

Meyer, Marian. "First U.S. Woman Arrives in Santa Fe." *Journal North* (Albuquerque newspaper), June 24, 1987, 6.

―――. *Mary Donoho: New First Lady of the Santa Fe Trail.* Santa Fe, N.M.: Ancient City Press, 1991.

The Mighty Chieftains. Alexandria, Va.: Time-Life Books, 1993.

Miles, Nelson A. *Personal Recollections and Observations of General Nelson A. Miles Embracing a Brief View of the Civil War or from New England to the Golden Gate and the Story of His Indian Campaigns with Comments on the Exploration, Development and Progress of Our Great Western Empire.* 2 vols. Chicago: Werner Company, 1896. Rpt., Lincoln: University of Nebraska Press, 1992.

―――. *Serving the Republic: Memoirs of the Civil and Military Life of Nelson A. Miles.* 1911. Rpt., Freeport, N.Y.: Books for Libraries Press, 1971.

"Military Item." *Dallas Herald,* August 10, 1872.

Miller, Flora May Starr. *The House of Starr.* College Station, Tex.: Starr Custom Binding, 1971.

Miller, Ray. *Eyes of Texas Travel Guide: Panhandle/Plains Edition.* Houston: Gulf Publishing Company, 1982.

―――. *Ray Miller's Texas Forts: A History and Guide.* Houston: Cordovan Press, 1985.

Mills, Betty J. *Calico Chronicle: Texas Women and Their Fashions, 1830–1910.* Lubbock: Texas Tech Press, 1985.

Mishkin, Bernard. *Rank and Warfare among the Plains Indians.* Seattle: University of Washington Press, 1940. Monographs of the American Ethnological Society 3. Lincoln: University of Nebraska Press, 1992.

Mondy, Robert William. *Pioneers and Preachers: Stories of the Old Frontier.* Chicago: Nelson-Hall, 1980.

Montgomery County Genealogical and Historical Society. *Montgomery County History.* Conroe, Tex.: 1981.

―――. *Early Montgomery County, Texas Marriages Found in the "Black Boxes," 1838–1872.* Conroe, Tex.: 1986.

Montgomery County Tax Rolls, 1838–1887. Microfilm roll 1. Clayton Genealogical Library, Houston, Tex.

Mooar, J. Wright. "Frontier Experience of J. Wright Mooar." *West Texas Historical Association Year Book* 4 (1928): 89–92.

Mooney, James. "Calendar History of the Kiowa Indians." *Seventeenth Annual Report of the Bureau of American Ethnology to the Secretary of the Smithsonian Institution, 1895–96.* Pt. 1. 141–468. Washington, D.C.: Government Printing Company, 1898.

Moore, Stephen L. *Taming Texas: Captain William T. Sadler's Lone Star Service.* Austin: State House Press, 2000.

Morrell, Z. N. *Flowers and Fruits in the Wilderness or Forty-Six Years in Texas and Two Winters in Honduras.* 3d ed., rev. St. Louis: Commercial Printing Company, 1882. Rpt., Texas Baptist Historical Committee, 1993.

Muir, Andrew Forest, ed. *Texas in 1837.* Austin: University of Texas Press, 1958.

Nance, Joseph Milton. *Attack and Counterattack: The Texan-Mexican Frontier, 1842.* Austin: University of Texas Press, 1964.

―――. *Dare-Devils All: The Texan Mier Expedition, 1842–1844.* Austin: Eakin Press, 1998.

Neeley, Bill. *Quanah Parker and His People.* Slaton, Tex.: Brazos Press, 1986.

Neighbors, Robert S. "The Nauni or Comanches of Texas; Their Traits and Beliefs, and Their Divisions and Intertribal Relations." In *Information Respecting the History, Conditions, and Prospects of the Indian Tribes of the United States,* ed. Henry

R. Schoolcraft. 2: 125–34. Philadelphia: Lippincott, Grambo and Company, 1852. Rpt., New York: Paladin Press, 1969.

Newcomb, W. W. (William Wilmon). *The Indians of Texas: From Prehistoric to Modern Times.* Austin: University of Texas Press, 1990.

Newton, Lewis W., and Herbert P. Gambrell. *A Social and Political History of Texas.* Dallas: Turner Company, 1935.

Northern Standard (Clarksville, Tex.), May 25, 1846, 2.

Norton, Herman A. *Religion in Tennessee, 1777–1945.* Knoxville: University of Tennessee Press, ca. 1981.

"Notice." *Telegraph and Texas Register* (Houston, Tex.), Jan. 20, 1838.

Noyes, Stanley. *Los Comanches: The Horse People, 1751–1845.* Albuquerque: University of New Mexico Press, 1993.

Nye, W. (Wilbur) S. *Carbine and Lance: The Story of Old Fort Sill.* Norman: University of Oklahoma Press, 1969.

Oates, Stephen B. "Texas under the Secessionists." *Southwestern Historical Quarterly* 67 (1963): 167–212.

Old Santa Fe Today. Albuquerque: University of New Mexico Press, 1966.

O'Quinn, Eugene Graham. "Quanah—the Eagle: Half White Comanche Chief." *Our Heritage* (Van Zandt County Genealogical Society, Canton, Texas) 2, no. 3 (1981): 11–28; 2, no. 4 (1981): 20–36.

"O'Quinn, James Rufus." 6 Texas Cavalry (Stone's Regiment, 2d Cavalry). *Texas Confederate Compiled Service Records.* M–P, M323, Microfilm roll 40, National Archives, 1960.

"Over 100 Indians Held Prisoners of War." *Fort Concho Report* 12 (1980): 16–17.

Parker, Ben J. "Early Times in Texas and History of Parker Family: Ben J. Parker Gives Events of Pioneering." *Palestine Daily Herald,* February 12, 1935.

Parker, Daniel. "A Short History of the Life and Progress of the Editor." *Church Advocate* 2 (1831): 259–88.

———. *A Public Address to the Baptist Society and Friends of Religion in General on the Principle and Practice of the Baptist Board of Foreign Missions for the United States of America.* Stout and Osborn, 1820.

———. "For the Intelligencer." *Illinois Intelligencer,* December 7, 1822, 1.

———. *Views on the Two Seeds: Taken from Genesis, 3rd Chapter and Part of the 15th Verse.* Vandalia, Ill.: Robert Blackwell, 1826.

Parker, Daniel, et al. "To the People of Illinois." *Illinois Intelligencer,* March 8, 1823, 1–2.

"Parker, Ira." *Texas Confederate Compiled Service Records.* 1st Infantry (2d Infantry) Mo–Pe, M323, Mirofilm roll 253, National Archives, 1960.

Parker, James W. *Defence of James W. Parker against Slanderous Accusations Preferred against Him.* Houston: Telegraph Power Press, 1839.

———. *Narrative of the Perilous Adventures, Miraculous Escapes and Sufferings of Rev. James W. Parker, during a Frontier Residence in Texas, of Fifteen Years; With an Impartial Geographical Description of the Climate, Soil, Timber, Water, &c., &c., &c. of Texas; Written by Himself. To Which Is Appended a Narrative of the Capture and Subsequent Sufferings of Mrs. Rachel Plummer, (His Daughter,) during a Captivity of Twenty-one Months among the Cumanche Indians, with a Sketch of Their Manners, Customs, Laws, &c.; With a Short Description of the Country over Which She Travelled Whilst with the Indians; Written by Herself.* Louisville, Ky.: Morning Courier, 1844.

———. *Parker's Narrative and History of Texas; To Which Is Appended Mrs. Plummer's*

Narrative of Her Captivity of Twenty-one Months among the Cumanche Indians. Louisville, Ky.: 1845.

———. to M. B. Lamar. Letter, February 3, 1844. In *The Papers of Mirabeau Buonaparte Lamar,* ed. Charles Adams Gulick, Jr. 4.1: 38. Austin: Texas State Library, 1924. Rpt., Austin: Pemberton Press, 1968.

"Parker, Lucinda, Admrx. of estate of Silas M. Parker, dec. To the Honl. Jesse Grimes, Judge of the Probate Court of Montgomery County." *Herald* (Montgomery County Genealogical and Historical Society) 11 (1988): 82, 100.

"Parker, Silas," 15 Infantry. *Texas Confederate Compiled Service Records.* P–Sm, M323, Microfilm roll 379, National Archives, 1960.

Pease, Theodore Calvin, ed. *Illinois Election Returns, 1818–1848.* Springfield: Illinois State Historical Library, 1923. Vol. 18 of *Collections of the Illinois State Historical Library,* 34 vols.

Peck, John Mason. "Historical Sketches of the Baptist Denomination in Indiana, Illinois, and Missouri." *Baptist Memorial and Monthly Chronicle* 1 (1842): 197–200. Eds. R. Babcock and J. O. Choules. New York: John R. Bigelow, n.d.

Perrin, William Henry, ed. *History of Crawford and Clark Counties.* Chicago: O. L. Baskin and Company, 1883.

Perrin, William Henry, et al., comps. *The History of Coles County Illinois.* Chicago: Wm. Le Baron, Jr., and Co., 1879.

Phelps, Bailey P. *They Loved the Land: Foard County History.* Quanah, Tex.: Quanah Tribune-Chief, 1969.

Pierce, Michael D. *The Most Promising Young Officer: A Life of Randald Slidell Mackenzie.* Norman: University of Oklahoma Press, 1993.

"Plummer, James Pratt." *Texas Confederate Compiled Service Records.* 15 Cavalry (2d Reg., Johnson's Brigade) Mi–S, M323, Microfilm roll 88, National Archives, 1960.

Plummer, Rachel. *Narrative of the Capture and Subsequent Sufferings of Mrs. Rachel Plummer during a Captivity of Twenty-One Months among the Cumanche Indians: With a Sketch of Their Manners, Customs, Laws, &c.; with a Short Description of the Country over Which she Travelled whilst with the Indians.* Houston, 1839. Rpt., Waco: Texian Press, 1968.

———. *Rachael Plummer's Narrative of Twenty One Months Servitude as a Prisoner among the Commanchee Indians. Written by Herself.* Houston: Telegraph Power Press, 1838. Rpt., Austin, Jenkins Publishing Company, 1977.

Price, Billie. "Elder John Parker and His Family." *Roadrunner* (Chaparral Genealogical Society, Tomball, Tex.) 10 (1984): 201–202.

Prince, L. Bradford. *Spanish Mission Churches of New Mexico.* Glorietta, N.M.: Rio Grande Press, 1977.

Puetz, C. J. *Tennessee County Maps.* Lyndon Station, Wis.: County Maps, n.d.

Putnam, A. W. (Albigence Waldo). *History of Middle Tennessee; Or Life and Times of Gen. James Robertson.* Nashville: Privately printed, 1859.

R. C. (Robert Cotter). "The Indian Fight on the Wichita—Graphic Sketch." *State Gazette* (Austin, Tex.), May 29, 1958.

Ray, Thelma. *The Reagan-Parker Family Genealogy.* Fort Worth: Miran Publishers, 1987.

"Record of Engagements with Hostile Indians in the Division of the Missouri form 1868 to 1882." *Journal of the United States Cavalry Association* 14 (1903–1904): 366–91.

"The Records of an Early Texas Baptist Church, 1833–1847." *Quarterly of The Texas State Historical Association* 11 (1907–1908): 85–156; 12 (1908–1909): 1–60.

Reid, Mary. "Fashions of the Republic." *Southwestern Historical Quarterly* 45 (1941–42): 244–54.

Republic of Texas, 5 Cong., 1 Sess., 1840–1841, House Journal.

Richardson, Rupert N. *The Comanche Barrier to South Plains Settlement: A Century and a Half of Savage Resistance to the Advancing White Frontier.* Glendale, Calif.: Arthur H. Clark, 1933.

———. "The Comanche Indians at the Adobe Walls Fight." *Panhandle-Plains Historical Review* 4 (1931): 24–38.

———. "Comanches." In *Indian Tribes of Texas.* Dorman H. Winfrey et al. Waco: Texian Press, 1971. 39–66.

———. "Cynthia Ann Parker." In *Women of Texas,* James M. Day et al. Waco: Texian Press, 1972. 73–89.

———. *Texas: The Lone Star State.* 2d ed. Englewood Cliffs, N.J.: Prentice-Hall, 1958.

Riddle, Roy. "Indian Survivors of Adobe Walls Visit Site 65 Years after Fight." *Amarillo Daily News,* April 26, 1939, 1, 13. Panhandle-Plains Historical Museum, Canyon, Tex.

Rister, Carl Coke. *Border Captives: The Traffic in Prisoners by Southern Plains Indians, 1835–1875.* Norman: University of Oklahoma Press, 1940.

———. *Border Command: General Phil Sheridan in the West.* Norman: University of Oklahoma Press, 1944.

———. *Fort Griffin on the Texas Frontier.* Norman: University of Oklahoma Press, 1956.

———. *Robert E. Lee in Texas.* Norman: University of Oklahoma Press, 1946.

———, ed. *Comanche Bondage: Beales's Settlement and Sarah Ann Horn's Narrative.* Lincoln: University of Nebraska Press, 1989.

Rittenhouse, Jack D. *The Santa Fe Trail: A Historical Bibliography.* Albuquerque: University of New Mexico Press, 1971.

The Roads of Texas. Fredericksburg: Shearer Publishing, 1988.

Robertson, Pauline Durrett. *Panhandle Pilgrimage.* Canyon, Tex.: Staked Plains Press, 1976.

Robinson, Charles M. *Bad Hand: A Biography of General Ranald S. Mackenzie.* Austin: State House Press, 1993.

Robinson, Lila Wistrand, and James Armagost. *Comanche Directory and Grammar.* Arlington: University of Texas at Arlington, 1990.

Rose, Victor M. *Ross's Texas Brigade: Being a Narrative of Events Connected with its Service in the Late War between the States.* Louisville, Ky.: Courier-Journal Book and Job Rooms, 1881. Rpt., Kennesaw, Ga.: Continental Book Company, 1960.

Ross, James. *Life and Times of Elder Reuben Ross.* Philadelphia: Grant, Faires and Rodgers, ca. 1881.

Ryland, Garnett. *The Baptists of Virginia, 1699–1926.* Richmond: Virginia Baptist Board of Missions and Education, 1955.

Sanders, Leon, ed. "A Letter from East Hamilton, Texas." *East Texas Historical Journal* 28, no. 2 (1990): 46–48.

"Says Cynthia Ann Parker Buried in Henderson [County]: Cousin of Quanah Parker Gives out Interview Regarding Burial Place of Noted Woman." *Wills Point Chronicle,* November 11, 1910.

Schmitz, Joseph William. *Texas Culture in the Days of the Republic, 1836–1846.* San Antonio: Naylor Company, 1960.

Schofield, Donald F. "W. M. D. Lee, Indian Trader." *Panhandle-Plains Historical Review* 54 (1981): vii–113.

Scott, Hugh Lenox. *Some Memories of a Soldier.* New York: Century Company, 1928.

Scott, Lorine Maud. "Daniel Parker and the First Baptist Church in Texas." Master's thesis, University of Chicago, 1931.

Semple, Robert Baylor. *History of the Baptists in Virginia.* Lafayette, Tenn.: Church History Research and Archives, 1976.

Sheridan, Philip H. "Record of Engagements with Hostile Indians in Texas, 1868 to 1882." *West Texas Historical Association Year Book* 9 (1933): 101–18.

Sibley, Marilyn McAdams. *Lone Stars and State Gazettes: Texas Newspapers before the Civil War.* College Station: Texas A&M University Press, 1983.

Simmons, Marc. *Along the Santa Fe Trail.* Albuquerque: University of New Mexico Press, 1986.

———. *New Mexico: A Bicentennial History.* New York: W. W. Norton and Company, 1977.

Simpson, Harold B. *Cry Comanche: The 2nd U.S. Cavalry in Texas, 1858–1861.* Privately printed, 1945.

Small, Guy W. "The Life of Daniel Parker." Master's thesis, East Texas Baptist College, Marshall, 1954.

Smith, Clinton L. *The Boy Captives.* Privately printed, 1927. Rpt., San Angelo, Tex.: Anchor Publishing, 1993.

Smith, F. Todd. *The Caddo Indians: Tribes at the Convergence of Empires, 1542–1854.* College Station: Texas A&M University Press, 1995.

Smith, Ralph A. "The Comanche Bridge between Oklahoma and Mexico, 1843–1844." *Chronicles of Oklahoma* 39 (1961): 54–69.

Smithwick, Noah. *The Evolution of a State, or Recollections of Old Texas Days.* Austin: Gammel Book Company, 1900. Rpt., Austin, University of Texas Press, 1983.

Some Southwestern Trails. El Paso: Carl Hertzog, 1948.

Sommer, Charles H. *Quanah Parker: Last Chief of the Comanches.* Privately printed, 1945.

Sonnichsen, C. L. (Charles Leland). *Ten Texas Feuds.* Albuquerque: University of New Mexico Press, 1957.

———. *The Mescalero Apaches.* Norman: University of Oklahoma Press, 1973.

Sowell, A. J. (Andrew Jackson). *Early Settlers and Indian Fighters of Southwest Texas.* 2 vols. New York: Argosy-Antiquarian, 1964.

Spearing, Darwin. *Roadside Geology of Texas.* Missoula, Mont.: Mountain Press Publishing Company, 1991.

Speer, William S., ed. *The Encyclopedia of the New West.* Marshall, Tex.: United States Biographical Publishing Company, 1881.

Spellman, Paul N. *Forgotten Texas Leader: Hugh McLeod and the Texan Santa Fe Expedition.* College Station: Texas A&M University, 1990.

Stanley, F. (Francis). *Ciudad Santa Fe: Mexican Rule 1821–1846.* Vol. 2. Pampa, Tex.: Pampa Print Shop, 1962.

Stanley, Henry M. "A British Journalist Reports the Medicine Lodge Peace Council of 1867." *Kansas Historical Quarterly* 33 (1967): 249–320.

———. *My Early Travels and Adventures in America and Asia.* 2 vols. New York: Scribner's Sons, 1895. Rpt., Lincoln: University of Nebraska Press, 1982.

Stephens, Ray A. "The Killough Massacre." *Texana* 7 (1969): 322–27.

Stewart, Omer C. *Peyote Religion: A History.* Norman: University of Oklahoma Press, 1987.

Sunder, John E., ed. *Matt Field on the Santa Fe Trail.* Norman: University of Oklahoma Press, 1960.

Sweet, William Warren. *Religion in the Development of American Culture, 1765–1840.* Gloucester, Mass.: Peter Smith, 1963.

———. *Religion on the American Frontier: The Baptists, 1783–1830.* Chicago: University of Chicago Press, 1931.

Tatum, Lawrie. *Our Red Brothers and the Peace Policy of President Ulysses S. Grant.* Philadelphia: J. C. Winston, 1899. Rpt., Lincoln: University of Nebraska Press, 1970.

Taylor, Alfred A. "Medicine Lodge Peace Council." *Chronicles of Oklahoma* 2 (1924): 98–118.

Taylor, Joe F., ed. "The Indian Campaign on the Stakes Plains, 1874–1875." *Panhandle-Plains Historical Review* 34 (1961): 1–216; 35 (1962): 215–362.

Telegraph and Texas Register (Houston newspaper), March 3, 1838.

Texas and the American Revolution. San Antonio: University of Texas at San Antonio, Institute of Texan Cultures, 1975.

Thoburn, Joseph B., and Muriel H. Wright. *Oklahoma: A History of the State and Its People.* 4 vols. New York: Lewis Historical Publishing Company, 1929.

Thompson, W. A. "Scouting with Mackenzie." *Journal of the United States Cavalry Association* 10 (1897): 429–33.

"A Thrilling Narrative." *Galveston Weekly,* February 5, 1861.

Thrall, Homer S. *A Pictorial History of Texas, from the Earliest Visits of European Adventures to A.D. 1879.* St. Louis: N. D. Thompson and Company, 1879.

Tillson, Christiana Holmes. *A Woman's Story of Pioneer Illinois.* Chicago: R. R. Donnelley, 1919.

Tingley, Donald F. "Illinois Days of Daniel Parker, Texas Colonizer." *Journal of the Illinois State Historical Society* 51 (1958): 388–403.

Trails West. Washington, D.C.: National Geographic Society, 1979.

Traweek, Eleanor Mitchell. *Of Such as These: A History of Motley County and Its Families.* Wichita Falls, Tex.: Nortex Publications, 1973.

Turner, Martha Anne. *Sam Houston and His Twelve Women.* Austin: Pemberton Press, 1966.

Twitchell, Ralph Emerson. *The Leading Facts of New Mexican History.* 5 vols. Cedar Rapids, Iowa: Torch Press, 1911–17.

———. *Old Santa Fe: The Story of New Mexico's Ancient Capital.* Chicago: Rio Grande Press, 1963.

Tyler, Ron C. *The Big Bend: A History of the Last Texas Frontier.* Washington, D.C.: National Park Service, 1975. Rpt., College Station: Texas A&M University Press, 1996.

———, ed. *The New Handbook of Texas.* 6 vols. Austin: Texas State Historical Association, 1996.

U.S. Department of Commerce, Bureau of the Census. *Eighth Census of the United States, 1860, Henderson County, Texas.*

———. *Eighth Census of the United States, 1860, Van Zandt County, Texas.*

———. *Fifth Census of the United States, 1830, Conway County, Arkansas Territory.*

———. *Ninth Census of the United States, 1870, Anderson County, Texas.*

———. *Seventh Census of the United States, 1850, Anderson County, Texas.*

———. *Seventh Census of the United States, 1850, Houston County, Texas.*

———. *Seventh Census of the United States, 1850, Montgomery County, Texas.*

Walker County Genealogical Society and Walker County Historical Commission. *Walker County, Texas: A History.* Dallas: Curtis Media Corporation, 1986.

Walker, Henry Pickering. *The Wagonmasters: High Plains Freighting from the Earliest Days of the Santa Fe Trail to 1880.* Norman: University of Oklahoma Press, 1996.

Wallace, Edward S. "General Ranald Slidell Mackenzie, Indian Fighting Cavalryman." *Southwestern Historical Quarterly* 56 (1953): 378–96.

Wallace, Ernest. "The Journal of Ranald S. Mackenzie's Messenger to the Kwahadi Comanches." *Red River Valley Historical Review* 3 (1978): 227–46.

———. *Ranald S. Mackenzie on the Texas Frontier.* Lubbock: West Texas Museum Association, 1964. Rpt., College Station: Texas A&M University Press, 1993.

———, ed. *Ranald S. Mackenzie's Official Correspondence Relating to Texas.* 2 vols. Lubbock: West Texas Museum Association, 1967–68.

Wallace, Ernest, et al., eds. *Documents of Texas History.* 2nd ed. Austin: State House Press, 1994.

Wallace, Ernest, and Adamson Hoebel. *The Comanches: Lords of the South Plains.* Norman: University of Oklahoma Press, 1952.

Walter, Ray A. *A History of Limestone County.* Austin: Von Boeckmann-Jones, 1959.

Washburne, E. B. (Elihu Benjamin). *Sketch of Edward Coles, Second Governor of Illinois, and the Slavery Struggle of 1823–4.* Chicago: Jansen, McClurg and Company, 1882.

Water, Oil, Sand and Sky: A History of Ward County, Texas. Monahans, Tex.: Monahans Junior Chamber of Commerce, 1962.

Wauer, Roland H. *Naturalists' Big Bend: An Introduction to the Trees and Shrubs, Wildflowers, Cacti, Mammals, Birds, Reptiles and Amphibians, Fish, and Insects.* College Station: Texas A&M University Press, 1973.

Webb, James Josiah. *Adventures in the Santa Fe Trade.* Glendale, Calif.: Arthur H. Clark Company, 1931.

Webb, Walter P. *The Texas Rangers: A Century of Frontier Defense.* Austin: University of Texas Press, 1965.

Webb, Walter P., and H. Bailey Carroll, eds. *The Handbook of Texas.* 2 vols. Austin: Texas State Historical Association, 1952.

Webster, Dolly. *A Narrative of the Captivity and Suffering of Dolly Webster among the Camanche Indians in Texas, with an Account of the Massacre of John Webster and His Party, as Related by Mrs. Webster.* Clarksville: McGranaghan and McCarty Printers, 1843. Rpt., New Haven, Conn.: Yale University Press, 1986.

Weiss, Harold J. "The Texas Rangers Revisited: Old Themes and New Viewpoints." *Southwestern Historical Quarterly* 97 (1994): 621–40.

West, G. Derek. "The Battle of Adobe Walls (1874)." *Panhandle-Plains Historical Review* 36 (1963): 1–36.

Wharton, Clarence R. *El Presidente: A Sketch of the Life of General Santa Anna.* Austin: Gammil's Book Store, 1926.

"Where Was Cynthia Ann Parker Captured?" *Crowell Index,* October 8, 1909.

"The White Captive." *Civilian and Gazette* (Galveston), February 5, 1861, 3.

White, E. E. (Eugene Elliot). *Experiences of a Special Indian Agent.* Little Rock: Diploma Press, 1893. Rpt., Norman: University of Oklahoma Press, 1965.

White, Gifford E., ed. *Character Certificates in the General Land Office of Texas.* Privately printed, 1989.

———, ed. *The 1840 Census of the Republic of Texas.* Austin: Pemberton Press, 1966.

———, ed. *1840 Citizens of Texas.* Vol. 3: Land Grants. Austin: Privately printed, 1988.

———, ed. *1840 Citizens of Texas.* Vol. 2: Tax Rolls. Austin: Privately printed, 1984.

———, ed. *The First Settlers of Houston County, Texas.* Austin: Privately printed, 1983.

Wilbarger, J. (Josiah) W. *Indian Depredations in Texas.* Austin: Hutchings Printing House, 1889. Rpt., Austin: Eakin Press, 1985.

Wilcox, Pearl. *Jackson County History* (Missouri). Privately printed, 1975.

"Wild as Coyotes." *Fort Concho Report* 17, no. 2 (1985): 21–27.

Williams, Amelia W., and Eugene C. Barker, eds. *The Writings of Sam Houston, 1813–1863.* 8 vols. Austin: University of Texas Press, 1938–43.

Williams, Jesse Wallace. *Old Texas Trails.* Burnet, Tex.: Eakin Press, 1979.

Williams, Robert H. "The Case for Peta Nocona." *Texana* 10 (1972): 55–72.

Williams, Villamae, ed. *Stephen F. Austin's Register of Families.* Privately published, ca. 1984.

Wills Point Chronicle, December 8, 1910. Van Zandt County Genealogical Society, Canton, Tex.

Winfrey, Dorman H., and James M. Day. *The Indian Papers of Texas and the Southwest, 1825–1916.* 5 vols. Austin: Pemberton Press, 1996. Austin: Texas State Historical Association, 1995.

Wissler, Clark. *North American Indians of the Plains.* New York: American Museum of Natural History, 1927.

Woolridge, J., ed. *History of Nashville Tennessee.* Nashville: Publishing House of the Methodist Episcopal Church South, 1890. Rpt., Charles Elder Bookseller, n.d.

Wooten, Mattie Lloyd, ed. *Women Tell the Story of the Southwest.* San Antonio: Naylor Company, 1940.

Wortham, Louis J. *A History of Texas from Wilderness to Commonwealth.* 5 vols. Fort Worth: Wortham-Molyneau Company, 1924.

Writers' Program. *Missouri: A Guide to the "Show-Me" State.* Rev. ed. New York: Hastings House Publishers, 1954.

———. *New Mexico: A Guide to the Colorful State.* New rev. ed. New York: Hastings House Publishers, 1962.

Wylie, Edna McDonald. "The Fort Houston Settlement." Master's thesis, Sam Houston State Teachers College, Huntsville, Tex., 1958.

Yoakum, Henderson K. *History of Texas.* 2 vols. New York: Redfield, 1855.

Zuber, William Physick. *My Eighty Years in Texas.* Austin: University of Texas Press, 1971.

INDEX

JO ELLA POWELL EXLEY is an independent writer who is the compiler of *Texas Tears and Texas Sunshine: Voices of Frontier Women,* which has become a modern classic. She lives with her husband and daughter in Katy, Texas.

ISBN 1-58544-136-8

90000

9 781585 441365

Earnest

St. Louis Community College
at Meramec
Library